Creating an American Identity

Creating an American Identity

New England, 1789–1825

Stephanie Kermes

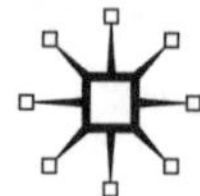

CREATING AN AMERICAN IDENTITY

First published in 2008 by
PALGRAVE MACMILLAN™
175 Fifth Avenue, New York, N.Y. 10010 and
Houndmills, Basingstoke, Hampshire, England RG21 6XS
Companies and representatives throughout the world.

PALGRAVE MACMILLAN is the global academic imprint of the Palgrave Macmillan division of St. Martin's Press, LLC and of Palgrave Macmillan Ltd. Macmillan® is a registered trademark in the United States, United Kingdom and other countries. Palgrave is a registered trademark in the European Union and other countries.

ISBN-13: 978–0–230–60526–8
ISBN-10: 0–230–60526–5

Library of Congress Cataloging-in-Publication Data

Kermes, Stephanie.
Creating an American identity : New England, 1789–1825 / Stephanie Kermes.
p. cm.
Includes bibliographical references and index.
ISBN 0–230–60526–5
1. New England—Civilization—18th century. 2. New England—Civilization—19th century. 3. Regionalism—New England—History. 4. Nationalism—New England—History. 5. Nationalism—United States—History. 6. National characteristics, American—History. 7. Popular culture—New England—History. 8. Political culture—New England—History. 9. New England—Relations—Europe. 10. Europe—Relations—New England. I. Title.

F8.K47 2008
974'.03—dc22 2007048026

A catalogue record for this book is available from the British Library.

Design by Newgen Imaging Systems (P) Ltd., Chennai, India.

First edition: July 2008

10 9 8 7 6 5 4 3 2 1

Printed in the United States of America.

To my daughter and husband, Lia and Tom, I dedicate this book with love

Contents

List of Figures ix

Acknowledgments xi

Introduction 1

Chapter 1 New Englandizing America 15

Chapter 2 A Prussian Monarch—an American Hero: Early Republican Royalism and Parallels between the Cult of Frederick the Great and Celebrations of the First American President 57

Chapter 3 Failed Republicans: Images of the British and the French 87

Chapter 4 Hero of Liberty: New England Celebrations of General Lafayette during His Visit in 1824–1825 117

Chapter 5 Separation for the Nation: The Movement for Maine's Statehood 145

Chapter 6 God's People: The Creation of a Protestant Nation 169

Conclusion 197

Notes 203

Bibliography 273

Index 287

List of Figures

Figure 1.1	Artist Unknown, *Contemplation by the Shore*, fireboard, 1790 (courtesy of the Peabody Essex Museum, Salem, Massachusetts)	30
Figure 1.2	George Ropes, *Crowningshield's Wharf*, 1806 (courtesy, Peabody Essex Museum, Salem, Massachusetts)	37
Figure 1.3	Francis Alexander, *Globe Village*, painting, ca. 1822	40
Figure 1.4	*View from the Green Woods toward Canaan and Salisbury, in Connecticut*, engraving, Columbian Magazine, 1789 (courtesy, American Antiquarian Society)	40
Figure 2.1	Norman, *The Justice of Frederick!* engraving, in *Boston Magazine* 1 (1783): 287 (courtesy of the Rare Books and Manuscript Department, Boston Public Library)	74
Figure 5.1	Lemuel Moody, *Signals at Portland Lighthouse*, watercolor 1807, collections of the Maine Historical Society	157

Acknowledgments

This book would have never been written without my professors and fellow graduate students in the history department and the administrators at the Graduate School of Arts and Science at Boston College. For me, Boston College has been the most supportive and inspiring scholarly environment that I could hope for, when I first came there as an international student from Germany, throughout my years as a Ph.D. candidate, and as a Postdoctoral fellow. Teaching and research fellowships from Boston College allowed me to become the teacher I wanted to be and to write the first draft of this book. Fellowships from the John Nicholas Brown Center and the Huntington Library also supported me during research and writing of my dissertation.

The expertise and generous aid from archivists and librarians throughout New England not only made this book possible, but also helped to complete it in a little less than ten years. I would like to thank the staff at the Massachusetts Historical Society, the Maine Historical Society, the Boston Public Library, the Society for the Preservation of New England Antiquities (now Historic New England), the Houghton Library at Harvard University, the John Hay Library at Brown University, the Huntington Library, the Amy Bess and Lawrence K. Miller Library at the Hancock Shaker Village, and the New Hampshire Historical Society. I especially appreciate the assistance of Peter Drummey at the Massachusetts Historical Society and Nicholas Noyes at the Maine Historical Society.

I need to acknowledge everybody who made it possible for this book to also include visual sources. James Patterson at the Jacob Edwards Library, Christine Michellini at the Peabody Essex Museum, Sean P. Casey at the Boston Public Library, Bethany Engstrom at the Farnsworth Art Museum, and Jaclyn Penny at the American Antiquarian Society made sure that I get reproductions of the images and permissions in a very short time.

Christopher Chappell, my editor at Palgrave McMillan, helped more to finalize this book than he probably realizes. It was a pleasure to work with him; his prompt and clear answers to my e-mails, which were numerous on some days, kept the process flowing at all times.

My greatest intellectual debt is to teachers and colleagues who accompanied this book and its author at different stages. Alan Rogers has been the best dissertation advisor one could wish for and a wonderful friend. I learned so much from him, not only about American history but also about teaching and writing in general. Observing his intelligent and at the same time entertaining lectures was as much a lesson for me as our long conversations about New England in the early republic. David Quigley, with his insight and dedication to American history, made me want to read, research, and write night and day and pushed me and this book further than I could have ever gone. It was always the best decision to follow his advice. Marilynn Johnson's classes, although they focused on a later period than mine, greatly influenced my thinking and made me a better historian. During the transformation from the dissertation into the book, Joyce Appleby, Joseph Conforti, Jonathan Sassi, and Alan Taylor all read a few chapters or the entire manuscript. I cannot thank them enough for their careful reading and inspiring comments, which helped me to make most meaningful revisions. I owe a large debt to my friend Joan Cashin. She was always there for me when I needed advice and remains my model as a teacher, scholar, and writer.

I also want to thank Jay Corrin, Polly Rizova, John McGrath, Tom Whalen, John Mackey, Susan Lee, and Kathleen Martin at Boston University for being wonderful colleagues and friends.

I dedicate this book to Tom and Lia, my husband and daughter. I am ever thankful for Tom's support, critical questions, and belief in me. This book became what it is because of their love and affection.

Introduction

The creation of American nationalism in the decades after Independence was paradoxically a distinctly regional process. At the same time the French Revolution brought about the emergence of modern nationalism in Europe, the founding of the new American republic led Americans to establish an idea of what it meant to be an American. Americans in New England thought that to be an American meant primarily to be a New Englander. They came to believe that in the creation of the new American identity their region should serve as a model for all other Americans. Taking the measure of this early American nationalism is essential to understanding the politics, culture, and identity of the new republic.

More than thirty years ago, David Potter reminded us that national and regional loyalties are intertwined. He emphasized that a national identity does not overpower regional and local identities, but that all these loyalties nourish and shape each other because they share a psychological pattern. My study returns to Potter's observation by focusing on New England between 1789 and 1825 in order to analyze the relationship between nationalism and regionalism.[1]

At the beginning of the twenty-first century, globalization evokes fears among many people that we are losing local, regional, and national traditions. In response to a situation where we share more information, consumer goods, and entertainment with others around the world every day, values connected with a more particular place gain new significance. Even if progressing rapidly, globalization does not remain unchallenged by local, regional, and national loyalties. Therefore, it is especially important for us to understand how universal and particular identities interact. This study looks at the relation between American nationalism, New England regionalism, and transatlantic elements that helped define those identities.

When I was a graduate student at the University of Munich in Germany, I was curious about how the size of the United States and its immigrant, multicultural, and multiracial character might distinguish American nationalism from its European counterparts.

All these factors turn American nationalism into a particularly interesting case for a study of the interaction between nationalism and regionalism. In a large nation, regional loyalties are strong. My interest in American rejections, adoptions, and transformations of European ways is deeply affected by my own experience as a recent immigrant to the United States from Germany. Living a transatlantic life, with a strong loyalty to my adopted country, the impact of European culture on the American national identity appeared to me as a natural question that has not been addressed by historians of American nationalism.

Already in the years of the early republic, the size of the American nation and its continuous expansion helped to secure strong local and regional identities. Growing economic, cultural, political, and personal exchange between Northern and Southern colonies in the half-century before the Revolution had made Americans aware of shared interests and characteristics, but at the same time Americans also started to develop a sense of differences between the regions. Westward migration, which became more and more part of the American experience with the turn of the nineteenth century, contributed to an awareness of regional distinction as well. The fact that people who came from Europe and, therefore, lacked an organic connection with the new "homeland" founded the nation of the United States adds another appealing component. The immigrant character of the young American nation complicated the process of creating images of the "other" and led to an ambiguous perception of everything European. When independent Americans struggled with shaping their collective identity, European cultural heritage and new-world experience sometimes clashed and sometimes merged.

With its provincial pride and transatlantic connections; New England is inviting for a study of early Republican regionalism and nationalism. Since Perry Miller, historians have long scrutinized regional characteristics and identities; but they did not place them into the context of other collective loyalties as David Potter suggested. Half a century after Miller introduced the term, the "New England mind" is still a useful concept in New England history. With its strong local roots and intense English contacts, the region affords an ideal test case for early American nationalism and its relationship with a regional identity. As this study shows, the invention of a New England regional identity was a pivotal step toward the emergence of an American identity. Strikingly, New Englanders defined this new American identity by employing a wide range of regional, national, and transatlantic ideas and images. This combination is remarkable because it shows that the nature of regional nationalism in the early American republic was not provincial, but rather cosmopolitan.

During the early years of the republic, the region's religious, intellectual, and political leaders successfully introduced ideas of New England virtues to their audiences of ordinary New Englanders and used them as a foundation for the popular imagination of the new nation. Loyalty to New England and the reinvention of New England traditions promoted by members of the New England elite shaped the new nationalism that was rising in the early years of the American republic. In contrast to colonial New England identity, the early national regional identity no longer just focused on New England and its comparison with Great Britain. Furthermore, the new ideology of republicanism played an important role in defining New Englanders' collective identity after the Revolution. The first generation of independent Americans in New England placed their region into the context of the new American nation. They compared themselves with their Southern countrymen and began to wonder about New England's role in modeling the culture, politics, and economy of the new federation. The founding of the United States led New Englanders to think simultaneously in regional and national terms.[2]

Ironically, in crafting an identity in opposition to the South, New Englanders were embedding their own regional values in a national context. They invented a national identity that excluded a large group of Americans from the South from their vision of America. Interestingly, New Englanders used some European symbols and characteristics as ingredients in the recipe for their new national identity. Southerners, however, never served as role models for an emerging New England American identity, nor did New Englanders imagine them to share many of their New England virtues. As New Englanders used European imperfections to create a sense of a unique American identity, they employed what they perceived as Southern shortcomings to demonstrate their own virtues and to define national ideals shaped by their own regional bonds. Early republican New Englanders did not envision the new American identity as a hybrid of Southern and Northern values and lifestyle. The creation of a national identity in New England did not follow the Constitution in its concept of compromise between the regions.

The works of David Waldstreicher and Linda Kerber add to Potter's generalization by suggesting that a collective national identity was nationally imagined, but performed locally. They emphasize that growing regionalism of the American nation was nevertheless nationalistic. Nations as communities are too big for their members to know each other personally. They can only be imagined. Their members can only experience the nation in their daily lives on the level of their local community; therefore, when the new American nationalism emerged, smaller communities such as the region or township became the stage for presentations of nationalist loyalties and an instructive pattern for early republicans through which they could imagine their nation. Observing their neighbors, their town, and surrounding landscapes, New Englanders thought that all that was a miniature of America. For them, their small community was simply an image of the entire nation.[3]

In recent works on early nationalism, Waldstreicher, Simon Newman, and Len Travers have focused on the partisan character of the emerging nationalism and emphasized how despite partisan differences, popular political culture played a vital role in the creation of national identity. Inspired by Joyce Appleby's important work, my study aims to add to their assumptions that sometimes national identity united New Englanders across party lines. Early American nationalism in New England provided collective values shared by Federalists and Republicans. Logically, both Federalists and Republicans contributed ideals to that new image of an American nation in New England. The ideal New England America combined values from both parties. It should be added that Jeffersonian Republicans in New England excoriated Federalists for the Hartford Convention in 1814, in which some Federalists aimed at New England's secession from the United States. Although the Federalist Party was tainted as the party for treason ever after and never really recovered, Federalist culture in a broader sense still survived in New England for at least another decade. Historians of the early republic still need to define to what extent New Englanders imagined the nation in terms of their own culture. By celebrating themselves as true Americans and true republicans, New Englanders claimed to embody the new nation. They introduced New England as the model miniature America.[4]

This enriches our understanding of early American nationalism by arguing that the interaction between nationalism and regionalism was an ambiguous process, at once inclusive and exclusive. New Englanders used transatlantic symbols that equated their region with the nation, but at the same time New England regionalism used "others" to construct their national identity. Timothy H. Breen, for example, suggests that an American identity initially emerged in an Atlantic world. He argues that it was Americans' exclusion from British nationalism that "forced colonists to imagine themselves as a separate people."[5] This study applies his approach to the post-Revolutionary period. I argue that after the Revolution New Englanders distinguished themselves from external enemies such as the English and the French and from Southerners whose values and characteristics served as the antitheses of New Englanders' emerging American identity. Although sometimes privileged Northerners and Southern planters admired each other and identified more with each other than with ordinary people from their regions, many New Englanders began to see themselves as better republicans and better Americans than their Southern countrymen. This growing sectionalist component of New England's nationalism shaped America's history of the nineteenth century. A sense of superiority and exclusiveness defined the New England national identity. Sometimes traveling strengthened bonds between early republicans from the North and the South.[6]

It was this sense of superiority and exclusiveness and their imagination of common virtue, which they thought distinguished them from Europeans and Southerners, that helped New Englanders to share a collective identity despite political, class, geographic, and religious divisions within the region. New Englanders split along party lines and as Waldstreicher, Newman, and Travers have shown, those partisan affiliations even shaped public celebrations. Wealthy coastal towns certainly differed in lifestyle and culture from the frontier settlements in the Western parts of Massachusetts and Maine, in New Hampshire and the new state of Vermont. In addition to isolation, lack of church or government authorities, and evangelical religion, class often distinguished hinterland settlers from coastal New Englanders.

Religious divisions played an important role in early Republican life. Traditional Congregationalism shaped Connecticut, while Rhode Island was home to a diverse set of religious communities. Evangelism dominated the new settlements in the Western parts of the region and set its inhabitants apart from their coastal counterparts. It is important to understand that in spite of these divisions New Englanders from different social backgrounds and different areas of the region, belonging to different religious sects or emerging political parties, were able to forge shared ideas about regional and national identity.

With the construction of a national identity in New England, the region's elite responded to the popular need for a definition of the character of the new American nation. New England leaders also attempted to answer the question of what role New England played in the new national environment. In the late eighteenth and early nineteenth century, migration from the old crowded centers to new frontier settlements and changes in social relations, living and working conditions created by the market revolution removed people from family, friends, and more personal relationships with their employers. These changes caused confusion, insecurity, anxiety, and sometimes loneliness among ordinary working people. By modeling and promoting the new regional nationalism, the elite offered their fellow New Englanders a feeling of security and a sense of community and belonging. That gave them a new identity molded to fit into the new social, economic, and political system.[7] These inventors of a New England American identity shared a vision of their region and nation, an interest in an intellectual and cultural exchange with Europe, and an activism to spread their own beliefs and values among ordinary people throughout the United States. Although they came from different places all over New England, worked in different professions, and belonged to different religious groups and political parties, they all aimed to convince New Englanders and Americans as well as Europeans of the superiority of the America that they saw embodied in their own region. They defined this superiority through religion and republicanism.

The New England nationalists were ministers, professors, lawyers, doctors, editors, publishers, statesmen, and artists. Although a large number lived in Boston, many came from other coastal centers such as New Haven, in Connecticut, Newburyport, in Massachusetts, Portsmouth, in New Hampshire, and Portland and Bath in Maine. Local elites from inland towns such as Hartford, Connecticut, Worcester, Massachusetts, and Concord, New Hampshire, also played an important role in spreading the nationalist ideology. Even leaders from small hinterland towns such as Weatherfield and Enfield, Connecticut; Groton, Massachusetts; and Merrimack, New Hampshire were involved in the process. Some came from traditional elite families, others were social climbers whose fathers had been tavern keepers or schoolteachers. The rising professions of editor and publisher often helped talented young men to work their way up in the new republican social system. Religiously and politically they were a mixed group belonging to various denominations and both political parties. Almost all of these New England nationalists participated in the reform movement and belonged to inter-denominational missionary societies. Often they were founders or leaders of these organizations. Inspired by the nationalistic mission, they also helped establishing the nation's early literary and scientific institutions. Many of these advocates of New England nationalism were educated at Harvard, Yale, or Dartmouth College and some continued their studies at European universities. Ironically, given their nationalist activism, they lived transatlantic lives. Many traveled in Europe and made friends among European intellectuals. As publishers and editors they read European newspapers and magazines. If they worked in other professions, they purchased European books and read articles by European authors that were published in their local journals. Probably because of their transatlantic lifestyles, they struggled with the classification of their own nation within the Atlantic world.[8]

Merchants, professional artists, itinerant painters, housewives, and schoolgirls also helped to forge and advocate regional nationalism. Images of New England landscapes and heroes in paintings, on coverlets, ceramic plates, silver tankards, and gloves turned New England nationalism into a big business. These nationalistic items increased sales in the new manufacturing sectors of the region. New England merchants even sold some of these souvenirs in Europe. Such an export of New England relics was probably quite satisfactory for tradesmen because it provided proof that their goods and New England values and images were good enough to please the taste of European buyers. Images depicting nationalist New England's characteristics and values on household utensils and artworks indicate that this imagery surrounded ordinary New Englanders in their daily lives.

The fact that early republican women themselves produced such pictures on household goods they made, sometimes copying the works of professional artists, but also contributing their own interpretation, shows what an important part of their life regional nationalism was. Jane Otis Prior from Maine, for example, painted a sewing box with an image of her hometown Thomaston. If ordinary women did not make wooden boxes, linens, or paintings on fireplace mantelpieces, they at least bought such items to decorate their homes. Children viewed images of a New England American culture on material goods provided by their mothers at home and presented in their books at school. The large amount of visual and material evidence of the New England nationalist culture shows that early republican New Englanders not only perceived the new ideology, but also supported the expansion of that nationalistic ideology and helped to spread it among their children and neighbors. Sometimes they actively shaped the images of New England American values, when they reproduced them. While men wrote the majority of the regional nationalistic accounts in books and newspapers, women dominated in the production of household goods decorated with visual interpretations of that collective identity. The material culture of New England nationalism gives us an insight on how and to what degree ordinary people absorbed and performed that ideology. It shows a manifestation of a New England American identity in the region's everyday life.[9]

In the first chapter; "New Englandizing America," I focus on depictions of the New England landscape and people in paintings, on ceramics, and needlework as well as in poems and travel accounts in books and newspapers. In the New England mind, the constructed New England village—the common and the plain meetinghouse surrounded by small farms— embodied republican virtues of liberty and equality. Of course, in this imagery the people of New England were model republicans personalizing these virtues. Such descriptions of New England demonstrate that early American nationalism and regionalism were intertwined. New Englanders were proud of their region and imagined it to embody the new nation. They defined America in New England terms. This New England nationalism included an ambiguity toward Europe. Even if European culture sometimes still served as a model and New England leaders struggled with the classification of their nation in an Atlantic context, by 1825 many New Englanders believed in American superiority.

To highlight the construction of a superior collective identity, New Englanders made an invidious comparison between their region and the Southern environment. Southern plantation agriculture with the luxurious lifestyle of the planters and the undemocratic institution of slavery were the trappings of an aristocracy, they said. According to New Englanders and their European visitors, Southern immorality, irreligion, and industrial backwardness contrasted with their own republican virtues. In their comparison of their own region with the South, New Englanders reinvented their own region as a place where African Americans and slaves did not exist. They denied their own history of slavery. Moreover, slavery continued to exist in New England even into the years of the early republic. Abigail Adams, for example, grew up in a household with slaves.

Idealized regional images not only allowed New Englanders to define themselves, but to create the North as well. The creation of a New England American identity was also an inclusive process; neighboring Northern states and European visitors, who often wanted to promote immigration, participated in this New England ideology. The New England identity became at once a Northern and a national identity, because as Joyce Appleby[10] emphasizes, the American nation was created in the image of the North. Publishers in New York and Philadelphia printed depictions of New England, which encouraged their audiences to adopt the New England ideal. The large number of such pieces in New York and Pennsylvania indicates how successful the enterprise of forging a Northern identity was in spite of images of money-driven Yankees who tricked their countrymen. This Northern identity was obviously dominated by New Englanders and their worldview. Although New Englanders and other Northerners shared a collective identity, sometimes New Englanders and even visitors from Mid-Atlantic states still claimed that New Englanders were better educated and less prone to drinking and swearing than their neighbors. New Englanders who migrated to Ohio and the Western parts of New York wanted to transplant and spread New England culture. Such migrants founded, for example, a New England Society in New York City promoting the region's values. Europeans who traveled in the United States celebrated this process, and so added a cosmopolitan theme. New England pottery manufacturers in turn exploited this transatlantic construction by selling dinner services to Italy and England, which pictured the republican Boston State House.

To achieve the goal of combining regional and national identity, New Englanders drew selectively on other transatlantic myths and symbols. Linda Kerber mentions that New England Federalists identified with Prussia, but the second chapter of this book "A Prussian Monarch—an American Hero: Early Republican Royalism and Parallels between the Cult of Frederick the Great and Celebrations of the First American President" is the first to flesh out New Englanders' celebration of the Prussian king Frederick the Great. Strikingly, anecdotes of the German monarch that made an important contribution to his canonization in German states after his death in 1786 crossed the Atlantic and were published in Massachusetts and other regional newspapers. In these articles New Englanders reinvented the enlightened Prussian despot Frederick II as a republican hero and a popular model for New England virtues.

The New England cult of the Prussian king serves as an example for transatlantic elements of the new American identity. The figure of Frederick II enabled the American literary elite to transform colonists into republicans in a way that very much appealed to ordinary people because it involved a popular Protestant hero with whom it was easy to identify. By introducing an idol who linked republicanism with a familiar culture of royalism and served as a powerful transatlantic role model, newspaper editors made sure that the shift in values would be successful. By transforming a European monarch into a republican hero who had raised his state of Prussia from one among many German states to a status as a great power, New Englanders communicated their own goals within the nation and for the entire country. Publications on the Prussian hero in neighboring Northern states confirm the existence of an emerging sectional identity dominated by New England culture. Such publications favorably compared New

England with Prussia and unfavorably associated the South with Prussia's enemy Austria.

In these anecdotes published in New England newspapers, Frederick the Great appeared as a personification of the new republican virtues: he lived a Spartan life, avoided all royal luxury, stood for religious toleration, showed self-discipline as well as generosity, justice, and sympathy toward his people. The boundaries between monarch and subject blurred. The king's main concern seemed to be the common good, and New Englanders ascribed the very same virtues to their first president. But while Frederick became a rather ordinary human being, the republican George Washington was celebrated in a quasi-royal way and many Americans thought to recognize even aristocratic features in his appearance. Striking similarities between the German cult of Frederick II and the American cult of George Washington expose the transatlantic character of modern patriotism. It also uncovers royalist tendencies of early American nationalism. This book claims that patriotism and nationalism are a hybrid of monarchical and republican culture and that this hybrid was a transatlantic phenomenon. Frederick was, of course, also perceived as a transatlantic Protestant ideal-figure.[11]

Chapter 3, "Failed Republicans—Images of the British and the French," analyzes depictions of the two European nations in New England publications. These images of the British and the French demonstrate New Englanders' ambiguity toward Europe, especially in the early years of the new republic. New Englanders simultaneously extolled republican political institutions and sought to mimic French and English architecture, dress styles, and furniture. At the same time, they thought that the British failed as republicans because they had restored monarchy after the civil war and succumbed to the siren song of luxury. Similarly, New Englanders criticized the French Revolution for giving birth to an oppressive government and a cluster of non-republican vices such as gambling and the theatre. In this portrait, French women who worked in male professions and neglected their duty as republican mothers were portrayed as defeminized by the violence of the Terror. In the first two decades of the nineteenth century, New Englanders overcame some of their insecurities about the status of their collective identity and felt increasingly superior to their contemporaries on the other side of the Atlantic. This process increased in scale and tempo after the war of 1812, when New Englanders were less tied to their former mother country and no longer felt bound to the French "sister republic." Fears that the British and French threatened their republican values led New Englanders to use them as juxtapositions for their collective identity. Competition with the new French nationalism and the importance of religion for the new regional American identity caused New Englanders to exclude the Catholic French even more aggressively than the English from their regional national identity.[12]

In chapter 4, "Hero of Liberty: New England Celebrations of General Lafayette during His Visit in 1824–1825," I describe a brief moment in the early republic that united the young American nation, which otherwise split increasingly along partisan and sectional lines, especially after the turn of the century. During Lafayette's visit, people of all classes, gender, and ages celebrated the French Revolutionary hero as a martyr for liberty, as a model republican, and as the last founding father. Emphasizing his attachment to the American people, Lafayette met veterans, children, and other ordinary citizens when he visited battlefields, schools, orphanages, and hospitals. Celebrations of the aristocratic French general provided powerful means to invoke the memory of the Revolution and to reinvent republican virtues. By praising Lafayette's benevolence and disinterestedness, New England leaders hoped to counter selfishness and individualism emerging with the commercialized society. Accounts in local newspapers reporting about Lafayette fetes in places near and far established a collective imagination of common national virtues and festivities.

Interestingly, celebrations of Lafayette and articles and books telling the story of his "heroic" life also opened another opportunity for New Englanders to depict his French countrymen—in contrast to Lafayette—as failed republicans. When New Englanders emphasized Lafayette's Americanism and American prosperity, which indicated in their minds American superiority, they excluded Europeans in general from their collective identity. A similar process appears in their portraits of Lafayette as an advocate for freedom for slaves. New England papers tried to exclude Southern slaveholders from their regional ideal of the American nation. Furthermore, worshiping the French guest as an American shows how everybody who shared collective American values could become an American. Unlike European identity, American national identity was not strictly connected to the land. The large number of Lafayette souvenirs, which crowded the stores during his tour, is another indicator of the important economic role of New England nationalism.[13]

Studying early republican American nationalism in New England also opens the opportunity to look at the effects of political pluralism. In chapter 5, "Separation for the Nation: The Movement for Maine's Statehood," I explain how Maine separatists, for example, made use of a nationalist rationale to justify separation from regional Massachusetts. Ironically, Mainers' separatism reinforced regional unity. New England nationalism played a crucial role in helping the movement for separation to final success in 1820 after a struggle that went on for more than three decades. While the movement for a state of Maine evolved immediately after the Peace of 1783, the majority of Mainers did not support it insistently until after the War of 1812, when a new generation of separatists employed older arguments for statehood in a more professional and inclusive way. Local conditions such as the lack of institutionalized authorities as courts and churches, isolation from the market, and religion molded the identity of Northern and Western New Englanders (Maine, New Hampshire, and Western Massachusetts). Such differences not only distinguished Maine from Massachusetts, but also caused divisions between coastal centers and frontier settlements in the district itself. After 1815, separatists won many followers by including Mainers who had settled at the frontier in their campaign for separation and by praising them for their contribution to the New England American task of civilizing the wilderness. Furthermore, in a series of newspaper articles and during personal visits to their friends and neighbors they promoted the argument that a state of Maine would turn the district into a model for New England virtues. The lack of celebrations of the new state of Maine in the spring of 1820 indicates the dominance of the regional national identity and how this loyalty had absorbed any distinctive loyalty to the new state.[14]

As preceding chapters already reveal, religion played a significant role in creating a regional-national identity in New England. In chapter 6, "God's People: The Creation of a Protestant Nation," I particularly trace the important role the New England ministry played in creating and promoting New England nationalism. The growing church membership during the Second Great Awakening and the religious leaders' political activism in missionary, temperance, and antislavery societies helped them to expose a large audience to their nationalist ideology. They participated in establishing many of the different elements of the New England national loyalty. In this process, ministers tightly linked New England nationalism and Protestantism. This allowed them to foment a feeling of New England American superiority that they justified with the image of New Englanders—and consequently Americans—as God's chosen people. It also helped them to exclude Catholic France from the very identity they promoted. At the same time, by preaching the importance of religion to their early republican audiences, ministers secured themselves an important role in American society. Especially after witnessing secularization in post-Revolutionary France, a fear arose among New England ministers that the American republic would become more worldly than religious as well. Although the clergy embraced republican virtues, ministers argued that some traditional values such as religious education and modesty had to be maintained in order to guarantee the survival and prosperity of the republic, about which everybody was so concerned. Only piety, they said, could prevent corruption, materialism, and self-interest, which all came with the market society, from destroying republican virtue. Some ministers wanted to make sure that traditional Puritan values would still have an impact on the new republican collective identity. Nationalism did not necessarily replace religion as Benedict Anderson indicated. At least American nationalism rather merged with religion and formed a strong ideological amalgam. The different worldview of Congregationalists on the one hand and the post-Revolutionary radical sects on the other hand did not lead New Englanders to imagine the nation in dissimilar terms. Despite the differences in doctrine and religious practices, Protestant New England nationalism remained a strong force that unified New Englanders across denominational, generational, gender, and class lines.[15]

In the decades from 1789 to 1820, elements selectively drawn from Europe and New England helped to forge an American national identity that was shaped by republicanism and Protestantism. It was a dynamic process, to which New England regionalism made an enormously important contribution. Collective images of New England landscapes, virtues, and ideal figures served to overcome partisan and religious divisions. New Englanders and their Northern neighbors imagined the nation in terms of this New England identity and claimed that everything American emerged from it.

CHAPTER 1

New Englandizing America

In the years between 1789 and 1825, New England and its people came gradually to embody America and, even more importantly, to define true American republicanism. Travelers touring the region described a land of picturesque, romantic landscapes, a civilized wilderness with neat, industrious, democratic towns inhabited by pious, hardworking, and educated people, and unified by a strong sense of community. In the view shared by these inhabitants with their foreign visitors, as well as with those from other Northern states, New England was, like Europe, civilized and educated but, in contrast to the old world, it was neither overpopulated nor corrupt. Both New Englanders and their guests spoke of another sharp distinction as well: the contrast between their region—its liberty, equality, simplicity—and the patriarchal society and luxurious lifestyle of the South. In short, many agreed that New England represented a notion of perfect harmony by uniting the best of the old and the new world.

During this period, a new collective identity was emerging from the ideals and virtues surrounding the Revolutionary War, an identity that would form the basis for the subsequent establishment of national political and cultural institutions. New Englanders—like all Americans of this first independent generation—were induced by these ideals and virtues to engage in the search for such a new national identity. Thus, as both native New Englanders and their visitors created and marketed images of New England landscapes, towns, people, and their characteristics, these were all called "American."

In prose and poetry, paintings, engravings, wall decorations and fireboards, writers and artists sang the praises of New England's American-ness. Schoolgirls copied pictures of New England landscapes and buildings into embroidered and painted mourning pictures honoring deceased relatives and family records. Housewives did likewise on quilts and coverlets. Manufacturers decorated clocks, boxes, pitchers, and ceramics with idyllic New England scenes. These images were exported to neighboring states and to the other side of the Atlantic through accounts of New England features and landscapes in Philadelphia and New York journals, travel descriptions published in London, and dinnerware sold in England and Italy decorated with pictures of the Boston State House.

In such ways, inhabitants of New England encountered images of their region everywhere in their daily life: in schoolbooks, newspapers, on their walls, textiles, and household utensils. In the process a strong regional identity emerged: New Englanders living in places as different as Boston, Massachusetts, and Thomaston, Maine shared these pictures of their region. And New Englanders wanted their region to embody the new nation. They celebrated New England virtues and landscapes and towns as truly American and truly republican.

Idealized images of New England not only served to define the nation to New Englanders but to Northerners in general. This process took place in spite of some cultural contradictions: for example, the often pejorative term "Yankee." This designation could describe money-driven New Englanders who exploited Southerners as well as their own Northern neighbors by playing clever tricks. But it could also denote the New York urbanites whose pleasure in dances, boat trips, horse races, and plays clashed with the Puritan virtues more traditionally associated with New England. Nevertheless, a powerful identification with New England virtues eventually came to shape the Northern states. It was the New England identity beyond any others that became available as the foundation of both a Northern and a national identity.[1]

The development of this New England/American identity was an ambivalent process. Although Americans, in these early years of the republic, defined themselves in contrast to Europeans, they also used European symbols in the creation of their new national identity. In its character as the "civilized" and "educated" region of America, New England could unify the old European and the new American ways. In the Northern mind, it was this fusion of both worlds that forged the new nation into a collective identity shaped by several factors: a Protestant and Puritan heritage; a common history of cultivating the wilderness; and the landscape and republican virtues of New England itself.

Sharing a Common History

American nationalism may well have undergone its earliest and most vigorous development in New England, a claim made by Wilbur

Zelinsky in his study *Nation into State.* Certainly New Englanders developed early on a strong sense of their past. In the years following the adoption of the federal constitution, patriotism combined with a reawakened interest in Puritan history and European influence in animating New Englanders to establish historical societies. And one of the first bodies of historiographic literature in the United States arose in New England; not surprisingly, it focused on the region's own history. The years between 1791 and 1815 saw the publication of no fewer than eight histories of New England. These included even a history of Massachusetts written by Thomas Hutchinson, the state's former loyalist governor. The most popular histories, such as Hannah Adams's *A Summary History of New England* and Jeremy Belknap's *History of New Hampshire,* went through several reprints and editions. Adams's history also appeared in an abridged version for use in the schools. Reprints in London brought these accounts of New England's history to a British audience. Numerous reviews of these publications and a large number of articles on the region's first settlement not only show New England's interest in its past, but also constitute the beginnings of a historiographical discourse.[2]

These early historians received support and encouragement from publishers who wanted to create for their general readership a New England history that was "correct, comprehensive and popular" and that would establish the collective image of a common past that distinguished the region from others. Some older "materials" they found "so complicated with facts and details" that they thought it was time for a history that would be not just valuable to the "historiographer" but also entertaining to the general reader. In order to increase the credibility of these histories, friendly reviewers described authors as pious, tender, and benevolent—qualities that, to the public mind, defined them as typical New Englanders and assured that their work was free of religious or patriotic bias.[3] Since history was meant to serve the common good it was especially important to picture historians as good republicans.

New England's most popular historians in the early republic, Hannah Adams, Jeremy Belknap, and Jedidiah Morse, can serve as examples. They were well educated and very religious, but still influenced by Enlightenment thought; and they all moved in Boston's high society. Hannah Adams, a distant cousin of John Adams, was a self-educated young woman, introduced to Latin and Greek philosophy by students boarding at her parents' house in Medford, Massachusetts. A religious scholar as well as a historian, her interest in ideas that transcended her own New England culture led her to become an advocate of religious toleration. Her liberal religious attitude put her at odds with Jedidiah Morse's Calvinist orthodoxy, resulting in a ten-year long controversy between the two historians starting in 1804. Prominent members of Bostonian society who were religious liberals helped Adams to survive the controversy financially by granting her an annuity. Among these supporters were Federalist congressman and later Boston mayor Josiah Quincy and Adams's cousin William Smith Shaw. Shaw published the *Monthly Anthology* and in 1807 he founded the Boston Athenaeum.

Adams's rival, Jedidiah Morse, was a historian, geographer, and Congregational clergyman. Following graduation from Yale College, he published his *American Geography*, which became very popular, selling 15,000 copies of the first 1789 edition. In 1799, Morse became pastor of the First Congregational Church in Charlestown, Massachusetts, where he would stay for twenty years. Besides his research and writings on American geography, his nationalistic efforts included participation in the establishment of the New England Tract Society, founded with the aim of disseminating religious information. Like many other New England nationalists, he also helped establish the American Bible Society.

Like Morse, Jeremy Belknap was a Congregational clergyman, serving as pastor in Boston's Long Lane Church. In spite of his traditional Puritan education at Harvard, Belknap was influenced in his historical writings by the Enlightenment emphasizing reason as the major force in history. He was also involved in founding institutions to support American arts and sciences. While he was devoted to the promotion of New England history through his histories of New Hampshire, Belknap helped launch the Massachusetts Historical Society and its national ambitions to collect and preserve documents of American history. The Massachusetts Historical Society was the first institution of its kind in the country.[4]

Many editors and publishers shared the cultural backgrounds of historians and other writers. William Emerson, the editor of the *Monthly Anthology* was theologically liberal and politically conservative. A Unitarian clergyman, Emerson became pastor of Boston's prestigious First Church in 1799. Like William Smith Shaw, Emerson moved in Boston's best circles and socialized with, among others, the governor of Massachusetts. The father of the famous transcendentalist Ralph Waldo Emerson became the city's most prominent clergyman. As a member of the Massachusetts Historical Society and the American Academy of Arts and Science, William Emerson also supported the new nation's literary institutions.[5]

Though they may have had shared cultural backgrounds, editors and publishers frequently enjoyed one striking advantage over historians and other writers: They could sometimes support themselves—and even make good money—in the fast-growing American printing and publishing industry without entering a traditional elite profession such as the ministry. Early nineteenth-century society, however, did not yet support writing as a profession. Charles Brockden Brown, for example, was much more successful as the editor of the *Monthly Magazine and American Review*, a Philadelphia magazine that reviewed histories of New England, than he was as a writer, although he is now regarded as one of the most talented early novelists of the United States.

Interest in New England was not limited only to the six states of the region. Mathew Carey, editor of the Philadelphia journal *American Museum*, was a staunch American nationalist who promoted New England history by publishing articles, as well as reviews of Belknap's work. Carey, a native of Ireland, was another foreign-born advocate for New England history and culture. On a trip to Paris in 1779, he had met Benjamin Franklin and the Marquis de Lafayette, whose accounts of the United States probably attracted the young Irishman. Five years later Carey boarded a ship to Philadelphia. Settling in the printing capital he wanted to start a newspaper, but lacked the necessary financial resources. Interestingly, his Paris friend, the Marquis de Lafayette, loaned him the money to establish the business. From the 1790s on, Carey, who quickly became an American nationalist, reprinted English books for the American market as a way of supporting the domestic publishing industry; to increase distribution, he employed an itinerant bookseller. More importantly, he organized the first national book fair of the United States, which helped establish a national distribution network.

In 1814, Carey's nationalism brought him further recognition in a time of political crisis during and just after the War of 1812, with the publication of his book *The Olive Branch*. There were some in New England at this time who had come to believe that they did not have sufficient interests in common with the South, and had thus begun to think about and discuss secession. It was a threat designed in part to encourage, forcefully, the adoption of New England virtues in the rest of the country by, if necessary, creating a "New England nation" without the recalcitrant South. This threat of secession, as Joseph Conforti has argued, could be viewed not so much as an alternative to "New Englandizing" the rest of the country but as a "strategy to restore its power in the Union."[6]

Carey's book, which took on the crisis by blaming it on both Federalists and Republicans, established his reputation as an intellectual, specifically one who wished to preserve the union. This desire did not prevent him, however, from clearly pursuing the expansion of Northern ideals, many of which, of course, continued to clash with Southern interests. An opponent of slavery, he favored colonization and the employment of blacks in factories; and to protect tariffs against Southern opposition, he founded, in 1824, the Pennsylvania Society for the Promotion of Internal Improvement. During that year his old friend General Lafayette visited America, and Mathew Carey publicly paid back the loan.

These writers, editors, publishers, and reviewers were all part of the new intellectual elite that was emerging along with the growing print culture. They believed that history could serve as a vehicle to establish and strengthen republican virtues. "The history of our native country," one reviewer stressed, "justly merits the highest place in our regard... because it relates... to ourselves; because we are fully qualified to understand it; because its lessons are of indispensable use in teaching us our duty, as citizens of a free state, as a guardian of our own liberty and happiness." New England history, these intellectuals hoped, would introduce a historical tradition in a country that lacked established institutions and customs. They wished to create a collective past that would evoke national pride. One commentator on Adams's abridged version of her New England history, for example, claimed that Americans and especially New Englanders had developed a particular pride in their country and its past. Their experience of settling in an "uncivilized" country distinguished New Englanders and their region's history from other national histories and made it especially relevant for the history of civilization in general:

> It is probable, that individuals of all nations think favourably and even fondly of their native country. Certain it is, that as Americans, and especially as children of Newengland [*sic*], we cherish a high reverence and a tender partiality for this land of our fathers. We regard it as the theatre of scenes, which are extremely interesting, instructive and honorary to human nature.[7]

For these intellectuals, it was not only the Revolution but also New England's prior history, from the first settlement, that had given birth to the young nation's institutions, virtues, and freedom. Thus, Adams believed her history was popular among her generation due to the fact that, for them, the very causes for the original migration to New

England had had an important impact on the civil and religious liberties of mankind.

According to these ideas a distinct American character was shaped when the Pilgrims and Puritans settled in the new world. In these early years of the republic, the myth of the errand into the wilderness still persisted. The *Columbian Phenix* praised Adams, who was the young nation's first professional woman writer, for her intention to "keep alive a due remembrance of the sufferings and heroism of her countrymen…which led to the establishment of this young and glorious nation." For that same reason, the author of an article on New England's first settlers in the *Connecticut Evangelical Magazine* considered his topic to be particularly important. "Few subjects can be more deserving of attention, than the character and history of our forefathers," he thought because they founded all the moral and civil institutions, which guarantied social happiness in the young republic.[8]

By writing New England's history, New England intellectuals aimed to establish the centrality of their section to American history. In their works they used "New England" and "America," "New Englanders" and "Americans" as synonyms. Their historical narrative introduced the idea that everything American had its origin in New England. This process did not stop at New England's borders; Americans could read about New England history in Philadelphia and New York periodicals such as *The Monthly Magazine and American Review*, *The American Review and Literary Journal*, *The American Museum or Universal Magazine*, and *Portfolio*. At the center of such articles stood the history and character of the Pilgrims and Puritans.[9]

Adams, Morse, and Belknap were all inventing a historical tradition that explained their view of the American character; they did this by arguing that what shaped the nation's people and distinguished them from Europeans was in fact the first settlement of the country. What had turned Englishmen into Americans was the collective act of civilizing a wilderness. Celebrations of the landing at Plymouth and Puritan Forefathers' Day in Boston brought this message to an even broader public. Again, accounts of these festivals in New York and Philadelphia newspapers extended the glorification of New England settlers to other Northern states. Strikingly, New York and Philadelphia each had a New England Society that joined in these annual rites.[10]

Lectures and articles about the first settlers centered on the wild nature of the new world's land and native population, tracing at length the hardships of a life in such an environment. Like many of his colleagues, an unnamed New York *Monthly Magazine* author turned to the Pilgrims' struggle to survive in the wilderness in order to explain the circumstances that had formed the New England character. He describes the harsh and wild nature of the land and of the aborigine people as readers in the early republic would find it in almost every issue of their journals. By reading such accounts they could imagine how their ancestors landed in an unknown country, wholly uncultivated, covered with woods, full of unwholesome swamps, and inhabited by ruthless and revengeful savages: a country, too, where the greatest part of every year was consumed in a winter no less severely cold than tedious in duration, a season that kept the earth out of the hands of husbandry and locked the coast in mountains of ice for a full seven months.

Historians and travel book authors shared in this sort of campaigning the idea that the new world's landscape molded the character of New Englanders. Yale president Timothy Dwight promotes a historical consciousness even in his travel books, appealing to tourists to consider the extraordinary achievement of the first immigrants to New England. Traveling through an area such as the White Mountains, according to Dwight, would make every American aware of this achievement. Early travelers could imagine, he says, how men, women, and even children fought "a combination of evils" every day, negotiating steep hills, riding through swamps, crossing deep rivers, and climbing over rocks.[11]

And an article in the *Monthly Register* is quite explicit on the notion that the American landscape inspired the first settlers to cultivation and civilization. With these historical accounts the elite communicated the idea of a challenging relationship between the Puritan settlers and the land. Many advocates of the emerging collective identity promoted traditional Puritan virtues because they hoped those religious ideals would coexist with the secular trends of the new republicanism. Some went so far as to reinvent Puritan traditions as republican virtues.

Their message was clear: Protestantism and New England's Puritan heritage were essential for the survival of the republic. In these New England histories, the wild landscape of the new world compelled the first immigrants to work hard while it strengthened their piety. At the same time Puritans were shaping this wilderness and creating the typical American landscape by building villages, commons, and harbors, putting up fences and planting fields. In a nation of immigrants, lacking any natural bonds with the land, the creation of such strong ties between the land and its people was especially important for the emergence of nationalism. In his *Topographical and Historical Description of Boston* Charles Shaw gave a sense of this connection.

"The fathers of New England," he explained were pious, moral, and "ready to endure every suffering, for the sake of civil and religious freedom." Although they first had to "level forests where savage beasts, and savage men had roamed for ages," their "sagacity and prudence," soon enabled them to live in a cultivated society. With all their virtues and talents, Shaw argued, "it is no wonder" that the first planters' character "shone light in the dark places of this American wilderness." The virtuous character of the settlers shaped the new American landscape.[12]

And such virtues, according to these early historians, were already in large part republican virtues. The collective experience of settling in an uncivilized country established and strengthened collective virtues such as industry, piety, equality, benevolence, and selflessness. By ascribing virtues of civic humanism to the first colonists, intellectuals were trying to invent a tradition of republican virtues and persuade their audience to adopt them. In a time when commerce and popular sovereignty seemed to turn benevolence into self-interest, the nation's intellectual leaders were urged to promote the idea that the settlement of New England had evoked civic virtue: "The whole enterprise by which they opened a pathless wilderness and laid foundations of civilized society in a savage dessert, evinced a public spirit...a disinterestedness...a readiness for personal sacrifices, which can scarcely find a parallel."[13] Moreover, they claimed that the virtues of the first settlers developed over time into organic American virtues. In these terms an article in the *Monthly Magazine* described how the character that emerged through the experience of the settlement in New England became a national character: "The tendencies which they thus receive are not only forwarded and encouraged by imitation and example, but handed down with increase from age to age." Finally they become "interwoven in the fabric of the hearts and minds of...society," as if they were inherent.[14]

Connected to this celebration of the Pilgrims and Puritans was a revival of the idea of New Englanders as God's chosen people. As Lewis P. Simpson argues, New England's claim to moral and cultural preeminence lay in the idea of its unique spiritual bond: "a world-historical covenant with God." This meant a covenant between God and the community of the godly building their City on the Hill. New England leaders used this idea to interpret the new national union as a continuation of the original project of the Puritans. As proof for the divine providence of their forefathers, eighteenth-century Puritans gave the fact that the first settlers after all survived in the wilderness. They found "the special Providence of God...strikingly visible in the first settlement of New England," because God prevented the Indians from attacking them and "the ferocious natives...in many instances disposed to show kindness."[15]

With their description of America and New England as a wilderness and their emphasis on the process of civilization, New England historians supported the image of New England and America drawn by artists, poets, and travelers as a middle landscape between overcivilized Europe and savage Native America. They wanted traditional Puritan virtues to play a role in shaping the new collective identity, to add a traditional element to the new republican virtues. The idealization of the first settlers coincided with the image of contemporary New England virtues as they were exhibited in poetry, literature, paintings, and home decorations.

Landscapes between Wilderness and Civilization

New England attracted the first wave of tourists after the founding of the new nation. Travelers native to the region as well as those from neighboring states and from Europe praised a much improved road system, along with friendly and comfortable inns. The Englishman John Melish was impressed by New England's infrastructure. What he said about the Connecticut roads he found true for other New England states as well: "The state is supplied with good roads and bridges, some of which have been constructed on an ingenious plan and at great expense." Like the French Brissot de Warville, Europeans saw roads and bridges as "monuments" to New England's industry. Tourists carried home silver tankards with views of the Charles River Bridge as a souvenir. Like many other travelers, the New Englander Benjamin Silliman was quite pleased with the comfort and hospitality of the region's overnight accommodations and praised them as comparable to England's. About his lodging in Lenox, Massachusetts, he wrote: "Our dinner and treatment at the inn, were such as a reasonable traveler would have been very well satisfied with, at a country tavern in England." Englishman William Strickland agreed only in part. He found New England accommodations very comfortable, but indicated that European inns offered a higher standard. Probably like many tourists, he nevertheless praised New England lodgings because they exceeded his expectations by far.[16]

Other English travelers confirmed Silliman's favorable comparison of the New England inns with European inns, adding that New England accommodations were superior to anything offered in the

South. In 1801, for example, the *Connecticut Magazine* featured an article by an English traveler commenting on New England hotels: "The inns have accommodation for travelers, superior to any I have seen in the southern districts of America."[17]

Although the background and motivation of New England visitors differed, they drew a surprisingly consistent picture. Bostonian artists, provincial amateur painters, schoolgirls, and artisans joined the tourists in creating a collective image of New England when they depicted New England countryside, towns, and buildings on paintings, fireboards, mourning pictures, boxes, and clocks. Painted on household ornaments or etched on utensils, the image of New England reached a broad audience and became a popular commercial theme, useful as well as ornate.

Early observers of New England landscapes were looking for distinct American features, elements that distinguished the region's scenery from its European counterpart. Nearly two hundred years after its first settlement New England could still be described as a wilderness, especially when compared to populated, industrialized European landscapes. Both European visitors and American travelers found the wild character of American nature impressive and even picturesque. The wild scenery of New Hampshire, for example, enchanted Timothy Dwight:

> When we entered the notch [he wrote] we were struck with the wild and solemn appearance of everything before us. The scale on which all the objects in view were formed was the scale of grandeur only. The rocks, rude and ragged in a manner rarely paralleled, were fashioned and piled on each other by a hand operating only in the boldest and most irregular manner.[18]

Rude and wild features became characteristics of New England landscapes. This helped the first cohort of independent Americans and their European visitors to create a picture of a distinct American landscape. The image of an unnatural and overcivilized Europe served especially for American observers as the antithesis of their own concept of nature. To New Englanders and their visitors the rugged American landscape suggested that in contrast to Europe the United States was free of corruption.

But some American travelers were ambivalent toward this wilderness. In 1809, Elias Boudinot journeyed from his home in Burlington, New Jersey, to Boston to visit some friends. Together they hiked New Hampshire's White Mountains. The former congressman had mixed feelings about the rugged terrain; while he found it beautiful, it also frightened him: "The picturesque appearance of the surrounding Hills—the beautiful Sheet of Water above the falls—the tremendous roaring of the stream down the awful precipice, and the apparent existence of an Earthquake in the beginning of the time, as the Cause of such dreadful confusion of huge Massy Rocks, fill the spectator at once with awe & delight."[19]

Elias Boudinot was the descendant of a Huguenot immigrant family, a prominent and wealthy member of early Republican society. As a Federalist, the lawyer and statesman had been elected to the First Congress of the United States and served as director of the U.S. Mint for one decade beginning in 1795. Believing in Americans' progress in civilizing the wilderness, Boudinot invested in Western lands. New England virtues appealed to him because as a philanthropist he was convinced that propagating such virtues would increase civic virtue among his fellow countrymen. As many other members of the Northern elite who helped shape a collective image of New England, Boudinot participated in the Reform movement. He played the most important role in founding the American Bible Society in 1816. His devotion to the promotion of a combination of republican and Protestant ideals led him to the celebration of New England virtues. Boudinot shared this motivation with many of his contemporaries, who lived like him in one of New England's neighboring states and involved themselves in the region's identity. They found in the praise of New England an effective means to promote their philanthropic and Christian ideals. Furthermore, they thought that the romantic, idealized image of New England could help Americans to solve some of the problems they faced in creating their collective identity, as, for example, their fear of inferiority to Europe.[20]

The problem early Republicans such as Boudinot confronted with the American wilderness was that they wanted to reject both the image of "decadent European civilization" and the "savage" American wilderness brimming with Indians. They solved this conflict by portraying New England as a middle landscape between European overcivilization and Native American savage wilds. Although New England travelers celebrated this combination of rough nature and civilization, some, such as Almira Deering from Portland, Maine, the wife of the wealthy shipbuilder and merchant James Deering, identified areas that did not represent that ideal. On her trip from rural Maine to Boston, she characterized Boston's North Shore simply as "rough and uncultivated."

When the first generation of the new American nation wrote about a New England landscape, for example, they emphasized the balance between the cultivated areas and the wild aspects. In this manner Timothy Dwight outlined his view at the valley of the Ammonoosuc River in the White Mountains:

> For a considerable part of this distance it runs at the foot of the hills on the northern side, whose cliffs and woods, overhanging the stream, form with their wild magnificence a fine contrast to the softer scenery by which they are succeeded. From this spot the river...winds with an elegant course through a chain of intervals parted into rich farms...promising...to become a residence of peace, industry, and posterity.[21]

Picturesque scenes with a variety of romantic settings of wilderness and agricultural communities, views from hill or mountaintops whose grandeur provoked awe and fear, dominated images of the New England countryside. Dwight perceived landscape as if it came out of a painting. English writers and landscape designers had defined this picturesque ideal in the mid-eighteenth century. They described the picturesque as an aesthetic quality between sublimity and beauty shaped by a pleasing irregularity. Dwight was one of the first writers who brought such aesthetic ideas of the picturesque landscape to America. At the time when the president of Yale College set out for his travels in New England and New York during his summer breaks in the years between 1795 and 1815, the cult of the picturesque had exploded into a mania in England. Dwight's descriptions particularly reflect the ideas of William Gilpin, the great English popularizer of the picturesque, who taught the traveler to gather various elements of a landscape into a composition. While spectators of English countryside combined the natural landscape with country homes and ruined castles, the American version of these Gilpinesque strategies was to place the wild nature, in paintings and written descriptions, in a harmonic picture with meadows and neatly arranged towns.[22]

The cult of the picturesque crossed the Atlantic and influenced observers of American landscapes. Dwight was not Gilpin's only American student: the Englishman's works were much in fashion in America at the end of the eighteenth century. Other early American tourists, such as Dwight's Yale colleague and close friend Benjamin Silliman, also looked at landscape in this new way. In fact, "picturesque" and "romantic" are the most frequent terms in early Republican travel books. Two decades after Dwight began to scout his beloved New England, Silliman went on a tour from Hartford, Connecticut, to Quebec and drew the same pictures of a wilderness perfectly punctuated by cultivated fields and towns. Like Dwight, he preferred an elevated position on a hillside, the view that gave him control over nature, turned that open country into a landscape gallery. "You look...into a valley of extreme beauty, and great extent, in the highest state of cultivation," he wrote describing the Farmington River in Maine:

> Through the whole of this lovely scene, which appears a perfect garden, the Farmington river pursues its course, sometimes sparkling through imbowering [sic] trees, then stretching in a direct line, bordered with shrubbery, blue, and still, like a clear canal, or bending in graceful sweeps, round white farm houses, or through meadows of deepest green.[23]

Benjamin Silliman was a professor of chemistry at Yale and a friend of the school's president. After Silliman lost his father in his teenage years, when he was a student at Yale College, Dwight became a second father to him. Like many other New England boosters, he was educated and involved in the foundation of the new republic's literary and scientific institutions and publications. By advocating for Yale's medical school, Silliman played an important role in transforming the college into a university. In 1818, he established the *American Journal of Science*. As a religious person Silliman insisted, in contrast to most of his European colleagues, that science and religion were compatible. A trip to England in 1805–1806 gave him the opportunity to meet leading British scientists and to import the latest European scientific ideas to the United States. In addition to academic exchange, he gained an impression of European society and culture, which enabled him to distinguish the old from the new world. It was probably this transatlantic experience and his involvement in the creation of American science, the drive to help the new republic to compete with European civilization, that led him to follow Dwight's lead in inventing the picturesque landscape of New England. The legacy of Silliman's father, who was a prisoner of the British when Silliman was born, and his heroic deeds in the American Revolution caused a feeling of inferiority, which many of Silliman's generation shared. This generational struggle also played a role in motivating the scientist to promote the new republic and his region.[24]

The New England frontier was a place, where advocates of the new collective identity could imagine that the region's history continued or repeated itself. The more recently settled areas of Western Massachusetts, New Hampshire, and Maine encouraged the early Republican observer to compose an ideal picture of a middle landscape between civilization and wilderness. In these new frontier settlements, they saw early Republicans clearing forests and building towns just as their Puritan ancestors had done when they first settled the coastal areas of the region. Emphasizing a pattern of settlement and cultivation in the landscape enabled Dwight and his companions to recall the Puritan rhetoric of the jeremiad. At the New England frontier the myth of the Puritan tradition of Christian civilization could be displayed as an American tradition. These newly settled areas showed that the Puritan effort to clear the forest and create a fertile and lovely countryside with self-sufficient towns was an ongoing project. When Dwight talked about the frontier areas in his travel books, he always drew a line from the Puritans to contemporary frontier settlers. Settling in a wilderness molded the New England character and made its sons and daughters distinct. "It is scarcely possible," he wrote, "for a European to conceive of the hardship of attending a new settlement even on our present frontiers, where the country which surrounds him is able to supply the planter's wants." He made the following point: "The difficulties . . . of forming a plantation in the wilderness are such as to demand not a small share of that resolution and enterprise for which people of New England are so remarkably distinguished."[25]

The idealized image of the civilized wilderness did more than distinguish the new American nation from Europe. By emphasizing the process of cultivation as the central issue early Republican writers took sides with the poor settlers, who cultivated land at New England's frontier in Maine and Western Massachusetts, in their struggle with the wealthy great proprietors who owned those lands. In their descriptions, the New England nationalists gave agency to the ordinary people who did the actual work of "civilizing" the land. Sometimes their pictures even depicted the process of cultivating the land, cutting trees, planting crops, building houses and roads. Settlers might have interpreted this as support for their argument that they owned the work they did and, therefore, had only to pay the proprietors the value of the wild land. Since the proprietors shared the ideal of a middle landscape between civilization and wilderness, such images increased perhaps their willingness to recognize the settler's contribution and to agree to a compromise. Some intellectuals hoped that the collective ideal might help to ease class conflicts.[26]

Landscape painters of the late eighteenth- and early nineteenth century absorbed Gilpin's aesthetics as well. Unlike the later Hudson River School painters who gloried in the rugged American wilderness, early Republican artists created a civilized countryside. Ralph Earl's 1800 painting *Looking East from Denny Hill* showed a cultivated agrarian landscape. Like all contemporary observers of a picturesque scene, the native of Worcester, Massachusetts, chose the panoramic view from a hill. Earl painted winding rivers and hills beyond the white church spires, orderly fields, and hardworking farmers. Such cultivated landscapes certainly gained popularity through professionals such as Earl, but the work of a large number of itinerant amateur painters also brought the civilized image of the New England landscape to the most isolated communities. These traveling artists painted rural scenes over fireplaces or on boards used to close the chimney in the summer. Their work was instrumental in creating a New England image.[27]

The work of these unskilled painters was especially helpful in creating a collective image because they often copied illustrations from books and periodicals and contemporary engravings by professionals. Sometimes they used elements from European pictures. An example of such a fireboard is *Contemplation by the Shore* (see figure 1.1), painted in 1790 by an anonymous artist. Illustrating the increasing interest in the picturesque, it combines the dark forest with the open sea and a mountain scene in the background. The pastoral scene with grazing sheep, ships, and an elegant young woman underlines the region's level of cultivation and commerce, but also gives the painting some European character. "A View of the Town of Haverhill," a popular print published in 1819 from an earlier drawing by the local artist Mrs. Green (as she signed it) also celebrated man's influence on the

Figure 1.1 Artist Unknown, *Contemplation by the Shore*, fireboard, 1790 (courtesy of the Peabody Essex Museum, Salem, Massachusetts)

land, by highlighting symbols of civilization such as towns, bridges, and roads. As in many New England scenes of the time, the town is rather in the background. Ordinary New Englanders emphasized the rural landscapes surrounding their towns and often framed their images with a tall tree on each side. Large ancient trees were probably used as New England and American symbols because after centuries of deforestation Europe was comparatively barren.[28]

New England natives and travelers often compared what they observed in New England to European scenery.[29] The comparison with Europe was a double-edged sword. It led some American tourists to recognize what the new world was lacking. Contrasted with Europe, New England's natural landscape was not only rude and wild, but it also lacked the medieval ruins that were thought to be quintessentially picturesque. Without apology, New England's landscape painters replaced Europe's castles and abbeys with a typical New England village. Dwight, for example, declared the New England village a picturesque element: "Neat farmhouses standing on the hills, a succession of pretty villages with their churches ornamented with steeples, most of them white and therefore cheerful and brilliant, lent the last touches of art to a picture so finely drawn by the hand of nature."[30] After the foundation of the American nation, European visitors also celebrated an idealized New England town with the meetinghouse and the common surrounded by farmhouses and meadows. They revived the Puritan idea of the New England town as a culmination in the history of civilization. In their eyes the New England town embodied New England and American virtues. Courthouses, schools, and other public buildings stood for democracy and education, shops and mills for progress and industry, while the white houses and church steeples indicated purity, sobriety, and piety. All these attributes, New Englanders believed, enabled their towns to nurture republican virtues among their inhabitants, which were so essential for the new nation to survive and succeed. Thus townscapes emerged, at least in New England minds, as the key New England landscape.

Towns as Symbols of Republicanism

While writers reinvented Puritan New England in their publications, townspeople used architecture and landscape designs to connect their new national identity with the colonial past. As Joseph Wood has convincingly argued, colonial New England villages as we imagine them today were actually built during the early national period. After the Revolution, elegant two- and three-story homes and ornate churches with tall white steeples increasingly replaced modest colonial one-story houses and simple barn-like meetinghouses. The end of the ascendancy of the Congregational establishment and the union between church and state at the turn of the nineteenth century also had an impact on the new design of churches. The old barn-like design with the door on one side and the pulpit on the other gave way to a plan where people entered at the tower side and the pulpit moved to the end opposing the tower, which was much more church-like. Other religious sects such as Baptist, Methodists, Quakers, and Universalists gradually achieved equality when the Congregational church lost its privilege of collecting taxes. These denominations started to build their own churches in New England towns. While Colonial meetinghouses had served as places of worship and had harbored town meetings, early Republicans believed that churches should be solely used for religious services and requested town meetings to be held elsewhere. They converted the grazing areas for their cows on the commons into carefully landscaped centers for recreational activities. In many towns, the meetinghouse lot became the town common. By redesigning their homes and public spaces and defining them as typical colonial, New Englanders invented traditions of civilization and sophistication. The architects as well as the adopters of these traditions assumed that they were meant to serve the common good and thus help consolidate republicanism. Early Republican travelers were already documenting that process. When Elias Boudinot returned to Boston after eight years in 1809, he was impressed by the dramatic improvements. Especially striking to him was Beacon Hill, where grand houses had replaced "rough, broken and barren" ones. This vision of the New England town and the virtues it manifested was a powerful means by which people could imagine the national community and hope it would take on the republican character of New England. These pictures and descriptions were stylized enough to fit any town. Therefore, they enabled people to use this consensual vision of local institutions and networks, which shaped their daily lives, to create their imagination of their nation. Without that imagined embodiment of the nation in the local community, the national community would have been a mere theoretical framework. It could not have served as a community to which early Republican Americans became attached. The same is true, of course, for New England as a region. Since their towns and surrounding landscapes defined New England and were a daily reality at the center of people's lives, New Englanders could only imagine the nation in terms of their region.[31]

Because for many the New England town was a symbol of American republicanism, travelers rarely tired of giving a detailed description of every town they entered. Their journals are filled with repetitive data listing each town's public buildings, courthouses, colleges, churches, as well as commercial and industrial sites. The travelers' focus on the town was meant to demonstrate that American civilization could easily and comfortably coexist with wilderness. Silliman's account of the Western Massachusetts town of Lenox celebrates the town in the wilderness:

> It has a jail, a woolen manufactory, a furnace for hollow ware, an academy of considerable size, and a courthouse of brick, in a fine style of architecture; it is fronted with pillars, and furnished with convenient offices and a spacious court room; this room is carpeted, and what is more important, contains a library for the use of the bar. Lenox has fine mountain air, and is surrounded by equally fine mountain scenery.

To drive home his point, Silliman concluded that "no small town in England is so beautiful as Lenox, nor have the Europeans, in general any adequate idea of the beauty of the New-England villages." In praising his favorite New England towns, which included not only Lenox, but also Burlington at Lake Champlain in Vermont, Silliman was pointing to the region's Western settlements. This glorification of the Westward movement can be seen as an embryonic form of what would later be called "Manifest Destiny." New Englanders felt that it was their divine providence to move Westward to civilize the land and establish Protestant and republican ideals. This attitude and regional enthusiasm it sought to promote must have certainly helped New Englanders to overcome doubts when they wondered about the quality of New England life in contrast to promises of the Western frontier, because many people left the region for it.[32]

In addition to travel accounts, observers could find depictions of towns in magazines and on household utensils and decorations. These townscapes present the typical features of the New England town as the meetinghouse and the common and often uncovered active elements behind the sleepy harmonious visage. An oil painting by the local artist Daniel Bell showing the center of Framingham, Massachusetts, in 1808, with the meetinghouse, which dominated the common, the brick academy, and the schoolhouse, also depicts the three-story tavern and passengers waiting for the stage coach, the shoe and the gun shops. The cult of the New England town becomes most obvious with the appearance of towns in portraits and as ornamentation on household goods. With such images of stylized New England towns, the region's artists wanted to prove that their towns did not lack any element of progress or civilization characteristic of European cities, but that their smaller versions of cities were at the same time free from the corruption, pollution, and poverty prevailing in places such as London and Paris, or the new industrial centers such as Manchester and Lyon. Furthermore, they aimed to indicate that the New England settlement ideal was superior to Southern and Western equivalents. Joseph Stewart's 1793 portrait of Maria Malleville Wheelock shows Hanover, New Hampshire, in the background. Jeffersonian Republicans probably identified rather with town views on household utensils than with depictions in upper-class style portraits. Jane Otis Prior equated New England with English country towns. In 1822 she decorated the two ends of a sewing box with copies of prints of English picturesque scenes. On the back she created her own drawing of Thomaston, Maine. This combination of images of English landscapes and Prior's hometown indicates that she might have risen above the struggle between employing European heritage and inventing a unique American culture by suggesting that views of New England could endure exhibiting next to English scenes.[33]

New Englanders could also admire the image of their typical town on quilts and embroidery, which must have had a broader appeal than portraits. When schoolgirls started in the 1790s to paint and embroider so-called mourning pictures and family registry, in order to memorialize deceased relatives, they often included town scenes. The very large number of works such as the sampler of fourteen-year-old Sophia Stevens Smith picturing North Branford, Connecticut, shows the popularity of such town views and how iconographic towns already were for young girls.[34]

In addition to these town views, images of individual public buildings were quite in fashion. Every New Englander was familiar with the Boston State House and Faneuil Hall. Amateur artists and schoolgirls copied the Boston artist Samuel Hill's well-known engraving of Faneuil Hall, published in 1789 in the *Massachusetts Magazine*, on wall paintings and needlework. Rebecca Davis represented it precisely in a watercolor that memorialized her two younger brothers Levi and Simon. In the mourning picture for her brothers, Davis relocated Boston's large market hall in pastoral surroundings. The young girl envisioned the famous building in midst of farm workers and a country idyll. Views of the Boston State House were in such high demand that pottery manufacturer John Rogers specialized in dinner services with that pattern. He sold them not only on the home market, but also in Great Britain and Italy. With the pictures of these buildings New Englanders exported symbols of their civilization and republican spirit.[35]

In the eyes of many New Englanders and their visitors Boston, with its large public buildings, a growing number of literary societies, and thriving commercial activity, was seen as a particular locus of civilization. Many described Bostonian houses, stores, and dress styles as elegant. All these characteristics, they concluded, made the New England "capital" comparable to European cities. Interestingly, some inventors of the New England national identity thought that in contrast to the New England countryside Boston had developed some of the drawbacks of civilization. Timothy Dwight, for example, saw the need for more effective "energetic" police in the city. He also complained that in its early days Boston, like some older European cities, was built without a plan and, therefore, had a narrow and confusing system of streets and lacked bright public squares. Dwight preferred an "American" city plan with straight, wide avenues. Whether they expressed only praise for Boston as a center of civilization or also found a few signs of corruption in the city, New Englanders imagined a "middle" landscape between wilderness and civilization with rural characteristics and urban elegance as the New England American ideal. John Rogers's dinner service indicates this by picturing the State House with two cows grazing in front of it, on the meadows of the Boston Common. The fact that at that time cows were no longer grazing on the common shows the mythic quality of such images. Although some inventors of the new collective identity tried to make Boston fit into their regional vision of an American landscape, the city really displayed the quality of civilization. If they combined Boston with the frontier areas, however, New Englanders in the early republic might have nevertheless been able to imagine the unique American combination of wilderness and civilization and, therefore, an appropriate place for Boston in the regional American scenery.[36]

The ideal of a nation that combined rural and urban elements, which was probably spread most successfully through visual sources, is a variation on the model of a landscape between wilderness and civilization. Images emphasizing the nature surrounding New England towns and picturing city buildings such as Faneuil Hall in the middle of imaginary rural landscapes with farm workers in front of it, demonstrate how powerful the ideal was, especially among ordinary people and especially women, who produced and purchased many household items with such pictures.

This image enabled New Englanders to feel superior to overcivilized Europe and more civilized than the Southern and Western parts of the republic. It also helped them to imagine a landscape that was free of Native American relics. Moreover, it appealed to both Jeffersonians, who envisioned a nation of farmers, and Federalists, who aimed for an industrially thriving homeland. Such New England images indicate that ordinary people actively participated in the invention of early American nationalism.

While authors could only give exaggerated and stylized accounts of New England landscapes, in their arts and crafts, however, men and women completely reinvented such landscapes by visually relocating some of its elements. In one of these imaginary landscapes Faneuil Hall stood in an agrarian setting close to a family tomb. As Joyce Appleby has pointed out, the lines between urban and rural, private and public, blurred in visions of the new American identity.[37] While written sources help us detect these contents of early Republican identity, material culture tells us more about the process of inventing it. Visual sources reveal young girls' and itinerant artists' conscious use of their imagination to design pictures that defined their nation. This kind of popular participation itself was an American characteristic. These images, whether they moved buildings into new settings or just depicted a town and its surroundings, were successful in popularizing New England national icons because of their realistic and reportorial style. Ordinary New Englanders could always find their local townscape and landscape in these pictures because they did not dramatize as later paintings and always included such icons as mills, courthouses, farms, trees, and workers. In the minds of ordinary people, symbols of prosperous Federalist commerce and harmonic Jeffersonian agriculture easily merged.

Travelers, writers, and artists also glorified the region's colleges. New Englanders and their visitors proudly bought views of colleges as souvenirs and put them on their walls. The Needham artist Alvan Fisher, who was one of early America's most talented portrait and landscape painters, created two pictures of Harvard College. As often in his prolific career, Fisher also sold these paintings as engravings, and ceramic manufacturers copied them later on china. Colleges signified the region's high level of education, which New Englanders saw as an essential precondition for a good republican people and, therefore, in the New England mind, justified the region's feeling of superiority.[38]

Town views competed with images of New England ports for popularity and for a role in defining the new collective identity. New Englanders produced a very large number of depictions of seaports, which were major centers of commerce, or coastal landscapes with trading vessels in the background. George Ropes's *Crowningshield's Wharf* from 1806 (see figure 1.2) depicts India Wharf in the port of Salem, Massachusetts, a major international port, especially at the peak of neutral trade during the Napoleonic Wars. Townscapes depicted virtues such as education, purity, and democracy. Such port or coastal scenes, however, always crowded with shipping, emphasized New England's industry and prosperity. In contrast to towns, which appeared almost as isolated communities, ports expressed New England's internationalism and global connections. Not all New England observers participated in the celebration of towns and ports uncritically. When he saw the large buildings and ships in Bath, Maine, the English writer Edward Augustus Kendall wondered whether the port had not grown too fast. The rapidly expanding American economy, he feared, was not strong enough to continue to flourish if it lost European trading partners and markets through a longer period of inner-European wars. New Englanders who lived in the region's hinterland and often resented the wealthy globally connected coastal towns had probably a difficult time identifying with such port scenes.[39]

Beside public and commercial buildings, the refined and beautiful architecture of private houses caught the eye of travelers and artists. Many visitors to New England commented on the impressive homes. Elias Boudinot made trips to the Boston area, which he found "crowded with very handsome Seats and rich, well cultivated Gardens." Later he wrote, "The Villas on the way are really superb & magnificent."[40] Americans were proud and Europeans quite impressed that the young nation had already created such symbols of civilization, refinement, and wealth. In his portraits Ralph Earl often included a view of the estate belonging to his clients. This conveys

Figure 1.2 George Ropes, *Crowningshield's Wharf*, 1806 (courtesy, Peabody Essex Museum, Salem, Massachusetts)

New Englanders' attachment to their land and houses and their pride in them. Earl's 1792 painting of Oliver and Abigail Ellsworth pictures a neatly arranged domestic landscape. The chief justice and his wife sit in front of a window that opens onto the view of a typical eighteenth-century white New England house surrounded by elm trees and a fence, the very house in which the Ellsworths are seated. Like towns, private homes were used as decoration on sewing boxes, fireboards, clocks, and embroidery. The fireboard found in the Banister House in Brookfield, Massachusetts, picturing the house as it looked in the late eighteenth century, is an example of this fashion of house portraits. The painting shows what an important role such artifacts played as a medium to enable people to share imaginations. Of course, these depictions of such symbols of wealth and upper-class refinement could also breed class resentment. Images of country estates and their owners certainly rather pleased the taste of Federalists. Jeffersonians might have disliked the aristocratic undertones in these works. Itinerant artists spread not only images of New England, but also European elements. The flute player in the Banister house appears in a mid-century needlework picture from Maine and was common in French engravings of the time.[41]

In an attempt to appear civilized, New Englanders copied English garden styles. Elias Boudinot enjoyed the refined gardens he saw on his trip. About merchant Stephan Higginson's Brookline villa he wrote: "The grounds around [it] laid out much in the English style—The... Forest Trees extremely well arranged [...] The Kitchen garden at a distance, & thro' Which Walks... all bordered with Grapes and Flowers." Strikingly, during the first decades of their independence New Englanders followed the traditional English model of terraced, fenced square gardens. These fenced enclosures contrasted the wildness of the American landscape and added to it the much desired civilized element. In a time when many people feared anarchy and chaos, geometric flowerbeds and straight walks represented order and civility. At the turn of the century, however, New Englanders began to imitate the new English design of "natural" landscapes. As is obvious, Alvan Fisher's 1820 watercolor *The Vale*, the country estate of Boston merchant Theodore Lyman, marks this transition to the English picturesque style. Lyman's country estate featured a natural garden designed by English gardener William Bell.[42] By 1820 this natural landscape style had almost replaced geometric gardens in New England. The fact that New Englanders employed such English picturesque conventions to promote an American identity demonstrates the ambiguity of their attitude toward Europe and more specifically in this case toward England. While they wanted to distinguish themselves from their former mother country, New Englanders at the same time used European features as models for their own landscape designs. Observers could, of course, interpret such landscape architecture in different ways. Federalists were more likely to be proud of the republic's ability to create sophisticated "English" gardens. Jeffersonian Republicans, however, may well have perceived them as "aristocratic" European displays of superiority, prone to corrupt republican spirit.

Mills and other factories also appeared as picturesque elements. When New England began to industrialize at the end of the eighteenth century, many of its inhabitants were excited about the new opportunities to leave their farms for the textile and paper mills and to supplement a family's farm earnings. Not surprisingly, given this warm reception, artists and writers turned these industrial sites into ornaments of the natural New England landscape. Dwight was already integrating the first symbols of industrialization into his pictures of the New England countryside. "This village," he wrote about Providence, Rhode Island, "is well built and wears a flourishing aspect. The river is a large millstream.... Directly under the bridge commences a romantic fall which... furnishes a number of excellent millseats." In the first decade of the nineteenth century, when more and more farming villages grew into industrial towns, the presence of mills in the images of New England landscape increased dramatically. Travel books, diaries, and even a tourist pocket guide added a detailed list of all industries to their repetitious accounts of state, school, and courthouses. Boudinot's description of Norwich indicates the ease with which New England accommodated the factory in its rural landscape: "Below the falls are the finest mills in the State. We took notice of an Oil Mill [...] a Paper Mill [...] a Fueling Mill, a Grist Mill, a Saw Mill...."[43]

Francis Alexander's 1822 view of "Globe Village" (see figure 1.3) visualizes this early local industry. The mill is located in the romantic setting of a small town surrounded by an agricultural landscape. The image thus includes Federalist ideals of industry and progress as well as symbols of Jeffersonian agricultural harmony. Like many amateur artists of his time, Alexander left his native Connecticut and traveled from town to town between Providence, Rhode Island, and Boston, where he in 1825 eventually met Gilbert Stuart, who recognized his talent and trained him as a professional painter.

The image of industrial sites as part of the picturesque landscape was also very present in newspapers. As early as 1789 the *Columbian*

Figure 1.3 Francis Alexander, *Globe Village*, painting, ca. 1822

Figure 1.4 *View from the Green Woods toward Canaan and Salisbury, in Connecticut*, engraving, Columbian Magazine, 1789 (courtesy, American Antiquarian Society)

Magazine published the "View from the green woods towards Canaan and Salisbury, in Connecticut" (see figure 1.4). The engraving shows a traveler walking down a mountain exposed to a view of the typical New England landscape of hills, meadows, churches, and black smoke signaling the location of the Salisbury Iron Works. In this picture, such rough natural elements as a steep hill and an approaching storm dominate again. The image of the mill in a typical New England town surrounded by idyllic farm properties introduced a middle landscape that offered a compromise between clashing partisan visions for the nation's future. With its emphasis on industrial progress as well as on pastoral idyll, the New England mill scene offered a collective ideal for Federalists and Republicans. This does not mean that some Federalists did not hope to use such depictions to slowly convince their opponents of America's need to industrialize. Those Federalists might have attempted to suggest that Americans were able to control industrialization and would thereby avoid its European ills. It does also not mean that some Jeffersonians did not always reject that middle landscape because of its manufacturing components. Still, to many people who lived with the reality of multiplying mill towns and family members leaving their farms to live there, such picturesque mill scenes must have been appealing. Bringing together industrial and agricultural elements in an ideal New England landscape, picturesque mills helped overcome partisan disruptions within the new collective identity.

Churches, schools, court houses, dwellings, and mills were in fashion in early republican portrayals of New England not only because of their picturesque quality, but even more because they served to indicate a high degree of civilization and posterity. They sought to demonstrate that although America was crude and less populated and did not produce works of art like Europe, it had still in a very short time created civil institutions, fine architecture, and industry that could easily compete with her. Moreover, these elements added up to the pious, educated, industrious, prosperous, and democratic New England way, the cornerstone of the whole country's well-being. By placing industries in romantic landscape settings, Americans emphasized again the ideal middle landscape between civilization and wild nature in the new world, whereas, in the old world, industry often replaced natural environments.

Moreover, such visions could still serve as a common ideal of Federalists and Jeffersonians. This was the case even after 1800, when Federalism started to decline, because New England travelers placed these industrial towns into picturesque rural landscapes. Such images appealed to Democratic Republicans as well because they seemed to combine progress, profit, and American superiority over Europe with an agricultural American character. It was the emphasis on both industrial commerce and agriculture that made them an essential component of New England's collective identity. New England maintained a

Federalist culture even after the political decline of the party. This is most obvious in Maine, where Democratic Republicans began to dominate soon after Jefferson's election. Although Jeffersonians gained power, the idea that a state of Maine would be able to industrialize remained a strong argument for the separation from Massachusetts.

The best example of celebrating the New England town in the years after the foundation of the American nation is Timothy Dwight's poem *Greenfield Hill.* From 1783 until 1795, when he was called to the presidency of Yale, Dwight served as the minister of Greenfield, a rural parish in the town of Fairfield in southwestern Connecticut. It was this experience of New England village life that inspired him to praise its goodness and announce his imperial dream for its spread outward across the entire nation. Although Dwight imitated the style of British poets, his poem is distinctly American. It celebrates the New England town as a way of life and the New England ideals of hard work, piety, and neighborliness as particularly American virtues. The basis for these New England virtues was the social, economic, and religious institutions of the town—the Congregational Church, the town meeting, the schoolhouse, and the family farm. In the poem, Dwight takes particular pride in them because they demonstrate the republican reforms undertaken in the new world. A comparison with their European counterparts is not favorable to the latter. Dwight finds New England churches, town governments, schools, and family farms the "noblest institutions, man has seen." Like many European visitors the New Englander praises the New England land tenure and emphasizes its nurturing effect on the republicanism of the people.[44]

According to Dwight and many contemporaries such as America's first geographer Jedidiah Morse, a close friend, education was a prerequisite for such a republican system. Molded by Puritan traditions of Bible-reading and self-government and the classical belief that a republic needs educated citizens to survive, Dwight saw universal education as a pivotal element of what constituted New England. Such a universal education was a necessary prerequisite for participatory democracy. Periodicals published in Northern cities outside New England joined the New England minister in praising New England town governments and schools. Journals such as the Philadelphia *American Museum* glorified New England as the embodiment of the American republic and more importantly contrasted its democratic structure with the unequal "aristocratic" organization of Southern society. In an article on

New England republicanism, the *American Museum* wrote as follows:

> The constitutions of the New England states breathe the spirit of pure republican equality. Elections are free—are frequent—and the right of suffrage is not confined to landholders, as in Virginia, but is extended to almost all the citizens of full age, who also may be chosen to office . . . the laws . . . protect no right or great man in his estate against his creditors; they provide for the poor, and what is far better, they prevent the increase of poor, by providing schools for the children.

Strikingly, this particular account claimed that even New England's natural landscape, the composition of the land, supported the democratic social structure: "A soil, too rugged for any but free hands to till, is found, on numberless trials, unprofitable when engrossed into great plantations." Jeremy Belknap even wanted to distinguish his beloved New England from the Southern states by emphasizing that European remarks about the unhealthiness of American weather were only true for the South.[45]

European visitors who came to New England to observe democracy also admired New England's "civil governments." Frances Wright, a Scotswoman traveling through North America in 1821, underlined education and democracy as typical benefits of New England society. In one of her letters back home, she wrote the following about Vermont: "In scrupulous regard to the education of her citizens, in the thorough democracy of her institutions, in her simple morals and hardy industry, Vermont is a characteristic daughter of New England." Wright came to the United States for the first time in 1818 as a young woman of twenty-three. When she returned to Great Britain two years later, she published her book on American society, probably hoping to provide provocative ideas for social reforms in her own country. Wright's praise of the new world led to her friendship with another European admirer of the new American nation, General Lafayette. She timed her second visit to the United States to coincide with Lafayette's return to America in 1824 and accompanied him on most of his tour. Together they met many political leaders of the new nation including Thomas Jefferson and James Madison. On their trip through Southern states Wright reaffirmed her rejection of slavery and, therefore, despised the South. Like many Northerners, Wright believed in America's mission to civilize the Western wilderness; she invested in land in Tennessee. In 1829, she finally settled in New York, where she saw better opportunities to pursue her activism for equal rights for women than in Europe. As an advocate for slave emancipation, Wright clearly identified with the emerging Northern identity and used her Western property to experiment with her ideas.[46]

Dwight and his fellow observers of New England believed in a mutually supportive relationship between the New England landscape and the character of its inhabitants. New England towns operated through the republican virtues of their citizens, while at the same time the towns' institutions produced good republicans. Travel books and periodicals told the first cohort of Americans that the unique New England landscape was molding the American character. This idea also included the uncivilized part of the landscape. In the popular imagination civilized towns and pasturelands were not to be separated from mountains, forests, and lakes. The American picturesque required both elements. Benjamin Silliman was pointing to this mutual relationship between the national landscape and character when he wrote that "national character often receives its peculiar cast from natural scenery," and continued, "natural scenery is intimately connected with taste, moral feeling, utility, and instruction."[47] He imagined the wild and rugged American landscapes as creating a people free from corruption. The population thus educated on the other hand, he thought, added some structured elements to the landscape and transformed it into a more beautiful, romantic, and productive countryside.

The People of New England as Model Republicans and True Americans

New Englanders proudly imagined themselves to be pious, orderly, industrious, simple, and educated. With their commitment to liberty and the common good they believed they were model republicans. Artists, writers, and tourists confirmed this view. Their praise of the region's social, religious, and economic institutions and democratic governments matched their description of New England virtues. Advocates of the New England national identity gave a romanticized description of the effectiveness of these institutions when they claimed that the region's republicanism embedded in them was so far-reaching that even people of lower ranks displayed these characteristics. Thus, Elias Boudinot was pleased to notice such benefits of republicanism. "An extraordinary Spirit of liberality & unbounded Charity," he recorded in his travel book, "seems to prevail among all orders of the Inhabitants. Their public Institutions of Charity & usefulness are very numerous, and the Christian Virtues seem to abound among them." Such praise of moral uniformity sounds like a defense against

Jeffersonian complaints of aristocratic attitudes among Federalists. New England's role as a model for other Northern states becomes clear, when Boudinot, who was visiting from New Jersey, contrasts New Englanders with his fellow citizens at home: "Neither profane Swearing or Drunkenness, prevail among the lower ranks of the people, as they do with us." Although such descriptions were dramatic oversimplifications, some journals and magazines sold in New York and Pennsylvania subscribed to these ideals and argued that New England virtues were components of a Northern identity.[48]

Strikingly, many foreigners, such as the Englishmen William Strickland, John Melish, Isaac Weld, the Scotswoman Frances Wright and her countryman John Goldie, as well as the Frenchman Brissot de Warville, also wrote glowingly about the people of New England.[49] In spite of their general praise for New England people, however, some travelers did not perceive New England virtues as consistent throughout the region. Even Boudinot, for example, was disappointed with the people of Rhode Island because he found them "not only ignorant, but careless & indolent." He explained their attitude by reference to the lack of schools and churches in the state. The Congregational clergyman Jeremy Belknap, in contrast, had no excuse for the small-mindedness he observed among the people of Dover, New Hampshire, where he served as a minister for nearly two decades. Boudinot and Belknap both expected model republicans to be model Christians as well and tended to exclude from the imagined New England nation everybody who was not perceived as such. Belknap also found his parishioners in Dover not well educated and was disappointed that they had failed to establish a public school. As a haven for Baptists, Rhode Island did not fulfill Boudinot's ideal of Puritan piety. His fellow New England boosters Jedidiah Morse and Timothy Dwight also evicted Rhode Island from New England because of its religious pluralism and secularism.[50]

European admirers of New England culture were often hoping to encourage their countrymen to emigrate to the new world. They especially praised New England because they adopted the belief that New Englanders and some other Northerners shared that the region was the best example of true American virtues. Just as some New Englanders wanted to counter a feeling of inferiority caused by emigration to the new Western territories, European New England boosters sometimes tried to promote the region for immigration. These travelers based their campaign for emigration on their own ideas of the opportunity to find economic or ideological freedom in America. Some eventually settled in the United States themselves. Isaac Weld, for example, published the journal of his tour through the United States and Canada in order to motivate large numbers of his Irish compatriots to leave for the United States. His book was also available for non-English speakers in French and German translations and introduced these people as well to his praise of the new world. As the president of the Dublin Royal Society, Weld was an influential figure. When he traveled through the United States, he met George Washington and Thomas Jefferson.[51]

European travelers who came especially from societies where language, manners, and style of dress indicated social status, and where coffeehouses and pubs were socially segregated, promoted the degree of social equality as most impressive. An article in the Boston *Monitor* comparing New England with old England claimed the former colony differed from its motherland even in its language structure. The article helped create a myth of linguistic equality in New England. Unlike Great Britain, where the English language divided the country along geographic and class lines, it said, in New England language was a unifying factor, as all inhabitants spoke Standard English. Different Saxon and Celtic dialects aggravated the communication among Britons, while upper-class Englishmen and women cultivated a distinctive form of speech. In New England, however, the article asserted, everyone spoke like the English upper class: "The bookish, polished or latinized Saxon, is scarcely known to one fiftieth of the British people, but it is, properly speaking, the only and vulgar language of New-England." This was, of course, pure New England nationalist propaganda that ignored the different, sometimes uneducated, dialects of the region. Like many Europeans, the Scottish tourist John Goldie participated in that kind of New England promotion when he expressed his fascination with the fact that people of all sorts spent their evenings in the same pub and interacted as equals, "the President and the poorest person mixing indiscriminately."[52]

Underlining the superiority of New Englanders, Dwight wrote in his *Travels*, "They are the only people on the continent who originally understood,...the inseparable connection between liberty and good order." A proof for Dwight was, he claimed, the almost total absence of capital crimes committed in the region. Dwight's point was, as in many cases, exaggerated. Proudly he added another exaggeration to the repertoire of New England advocates: "There have been fewer capital crimes committed in New England since its settlement than in any other country on the globe." An Englishman writing for the *Connecticut Gentlemen's and Ladies' Monthly* drew the same picture of orderliness. He felt very safe in Boston: "The police of the town is well regulated; disorderly houses and fragrant breaches of the public peace being rarely met with or taking place."[53] This social harmony New England travelers referred to in their enthusiastic accounts was extremely exaggerated, but the early republic was indeed one of the calmest periods in New England history. A comparatively even distribution of wealth contributed to the consensual atmosphere indicated in the travel descriptions.

In the eyes of contemporary observers, one reason for the orderliness in New England was, of course, that New Englanders even of the lower sorts were very well educated. New England advocates claimed that republicanism in New England had advanced further than in the Mid-Atlantic and Southern states because the lower classes were much better educated. In this theory education made the lower sorts better republicans who contributed to the common good and deserved more political participation. Dwight contrasted his native land with New York and found the level of education in New England superior: "Accordingly, [in Boston] there are many more men in proportion to the whole number liberally educated than in New York, and far more than in any other town in America. There is also much more extensive diffusion of intelligence and information among all classes of people." Also, Dwight felt Europeans could not compete with the educated New Englanders. An Englishman joined his New England contemporaries in amplifying the superiority of education in the region when he informed his readers that "every native of New-England can read and write. This cannot be said of natives of Britain." Although literacy in New England was very high, it was certainly not the case that every single New Englander had learned to read and write.[54]

Many observers also believed education tempered New Englanders' religious zeal and encouraged liberal and democratic attitudes. The English tourist John Melish, for example, said the following about New Englanders: "Though, much attached to the subject of religion, they are more liberal . . . than any people I have been yet been amongst."[55] After his travels through the United States in the years between 1806 and 1811, Melish, who shared many Northerners' enthusiasm for New England, settled in Philadelphia. He decided to stay in the United States because the idealized image of the young republic as a land of opportunity was, of course, true for some people. Talented people in occupations that were needed did indeed have opportunities to prosper. Melish was a merchant and geographer and a gifted draftsman. When his cotton business in England declined, he saw new opportunities in

Philadelphia's expanding print sector. Beside his own travel notes, which he published in 1812, Melish published and printed maps. Among the maps he created in his shop were the ones he drew for the illustration of his own writings. His maps sold so well that he was able to employ thirty people. Encouraged by his own professional success in the United States, the Englishmen published his travel notes in order to convince his former countrymen to follow his example and emigrate to America. In his books, he especially praised New Englanders because he shared the common Northern belief that the region embodied the new American nation. Descriptions of New England virtues, he assumed, would be particularly effective in attracting new English immigrants. Melish probably hoped that New Englanders' piety would promise a religious refuge from the secularized society of nineteenth-century England.

New Englanders' piety was regarded as another characteristic that made them good republicans. Contemporaries believed it inspired a high level of morality and motivated people to work toward the common good. Journals and books published at the turn of the nineteenth century routinely compared New Englanders and Southerners, arguing that religion—like democracy, good manners, and education—was far advanced in New England. An English traveler's analysis connected a decay of religion, which he perceived in the South and Mid-Atlantic States, with immorality. "In the midland and southern provinces of the United States," he wrote, "irreligion, with its usual attendant, immorality, seems to be advancing with hasty strides." New England travelers Boudinot and Belknap also identified areas in New England where people were not as religious as they had hoped. Such statements were, of course, exceptions to the general praise of New England religiosity.[56]

Another highly praised New England virtue related to religion was the simple lifestyle. In a time when displays of social superiority had fallen into disrepute, American observers of early Republican New England found expressions of the plain and simple character everywhere in the people's manners, clothing, and language. When he visited the Northington Valley in New Hampshire, Benjamin Silliman liked the modest lifestyle of the people gathering there: "The people, evidently agricultural, had scarcely departed from the simplicity of our early rural habits." Like many contemporaries, he was especially pleased with the local use of domestic instead of imported European goods. European commentators also found the simple New England ways remarkable. In her summary of the virtues that fueled her admiration for New England, Frances Wright spoke, probably unaware of this fact, for most of her European fellows who came to discover the other side of the Atlantic:

> There is not a more truly virtuous community in the world than that found in the democracies of the east. The beauty of their villages, the neatness and cleanliness of their houses, the simplicity of their manners, the sincerity of their religion . . . their domestic habits, pure morals and well administered laws, must command the admiration and respect of every stranger.[57]

New England women also won their share of praise. They were seen as personifications of republicanism, manifesting New England virtues such as sobriety, plain beauty, and education. They served especially as symbols of refined New England manners. Almost every New England tourist enthused about the respectable, handsome, and intelligent women of the region. They praised working women with whom they came into contact—a hostess at an inn, a widow who supported herself by running a bed and breakfast, a daughter who helped in her father's tavern. Sometimes visitors talked about women they met at dinner or at a tea reception. After attending a dinner party in Boston, Elias Boudinot praised the women's sophisticated manners: "The fine understanding, displayed at dinner, and the elegance & beauty of the Ladies at Tea gave us a high Idea of the cultivated manners of Massachusetts." Others found the level of women's education remarkable: "The ladies of Boston . . . are handsome, with fine complexions . . . [and] have a richness of intellect." Likewise, Benjamin Silliman was so delighted by the female hosts in hotels and restaurants that he frequently mentioned their correctness and sobriety. At a New Haven stop he wrote: "We dined pleasantly; every thing was good, and neatly and well prepared, and we were attended by one of those comely respectable young women, who, so often, in our public houses, perform these services, without departing from the most correct, respectable, and amiable deportment."

Silliman's point was unmistakable: in a republic working New England women retained their virtue and respect. It has, of course, to be considered that Silliman stayed at the more upscale inns in New England, which certainly lent his view of the region's hostesses a certain class bias.

New Englanders also praised their women's contribution to the War of Independence. In his patriotic "New England Poem," poet William Tappan accentuated the general admiration and gratitude for

New England's leading role in the Revolution and especially stressed the sacrifice of New England "daughters" in giving up imported luxury goods. In this formulation, women actively participated in supporting the republican cause. And they indeed did: In the early republic, New England mothers took their task as "republican mothers" seriously. Mary Spence, the wife of a wealthy Boston merchant, for example, instructed her son Keith, who attended a boarding school, in pursuing proper New England manners. In her letters she advised him that he should never drink, fulfill all his duties carefully and in an orderly way, study hard at the academy, and always go to church on Sundays.[58]

Although the early Republican image of New Englanders was pretty consistently favorable, Yankees did also have a notorious reputation. Some anecdotes and plays described the typical Yankee as ambitious and unscrupulous in pursuing his goals of making money, running manufactories, and seeking public office. The "Yankee trick" was a common term in such material and indicated that clever Yankees cheated on everybody else in order to make money through all kinds of different ventures. Especially the Yankee peddler traveling to the South and to the new Western settlements, where he sold household items, toys, and books, was connected with fraud. "A Yankee Trick," published in the *New England Farmer*, is typical for such anecdotes. In this story a host at a Southern tavern refuses a Yankee peddler because of Yankees' bad reputation. When the peddler promises to show the host a Yankee trick, the curious Southerner allows him to stay at his tavern. The next day the Yankee urges the landlady to purchase a bed coverlet from him and she convinces her husband to buy it because it exactly matches her other coverlets. When the Yankee is about to leave, the host protests that he has forgotten his trick, but the peddler assures him that he would soon find out what the trick was. It is up to the reader to conclude that the Yankee has sold the host the coverlet from the very room where he spent the night. While stories such as this indicate how Americans from other regions felt threatened and exploited by Yankees, they also show that at the same time they admired the cleverness and business-mindedness of their Yankee countrymen. Interestingly, New England newspapers in such places as Boston, Providence, and Portsmouth as well as other Northern publishers in New York City, Albany, and Philadelphia printed these stories. The notorious Yankee reputation grew in the decades after 1830, when the number of anecdotes and plays depicting them as money-driven, clever, exploitive, and unscrupulous increased noticeably. Southerners certainly performed such plays and bought collections of Yankee anecdotes. Perhaps New Englanders read the Yankee stories as statements of the naiveté, backwardness, and inferiority of people in other regions, while some of their neighbors and especially Southerners focused on Yankee fraud and other negative characteristics.[59]

As New Englanders attempted to create their New Englandized America, they did so with an ambivalent attitude toward the old world. On the one hand, they used Europe, and especially England, as a model for the invention of their nation. Northern periodicals proudly published travel accounts of Europeans underlining the similarity between New England and Europe. American tourists in New England constantly compared what they observed with Europe. But to complete their independence from Great Britain, Americans had to develop a collective identity that differed from the previous English one. While during the Revolution colonists had claimed to defend true English liberties and virtues, in the early years of the republic they began to develop distinctly American virtues. According to this new image of the nation, the United States had surpassed Europe by preserving its standards of civilization, but avoiding its corruptness, overpopulation, and social segregation.[60] Although the French Revolution had caused some enthusiasm among Americans because it enabled them to interpret their own Revolution as the beginning of a general republican movement, Protestantism and the colonial heritage linked young republicans rather with England than with France. Timothy Dwight, for example, reminded his countrymen to take pride in their British origin, because it was that heritage which had laid the path for present American virtues:

> The present race of Americans can never be sufficiently thankful that their ancestors came from Great Britain and not from any other country in Europe. In Great Britain they formed most of their ideas of liberty and jurisprudence. There also, they found learning and their religion, their morals and their manners. The very language which they learned in that country opens to their descendants, as in a great degree it had opened to them, more valuable literature, science, and some wisdom than could be found in all the languages of Europe united.

Dwight's nationalism displayed the sort of anti-Catholic and anti-French tendencies that helped also to distinguish the character of the American nation from that of its Canadian neighbor. The New England College professor contrasted his own people with uneducated, drinking, and oppressed French Catholics:

> Had the American states been colonized from France, the lands [would] have been parceled out, as were those of Canada, between numerous

> noblesse and a body of ecclesiastics probably not less numerous. The great body of the New England people, instead of being what they now are, an enlightened independent yeomanry, would have been vassals of these two classes of men, mere Canadian peasantry, sunk below the limits of civilization, unable to read or to think [. . .] with an occasional draught of whiskey; Roman Catholics of the lowest class, their consciences in the keeping of ecclesiastics prostrating themselves before a relic and worshipping a crucifix or a cake.[61]

The European nationalism that emerged after the French Revolution simultaneous with the American collective identity turned into an intellectual problem for the young American republic. Europeans equated nation, land, language, and history, but the United States lacked a distinct American language and white Americans had neither an organic connection with the land nor a long history there. New Englanders had thus to rely even more on the invention of more recent historical traditions as well as landscapes and virtues that were uniquely American and clearly distinguishable from everything European. Because of their European origins and colonial past, Europe served nevertheless as a model for the young nation, but America was at the same time imagined to exceed the European example. While the new national identity included at least some European characteristics, the South was completely excluded from the image of the new American nation. During the nation's first three decades Northerners were already starting to demand that the South "Americanize" by adopting New England virtues in order to become part of their construct of the American nation. It was a nation, as Joyce Appleby has shown, created in the image of the North. But it is important to specify this argument even more narrowly by emphasizing that New England stood at the center of that Northern identity. Northerners believed that New England was the true America. New Englanders were willing to include their New York and Pennsylvania neighbors in their vision of America, but they insisted on their own superiority.[62]

New England Embodies the Nation

When tourists praised New Englanders' work ethic, proud Yankees thought that this clearly distinguished them from their Southern and even mid-Atlantic countrymen. As early as 1794–1795, the Englishman William Strickland found New Englanders to be: "the most active and enterprising people . . . and best calculated on account of their sobriety, hardihood, spirit and knowledge to form and carry on a new establishment." Although England's industrial revolution was decades old, English tourists defined the drive to prosper as an American characteristic and New Englanders welcomed the opportunity to put their stamp on the entire nation. An article in the *Massachusetts Magazine* stated: "It is indeed to be wished that the sober industry here so universally practiced may become more extensive through the union, and form the national character of several Americans."[63]

Tourists, writers, and artists established New England as the republican and commercial model for the new nation. This image of the region as the leading member of the union excluded the slave South from New England's imagined nation. The creators of New England America also left out the history of New England slavery and the region's slave trade because they feared that it would weaken and conflict their newly invented identity. Emphasizing business-mindedness as a typical New England characteristic, Timothy Dwight described the inhabitants of the Mid-Atlantic States as less active and less gifted. "Boston is distinguished for its habit of business. A man who is not believed to follow some useful business can scarcely acquire or retain even a decent reputation," the Yale president recorded in his *Travels*, "A traveler passing through is struck with the peculiar appearance of activity everywhere visible. Almost all whom he meets move with a sprightliness differing very sensibly from what he observes in New York and Philadelphia." Residents of the Southern states seemed not to share New England virtues at all. New Englanders have "great solidity, of character in conducting business," an Englishman wrote, "whilst innumerable mischiefs have resulted in the extensive speculations too frequently occurring among the people of the south." A 1791 article in the Philadelphia *American Museum* agreed: "New Englandmen are more industrious, thrifty, and frugal than the citizens of the Southern states—they have long engrossed the principal part of the coasting trade of the two Carolinas and Georgia."[64]

The primary reason for the South's commercial and industrial backwardness was held to be slavery. Slaves, an article in a Philadelphia newspaper explained, were, of course, not interested in making profit for their owner and were, therefore, lazy and did a bad job: "A Carolinian planter owns a schooner worked by Negroes. Those poor wretches are not so much interested in the profits of the vessel, and make little or no exertion to expedite the trip. On the contrary, they will sleep whole tides in their favour." New England vessels, however, were successful and profitable because free African-American laborers motivated by the promise of their own profit worked very hard.

> The New England vessels, on the contrary, are some of them very elegant, beautiful pictures to the eye, all of them well found and fitted, and worked by temperate, industrious, bold, and hardy seamen. To their transcendent and lasting praise spoken, they are the only seamen in the universe, who are generally interested in their vessels. They are all owners.... Is it any thing surprising, at this time of day, that temperate and industrious freemen, sailing in vessels in their own property, should take the coasting trade from wretched, enslaved Africans? Surely no.[65]

The implication is that free African Americans had adopted New England virtues. As this model suggests, the South was excluded from New England nationalism. New Englanders and their visitors portrayed the South as antithesis of the New England epitome. Especially for people such as Dwight and Jedidiah Morse, the South became an "anti-image of sober, republican" New England. They thought that slavery and the absence of Sabbatarianism prevented republicanism from flourishing in the South. In the New England mind, the South's aristocratic slave society and leisurely lifestyle was a threat to the republican New England ideal. The only way for the South to become part of the imagined American community would have been to adopt New England virtues. Remarks distinguishing New England vehemently from the South, which occurred in travel books and magazines written and published by Northerners throughout the 1790s and first two decades of the nineteenth century, show that a sectionalist identity already emerged before the Hartford Convention of 1814–1815 and the crisis of 1819. Already in the 1780s, Morse and Noah Webster found moral landscape of model homogeneous New England villages lacking in the South and described it as raw and diverse. It was this sectionalism emerging over the first thirty years of the American nation that brought about the conflict between North and South whether new Western territories should become slave or free states. Even if temporarily resolved by the Missouri Compromise, these sectional tensions would grow over the course of the century.[66]

In the winter of 1814–1815, New England Federalists who had been talking about New England's secession from the United States during the War of 1812, met in Hartford, Connecticut, to discuss the issue of their region leaving the union. Although Moderates were able to prevent a resolution of succession, many Federalists wanted to push for changes in the Constitution. They declared that they wanted to restrict the presidency to one term, which was obviously aimed at Jefferson. They also hoped to abolish the three-fifth clause, which benefited all states with slavery. The timing of the Hartford Convention worked out to the Federalists' disadvantage: The victory of New Orleans increased nationalism throughout the United States and the Federalists' secessionist aims made them appear treasonous, even in the eyes of many fellow New Englanders. Even if the idea of New England secession failed to turn into a triumphant reality and New Englanders seemed to accept the union more easily after the Hartford Convention, their aspiration to force their own values onto Southerners grew more and more ambitious in the years between 1815 and 1825. Once New Englanders parted from the idea of secession, they started to promote their culture even more vehemently.

While New Englanders used the institution of slavery to distinguish themselves from Southern slaveholders, they tried at the same time to erase both their own history of slavery and the history of black New Englanders. New Englanders were hypocritical in their feeling of moral and cultural preeminence and superiority over the South. Even if New England had a relatively small number of slaves during the 150 years of New England slavery, the institution of slavery had shaped the region. Slaves clustered on the seacoast and lived in the same places were the region's political and cultural leaders. The society of Newport, Rhode Island, for example, had evolved around slavery. Moreover, slaves made an important contribution to the New England economy. The work slaves provided in New England households enabled their masters to get involved in new business ventures and to turn the region into the industrial and commercial center that it became in the late eighteenth and early nineteenth century. Slavery, as Joanne Pope Melish points out in her book on race and gradual emancipation in New England, contributed immensely to the "expansion and diversification of the New England economy."[67] Some New Englanders such as John and Nicholas Brown, the founders of Brown University, had made a lot of money in the slave trade. Moreover, when slavery in New England was gradually abolished after the Revolution, New Englanders did not welcome free blacks in their society, but rather wanted to remove them mostly through colonization.

New Englanders replaced the history of New England slavery with the myth of white New Englanders' republicanism and reinvented the institution of slavery as a purely Southern evil. This neglect of black New Englanders and their history helped white New Englanders to feel superior to their Southern countrymen and to imagine their region as the true America and a true republic. During the years of the early republic, New Englanders denied their own involvement in

American slavery and their emerging racist and discriminating attitude toward free black New Englanders.[68]

New Englanders nurtured a vision of New England ways spreading across the union. In the wake of the Revolution New Englanders left their old thickly populated communities and moved to the unsettled areas of upstate New York and the Middle West where they founded churches, schools, and civil governments. An article in the Boston *Gentlemen and Ladies' Town and Country Magazine* celebrated a New Englandization of America through migration by turning a sometimes frightening process into a positive event. "Our country-men and kinsmen of New England, for such I am proud to call them," an author explained in 1789, "are like herbs and trees, which encrease [*sic*] in beauty and vigour, by being transplanted." Dwight labeled the western part of New York "a colony from New England." Because of this phenomenon New Englanders believed their vision of the republic could be extended throughout the North, to "that part of the American republic in which its strength is principally found." New Englanders' vision of a New Englandization of the rest of the United States was so strong and apparently well articulated that the Philadelphia journal *The Reformer* aimed to raise awareness of it among its readers. The newspaper's editor warned of a plot by New England ministers, especially Lyman Beecher, to create an American culture that was dominated by the Yankee image. Importantly, many New York and Pennsylvania periodicals, nevertheless, promoted the idea of a nation defined by New England characteristics.[69]

The image of New England as the embodiment of the United States was especially forceful because many tourists shared New Englanders' infectious enthusiasm for their republican lifestyle. Books and articles, household decorations, and utensils idealized New England and created an image of republicanism that gloried in the region's plain spoken, pious, industrious people. This republicanism was closely tied to the new nationalism. It was the most obvious and effective difference between Europe and the United Sates and seemed to be the basis for all New England national characteristics. Furthermore, it helped New Englanders to justify their feeling of superiority against other regions, especially the slave South, and to turn their own region into the model for all others to follow. The evolution of small town republican America had begun.

CHAPTER 2

A Prussian Monarch—an American Hero: Early Republican Royalism and Parallels between the Cult of Frederick the Great and Celebrations of the First American President

After his death in August 1786, Europeans and Americans reinvented the Prussian king Frederick the Great, transforming him simultaneously into a mythical figure and an ordinary man. All over the German states, magazines published engravings and anecdotes depicting scenes from Frederick's life. Strikingly, such anecdotes of the Prussian king, which made an important contribution to his canonization in Germany, crossed the Atlantic. Between 1786 and the early 1820s, New Englanders perceived a glorious picture of the German monarch. Early Republicans in Pennsylvania and New York joined their New England neighbors in their celebration of the Prussian king.

Anecdotes, short amusing tales often illustrating the characteristics of well-known people, appeared frequently in eighteenth-century newspapers. With their sense of confidentiality and humor, these short stories served as entertainment for ordinary people who could easily remember and repeat them because they usually did not exceed one paragraph in length. Ninety-four percent of the American anecdotes on the Prussian king appeared in Northern states. This does not necessarily mean that Southerners did not show so much interest in Frederick II. While most of the increasing numbers of periodicals were published in the North, literate Southerners often read them as well. Literary elites used anecdotes as an effective tool to propagate collective values, which shaped society in the way these elites envisioned it.[1]

Federalists favorably compared New England with Prussia, and the South unfavorably with Prussia's enemy, Austria. New Englanders embraced Frederick as a model for nationalism because he had raised Prussia from one among many German states to a great power. It was precisely this rising status to which the young republic of the United States aspired. Americans saw Frederick of Prussia as an example, and the emergence of Prussia under Frederick was established as a model for the United States. Moreover, the example of Prussia's ascendancy was especially appealing to New Englanders because it fit perfectly with the idea of New England's dominance within the new nation, with the myth of the "city on a hill" and an eighteenth-century version of New England's "Jeremiad." Some New Englanders viewed their region as the American Prussia. New Englanders identified with Frederick the Great and his state because these anecdotes ascribed specific New England values to the Prussian king—self-discipline, hard work, and education. Prussians and New Englanders indeed shared those ideals. As their like-minded American contemporaries, eighteenth-century Prussians strove for a modest lifestyle and despised laziness and luxury. Ironically, the elite of the young United States employed this European monarchical cult to foster loyalty to the new republic.

Frederick II was king of the German state Prussia from 1740 to 1786. He was an enlightened despot and a brilliant military campaigner. During his reign he more than doubled the size of his state of Brandenburg-Prussia and transformed it into the foremost military power in Europe. In response to this achievement, a cult of the Hohenzollern king emerged in all German states in his lifetime. Later in the nineteenth century, Frederick II became a German national hero, although he himself was always a Prussian, and never a German nationalist.

Frederick started his military campaigns to enlarge Prussia immediately after he inherited the throne in 1740. First, the twenty-eight-year-old king annexed Silesia, Austria's richest province, and started the Wars of Austrian Succession (1740–1748). After the death of the Holy Roman Emperor Charles VI earlier in the year, France and Bavaria had refused to guarantee the succession of the emperor's daughter Maria Theresia. Frederick took advantage of the conflict and strengthened his own kingdom by taking possession of Silesia, which had a strong agriculture and industry, twice the size of Brandenburg-Prussia and with double the population. Feeling threatened by a Franco-Austrian defense alliance that had been concluded in connection with the beginning struggle between Great Britain and France in the American colonies in 1756, Frederick invaded Saxony.

This extended the French and Indian War, which Europeans call the Seven Years' War (1756–1763), to the other side of the Atlantic. Frederick played a major role in the Seven Years' War. While Prussia's ally England was busy fighting France in North America, in Europe Frederick battled the strong coalition of Austria, Russia, France, and Sweden. In spite of initial victories and the superior tactics and discipline of the Prussian army, by 1762 the war brought Prussia to the verge of ruin: Frederick's state was almost bankrupt and Russia occupied Berlin. Unexpectedly, a change in the Russian throne, the succession of Frederick's admirer Peter III, enabled the Prussian king to restore the status quo in the Treaty of Paris that ended the war in 1763. Another strategic accomplishment of Frederick II securing Prussia's status as a great power was his diplomatic maneuvering that led to the division of Poland between Russia, Austria, and Prussia in 1772. The western part of Poland, which now became Prussian territory, connected the separated provinces Brandenburg and Prussia.[2]

As an absolute monarch, Frederick the Great dominated the Prussian economy, administration, and social policy. His Prussia was a military state centered on the army. Even the administration followed a military structure and its major task was to run the army, where more than 4 percent of the Prussian population served. Even if he ruled authoritatively, Frederick was also an enlightened thinker who encouraged industry, education, and immigration. He published political and historical studies, as, for example, the *Anti-Machiavel*, wrote poems, composed music, and supported the arts. His castle San Souci emerged as a cultural center, where he invited ballet and opera companies and orchestras from all over Europe. Leading French philosophers such as Voltaire and Mirabeau came to Prussia as guests of the king as well. Although he maintained the system of serfdom, he abolished torture and granted religious freedom.

The wave of anecdotes about the Prussian king in American papers shows that colonial monarchical culture merged into the young republic and gave birth to a compound of royalism and Republican patriotism. Indeed, colonists had admired the Prussian royalty. As in England and in the German states, Frederick had been a celebrated figure in the American colonies during the Seven Years' War, because his victories over the French in Europe had enabled the English to win the war on the other side of the Atlantic. During the French and Indian War, Americans admired the Prussian king as a military hero who fought for Protestantism. A poem in a 1758 A*merican Magazine and Monthly Chronicle*, for example, praised him for his strategic talents and compared him with ancient heroes such as Hannibal and Julius Caesar.

Like their European contemporaries, colonists even ascribed divine qualities to Frederick. One author, who gave himself the name "Annandius," called Fredrick II a "godlike MAN." For Prussians, Englishmen, and colonists alike, Frederick's victories over the Catholic power France turned him into a universal protector of Protestantism. "Philandria's" ode emphasized this religious dimension of the celebration of Frederick II. The author described Frederick's warfare against the Catholic powers, France, and Austria, and concluded that Frederick was fighting for "PROTESTANTS unborn."[3]

During the French and Indian War, North American colonists had admired the German monarch so much that many collected Frederick souvenirs. Tobacco boxes depicting the king and his battles were not only popular items in Germany and England, but also in the American colonies. A Salem, Massachusetts, family, for example, owned a copper box that bore portraits of Frederick II and his brother Prince Henry. In this picture both princes looked at a battle scene of the Prussian victory over the French at Rossbach and Merseburg in November 1757. Another Frederick souvenir that crossed the Atlantic was a jug with a portrait of the "King of Prussia."[4]

In the late eighteenth and early nineteenth centuries Frederick the Great was still perceived as a transatlantic Protestant ideal-figure, but his celebration now developed into a cult. In contrast to the earlier image he was not just a political and military hero. The later anecdotes chosen by American papers stressed the king's human qualities. In these images Frederick appeared as a personification of the new Republican virtues: he avoided all royal luxury, lived a Spartan life, stood for religious toleration, showed self-discipline as well as generosity, justice, sympathy, and closeness toward his people. Like every good patriot, the king was most concerned about the common good. In this portrait the boundaries between monarch and subject blurred, so that Americans could imagine Frederick the Great as a Republican patriot. Not surprisingly, the young nation ascribed the very same virtues to its first president. But while Frederick became a rather ordinary human being, the Republican George Washington was celebrated in semi-royal ways and many Americans thought to recognize even aristocratic features in his appearance. Early Republican publishers and artists selectively used elements of European royalism to establish a collective value system that would turn Americans into model Republicans and to introduce a vision of a future American empire. By comparing themselves with the Prussian hero, New Englanders used the cult of Frederick to confirm their claim of dominance within the new American nation.

Frederick the Republican: The Prussian King's Meaning in New England

The death of Frederick II on August 17 in 1786 revived the enthusiasm for the German monarch in the Northern United States. It triggered a wave of anecdotes in New England periodicals that lasted till the early 1820s. The journals sometimes illustrated their stories of the German monarch with etchings and engravings. New York and Philadelphia publishers followed their countrymen in copying numerous anecdotes about Frederick from German books and journals. Often, the same anecdote appeared in several magazines. The publication of the same article in different places contributed to the emergence of a collective image of the Prussian king in New England and its neighbors in New York and Pennsylvania. Just as other Northerners participated in the celebration of New England landscapes and people, they also partook in New England's creation of Frederick as a New England national hero demonstrating once more how New Englanders and their neighbors in other Northern states shared a collective identity. The repetition of German anecdotes in American periodicals also shows that in addition to several domestic papers, editors received European journals and checked them for contents to publish again in their own papers. The stories of Frederick in American publications indicate a lively transatlantic culture.[5]

Theaters in New York City and Philadelphia even performed plays and operas on the popular king. The printed version of Thomas Cooke's opera *I'll Love You Ever Dearly* was so successful that it appeared in four Philadelphia editions between 1815 and 1819, and in an additional New York edition in 1817. Southerners also enjoyed plays on Frederick the Great. Playhouses in Fredericksburg, Virginia, for example, performed such royalist pieces of entertainment. New Englanders, in contrast, with their dislike of theatrical performances, preferred to read about the Prussian monarch. In his study of reading habits in rural New England, William Gilmore found Frederick the Great one of the most popular themes represented in the region's private libraries. The English translation of the collection of Frederick anecdotes by the Frenchman Dieudonne Thiebault, a member of the faculty of the Ecole Militaire at Berlin and a friend of the Prussian king, was in great demand when it became available to American readers in 1806. Publishers in New York and Philadelphia put it on the market in the same year. The book obviously still sold in 1816, when one of the Philadelphia companies printed it again.[6]

George Washington owned the works of Frederick II and Gillies's history of his reign. Moreover, the president wanted to decorate his house with a bust of Frederick II. Like early Republicans generally, Washington admired the military talents of the Prussian royalty, but was especially impressed by the king's focus on the common good. In response to General Lafayette's report on his visit to the Prussian court, the president wrote: "It is pleasing to hear that a due regard to the rights of mankind, is characteristic of the later [Frederick the Great]: I shall revere & love him for this trait of character."[7] New Englanders probably interpreted Washington's enthusiasm for the Prussian king as his participation in their cult of Frederick. They did probably not assume that Southerners were able to identify with the Prussian hero. This shows that New Englanders and their Southern countrymen might have shared more common values than what New England nationalists admitted.

When word of the death of Frederick the Great reached Boston and other New England towns in the fall of 1786, New Englanders perceived it as an important event and reported how deeply Prussians were mourning. They did not, however, join the German emotional outburst that followed the great man's death. On November 6, the *Boston Gazette* informed its readers: "The death of the King of Prussia will considerably affect the politics of Europe. It is an event for which the nations have been preparing for many months and which will not be suffered to pass over unimproved." The *Connecticut Journal* gave a detailed report of the monarch's death including the time and day, his age, the number of years, month, and days he had reigned as well as a description of his funeral. It also reported that 20,000 people attended the wake and that even his "brave" guards could not "restrain from tears on beholding the corpse of the hero who had so often led them to glory."[8]

The large number of Frederick anecdotes transferred from European books and periodicals to American publications in the three decades following Frederick's death may be surprising, considering this unemotional reception of the event. But, as the extensive newspaper accounts on his death indicate, New Englanders were nevertheless keenly interested in the king's fate. Americans could still get enthusiastic about European royalty, but their celebration of the Prussian monarch was selective. They did not mourn for the king and they decided to publish only those among the countless anecdotes that in their opinion matched their own Republican ideology. While Germans pictured the king as a divine-like figure and transfigured his death into an apotheosis, New Englanders ignored this genre of

Frederick stories.[9] Anecdotes that portrayed Frederick II as an ordinary human being and stressed his human qualities suited their taste and these were the stories that found their way into American newspapers. The American public felt affection for a monarch who, they thought, personified Republican values of disinterestedness, simplicity, and public virtue.

After 1786, Boston, New York, and Philadelphia publications still celebrated the Prussian king as a military hero, but his military achievements no longer lay at the center of his American commemoration. Shortly after the news of Frederick's death arrived in November 1786, the *Boston Gazette* recounted all of the king's territorial conquests and every single battle he had won. In the following year the *New Haven Gazette and Connecticut Magazine* told an anecdote that was very well known in Germany. Like every war story, this sketch emphasized that the Prussian king fought like any ordinary soldier and shared all dangers with common soldiers. He did not seek special protection because of his royal origin. But the newspaper added a characteristic that distinguished Frederick from the other soldiers; it depicted Frederick as an immortal, superhuman person. The story told about how after the battle at Torgau, against the Austrians, the king and his grenadiers were sitting around the fire and discussing the battle. The fire and the conversation warmed the king and he, therefore, unbuttoned his jacket. To his grenadiers' big surprise a musket ball fell out, which "pierced his [. . .] uniform and grazed his breast."[10] The shot obviously did not kill the king.

Stories picturing the Prussian king as a military genius appeared sporadically; and Frederick's military writings and theories enjoyed some popularity.[11] But in contrast to Germany, where the celebration of the military hero was still an important part of the Frederick cult, American publishers shifted the focus and chose to import those anecdotes that illuminated civilian virtues of the king. The anecdotes American newspaper publishers chose to publish emphasized that Frederick II was eager to avoid royal pomp and luxury and lived a Spartan life. New Englanders could identify with him because he appeared to have shared their aversion for aristocratic manners. Simplicity was a key element of the New England collective identity. The figure of Frederick enabled the Northern elite to transform colonists into Republicans in a way that very much pleased ordinary people. By using a European royal hero, newspaper publishers and editors made sure that the shift in values, which they directed, would be successful. The Republican virtues that the elites wanted to promote became popular because they introduced an idol that linked these new Republican values with a familiar culture of royalism and a powerful transatlantic role model.

In 1787 the *American Magazine* introduced an anecdote of Frederick asserting that "nothing was more irksome to the king than state ceremonies, and he avoided them as much as possible." The story ridiculed French court ceremonies and contrasted them with Prussian simplicity. Besides revealing Frederick's disdain for French etiquette, the story was meant to underline the king's sense of humor. It said that Frederick's friend the Marquis D'Argent accompanied the king to receive the homage of the Prussians. Following the Frenchman's advice, Frederick adopted French etiquette and asked the Marquis how he had acquitted himself. The Marquis responded that Louis XV would have done better. Frederick was not embarrassed and said, "and I know somebody that [*sic*] would have acquitted himself better than Louis XV: Baron, the actor."[12].

Other stories such as "The King of Prussia's Skill in Revenue," published in 1786 in the *New Haven Gazette and Connecticut Magazine*, described Frederick's simple and modest lifestyle. In the image of Frederick that Americans imported from Germany, the Prussian king did not surround himself with diamonds and gold like other European monarchs although generously gave such luxuries to his family and to his people. In his two volumes of anecdotes of Frederick the Great, Dieudonne Thiebault stressed again and again the plain appearance of the king. "I never saw him more than three or four times in coloured [*sic*] coats," he assured his readers, "and these were old and simple in their form." Young Republicans admired not only Frederick the Great for his plain style, but Prussian royalty in general. When John Quincy Adams was minister to Prussia in 1786, he got the same unassuming impression of Frederick's successor Frederick William III. He noted in his diary: "The appearance of the King has a great degree of simplicity; a plain uniform and boots."[13]

Post-Revolutionary Americans expressed ambivalence toward everything European and especially toward European monarchy. But for Frederick II the country felt near unanimous enthusiasm; only about 2 percent of the anecdotes published in the United States drew an unfavorable image of the king.[14] Boston, New York, and Philadelphia publishers found the Prussian monarch an ideal object of American admiration because German anecdotes pictured Frederick as representing himself as not monarchical, but in a plain style much in contrast to the common aristocratic display of other European kings and queens.

While New Englanders usually simply printed translations of German stories on Frederick the Great, they added one original

American anecdote, which they had not found in a German magazine. It pointed to another aspect that distinguished the Prussian king from his fellow European monarchs. The anonymous American author traced Frederick's favorable attitude toward the American Revolution. Interestingly, he created the image of a monarch who was at heart a Republican. "The late Frederic, king of Prussia, though a tyrant, had, in many parts of his character, the cast of a republican," the author began the story, which described Frederick's conversation about the American Revolution with an English philosopher, the American commissioner to European courts General William Lee, and a German philosopher. The English philosopher made the king suspicious, because in contrast to the enlightened monarch, he "had not penetration enough to see that a new era of things was about to take place among mankind." Frederick instead trusted Lee, who predicted that people will at some point "dispense with the services of monarchs." When the German philosopher agreed with Lee on the glorious future of Republicanism, Frederick proved his open-mindedness toward the new political system and answered: "In God's name, so be it: for my own part, I am a royalist by profession—and am determined to live by my trade as well as the best of them."[15]

By picturing Frederick as regarding kingship as nothing more than a profession, distancing himself from divine right ideology, and accepting Republicanism as a form of government, New Englanders reinvented him as an American Republican hero. The fact that Prussia had remained neutral during the Revolutionary War, that Lee was warmly received at the Prussian court, and that Frederick already considered a treaty of amity and commerce in 1774, might have inspired early Republicans to create this myth. George Washington's view of the treaty with Prussia reflects the impression many Americans had at that time, and later nurtured the celebration of the Republican Prussian king. On July 31, 1786 the future president wrote to the Comte De Rochambeau: "The Treaty of Amity which has lately taken place between the King of Prussia and the United States, marks a new era of negotiation. It is perfectly original in many of its articles. It is the most liberal Treaty which has ever been entered into between independent powers."[16]

The same kind of rumor about Frederick's support of the American War of Independence may have led Pennsylvanians to name a tavern and later a town after Frederick II. The town *King of Prussia*, near Philadelphia, was named after a tavern by the same name during the later part of the eighteenth century. Opinions divide on the reasons for naming the tavern after Frederick the Great. Some say the name was given during the French and Indian War to honor Frederick's assistance to the British. Others argue it was given during the Revolution, inspired by word of Frederick's support of George Washington. The most convincing opinion seems to be that the innkeeper George Elliot gave the town the name in 1786 when Frederick II died, because at this point a real cult of Frederick emerged in the new world. Gilbert Stuart painted the signboard of the tavern, showing Frederick on his horse.[17]

In American political discourse, the ideal Republican subordinated individual self-interest to the common good, was benevolent, religiously tolerant, self-disciplined, and educated. In the eyes of American publishers, the Frederick anecdotes that they themselves imported from Germany described a Prussian king who embodied all the Republican virtues that the American elite hoped would emerge as the collective values of the new nation. Ironically, New Englanders and other Northerners turned the Prussian king into a model of a good Republican, while Germans on the other side of the Atlantic saw Frederick as a role model for a good monarch. In a time when American leaders realized that not every American was a born Republican willingly fulfilling his civic virtues, but that instead self-interest increasingly replaced benevolence, they hoped that the example of the popular Prussian king would strengthen Republican sentiments among their people. Frederick became a widely used tool for the elite to invent a national identity.

The popular figure of Frederick, some editors believed, also helped early Republicans to avoid the vices emerging with economic transformation. Beginning in the early 1790s, the market revolution turned the struggle for wealth into a more widely accepted social norm. American economy shifted from household production, moral economy, and commodity exchange to production for the market. Commercialization changed lifestyle and culture. Through this economic change, the ideal of independence lost its connection with benevolence, which included the motivation to work toward the common good. By the early nineteenth century, the political and intellectual elite thought that materialism and selfishness prevailed. They feared that chaos, ambition, and greed would destroy the republic.[18]

The anecdotal depiction of Frederick supported the ideal of self-control, which would have served as an antidote to these vices. Frederick's dislike of luxury and royal display also served as an antithesis for materialism. Furthermore, this characterization of Frederick was meant to prove that it was civic virtue that helped a country to rise to the status of a great power. If young Republicans followed the example of the Prussian king, the United States would soon become a great power. The German anecdotes of Frederick that American newspaper editors selected for publication in their own country became a powerful instrument for Northern elites in the process of inventing an American identity shaped by New England values.

Many Frederick anecdotes ascribed the virtue of benevolence to the Prussian king. Interestingly, such myths of Frederick the Great overlapped with contemporary characterizations of George Washington, whom early Republicans also imagined as a benevolent man working toward the common good. Two stories of Frederick the Great, which probably every contemporary German was able to tell, also appeared in several American magazines. One was about a corporal in the king's bodyguard who could not afford to buy himself a watch and instead "fixed a leaden bullet to a chain, and wore it to his fob." When the king asked him for the time, the loyal corporal responded, "Sire, my watch neither points to five o'clock nor to six o'clock, but it every moment informs me that I must die for your Majesty." Frederick was so pleased by his servant's loyalty that he gave the corporal his own watch as a gift and said: "Take this, that you may also know the hour when you do die for me." The other anecdote is about a page at the Prussian court who fell asleep on a chair. The king found his sleeping servant with a letter from his mother peeping out of his pocket. Curious, the king read the letter and found out that the page's mother lived in poverty and that her loyal son tried to support her. The king felt sympathy for the poor mother, and impressed by her caring son, he filled a purse with gold ducats and put it into the page's pocket. When the servant woke up, the king said to him: "My friend [...] God often sends us blessings while we are asleep: send that purse to your mother, give my compliments to her, and assure her at the same time that I shall in future take care to provide for you both."[19]

The ideal of sacrificing self-interest for the common good linked American Republicanism and European patriotism. European historians use "patriotism" to describe the *Zeitgeist* of the second half of the eighteenth century. They define it as a moral-political attitude that obliged the individual to neglect selfish interests in favor of the common good. Ironically, a German king became a role model for the new Republican patriotism in New England and other Northern states.

With the democratization of society through the American Revolution, talent increasingly replaced social origin as qualification for leadership. Even in this respect New Englanders could identify with Frederick II and again regard him as a Republican. A story that publishers copied from a French source told how the monarch bestowed on an ordinary man the title of a count because this ordinary man seemed to be wise and talented enough to serve as a minister to the king.

Another Republican ideal that the revolution had established, and which New Englanders were able to find in the German anecdotes of Frederick the Great, was religious toleration. Frederick was not only celebrated as the protector of Protestantism, but also as an advocate for religious freedom. A number of anecdotes described how the king supported a minister who disagreed with traditional religious thoughts and expected his people to be tolerant of religious dissenters.[20]

American readers of stories on Frederick the Great idealized the Prussian king as a personification of Republican virtues and specific New England values. New Englanders shared some ideals of modesty, discipline, and education with Prussians. These common ideals enabled New Englanders to turn Frederick into one of their Republican heroes and identify with him. "A Faithful Lad," published in the *Boston Magazine* in 1802, described how disciplined the king was not to fall into laziness. The story said that even at an old age the king was eager to spend long hours working. Like many of these anecdotes, this story had a twofold didactic intent. It posted Frederick as a model and at the same time emphasized how important it was for the king that his people followed his example and also acted brave, loyal, and virtuous. When one morning the king's page woke him up, the story reported, the king asked the page to let him sleep just a little longer. The page insisted that he had orders to allow the king not one more minute of rest. "Well," said the king, "you are a brave lad; had you let me sleep on, you would have fared ill for your neglect."[21]

The editor of the *Boston Magazine,* Samuel T. Armstrong, was born in Dorchester, Massachusetts, in 1784. His parents had died before he turned thirteen and he entered the rising sector as a printer apprentice. As many of his colleagues in the publishing business, Armstrong worked his way up and successfully pursued a political career in addition. Armstrong became such an influential public figure that in the 1830s he was elected governor of Massachusetts, mayor of Boston, and state senator. He was part of the elite circles of statesmen, professors, lawyers, and ministers who promoted values such as self-control, which was emphasized in this anecdote. After the Revolution, self-control emerged as a new collective value in the American political culture. Republican leaders thought it would protect liberty from licentiousness and prevent chaos. Furthermore, like education, self-control had been an old Puritan value, which was embedded in New England culture.

New Englanders believed in a general education as a prerequisite for citizens to become good Republicans. Their emphasis on education was another reason for New Englanders to admire Frederick II because anecdotes pictured the king as a philosopher and a patron of the arts and sciences.[22] Being especially proud of their tradition of public education and fine colleges, New Englanders glorified the Prussian king for his effort to educate his people. John Quincy Adams, for example, saw Frederick as the personification of the enlightenment ideal of the genius, a combination of a talented commander and philosopher, but was most enthusiastic about his role in the education of his subjects. On his tour through Silesia during 1800 and 1801, he wrote to his younger brother Thomas Boylston in Philadelphia:

> Immortal Fredric [*sic*]! when seated on the throne of Prussia, with kneeling millions at thy feet, thou wert only a king; on the fields of Lutzen, of Torndorff, of Rossbach, of so many other scenes of human blood and anguish, thou wert only a philosopher, a historian, a poet; but in this generous ardor, this active, enlightened zeal for the education of thy people, thou wert truly great—the father of thy country—the benefactor of mankind!

The preceding section pointed out how impressed Adams was by the Prussian monarch's effort to secure intellectual welfare for his people. These lines are especially remarkable, because the emotional colorful tone was usually not Adams's style. His account of Frederick reads like one of the large number of eulogies written by German intellectuals and published in German periodicals.

> But how much greater still is the tribute of admiration, irresistibly drawn from us, when we behold an absolute monarch, [. . .] eminent as a writer in the highest departments of literature, descending, in a manner, to teach the alphabet to the children of his kingdom; bestowing his care [. . .] in diffusing [. . .] knowledge among his subjects, [. . .] in filling the whole atmosphere they breathed with the intellectual fragrance which had before been imprisoned in the vials of learning, or enclosed within the gardens of wealth!

Adams's opinion reached a larger audience than just his brother. His letters from Silesia were printed in the Philadelphia weekly paper *Portfolio* and they appeared in book form in London.[23]

Strikingly, on his tour through Silesia, which Frederick II had seized from the Austrians during the Seven Years' War, John Quincy Adams found people and towns quite similar to his native New

England. About the small town of Schmiedeberg, he said, for example, "It is about a German mile in length, consists of one street, in which there are many very handsome buildings; in both respects it has a considerable resemblance with the town of Salem in Massachusetts." Such a comparison of the backward Silesian farm town and the wealthy seaport Salem certainly required strong powers of imagination. Admiring the Prussian king, John Quincy had no doubt about the fact that Silesia had only profited from the Prussian conquest. In his mind it became the king's favorite province. Supplied by the Prussians with new roads and schools, in his opinion Silesia enjoyed all advantages of being Prussian. John Quincy Adams also emphasized the Republican ideas of the Prussian monarch. In his eulogy on Frederick, he underlined that the king intended to care equally for all his subjects. Frederick brought "knowledge to all classes of his subjects," he wrote to Philadelphia.[24]

New England's identification with Prussia linked regionalist and nationalist loyalties. New England elites liked to compare their region with Prussia because they imagined New England to rise like Prussia within the German states to the dominant region within their own country. Furthermore, they saw Prussia's rise as an example for the development of the entire nation. And it was, of course, New England that would lead the nation into that glorious future. New England nationalism shows its regionalist face; clearly the South was not part of the image. New Englanders regarded their region as the American Prussia and the South as the American Austria, Prussia's archenemy. Shortly after Adams's tour through Silesia in 1802, his friend, the diplomat William Vans Murray wrote to him: "Virginia will be our Austria. So make up your impatient mind to it. You may talk, like Prussia, of being the Spartans of the north, but the turkey cock has too wide spread a progeny for the black or blue eagle to oppose him, now that voices decide. The wilderness is hers and those who emerge from it."

Educated and well-traveled elites such as the Maryland Federalist Vans Murray and John Quincy Adams were aware of the cultural division between North and South. For them a comparison with Prussia and Austria was self-explanatory. As Prussians found their Spartan life contrasting with the leisurely Austrian way, New Englanders similarly held the luxurious lazy life of Southern planters in contempt and contrasted it with their own strong work ethic.

During the years of the early republic, Prussia and its famous king emerged as a collective example within the Northern states. New Englanders transformed Frederick II into a reflection of their own virtues and used him as antithesis to everything that contradicted their Republican and patriotic ideals. As a creator of this symbolism, John Quincy Adams criticized Thomas Jefferson for having tried to disguise his flight from Monticello to Mount Carter in order to escape British troops during the Revolutionary war. The ex-president contrasted the Southerner Jefferson with the New England role model Frederick the Great, who through self-criticism and -discipline had learned from such a mistake and admitted it:

> Frederick the Second [Adams noted in his diary on January 19, 1831] made a precipitate retreat from the battle of Mollwitz, which after he was gone, his General Schwerin, won for him. He neither conceals nor slurs over this incident in his memoirs of his own times, but says it taught him a lesson for all his after-life never to despair. Jefferson may have learnt the same lesson.[25]

Frederick the Philanthropist

In the mind of young Republicans, Frederick II not only became a model Republican and a patriotic leader, who turned his country into a great power, but also a philanthropist. New Englanders and their neighbors liked stories that depicted the Prussian king as an ordinary human being. In early Republican periodicals, interested readers could follow the Prussian king when he suffered the death of his brother; fondly played with his little nephew, pardoned prisoners, and defended a poor miller against his exploiting landlord. In these stories the king felt sympathy for other people, was just, upright, and humane. Such images of Frederick promoted New England Republican virtues of benevolence and patriotism. Moreover, they indicated that in a nation-state every citizen, including the leaders, was obliged to serve their country. By transforming the Prussian king into a human being suffering for his country, such anecdotes emphasized that the king sacrificed his own interests for the common good and the state as everybody else. The image of Frederick sacrificing his health, family, and royal privileges for the well-being of his country helped to introduce the European cult of service to the state, which was an important element of the emerging Prussian and British patriotism, to the new world. Such a cult of service to the state had not existed in the American colonies. At least since the 1750s colonists had felt excluded from a new British nationalism and, therefore, lacked a strong enough loyalty to the British kingdom.

Stories about Frederick's deep feelings of mourning when he lost his beloved younger brother Henry turned the strict military leader and hardworking Spartan king into an ordinary human being, a man with a good heart. As in Germany, a few intellectuals in the United States rather saw the Prussian king as a warmonger who was untouched by his brother's death in the battlefield. Such a negative view was still only presented in one anecdote published in 1813 in the *Ladies' Weekly Museum*. Frederick's human qualities in contrast were emphasized in numerous stories about his love for his nephew. These anecdotes served as evidence that Frederick II was fond of children, although he did not have any of his own. They supported the image of the king as the father of his country, which was a common depiction of eighteenth-century monarchs. It not only created a positive popular picture of the king, but also obliged him to live up to such expectations. Americans used the metaphor for another man who was not a biological father and whom they liked to compare to Frederick II, George Washington.[26]

The metaphor of the family played an important role for Americans when they created their national identity in the decades after the Revolution. In the minds of early Americans, Republican virtues served as common ground holding them together, but family was a metaphor and model for the new nation that nurtured these values. Early Republican leaders promoted the idea of the family as an "incubator" of Republican values and an institution that was essential for the survival of the young republic. Within this family imagery the idea of a Republican father was a powerful tool evoking loyalty to the new nation. At a time when Americans did believe that an absolute monarch could or should not protect and unite them, they felt comfortable celebrating Republican father-figures who were obliged to work for the best of their people even if it included a European king.[27]

As the father of his people, Frederick served as an example for humanity. An anecdote on the "Opinion of Frederick II on the Field of Sports," in an 1806 *Christian Observer and Advocate* told Republican readers that they were not supposed to do anything just for pleasure. The story argued that the king rejected killing for pleasure. In this anecdote, Frederick said: "Even the butcher does not kill animals for his pleasure; he does it for the necessities of man: but the sportsman kills for pleasure; this is odious! The sportsman, therefore, should be placed below the butcher in the order of society." Frederick anecdotes included several stories that described how the Prussian monarch freed prisoners because he felt sympathy for them. A popular one was the anecdote about a Prussian general who had killed his opponent in a duel. Frederick personally liked the man and when he was imprisoned, arranged everything for him to escape. Moreover, the king was pictured as so forgiving that after he succeeded on the throne, he even pardoned the general who had advised the king's strict father to whip Frederick's mistress when he was a young prince.[28]

Frederick's virtues of justice and closeness with his people stood at the center of the famous story of the miller Arnold. In 1784, the *Boston Magazine* published the anecdote accompanied by an engraving entitled *The Justice of Frederick*. The popular story appeared in slightly different versions in several regional New England papers during the late eighteenth and the early nineteenth centuries. It shows how the image of Frederick the Republican connected with the image of Frederick the philanthropist. The story is about a miller from the town of Custrin, who had lost the use of his mill because his landlord had redirected the river. Although the mill could now only be used twenty-eight days a year, the aristocrat still requested the full rent from the miller. The court of Custrin decided in favor of the landlord, but the issue was laid before the king. The king's response portrayed him not only as a humane king who had a heart for the poor and as the father of his people, but also as a true Republican establishing a judicial system that treated everybody equally. The story said that Frederick called the sentence a "shameful injustice," which was "contrary to the paternal intentions of his Majesty." The king removed the judges in order to teach them "that the meanest peasant, and even the beggar, are men as well as the king."[29] The engraving (see figure 2.1) supported this image and helped the eighteenth-century observer to envision the king as a father figure and as a caretaker of the poor. It pictured a peasant family kneeling before Frederick, who is serving as a judge and carrying a scale, the symbol of justice. A warrior figure flying down from the clouds above indicated Frederick's strong intentions to fight for justice for everybody. New Englanders, who prided in the justice of their courts and the libertarian nature of their land tenure, saw Frederick defending their own values and found parallels between their own region and Prussia confirmed.

Another group of Frederick anecdotes that clearly reveals the idealized image of Frederick as the Republican patriot and philanthropist are the stories of the king and General Ziethen, a Prussian hero of the Seven Years' War. An 1817 anecdote in the *Boston Weekly Magazine* included two often-told stories of the famous veteran. It traced Frederick's appreciation of the general's service to his country and the king's caring attitude toward the old Ziethen. Typically for a Ziethen story, the Boston periodical described Frederick's reaction to the old general falling asleep. After a long march during a military excursion, Ziethen and the king warmed up on a fire. Both were tired and fell asleep. When Frederick

Figure 2.1 Norman, *The Justice of Frederick!* engraving, in *Boston Magazine* 1 (1783): 287 (courtesy of the Rare Books and Manuscript Department, Boston Public Library)

woke up and saw that the general was sleeping, he was very pleased and immediately told a soldier who accidentally touched the general's foot to be very careful not to wake Ziethen up. The article continued with another story of Ziethen sleeping, this time at the king's table. When somebody intended to wake the general up, Frederick said: "Let him sleep, he has watched long enough that he can rest."[30]

In addition to displays of the Prussian king's caring and humane attitude toward his officers and soldiers, these stories highlighted the fact that the elite was also willing to sacrifice their own lives and interests in the struggle for their country. Anecdotes picturing the king and other aristocrats sharing all exigencies and dangers of war with the ordinary peasant soldier and fighting for their country with the same devotion helped to create and foster the new Republican patriotism. In Europe as well as in the United States, they heralded the collective ideal of selfless service to the nation. The very small number of stories describing Frederick as "the most savage monster" and a harsh commander to his soldiers among all the publications glorifying him confirms this. One example of the unfavorable stories is an 1811 anecdote in the Boston newspaper *Cabinet* about the king's abuse of his loyal general Ziethen. During the first Silesian war, the story says, Frederick forbid his soldiers under death penalty to keep a fire after a certain hour. When General Ziethen broke that rule because he wanted to write a letter to his wife, the king cruelly gave orders to execute him.[31]

German anecdotes of Frederick the Great in New England newspapers helped a transatlantic cult of patriotic service to the state to emerge quickly after Independence. The Prussian state with its well-organized bureaucracy, discipline, and obedience certainly impressed many New England statesmen and provided a model in avoiding anarchy and creating loyalty. In Great Britain, the American artists Benjamin West and John Singleton Copley encouraged the cult of heroism and state service, when they pictured members of the British elite gloriously dying for their country. New Englanders shared this glorification of service to the nation when they published and read anecdotes on the Prussian king, but also when they decorated their homes. West's painting *The Death of General Wolfe*, which was made into a best-selling print in England, also inspired Americans. A New England woman, for example, wove a bedspread with a pattern depicting the battle scene.[32] The subject was present in early Republican life. Household decorations such as these brought the patriotic message into many American homes. British iconography still had an impact on the first independent generation of the United States. A student of West and Copley, the New England-born John Trumbull painted the American elite, more precisely Revolutionary War heroes, in the same manner. In his painting *Death of General Warren at the Battle of Bunker's Hill*, finished in 1786, he depicted the death of the American general Joseph Warren.[33] Like the heroes in the British paintings, Warren is dying in a Christ-like pose, sacrificing his life for his country. Although a modern painting that no longer depicted a hero in ancient costumes, this celebration of a virtuous death as man's greatest triumph is still a phenomenon of the Enlightenment. In contrast to the British battle scenes, the American imitation was not a depiction of military victory; but although the Americans lost Bunker Hill, it was a battle that evoked national pride. Trumbull's main intention, however, was to symbolize the morality of the elite and Republican ideals of self-restraint, magnanimity, and generosity. Despite being a staunch patriot, the artist applied these virtues even to the British general Major Small. In his painting Small prevented a grenadier from bayoneting the helpless Warren.

Trumbull's hopes to emulate the success of West and Copley were not fulfilled. His celebration of the virtuous elite did not reach a large audience in the United States. His idea of mass-producing engravings after his paintings failed. But works such as *Bunker Hill* evoked nationalistic feelings among their elite observers. And the American elite recognized the nationalist potential of this glorification of the nation's leaders. When Abigail Adams saw Trumbull's work for the first time, she wrote to her sister Mary Smith Cranch that when she looked at it her blood shivered and she felt "faintness at her heart" because Trumbull was the first painter who tried "to immortalize by his pencil those great actions, that gave birth to our nation."[34] New England's intellectual leaders hoped the idealization of service to the country would help every individual and every former colony to sacrifice their own interest and to grow close to one nation. Moreover, it legitimized the elite and emphasized their patriotic devotion.

The cult of state service also promoted the Northern Federalist culture and ideology. Whether Frederick II risked his life on the battlefield, fulfilled his governmental duties from sunrise to midnight, or fought for justice and well-being of the people, in all these stories it is clear that he sacrificed his own interests for his country. The image of the king serving the state as anybody else should fostered the cult of state service. Although anecdotes of Frederick the Great communicated Republican values to the American audience, they conveyed a sense of hierarchy that was very much in the interest of the members of the elite who published Frederick anecdotes. In all these images, it was always the social leaders who served as a model and symbolized Republican virtues. Moreover, by celebrating devotion to the state, the cult of state service promoted a strong federal government. The glorification of state service in early Republican newspapers, paintings, and household goods supported the Federalist argument that a strong central government was needed to maintain order, liberty, and dignity.[35] New Englanders' interest in Frederick anecdotes and images shows that they partly relied on transformed European ideals in their invention of their new collective identity. Even remains of Colonial royalism such as the image of the monarch as a father figure merged into the new Republican patriotism.

The King and the President

In the image of the Prussian king as the Republican patriot, an ordinary human being who lived a simple life and worked hard, the boundaries between monarch and subject blurred. Not surprisingly, the young nation ascribed the very same virtues to its first president. During the late 1790s and early 1800s George Washington became a national icon and a profitable symbol on the American mass consumer market. Depictions of Washington on paintings, prints, pitchers, quilts, and wallpaper show an astonishing similarity to contemporary German artifacts picturing Frederick II. Strikingly similar was the canonization after the president's death, which shared the same pattern with the German imagery of the Prussian king. However, New Englanders did not import German depictions of Frederick as a divine-like figure, while they did adopt that theme in the celebration of their first president. While the monarch Frederick II became a rather ordinary human being in the American imagination, the Republican president George Washington, ironically, was celebrated in a semi-royal way.[36]

George Washington refused the crown, but all over the young nation he was celebrated like a European monarch. On his tours through the states in 1789 and in 1791 the country's first president often appeared in public on the back of his famous white horse accompanied by militia groups. When he crossed the line between Massachusetts and New Hampshire on his tour through New England in 1791 "pomp and circumstance were not left behind." Four hundred cavalry of Massachusetts escorted Washington to the state line and when he arrived there, another 700 awaited him.[37]

Washington was adorned with laurels and flags. The *Massachusetts Magazine* reported that at his entry into Trenton, New Jersey, in

1789, a triumphal arch was raised, which was twenty feet wide and supported by thirteen pillars. Each pillar was entwined with a wreath of evergreen and the arch was covered with laurel and flowers. New England newspapers kept their readers informed about Washington's reception in other parts of the country. Like the *Massachusetts Magazine*, the *Boston Courier* described how New England's southern neighbors celebrated the president. When he came to New York, New Englanders read as follows: "The whole city was brightly illuminated during the evening." This indicates the important role newspapers played in creating an American identity. By printing accounts of patriotic celebrations from near and far, local papers established a collective imagination of the emerging nationalistic culture.[38]

Early Republican royalism appeared in an even more direct form. The people of Portsmouth sang an ode on Washington in the tune of "God Save the King." After the president's election in 1789, Philadelphia's inhabitants even simulated a coronation: A little boy put a "civic crown of laurel" on the president's head. The painter Gilbert Stuart sold portraits on which Washington was looking "every bit an American George I." And people compared the president with the former king. Abigail Adams wrote to her sister that during receptions the president came to speak to her with such "grace dignity & ease, that leaves Royal George far behind him." It was important that the country's first man had "royal manners." Royal culture played an important role in Washington politics throughout the early republic. Although Jefferson made an effort to introduce a new Republican culture to Washington politics, Washington women and especially First Ladies such as Dolly Madison and Luisa Catherine Adams successfully used court rituals to participate in politics and often to support their husband's interests.[39]

The comparison of Washington with European monarchs shows that majesty still served as a model. Admiring Frederick the Great, New Englanders especially found similarities between the Prussian king and their first president. They drew parallels to Frederick II in order to signal Washington's greatness. A verse in the *American Journal* of January 20, 1781 emphasized that Frederick cheered Washington:

> etraction drops the guilty pen,
> Thy [Washington's] name without a stain
> So! Frederick* hails thee, first of men,
> All other praise is vain.[40]
>
> *of Prussia

The new American nation ascribed the same virtues to its first president as German anecdotes ascribed to Frederick the Great. Interestingly, the depictions of George Washington not only bore resemblance to those images of Frederick II that Americans copied from German publications, but were also similar to the genre of Frederick portraits that did not appear in American publications. As the American Frederick, Washington added the second half of the reincarnated Frederick persona to the American market, the mythical Frederick figure.

Although both the monarch and the president had been celebrated during their lifetimes, real cults around them developed only after their deaths. Like Frederick the Great in Germany, George Washington experienced a reincarnation portrayed on jewelry, household goods, and paintings, as well as in books, journals, and almanacs of the new nation.

Governments on both sides of the Atlantic encouraged such expressions of admiration. Frederick's successor William III instructed special exhibitions in memory of the great king, and Prussian academies of arts and sciences designed monuments to him. The U.S. Congress declared that Americans should express their grief over the president's death in eulogies. Furthermore it appointed committees to propose monuments in memory of Washington.

In the decades after their deaths, biographies and pictures on canvas, wood, copper, and porcelain embedded Frederick II and George Washington as part of everyday life. Depictions in schoolbooks introduced them as models to children. Portraits on household goods enabled the less-educated masses to participate in the celebration of the hero. Like the Prussian king, Washington was portrayed as a military hero, the father of his country, as benevolent, selfless, and trustworthy. Portraits of the king and the president, whether in visual or verbal form, were often identical images of each other. Despite their different political systems the old and the new world shared cultural elements of the enlightenment and modern patriotism.[41]

The celebration of Washington as a military hero was molded by enlightenment allusions to classical antiquity. Like his fellow war hero Frederick II, Washington was compared to ancient military leaders such as Caesar, Alexander, Cincinnatus, or Hannibal. In his "Ode on General Washington's Birthday," Thomas Thornton called Washington the "frantic son" of Julius Caesar. The Roman hero Americans probably used most to describe Washington was Lucius Cincinnatus. For early Republicans the parallel seemed obvious. Both generals were farmers who left their plows to rescue their country from the enemy only to return to simple rural life. Here the classical allusion merged with the Republican depiction of the leader as an ordinary citizen, the simple farmer.[42]

Germans depicted Frederick the Great as an ancient hero in drafts for his monument, as well as in etchings and paintings. They imagined him, for example, as Roman emperor or wandering through the Elysium accompanied by Caesar, Marcus Aurelius, and Alexander the Great. Washington also appeared as an ancient hero on engravings, ceramics, and needlework. Cornelius Tiebout's engraving "The Bowling Green Washington" pictured the American president in an ancient oratorical pose, a position in which German artists often depicted the Prussian king. In Tiebout's work Washington is standing between the obelisks "Liberty" and "Independence" in front of the empty pedestal on the New York Bowling Green, which once carried the statue of George III.[43]

Frederick II was not the only eighteenth-century idol that crossed the Atlantic. Images of George Washington appeared on the European consumer market as well. English, French, and Germans also bought prints and household goods with images of the American president. As the *New England Galaxy* proudly reported, newspapers such as the *London Courier* printed eulogies of the famous American. Tiebout's engraving, for example, was printed on Staffordshire and on handkerchiefs made in Glasgow.[44] This reveals less about British enthusiasm for Republicanism than about the extent of a general transatlantic culture of patriotism.

In the eyes of the young American nation, like Frederick the Great, Washington fulfilled the ideal of the enlightened genius. In this context early Republican writers and artists presented their first president as a philosopher, for example, when William Rush made a sculpture of the president and Revolutionary War hero in 1815, he emphasized the role of the learned statesman and general with attributes such as books, column, and a scroll.[45]

But the parallel with antiquity was just one element of the Washington cult. Like the Prussian king, the first American president was portrayed as a benevolent man working for justice and the common good. In 1810, the Boston magazine *The Panoplist* gave a detailed account of Washington's care for the poor. It reported that he always "ordered the baker to supply the poor with bread at his expense," and that "the poor near his own plantation were constantly supplied with wool, corn, flour, bacon, clothes, &c." The same article, which was introduced as possible reading material for schoolchildren, pointed out that Washington had been brought up not to be selfish.

Another anecdote pictured even the six-year-old Washington as an advocate of justice.[46]

All these virtues contributed to the father-image that Washington shared with Frederick II. When the president died in December 1799, all over the country similar grieving was to be heard: "Our Father, our Father ... we mourn that we see his Face no more." Thirteen years before, German intellectuals had published identical words of mourning following the death of the Prussian king. Erich Biester and Friedrich Gedicke, the editors of the Prussian periodical *Berlinische Monatsschrift*, had written: "He is no more the loving father of his people, the patron of his provinces."[47] The father of the American people was not only called "father of his people" and "Father of America," but also painted as paterfamilias.[48] The artist Edward Savage himself engraved the image in 1798, two years after he finished the painting. It was the most popular depiction of the Washington family. Copies of other images by painters and printmakers flooded the American market in the early nineteenth century. The figurative meaning of the theme of the Washington family in contemporary prints and paintings is so much more obvious because of the fact that the children were not Washington's own; Martha Washington brought them into the marriage.[49] The images of the American president with his stepchildren fulfilled the same purpose as the stories of Frederick and his little nephew. Whether in absolutist Prussia or Republican America, the father-image of the country's first man reflected traditional, even patriarchal, and familial political ideas. Some of these patterns might have survived the American Revolution and persisted in the early years of the republic. But above all, it signaled the advent of the new patriotism that demanded the monarchical as well as the Republican leader to care for the welfare of his country.

The deaths of Frederick the Great and George Washington were popular themes decades after they died. In New England as well as in Prussia, images of the death of the country's first man appeared on all kinds of different media; in almanacs, on paintings, jugs, and quilts. These German and American depictions show the most striking similarities. Although New Englanders did not import the German images of Frederick, they adopted the genre for the creation of a myth around their first president. German artists invented two almost opposing images of the death of the famous king. One transfigured the death into an apotheosis, the other, in contrast, showed an ordinary old man dying an ordinary death. The American adoption of the apotheosis theme is the most remarkable, because they had rejected such depictions of the Prussian king. A humanization as in the images where the hero is dying an ordinary death, however, appeared in a different context in many American Frederick anecdotes and it is not surprising that American Republicans applied it to Washington.

In his popular etchings the Prussian artist Daniel Chodowiecki celebrated Frederick II as a divine-like figure carried to heaven by angels. Contemporary American artists produced images that followed the very same pattern. In his popular 1802 engraving *Commemoration of Washington* the Irish immigrant artist John James Barralet also transformed Washington into a godlike figure. Like Christ, the president is raising from tomb to heaven. Father Time puts him in the hands of the figure of eternity. The three mourning women attending Washington's transport into heaven personify the virtues faith, hope, and charity. John Trumbull's sketch of an apotheosis of Washington underlines this parallel to Jesus by picturing the president as a nude man ascending to heaven. Even if the eagle in the Barralet engraving emphasized Washington's service to the republic, it does not distinguish his work from similar German depictions of Frederick. In the eyes of German observers, the apotheosis of Frederick suggested that he had sacrificed his self-interest for the Prussian state and finally came to an ordeal. With their Christ-like poses and indications of martyrdom, such Frederick and Washington death scenes topped the same themes of West and Trumbull's paintings of the elite dying for their country. Interestingly, Republican elites welcomed such imagery in order to secure hierarchy as part of the new political system.[50]

Such popular allegorical images of the death of patriotic heroes were elements of a transatlantic culture. But these pictures also must be understood in an American context. The celebration of Washington as a demigod is another indication of Puritan ideology as an element of early American nationalism. Depictions of Washington's divine providence and qualities supported the vision of the United States as a second Israel and Americans as latter-day elects. Moreover, the combination of allusions to classical antiquity and biblical apotheosis in these pictures shows that Republican virtue intermingled with ideas of Christian good.[51]

During the early years of the new republic, Enlightenment culture survived and some Americans shared the taste for divine attributes, at least when the hero was their first president. Almost a cult around the death of Washington emerged at the turn of the century. Early Republicans bought copies of Barralet's engraving on Chinese glass and Staffordshire pitchers. Charles Rembrandt Peale's

Apotheosis of Washington was exhibited repeatedly in the first years of the nineteenth century and later engraved by David Edwin. The popular pattern *The Apotheosis of Benjamin Franklin and George Washington* decorated bed curtains and coverlets. Strikingly, this English fabric print was not just produced for the American market. English inns also wanted to impress their guests with linens printed with this Washington allegory. So-called tomb mourning pictures, which depicted Washington monuments with patriotic and nationalist inscriptions such as "Pater Patria" and "Washington in Glory, America in Tears," flooded American households in the beginning of the nineteenth century. The pictures, which often included ancient symbols, even decorated wallpaper.[52]

German artists created a very different image of the death of Frederick the Great. This was a very human picture of an old man dying in his chair or in his bed. In these depictions there was no classical or religious imagery, the king looked like an ordinary old man doomed to death. He was not surrounded by angels, but by mortals as his servants and doctor. Like the enlightened picture of the apotheosis, Americans adopted this modern secular image to memorize the death of George Washington. Early Republicans even decorated their homes with such Washington deathbed scenes. The centerpiece of an early nineteenth-century quilt, for example, is a printed handkerchief that shows Washington on his deathbed accompanied by his wife, her children, and his doctor. The Sleeper-McCann House in Gloucester, Massachusetts, has an 1800 engraving with a similar depiction of the dying president.[53]

The modern patriotism and nationalism that emerged in the United States in the late eighteenth and early nineteenth century still comprised enlightenment symbols. Like their European contemporaries, Americans expressed loyalty to their country with figures and symbols from classical antiquity and images of the apotheosis of their greatest hero, George Washington. Such images of Washington are not, as Barry Schwartz argues, just part of the Anglo-American Whig tradition. The imitation of German Frederick portraits indicates a broader transatlantic culture of modern patriotism that emerged after the French Revolution. The assumption that the old and the new world shared common patterns of modern patriotism is strengthened by the fact that early American nationalism and patriotism included a German cult figure.

When New Englanders copied German anecdotes of the Prussian king Frederick the Great, they suppressed those who turned his death into an apotheosis or depicted him as a divine-like figure of any kind.

But they imitated this form of glorification to memorize their first president. This shows again that Europe sometimes still served as a model for the young American nation. By celebrating Washington in the same way as Europeans celebrated Frederick the Great, young Republicans wanted to put their president on the same level with the famous Prussian king. They sought to express that Washington was as great as the most popular European hero. The fact that young Americans celebrated their first president in royal ways and admired a German king identifies early American patriotism and nationalism as a hybrid of monarchical and Republican culture. Moreover, it shows that this hybrid was a transatlantic phenomenon. Americans did not want to imagine Frederick the Great as a divine-like figure because he was a European and a king, but they had no problem with the deification of their own national hero. Being aware of such popular perceptions, the architects of the new national identity picked and created the images that shaped that identity very conscientiously.

New Englanders certainly interpreted the numerous anecdotes of Frederick II differently from German readers. They reinvented him as a Republican hero. The humanization of the Prussian king in American publications made it easier for young Republicans to identify with the Prussian king. Northern publishers provoked this process by selecting those stories, which seemed to fit their country's Republican ideology and manipulated it in their own interest. But even if some interpretations varied, New Englanders and their countryman in New York and Pennsylvania shared images of Frederick the Great with their German contemporaries. A transatlantic culture of modern patriotism emerged. Frederick the Great was present in early Republican periodicals because he could be glorified as a model Republican. Furthermore, the myth of New England's resemblance of Prussia was based on some real similarities. New Englanders indeed shared some traditional collective values with their Prussian contemporaries. Both people considered education, modesty, simplicity, and hard work as important values. Furthermore, Prussia's history, its rise to become a dominant European power whose political stability and military strategy were admired all over the continent, described exactly what New England aimed for on a regional and national level. First, the New England intellectual elite wanted their culture to dominate within the United States. Then they imagined the entire nation rising to a great power following the Prussian example. They imagined America under New England leadership to glory just as Prussia. The fact that other Northerners participated in the New England cult of Frederick the Great shows that the people living close to the region identified with New England's vision of the nation. The collective celebration of the Prussian indicates the strong sectional Northern identity that emerged in the early republic.

In contrast to any comparison with England or France, the comparison with Prussia was not as problematic for young Republicans. During the time between the Revolutionary War and the War of 1812, some Americans developed an antipathy to Great Britain. Others disliked Revolutionary and Napoleonic France. With all the anecdotes available on him in German publications, the Prussian king Frederick offered a neutral alternative for a transatlantic hero. Besides establishing the German monarch as an American role model, anecdotes of Frederick the Great in New England journals implied that New Englanders already shared the described Republican virtues with the German hero. The Frederick stories are another indicator of the regionalist vision of New England as the embodiment of the new nation.

CHAPTER 3

Failed Republicans: Images of the British and the French

"John Bull vented a principal portion of spleen against the Pope and the Frenchmen. But for the present little while, the cock and the lion repose together most lovingly... to repress the struggles of freedom." With these words the New England nationalist James Kirke Paulding warned his fellow Americans about the anti-Republican national characteristics and politics, which he thought united the historical foes England and France. With a population unable to adopt civic virtue, in his mind, both European countries constituted a contraposition to all the Republican values that were so deeply embedded in his beloved New England.[1]

Nations invent their collective identities by distinguishing themselves from other nations, from political and economic competitors and neighboring countries.[2] In order to define their national identity, early Republican New Englanders compared themselves with Europeans—and particularly with the British and the French. Their comparison focused on these two nations because they were the dominant European powers that had a colonial history in North America and continuing economic interest in the new world. It was an ambiguous process, in which New Englanders both imitated European culture and rejected European characteristics in order to define their own American identity. The colonial history of the United States, the Revolutionary War, and the French support of the American colonies in their struggle for independence, complicated the process of creating images of the British and the French in New England. The century-old conflict between Great Britain and France certainly affected New Englanders' idea of the character of these two nations.

The process of identification and rejection on a broader cultural level, however, was rather fluid. When New Englanders looked at Europeans in order to define their own national identity, they sometimes liked or disliked both, and viewed them regardless of party affiliations. Generally, New Englanders felt that affection for one of the two European countries almost automatically forced them to dislike the other. In the political sphere, early Republicans split into Francophiles and Anglophiles; Republicans favored the French, Federalists the English. political events and changing relationships between the United States and their European counterparts molded the New England image of English and French characteristics. In reaction to these events, New England's disaffection sometimes shifted in seemingly contradictory ways. In their books and periodicals, New England authors and editors employed a picture of European characteristics in order to offer an antithesis to American virtues. By describing European vices, they hoped at least indirectly to emphasize New England virtues, which they thought proposed an American identity.

Disputes over trade and fishing rights, compounded by the War of 1812, had an impact on New England's image of the English. The French Revolution, the Quasi War, and the Napoleonic Wars added an intricate tension to early Republicans' distinction between themselves and the French. Both the English and the French served as a model, but even more as an antithesis for the new American identity. Considering the difference between the long history of European nations and the much shorter life of the young American nation, it is not surprising that New Englanders on the one hand selectively imitated French and English architecture, gardens, dress styles, furniture, cooking, and manners, but on the other hand wanted to distinguish themselves from the Europeans to invent explicit "American" characteristics. The most important difference between Europeans and Americans, in New Englanders' view, was French and Englishmen's lack of Republican virtues. Early Republican New Englanders thought the French and the English were not able to enjoy civil liberties because their national characters did not support a Republican political system. The idea of French and English inferiority in that respect strengthened New Englanders' self-consciousness and pride in their own political and social system.

When New Englanders pictured the English and the French in newspaper articles and travel books, they often portrayed Americans particularly virtuous in contrast to their European contemporaries. They were well read in characterizations of the British and the French, and used many different sources for their own descriptions of the British and French national character. Newspaper editors and publishers did not limit themselves and their readers to accounts written by Americans. They published essays by French and English authors, and even German commentators. New England publications presented the European perspective, as long as it supported their argument that the English and French had failed and continued to fail as Republicans. In reaction to European doubts that the American republic would last longer than a few years, the early Republican generation strengthened their self-consciousness by convincing themselves that they possessed Republican virtues that even civilized European nations lacked; which would help their young nation to prevail. A pivotal step to create this self-image was to contrast themselves with the British and the French over and over again, and to define and redefine them as antitypes of Republicans. Published in various journals with different readerships, such portraits of the British and the French reached a broad audience. They appeared in women's magazines, religious periodicals, farmers' journals, and also in newspapers addressing a more general audience.[3]

Authors and newspaper editors argued that the British had failed as Republicans because they had restored monarchy after the civil war and fell for the vicious seduction of commercialism. In their eyes, their British contemporaries constituted the antithesis of a virtuous Republican people by living a leisurely, luxurious life in an unequal society. Early Republican readers had access to extensive explanations of how the English society was split along class lines and how this led to poverty and discrimination. Moreover, New Englanders imagined the English to lack Republican virtues. New Englanders contrasted English drinking habits, immorality, and sensationalism with their own soberness, morality, and disinterestedness. Accounts on the English also traced issues such as corruption within the Anglican Church and the absence of religious freedom in Great Britain. Such depictions underlined religious diversity and freedom as an important element of the new American nation.

While they saw the English as anti-Republican lovers of luxury, New Englanders imagined the French in similar terms as a people that spent its time in extravagant theatres and gambling houses. With the turn of the century, the cruelties and chaos of the French Revolution evolved more and more at the center of the New England picture of the French. Strikingly, thirty years after the revolutionary events in France, New England papers still traced the horrors of the Terror and paid particular attention to the inhumane treatment of French aristocratic women during that time. In this imagery, the Revolution had destroyed French femininity by ignoring women's right to protection. Consequently, newspaper articles and books also portrayed French women living a masculine life style. Many commentators on French post-Revolutionary society drew a picture of French females working in traditional male occupations as shopkeepers and accountants. Distinguishing themselves explicitly from Catholic France and glorifying Protestantism, New Englanders idealized French Huguenots as martyrs for the Protestant cause. Another component of New England's picture of the French was the caring, philanthropic French soldier. This idea has to be seen in context with the American cult of the French general and American Revolutionary hero, the Marquis de Lafayette.

Dandies, Corruption, and the Inequality of English Society

New Englanders presented their image of the British in periodicals, in published and unpublished travel journals, and in letters written to friends and family at home during trips to Great Britain. The authors of such pieces, and the editors of the newspapers that published their writings, came from both political parties and belonged to different religious denominations. The orthodox clerical writers from the *Christian Spectator* joined Unitarians such as the *North American Review* editor Edward Everett and Harvard physician Walter Channing in publishing these images.[4] But this educated group of New Englanders also shared a large number of experiences and interests; many graduated from Harvard, traveled in Europe, and got involved in the nation's new literary institutions in order to help creating an American literature and history. Part of this process of inventing American traditions was to destroy remains of the previous English identity, which dominated among American colonists until mid-eighteenth century. In addition to their newspaper editing and writing, the engineers of New England's images of the British and the French filled leading positions in the region's society either as clergymen, professors, doctors, lawyers, or government officials. In these positions they served as models for more ordinary New Englanders, farmers, and artisans.

William Tudor, the editor and founder of the Boston *North American Review*, for example, traveled to places such as France and the West Indies in the late 1790s and early 1800s after he graduated from Harvard. In 1809, he was elected to the Massachusetts legislature. Tudor helped found the Boston Athenaeum. The Massachusetts lawyer and writer William Austin, who published his private letters from London portraying the English character, was also a Harvard graduate. Austin wrote these letters while he studied law in London.

As many New England intellectuals, Austin was also interested in public service. For many years he represented his hometown, Charlestown, in the Massachusetts General Court. In 1801, he was chosen to give the Bunker Hill anniversary speech. Like William Tudor, Austin wrote short stories describing the American way of life. The nationalistic activity of the Democratic Republican shows that members of both political parties subscribed to an emerging New England American identity.[5]

The accounts of these authors emphasized the British love of luxury and how wealthy Englishmen used luxury items to display their superior social status. Although New England travelers participated in the upper-class English lifestyle when they toured the British islands—at theatres, dances, and parties—this kind of entertainment nevertheless clashed with their Republican ideals and reinvented Puritan values such as simplicity and modesty. As Europeans came to visit the new world to experience the young republic, New Englanders journeyed to Great Britain as spectators of a monarchical society. Their scrutiny of English society made them especially aware of the social inequality in Great Britain, and they prided themselves on the social equality in their own country. By publishing their own as well as foreign accounts on such British characteristics, New Englanders created a convincing collective image of their former mother country.

In the eyes of early Republicans, the appetite for luxury molded the British national character. The image of the English "dandy" living on his fortune, and spending his time gambling and drinking, not only offended New England values of simplicity, modesty, and soberness, but also the ideal of hard work. In an 1823 review of *A Foreigner's Opinions of England*, written by the Prussian author Christian August Gottlieb Gohde, the reviewer in the New Haven *Christian Spectator* criticized this attitude of wealthy Englishmen. "Dandies," he explained "are commonly wealthy, loitering about the streets, yawning in the face of all that is worthy, and laboriously busy...in killing their great enemy, time."[6]

Travel books and articles on the English declared greed and luxury the major evils of British society. A contribution to the Boston *Monthly Magazine* thought British desire for luxury and display of wealth destroyed friendship bonds and turned social gatherings into competitions for social status. The reason to give a dinner party, the author claimed, used to be that people wanted to enjoy the company of their friends, but now they invite them to show off their luxury goods, which rather turns friends into enemies.[7]

New Englanders found these vices not only among the wealthy. The English Romanticist, popular writer and poet, Robert Southey, was one of the best analysts describing such characteristics of British society. His ambition to reform British society as well as his criticism of British political corruption and the emergence of the industrial poor in towns such as Manchester and Birmingham attracted the Bostonian publisher Munroe, Francis, and Parker. The company was eager to reprint his *Letters from England by Don Manuel Alvarez Espriella*. Southey's fictitious letters from Great Britain written from the point of view of a "naive" Spanish traveler described how Englishmen of all classes followed their desire for luxury items. In other countries, he observed, "the shops themselves are mere repositories of goods, and the time of year of little importance to the receipts. But it is otherwise in London; luxury here fills every head with caprice, from servant-maid to the peeress, and sops are become exhibitions of fashion."[8]

The reason for this materialism and selfishness, New Englanders thought, was Britain's all-consuming commercialism. While their own region was experiencing an economic transformation into a more industrialized society, they feared that the same vices ensuing from commercialization would lead to anarchy and chaos, and, ultimately the destruction of Republican virtue in the United States. By linking greed and ambition with the British, Americans converted their fears into a creative process in which they defined themselves in contrast to their image of the British. Moreover, with the picture of all these evils in British society, New England's elite appealed to their readers to maintain their Republican virtues and to prevent greed and corruption from crossing the Atlantic. In his *Letters from London*, published in 1804, Massachusetts lawyer William Austin summarized his observance of selfishness resulting from commercialism in England when he pointed out that in a "commercial country" the interest of each individual interferes in some form with the neighbor's and, therefore, people thrive at each other's expense.

Comparing this British commercialism with the rural and agricultural character of his own nation, Austin felt relieved. If America lost its unique virtuous rural character, he warned his countrymen, it would follow the destructive path of Great Britain and sacrifice its freedom and Republican equality. "Thank God, the United States are rather an agricultural, than a commercial country;" he wrote, "otherwise, in spite of its constitution, our republic would soon be lost in an odious aristocracy, and what is still worse, a commercial aristocracy, which experience proves to be the most inexorable, relentless, and coldblooded [*sic*] of all tyrannies."[9]

In the New England imagination, the old landed British aristocracy imitated the new commercial nobility and intermingled with successful merchants. Together they formed a new social class corrupted by extravagance. An "Anecdote of an English Nobleman" in a 1794 *Massachusetts Magazine* traced this social transformation: "An English Nobleman once asked Dr. Johnson, what was become of the gallantry and military of the old English nobility? He replied, 'Why my Lord, I'll tell you what is become of it; it is gone into the city to look for a fortune.'" Supporting this picture of the new upper class in his book *A Sketch of Old England, by a New-England Man*, James Kirke Paulding stressed the political corruption of these Englishmen. He saw traditional English virtues "daily mouldering away." Virtuous British people, he wrote, "cannot keep pace with the more numerous class of nobility and gentry, because their pride will not stoop to an alliance with vulgar wealth, nor their principles bend to earn the rewards of the government by the sacrifice of their integrity."[10] Significantly, the New York writer and government official called himself a "New-England Man." By linking himself with the New England identity that was so popular among his fellow New Yorkers, Paulding marketed his book and promoted New England nationalism outside the region. As a devoted nationalist, Paulding started to satirize the British in 1812, when the political and economic rivalry between Great Britain and the United States had much increased and soon escalated in the War of 1812. He published his popular book *The Diverting History of John Bull and Brother Jonathan*, the first of a series of publications on this topic, which he continued until the late 1820s. With his writings examining the American way of life, the New Yorker wanted to create a distinctive American literature. In addition to his career as a writer, Paulding also successfully pursued recognition in public service. When he was only seventeen years old, he became a clerk in the U.S. Loan Office in New York. Later, in 1828, Martin Van Buren chose him as secretary of the U.S. Navy.

New Englanders identified British places of leisurely amusement, such as gardens and theatres, as "schools of corruption." At least this is how Benjamin Silliman put it, when he described his visit to the dances at the gardens of Vauxhall in London. Stories of excessive feasting at dances and parties symbolized the insatiability of the British in their struggle for wealth. An 1818 *New England Galaxy and Masonic Magazine*, for example, published a poem on the rapacity of an English judge:

> A Pot-bellied Justice, who thought a good feast
> The best thing this world could afford,
> Commanded his cook, for that day's repast
> A Sturgeon to send to his board.

Three parts of the fish he dispatch'd with such speed
That one scarcely can credit the tale;
And had not a sickness prevented the deed,
This Jonas had eat up the whale.
The Doctor arrives—and, with countenance sad,
Assures him assistance is vain;
And to tell him the truth "his complaint was so bad,
He would ne'er eat a sturgeon again."
"If 'tis so," quoth the Justice, "what signifies care?
"And now I have only one wish:
"That as you're convinced I have no time to spare,
"You will send me the rest of my fish."[11]

The inequality in British society and its sharp divisions along class lines struck New Englanders as another British feature that distinguished the European power from the new American nation. The display of social status in everyday British life startled New England travelers, and they could not stop commenting on it in their journals. Their reaction to the poverty they observed in the streets of London and other British cities was even stronger. In their writing, they maintained a sense of ongoing shock. Contrasting British class hierarchy and indigence with their own social system helped New Englanders to define their nation as a land of opportunity and equality. In order to emphasize how different their native New England was from this European society, some early Republican observers of Great Britain argued that their American countrymen lacked any imagination of such social divisions. "I have lately made a most important discovery one of the great secrets of English rank," William Austin reported to a friend in Massachusetts, "you, in the United States, knowing nothing of this, will consider the following authentic history of rank a singular curiosity." The life of the English, he explained, is so clearly shaped by class that they know whether "a servant, a postman, a milkman, a half or whole gentleman, a very great gentleman, a knight, or a nobleman" is knocking at their door.[12]

During his 1811 trip through England, Harvard medical professor Walter Channing noted in his diary what a Prussian traveler had told him about the oppression of the British lower classes: "The distance between them and their supposed superiors was a far way farther than in the most acknowledged despotism." New Englanders took pride in the idea that the poor in the new world had a chance to work their way up, while the corrupt and oppressive British system did not give the lower ranks any chance to improve their position on the social ladder. Building on this contrast between England and his native country, Austin praised America's social flexibility: "If a man is born poor, he is not born to poverty; or if born to labour, he is not born to servitude."[13] Especially those members of New England's intellectual elite who were often involved in the nineteenth-century reform movements found the social conditions in England clashing with their own philanthropic ideas. Walter Channing, for example, was an ardent temperance reformer and devout Unitarian. As a leading member of the Boston medical community he filled the position of Harvard's first professor of obstetrics and remained at the university for forty years. He wrote his reports on British society during his studies in London and Edinburgh in the early 1810s. Like some other commentator on the British and the French, he was also a member of the American Academy of Arts and Science.

Comparing Great Britain with their own imagined nation, New Englanders could only view it as a country of corrupt wealth and hopeless poverty. By expressing their dismay and unfamiliarity with the large number of beggars in the streets of British cities, New England writers encouraged their readers to imagine their native country as a superior place, where the people enjoyed Republican equality. The founder and editor of the *North American Review*, William Tudor, argued that this equality made even the lower classes in America superior to their English counterparts.

> "I know that we have narrow-minded farmers and planters, paltry attorneys, and sordid traders," he explained, "but, take the same classes of men in the same circumstances,—suppose them to possess the same degree of good sense, education and liberality,—the consciousness of equality will make the American superior...than the Englishman, who acknowledges,...that he holds a subordinate station in society."

This attitude did not only help the elite to create a collective identity, but also to respond to many New Englanders' fear that social factions in their own country would destroy the republic. Descriptions of social inequality in old England allowed New England to appear as a place of peaceful equality. Furthermore, these publications made Federalists, who sometimes saw too much social equality as a source of chaos and anarchy, aware of the inhumane consequences of strict social divisions. This was an effect that might have satisfied Jeffersonian readers with more democratic attitudes. Appealing to his readers to condemn such English inequality, Gohde's Bostonian reviewer disagreed with the Prussian author's praise of the British welfare system.

He wondered how Gohde could have been ignorant of the threatening numbers of starving and homeless people in British cities. He wrote that he did not know whether Gohde "entirely forgot himself," or did not see "that tide of floating, starving poor, which almost clogs up some of the streets of London, and which threatens to sweep down even pillars of the country." The explanation for Gohde's ignorance was his lack of knowledge about British inequality and the terror of press gangs, which prevented the publication of reports on poverty.

In contrast to a British press, which some Americans did not imagine to possess the freedom do so, the early Republican travel reports often traced British poverty. Poverty indeed had evolved as a big problem in England, especially in eighteenth-century fast-growing London. Paulding, for example, wrote about Britain's capital: "One thing that has disgusted me most in this city, is the incredible quantity of wretched and profligate beggar's, [. . .] whose ragged, filthy, and debauched appearance turns pity into absolute disgust." To an American who is not used to see such scenes and signs of poverty, he felt, they destroy every "pleasing illusion" evoked by English monarchical culture.[14]

New England authors such as Austin believed that the social system had a strong impact on the British national character, which he defined as a combination of obedient servility and corrupt arrogance. The English character, he argued, combined dignity and servility: "The moment a man is addressed, he either disciplines himself to a demeanour [*sic*] of inferiority, or assumes an air of importance, suitable to the opinion he thinks is entertained of his presence."[15] In the New England mind, the British national character included elements such as sensationalism, immorality, gambling, drinking, rudeness, and egoism. Numerous newspaper articles and travel books gave examples of such English vices. These publications played an important role in creating a collective New England image of the British. When New Englanders contrasted Britons with their own people, they often talked about "Americans" and "America" instead of "New Englanders" and "New England." This indicates again that they imagined their region as the embodiment of the entire nation.

English Vices: Drinking, Gambling, Immorality, and Selfishness

New Englanders described the British as anti-types to themselves. In this picture, the British were exactly opposing New England virtues of sobriety, discipline, morality, disinterestedness, and selflessness. As in their depiction of New England landscapes and characteristics, New Englanders combined traditional Puritan values and new Republican virtues when they contrasted their own collective personality with the national characteristics of their former mother country. Instead of being hardworking, reading and self-reflecting like later-day Puritans, the English gambled and drank. In 1816, the *North American Review* agreed with a French traveler's description of Bath: "The concise sketch of Bath is correct," the anonymous reviewer wrote, "it is the paradise of invalid men and women, whose most important occupation is playing at whist." Although he found the French travel journal a valid source on the English character, the New Englander still suggested his readers look at works of New England and English authors Benjamin Silliman and Robert Southey. He found them "the best" and "most complete" literature available.[16] Descriptions of English vices often combined remarks on gambling with more frequent comments on how excessively Englishmen drank. New Englanders considered drinking one of the worst vices and a danger to Republican ideals of order and stability. In an 1823 article on "English Manners" the Boston *Atheneum* called the English "great drunkards." Especially on holidays such as election days, early Republican Puritans argued, British drunkenness caused chaos and violence. Like many New England observers of British elections, Silliman stressed that he had never before witnessed "such a scene of drunkenness, uproar and riot."[17]

The New England idea of British vices seemed to be confirmed by the immoral and improper behavior of English women. The picture early Republican periodicals and books drew of English women clashed with their depiction of New England women as personifications of New England virtues such as sobriety and simplicity. New Englanders thought that British women displayed extravagance, lost innocence, and increased immorality by wearing provocative, ornamented dresses. In 1808, the *Emerald* humorously commented on the immodesty of British women's dresses: "The dress of English women is perfect, as far as it goes; it leaves nothing to be wished, except that there might be a little more of it." Accounts of British leisure activities also traced the immorality of English women. Although a poem on "Packing Up after an English Country Ball" first pictured English men as immoral in a scene where they try to seduce women after the dance party was over, it particularly stressed the women's viciousness in the following verses. These illustrated how the young women willingly engaged with the male guests.[18] In addition to supporting the image of an immoral, chaotic British society, this portrait of British women helped to manifest the central role of idealized New England women in shaping the new national identity. At the same time newspaper editors hoped that such descriptions of English women would warn New England women not to lose their morality and simplicity and adopt British female vices.

In the eyes of late eighteenth- and early nineteenth-century New Englanders, Americans not only distinguished themselves from the former mother country through their Puritan virtues, which helped to prevent anarchy and chaos, but also through their Republican hospitality, selflessness, and interest in the common good. Britons, however, pursued their own egoistic goals and were consequently rude and inhospitable. The first generation of independent Americans wanted to prove that their manners and civility were superior to British behavior. With this intention, the Salem *Weekly Visitant* derided British politeness and civility as superficial public display. An 1806 article said that in England "much formality, great civility, and studied compliments, are exhibited in public; cross looks, sulky silence, or open recrimination, fill up their hours of private entertainment." Supporting this image of the rude and selfish Englishmen, Paulding contrasted British inhospitability with the warm reception he experienced in New England. He contrasted his experience at a castle in North Wales with traveling in his own small New England, where he often had stopped at private homes and asked for a glass of water and was offered a glass of cider or milk for which nobody ever expected him to pay. At the "stately" English castle he felt rejected and mistrusted. The *Merrimack Miscellany*, a Newburyport newspaper, explained to its readers how such selfishness resulted in national catastrophes. An 1805 article on the "Character of the English Nation" argued that the reluctance of the British to sacrifice their egoistic interests to the common good had led the country into civil wars: "A natural restlessness, and an extreme jealousy for their rights and their liberty, have often plunged them into the horrors of civil war, and brought them to the brink of ruin."[19]

This portrayal of the British national character served New Englanders as antithesis for their own collective identity and helped them to create an image of the ideal American whom they defined in New England terms. To early Republican readers, the description of such British characteristics must have above all indicated that Britons failed as Republicans because they lacked Republican virtues and possessed vices that provoked disorder and violence. Americans' urge to imitate and adopt European style, and their constant comparison of themselves with Europeans, reveal a feeling of American inferiority.

By declaring the American character superior to the British, New England writers and editors wanted to eradicate this tension. Moreover, they hoped to solve the conflict between imitation and rejection of European characteristics. Some advocates of New England nationalism warned early Republicans not to copy the British. Paulding, for example, predicted that admiration of the British would lead to imitation and finally to the destruction of American liberty: "It seems to me that our admiration of English government, English institutions, English genius, and English every thing else, will eventually harness us in the trammels of a servile imitation, that will not only fetter the genius of Americans, but lead to the commission of political errors, fatal in the end to our freedom and happiness."[20]

New England writers assured America's first generation that they should not imagine American intelligence and education as inferior to the British. Rather, they maintained that in contrast to ignorant Englishmen, Americans were knowledgeable and independent-minded, abilities that they saw as essential for good Republican citizens. William Austin tried to evoke pride and self-confidence in his American readers when he compared British and American intellectual abilities and qualifications for popular sovereignty. He was convinced that the British were not more intelligent than the Americans. Rather to the contrary, he claimed, because of the Republican system; because Americans had the opportunity to think independently and to participate in politics, they were better informed and there was more common sense among them. Sixteen years later, an article in the *New England Galaxy* treated the subject of British ignorance more expansively. The author, F. Hopkins, claimed that the English hardly understood anything that was unrelated to their profession, which was chosen for them by a parent or the parish. Moreover, the English were not only ignorant about the new world, but they even did not know their own constitution. Talk to an Englishman about the British constitution, Hopkins suggested, "he will tell you 'it is a glorious Constitution!' Ask him what it is, and he is ignorant of first principle."[21]

The *New England Galaxy* published a number of anti-British articles. Its editor, Joseph Tinker Buckingham, was born in Windham, Connecticut, as the son of a tavern keeper in 1779. Buckingham is another example of a social climber in the rising publishing and printing industry. After his father's death left the family in poverty, he worked for publishers in different New England towns. Membership in the Massachusetts Charitable Mechanic Association brought Buckingham the support of prominent Freemasons such as Samuel Knapp, and this enabled him to establish his own newspaper, the *New England Galaxy*, in 1817. His magazine focused on Masonic and agricultural news, but also included politics and poetry and enlisted prominent Boston writers. As an active New England patriot, Buckingham held different offices in the Bunker Hill Monument Association.

The combination of descriptions of New England virtues and opposing British vices in early Republican publications constituted a strong force in the emergence of a New England national identity. Bad English characteristics seemed to underline New England American righteousness. The fact that writers such as Austin and Paulding appealed to their countrymen to resist feelings of inferiority signals the first American cohort's struggle with the reputation of their nation. New Englanders, who were sure of their superiority within their own country, sometimes still viewed the British as a role model. But the discourse on the British character not only indicates American insecurity, it also shows how New Englanders proudly forged their new national identity by contrasting their own imagined virtues with British vices. Furthermore, they reacted to what they perceived as British arrogance.

For decades before the Revolutionary crisis, New Englanders had thought of themselves as Englishmen. Their ambiguous feelings about the British were partly rooted in this history of their collective identity. They still felt culturally closer to the British than to the French. But this ambiguity was certainly reinforced by changes in their foreign relationships with Great Britain and France. When in the early 1790s they saw the French Revolution as a continuation of their own, New Englanders rather identified with the French. Their struggles with the French in the late 1790s, however, revoked a consciousness of their British heritage that even lasted through the War of 1812. In their response to their shifting sympathies, New Englander rather sought an explanation in the British character than in their own inconsistency. As part of their characterization many authors stressed the obscurity of English values. In their mind, Englishmen personified contradiction. "The spirit of contradiction is the character of the [English] nation," Southey wrote. They love to fight wars, he said, but then do not want to pay for them. They love their royal family more than any other people on earth, but still openly caricature them constantly. Like Southey, many New England commentators sought to uncover contradictions in British values and behavior. In their depiction, Britons lacked principles and consistency because they once admired their king and then killed him; sometimes they benevolently supported the poor, but were also selfish and avaricious.

In addition, they seemed to apply double standards by defending liberty at home and oppressing colonists abroad. Hopkins expressed common sense when he concluded, "In a word contradiction and obscurity make an Englishman."[22] By introducing this idea, New England nationalists powerfully delineated their own image of the British. This process enabled them to declare every divergent depiction of Englishmen a result of such contradictions: somebody who drew a virtuous picture of the British must have experienced them in a moment when they switched values. New Englanders degraded English virtues by highlighting their inconsistency.

British Protestantism: A Different Kind of Protestantism

Protestantism played on important role as an element of New England nationalism. Since Great Britain was also a Protestant nation, and used religion as a major force to create their national identity, New Englanders could not define themselves as easily against Great Britain in religious terms as they could against Catholic France. They solved this problem by classifying English Protestantism as a different kind of Protestantism. Early Republican reports on British religion extricated the same vices, corruption, and greed that in the New England mind molded British society in general. Moreover, New Englanders thought that their Protestantism distinguished itself from British Protestantism through the religious freedom to choose among different denominations. As a strong advocate of the idea of English Protestantism as a different religion, William Austin wrote about England: "I seem to have found a new religion, so different is its aspect, in this country, from that which it discovers in New England."

New England publishers praised their own Republican Protestantism by describing the oppressive nature of financial obligations to the Church of England. Such publications implied that the Episcopalian Church, as which the New England Anglican Church reemerged after the Revolution, might constitute a threat to the religious liberty of the new republic. An 1821 article in the *Atheneum* rejoiced at the combination of religious and economic freedom in the new world: "In America there is no established religion. The law, though it compels every man to contribute a certain proportion to the support of some religious teacher, leaves it to the discretion of each individual to appropriate his quota to whatsoever sect may please him best." It further explained that Englishmen, however, had to support the Anglican Church, even if they did not share her ideology.

In the opinion of these authors, this system contributed to the general social inequality in Great Britain. The privileges of English bishops and greed and corruption of the English clergy appeared as a central theme in New England descriptions of the former mother country.

New England newspapers printed poems and articles that illustrated the greed, insatiability, and royalism of the English clergy. The poem "The Happy Life of an English Parson," published in 1825 in the *New England Farmer*, pointed to the English clergy's worldly interests and material privileges. The first two lines "Parson! These things in thy possessing, / Are better than a bishop's blessing," referred to the minister's non-spiritual priorities. After listing possessions and privileges of the parson, the poem ended with an allusion to his leisurely life and pointed out that he did not take his ministerial duties seriously:

> He that has these, may pass his life,
> Drink with squire, salute his wife,
> On Sundays preach and eat his full;
> And fast on Fridays—if he will;
> Toast church and queen; explain the news;
> Talk with the church wardens about pews;
> Pray heartily for some new gifts,
> And shake his head at Doctor SWIFT.

The image of the parson shaking his head at his fellow clergyman, the popular writer Jonathan Swift, indicated his own neglect of Swift's ideas. This portrait of corrupt English clergymen that the Boston paper introduced here gave the impression that Swift was rightly concerned about British Christianity losing its simplicity and coherence. Like Swift, New Englanders found similarities between the Church of England and Great Britain's political institutions. Austin noted: "The Christian [*sic*] religion in England might induce a stranger to believe it was a political institution," because it was as worldly and corrupt.[23]

The number of publications drawing a negative image of the British grew in the period between 1789 and 1825. Only very few pieces appeared before the turn of the century; ten of the thirty-three publications scrutinized in this chapter appeared between 1800 and 1810, and twenty-two between 1815 and 1825. Interestingly, New Englanders avoided such publications during the War of 1812. The reason for this was New Englanders' opposition to the war, which they thought damaged their trade and put an end to their prosperity. The region protested vehemently. Their clergy spoke against

"Mr. Madison's War" in their sermons, governors refused to release militia troops, bankers loaned money to the British, and publishers stopped printing accounts of English vices. In a letter to his Southern friend George Keith Taylor, the prominent Boston lawyer William Sullivan explained that the war was so unpopular in New England because it damaged the region's commerce, and New Englanders considered it as "unnecessary, impolite, and ruinous." In their statements of dissent to the war, New Englanders reinvented the Puritan myth of religious superiority of the region, and the American Revolution as a New England achievement. In this process, they excluded Southerners and Westerners by defining them as Francophile "infidels." The New England elite could not speak against the war with Britain and at the same time publish anti-British portraits. The war of 1812 brought the portrayal of a negative image of the English to a halt.[24]

After the War of 1812, however, such publications increased dramatically, signaling a growing self-consciousness and strengthened New England nationalism. Even if New Englanders had not wanted the war with the former mother country, its outcome still affected them as it affected Americans in other regions. American victory, especially Andrew Jackson's Battle of New Orleans that triumphantly ended a controversial war, evoked American pride and stabilized American self-confidence; the republic had survived, and Americans had once more defeated Great Britain. New Englanders had earlier taken pride in their own Oliver Hazard Perry's victory on Lake Erie in 1813. In spite of their opposition to the war and their reluctance to publish negative depictions of the British, they celebrated the Rhode Islanders' naval defeat of the British as a New England triumph. In their minds Perry's victory connected with the myth of New Englanders winning the Revolutionary War. The final defeat of the British in 1815 encouraged New Englanders more than ever before to project all the vices they saw themselves struggling with into their former enemy.[25]

French Vices and the Failed Revolution

In New Englanders' imagination, the French lived lives as luxurious and leisurely as the British. In their New England portrait, the French loved glory and pomp, extravagant and expensive dresses, jewelry, furniture, and food, and wasted their time in theatres, concerts, the opera, and on gambling tables. Publications on the French again defined such institutions of entertainment—and especially theatres—as places of immorality, where the French arranged and rearranged marriages and adulterous affairs. Unlike their descriptions of the English, in articles and books on the French, New Englanders did not treat this as the behavior of the new commercial classes, but rather as the cultural remains of a feudal system. On his trip to Paris, young Bostonian Theodore Lyman considered these amusements and luxuries an essential element of French patriotism. In his view, the French were prone to materialism because they lived in a military state under Napoleon and lacked the independence that evoked plain love for their country. "The French are born brave and high spirited, and have great love of their country," the twenty-two-year-old Harvard graduate wrote in his travel book, "but they have no independence." Their patriotism, he observed, was not founded on pure affection to their country. The French were more attached to material things than their motherland. "It is those promenades, those theatres, those bons plats, those jolie femmes, those demi tasses, those petit verres, and those thousand petit plaisirs," Lyman explained in great detail, "which have enslaved the French nation."[26]

Lyman came from a prominent Boston family with close friendship ties to Massachusetts political leaders such as Harrison Gray Otis. He was a die-hard Federalist. In the 1820s, he led the opposition against John Quincy Adams. Later, in the 1830s, then as a member of the Whig Party, he became mayor of Boston. Lyman studied the French character when he traveled in Europe for almost a decade between 1810 and 1819.

As with the image of the British, such portraits of the French served the New England elite as means to appeal to their own countrymen not to adopt such an un-Republican lifestyle. To drive home their point, editors published articles by Englishmen complaining how French influence in Great Britain destroyed English virtues. An 1817 article in the Boston *Atheneum,* which the editor had copied from an English journal, regretted that Britons were so attracted to French-language phrases, food, and dress. "It cannot have escaped persons of observation that in the higher orders of society, in this country, the French mode is predominant in the dress, at the table, in the social amusements," it said. "Among women, the glittering silks of the continent have supplanted the less showy, but not less elegant, garments of our own looms, our tables are now covered with ragouts and fricassees, instead of plain English dishes." By publishing articles such as this, editors implied that the licentious English lifestyle partly originated in the British adoption of French ways. The image of a persisting aristocratic lifestyle in France during the first two decades of the nineteenth century also led to the idea that the French

Revolution had failed to introduce any Republican virtues. Publishers emphatically and increasingly emphasized this in their accounts on the French.[27] According to New Englanders, the reason for this failure was the French character, which in their view did not create Republicans. Numerous stories of cruelty and chaos during the French Terror substantiated this image of the French as failed Republicans.

Interestingly, general accounts on violence during the French Revolution did not appear before the Napoleonic era and some were printed as late as in the 1820s. In the first four or five years of the French Revolution, New Englanders endorsed it as a continuation of the American Revolution. During the Jacobin Terror daily newspapers all through New England reported about the imprisonment and executions of the royal family, but it was not until a decade later that New Englanders read more specifically about the brutality against individual aristocrats during the mass executions. Although several New England towns celebrated the French triumph over the British in Valmy at the same time, these reports on regicide nevertheless provoked the first protests against the French Revolution.

In the spring of 1793, when news about the royal executions arrived, regional New England papers sympathized with Louis XVI and his family. By praising the humane virtue of the king and extensively picturing the maltreatment of the queen and her children in improper prisons, these reports implied that the revolution had turned France into a violent, anarchical state. News on the execution of Louis XVI humanized the king and underlined his boldness and dignity. The spectators around the guillotine, however, were portrayed as pitiless and bloodthirsty. Particularly the picture of the crowd dipping their handkerchiefs in the king's blood communicated their enthusiasm for the killings. Accounts similar or identical with the following report in the *Connecticut Courant* of Hartford appeared in the local New England press through April and early May of 1793:

> The unfortunate Monarch arrived at the foot of the scaffold at twenty minutes past ten. He mounted the scaffold with firmness and dignity—he appeared desirous of addressing the people, but even this last wish was denied him—Drums and trumpets gave the signal;...After his death, the nearest spectators divided among them what of his hair had been cut off by the stroke of the guillotine! And several persons were so inhuman as to dip their handkerchiefs in his blood.

Some papers, as, for example, the Massachusetts *Columbian Centinel* and the New Hampshire *Concord Herald*, appealed to their readers not to believe the bad characterization of Louis circulating in the Atlantic world. Moreover, by describing him as a good king with "magnanimity, finest... human virtue" and "pure pattern of morals," who had become a victim of his people's cruelty and ingratitude, they portrayed him as a martyr. Heartbreaking stories about the bad physical and spiritual conditions of the queen, princesses, and prince supported this image of the innocent royals as victims of an inhumane French people.[28]

New England daily papers dramatized the event of the king's execution by publishing anecdotal accounts about the reaction of his family. The *Salem Gazette* gave its readers the impression that they witnessed how the little crown prince attempted to rescue his father by begging the Parisian mob not to kill him. The story ended with a tearful farewell scene between father and son, which accordingly put the queen in a "raving delirium." Furthermore, Salem and Boston readers learned how the queen, the king's daughter, and sister became "dangerously ill," turned gray, and could neither eat nor speak as a result of the regicide and their own inhumane treatment in prison. Another story printed in the *Concord Herald* as well as in the *Salem Gazette* described more specifically the royal prisoners as so melancholic at the death of their father and brother that they refused to go for a walk in the gardens because they had to pass Louis's former room on their way out. News that the little prince was not allowed to see his mother and that the committee might even decide to guillotine him as well were also used to show the inhumanity of the French revolutionaries. These reports depicted the French royal family as human beings with strong family bonds. By emphasizing Marie Antoinette's role as a mother and the crown prince's childlikeness, editors underlined the royal family's innocence and the cruelty of the French people at not even protecting women and children from terror. The rather short accounts on the queen's executions supported the same imagery.[29]

These sympathetic reports of the royal executions, along with a violent image of the French people, indicate an early Republican royalism, and were first signs of disillusion with the Revolution. However, not before the turn of the century did numerous horror stories of the mass executions, and especially the suffering of aristocratic women under violent physical and verbal insults, appear in books and periodicals. New England Federalist clergy applauded the French Revolution as late as 1795 and some Bostonians still celebrated Bastille Day in 1796. According to David Waldstreicher, even until 1798 New England Fourth of July orators interpreted the French Revolution as a continuation of the American Revolution. Although

Democratic Republicans turned celebrations of the French Revolution into partisan events, most inhabitants of Federalist New England seemed to share their enthusiasm in spite of their political affiliation. Most New Englanders remained sympathetic to the French cause until the conflict over the Jay Treaty, French provocations, and finally the XYZ-Affair, and the Quasi War with France stopped Americans from connecting the French Revolution with their own. During the years between 1796 and 1800, America's conflicts with France reshaped New Englanders' attitude toward the French Revolution and they reconsidered whether its cruelties could be excused as liberating acts. After the end of the Quasi War in 1800, New England magazines and books described the French Revolution as violent and chaotic. This time, stories not only focused on the sufferings of the royal family—which readers could have seen as horrible but necessary actions of liberation—but talked about the tortures to which the Revolution exposed helpless French noble women.[30]

Building on the imagery of the reports on the royal executions, the stories published in the first two and a half decades of the nineteenth century showed how the French Revolution did not shy away from terrorizing women. Moreover, these publications gave the impression that women in particular became victims of the Terror. An article published in the *Literary Tablet* described how an English convent in Paris was misused as a women's prison and as a place for executions: "During the time of terror, it was converted into the crowded prison of the female nobility, who were here confined, and afterwards dragged from its cloisters, and butchered by the guillotine, or the daggers of assassins." The small town New Hampshire paper furthermore introduced its readers to the scrupulous bureaucratic procedure that the French followed to organize their mass killings. It outlined how the French created a list of all the names of the women to be guillotined and how once there was only one woman listed, when both she and her daughter should have been named. The executioners corrected their list and beheaded both, mother and daughter. A similar mother and daughter story in the *Ladies' Port Folio* was about a noble woman whose husband was killed although he had been willing to retire from nobility and to give up all his privileges. After losing her husband, her teenage daughter was guillotined because she fainted when she was forced to watch the execution of a friend. By including details about the execution, such as that the guillotine did not work properly in the daughter's case and so the executioners sawed her head off with a knife, the author tried to horrify his readers. In contrast to the early 1790s, at the turn of the century such images became very effective and new Englanders imagined the French Revolution as a cruel event that failed to provoke Republican virtues among the French people.[31]

With these stories, New Englanders did not necessarily aim to glorify French women; they rather wanted to emphasize the inhumane and chaotic nature of the Revolution. New Englanders did not imagine the French Terror as chaotic in the way the French carried out the killings, but as chaotic in the anarchical structure of the regime. Early nineteenth-century depictions of the French also implied that the Revolution was a chaotic event because of its social results. To New Englanders, the French Revolution had turned gender roles upside down. In contrast to their own New England women, authors depicted French women in traditional male occupations. A travel report in the *Atheneum* stated: "At the hotel…you may find the husband in the habit of going to the market or keeping the books; but all other business, such as receiving travellers [*sic*], adjusting the bills, superintending the servants…falls under the province of Madame." The anonymous author continued giving more details about French women's work: "In short women in France are expected not only to lend an assisting hand to their husbands in business, but to take a lead in the management, to keep the correspondence, to calculate the rate of price."

In the eyes of New England observers, French women's occupation of male roles led to the neglect of their children and homes. The author of the piece in the *Atheneum*, for example, thought the result of women managing their husband's business was "the almost universal neglect of neatness in the interior of the house, and the more serious danger of inattention to the health of their children." New Englanders imagined the lifestyle of French women as the opposite to their ideal of Republican motherhood, in which women contributed to the common good by raising healthy patriotic Republicans. In their everyday life, early Republican New Englanders lived more and more in a separate male and female sphere. The industrialization ended the household production unit and the bond of women to traditional jobs at home, while men went to work in modernized jobs in the new factory system. The combination of stories about cruelties against women during the French Revolution, and stories about early nineteenth-century French women working in male jobs, implied that the Revolution had defeminized French women. New Englanders reading both kinds of narratives probably combined that the denial of respect to the female right to protection during the Terror had masculinized French women and transformed caring mothers into accountants and managers.[32]

Images of an unstable French political system, obedient French peasants, and a French people who were satisfied with only limited liberties under Napoleon and the restored Bourbons manifested New England's picture of the French as a nation that lacked Republican virtues as a result of their Revolution. By the early nineteenth century, New Englanders had replaced the idea of the American and French sister republics with the image of France opposed to Republican ideals. An anonymous reviewer of John Scott's *A Visit to Paris in 1814* recommended the book to his readers because he agreed with the English author's description of an unstable French social system. He quoted Scott:

> From all I have said of the French character...it will be seen that I have the worst idea of their social system, as it is at present constituted. It seems to me to be without foundation or compactness. There are no generally recognized principles in the public mind,—there are no great bodies to give gravity, and steadiness, and impetus to the state.

According to New England publishers, the reason for the instability and unfairness of the French social system was that the French people accepted their living conditions and social opportunities. A poem in the *New England Farmer*, for example, ridiculed French peasants' joyfulness even when they were exploited and starving. Observing such an obedient attitude among the French in general, Theodore Lyman wrote: "The only liberty they [the French] have or deserve is the liberty of praising the government. They were satisfied with this liberty under Napoleon, and they begin to content themselves with it under Louis XVIII." In Lyman's view, the French showed their lack of Republican abilities by accepting tyrannical leaders such as Napoleon Bonaparte and consenting to the restoration of the Bourbons.[33]

Looking at French characteristics and lifestyle in the early nineteenth century, New Englanders found little resemblance of their ideal vision of a post-Revolutionary society in France. In their view, the French wasted their time and money on a pompous aristocratic life style, neglected the care and education of their children, accepted limitations on their liberties—and worse, still restored the monarchy. To New Englanders, the corrupt nature of the French national character diverted that nation from following the glorious Republican path blazed by the United States. The only group of Frenchmen New Englanders did not see in this image were French soldiers and Protestants. Early Republican newspapers celebrated French

Huguenots as heroes who had defended Protestantism against the Catholic threat.

French Heroes: The Virtues of Huguenots and Soldiers

In the 1810s and 1820s, editors of New England periodicals thought anecdotes of French Huguenots would entertain their Protestant readers and increase their pride in their own Protestant religion. Praising the heroism of the Huguenots created another opportunity for New Englanders to establish Protestantism as a central element of the New England national identity. These stories described the cruel persecution and discrimination of the Protestant minority in Catholic France, especially after Louis XIV in 1685 had revoked the Edict of Nantes that had guaranteed freedoms to French Protestant communities. They pictured the Huguenots as devoted believers who were willing to sacrifice their lives for their religious cause and often did not withdraw from their religious principles even under torture. An 1819 anecdote of a French officer who converted to Protestantism, which the editor of the Enfield *Religious Informer* copied from the *London Magazine*, was meant to show New Hampshire readers how French Protestants believed in their salvation. The officer in the story became a Protestant after he had read the Bible in a British prison camp. When his fellow French prisoners ridiculed his religious conviction, he compared himself with Napoleon's marshal Jean Baptiste Bernadotte. Bernadotte became a Lutheran after the Swedish general consul had declared him successor of the Swedish throne in 1810. "My motif is the same," explained the French officer referring to Bernadotte, "we only differ as to place. The object of Bernadotte is to obtain the crown in Sweden—mine is to obtain a crown in heaven."[34]

Most articles on French Protestants emphasized the violent and expansionist nature of French Catholicism and praised the Protestants' loyalty to their religion. By picturing the Huguenots resisting conversions to Catholicism, even when their Catholic persecutors tortured them and chased them out of their homes, New Englanders glorified their fellow believers. An anecdote in the New Haven magazine, *The Guardian*, celebrated the courage and religious steadiness of a teenage girl named Jeanneton. It reported how in an attempt to force her to convert, a priest wanted Jeanneton to sign a paper that she had become a Roman Catholic. Although his cavaliers employed "menaces and the most unmanly violence," the girl refused her signature. In particular the ending of the story emphasized the girl's brave resistance to Catholicism. When the priest, weary of her resolute defiance, proclaimed that she refused to sign because she was illiterate, the Protestant heroine "undauntedly and distinctly declared" that she knew how to write, but wanted to remain faithful to her religion.[35]

Anecdotes of the French Protestants' heroic defense of their religion and devotion to their beliefs underlined their courage, honesty, and loyalty. Early Republican Huguenot stories also contrasted the Protestants' humanity with their Catholic persecutors' cruelty and lack of sympathy with their victims. A story in the *Ladies' Port Folio* claimed that the Catholic French were so inhumane in feeling that they sacrificed the lives of their own children in order to defeat the Protestants. The Huguenot antagonist in this anecdote, however, rather saved the life of a Catholic boy than win the battle against the Catholic opponents. In this "Anecdote of a Noble Huguenot," the Huguenots surrounded a Catholic stronghold and demanded that the Catholics surrender. The Catholic governor answered that he would blow up the fortress before he surrendered. In the meantime the Huguenots had captured the governor's twelve-year-old son and threatened to shoot him in front of the governor if he did not give up the fortress. The Catholic governor replied that he could not neglect his duty only to save his son's life. Humanely, the Huguenots set the governor's son free and lost the fortress. In contrast to the Catholic leader, the Huguenot leader sacrificed his troops' victory to prevent the killing of the Catholic boy.[36]

Similar to the stories on the horrors of the French Revolution, most anecdotes of French Protestants appeared after the turn of the century. During the early 1790s, New Englanders trumpeted that the French Revolution overthrew the Catholic Church and Popery, and assumed that the consequence would be akin to a French mass conversion to Protestantism. Throughout the 1790s, *The French Convert*, a dramatic story about the conversion of a French noble woman to Protestantism, was among the most popular books in New England. Originally published in New York in the early 1720s, publishers in Boston and small town print shops throughout rural Massachusetts and New Hampshire also sold and often published it in the 1790s. The poem described a chain conversion from the gardener, to his mistress and then to the master. It introduced New England readers to Protestant heroes, who suffered through kidnapping, attempted murder, slavery, and a hard life in the woods before they could peacefully pursue their religion. The story began with the noble protagonist detecting her gardener reading the Bible, a "Protestant book," that she told him to burn. The servant convinced her to read it first and she became a Protestant as well. In revenge, Jesuits captured the gardener and sold him into slavery in Tangier. When the Catholic husband of the Protestant convert rescued the servant and brought him back home, the Jesuits kidnapped the Protestant lady and tried to kill her, but she escaped when her kidnappers got into a fight. The noble woman lived in the woods for two months until her husband finally found her, rewarded the gardener with gold, and converted to Protestantism.[37]

New Englanders grew disillusioned about the prospective French conversion in the late 1790s, when they discovered that deism and atheism had replaced Catholicism and Protestantism. The New England clergy feared French secularism crossing the Atlantic and perceived the growing deism in New England as an import from France. Moreover, in New Englanders' perception French atheism was not the only danger facing Protestantism; although the French Revolution had secularized France, it was still a Catholic nation. French expansionism under Napoleon aroused Protestant fears and strengthened the feeling of a transatlantic Protestant unity. In this atmosphere, New Englanders defined themselves against France particularly in religious terms. They propagated the evils of French Catholics, which supplemented the image of the French they created in the stories on the French Terror. In the New England imagination, the French were cruel and inhumane. They had brutally killed women and children in their attempts to destroy Protestants and later their aristocratic countrymen. Stories of the persecution of the French Huguenots linked such French vices explicitly with Catholicism. The contrasting description of Protestant Frenchmen as loyal and humane underlined the Catholic component of the wicked French characteristics. In the New England mind, Protestantism stripped Huguenots of French vices.[38]

New England's glorification of the French Huguenots also opened up an opportunity to celebrate Protestant virtues and to link American nationalism in New England with Protestantism. When they read such stories, New Englanders took pride in their Protestant nation, but the anecdotes also woke a larger sense of belonging to a transatlantic Protestant community. By turning French Protestants into role models, newspaper editors and authors appealed to their readers' own loyalty to their religious beliefs. In a time when the Second Great Awakening made some New Englanders worry about religious inconsistency, panegyrical newspaper articles on the French Huguenots connecting Protestants on both sides of the Atlantic communicated the idea that it was Protestantism in general that was virtuous.

Furthermore, New England had historical reasons to glorify French Protestants. After the revocation of the Edict of Nantes in 1685, a number of Huguenot refugees fled to Boston, and founded towns such as Oxford, Massachusetts, and Frenchtown, Rhode Island, and had settled on the Kennebec River in Maine. New Englanders liked them because they were industrious and inventive, and welcomed them as a group sent by God. Even if the French Protestants had rapidly integrated into Colonial society, some New Englanders were still aware of their Huguenot heritage in the early nineteenth century.[39]

Among the numerous stories on the French in early Republican books and magazines, there were a few that drew a positive image of the French in addition to those glorifying Huguenot martyrs. These pieces focused on French soldiers. In contrast to the French pictured in articles on the Terror and the persecution of the Huguenots, the soldiers in these stories risked their lives to save women and children. In 1819 the *Boston Weekly Magazine*, for example, published an anecdote about French troops in Germany, who even helped a Huguenot refugee who fell into their hands. During the Napoleonic Wars the Protestant mother, who was one of many Huguenot refugees who had settled in Berlin, mistook the French troops for Austrians and mistakenly fled to what she thought were her worst enemies. Against all odds, the author stressed, the French soldiers cared for the mother and her infant, and helped them to return to their home without being harmed.[40]

Anecdotes describing the French as humane and caring constituted the minority among early nineteenth-century publications in New England. Most likely, editors did not publish them to even out the horror stories on the killings of Huguenots and aristocrats. Positive characterizations of French soldiers rather indicated New Englanders' fascination for militarism. This military enthusiasm was most obvious in their glorification of Frederick the Great and in their interest for Napoleon, but also turned up in a few stories on ordinary French soldiers.

Although they admired him for his military talent, New Englanders had an ambiguous attitude toward Napoleon. Their libraries contained books about his military achievements and they collected snuffboxes with his portraits and chess games with Napoleon figures, but many newspaper articles ascribed all the vices that they ascribed to the French in general, also to the emperor. They pictured the French leader living in luxury himself and fulfilling the greed of his wife, officers, and ministers. Englishman John Scott, whose book on Paris was widely published in New England, claimed that the Bonaparte replaced hereditary attachments of the old regime with wealth and luxury for his officers and courtiers in order to bond them to his empire. An article in the *Merrimack Magazine* portrayed the French empress Marie Louisa as lavish and pompous, the contraposition of the glorified New England woman. According to the anonymous author, Napoleon's young wife never wore a gown twice, changed her dresses five times a day, replaced her diamonds every three months with the newest fashion of jewelry—and her furniture, china, and pets four times a year according to the season. Furthermore, the New England press accused Bonaparte of vindicating Republican principles and the rights of neutral nations with his antisocial and tyrannical government and ruthless annexation of other European countries. He was great only, as *The Boston Spectator* put it, "by making himself the instrument of men's worst passions."[41]

New Englanders hardly published any images of the French before the turn of the century, when the violence of the Terror and conflicted foreign relations with French had transformed the initial enthusiasm for the "sister republic" into dismay. The death of Louis XVI, to whom Americans felt obliged because of his support during their struggle for independence, and the frequent change of governments that lacked such connections to the United States, might also have played a minor role in this transformation of the New England image of the French. The expansionism of Napoleonic France strengthened emotional ties with Protestant European powers such as Prussia and Great Britain. The increasing number of books and articles defining British vices after the end of the Napoleonic Wars in 1815 underscore this conclusion. The results of the French Revolution New Englanders saw in the first two decades of the nineteenth century opened them up to the opportunity to project their own fears about political chaos and anarchy into the French political and social system. They used their image of post-Revolutionary France to visualize the consequences of a people failing to manifest Republican virtues. This mental image of the anti-Republican character of the French served the New England elite as a forceful means of propaganda for the collective virtues they wanted to establish among their fellow New Englanders, and finally all Americans. Moreover, the combination of publications describing French vices and of publications describing New England virtues helped them to create a feeling of American superiority. Using such language, a reviewer of George Ticknor's popular book on the Marquis de Lafayette, the French hero of the American Revolution, compared the outcome of the two Revolutions: "The French people had neither the intelligence nor the virtue of the American people. And the same degree of liberty, which was a blessing to the latter, would have been the greatest curse to the former." In his *Letters of the Eastern States* the Boston author William Tudor extensively admired the Republicanism of his fellow New Englanders. "The truth is, that the people of these states are all essentially democratic republicans," he wrote "in their civil and political code, their religion, education, laws respecting property, habits, prejudices, every thing. Even those who from mere wantonness and foppery talk lightly of republicanism, are all republicans in grain, and inveterately so." Then he pointed to the Republican inability of the French to set them off against his model Republican countrymen. "To make a monarchy here," Tudor tried to convince his readers "would even be more impracticable than to make a republic in France."[42]

In the late eighteenth and early nineteenth century, New Englanders saw themselves as model Republicans within their own country. Their articles and books tracing the character of the British and the French confirmed the image of the exemplary Yankee by emphasizing Britons' and the Frenchmen's lack of such New England virtues. According to New England observers, both the British and the French failed as Republicans because the national character did not support virtues of selflessness, modesty, and interest in the common good. The failure of the English Civil War and the French Revolution as it was still visible to traveling New Englanders in the oppressive, hierarchical, and pompous European societies, proved their argument. "The English and French have both had an opportunity of establishing an equal government," William Austin reminded his readers. But unfortunately, he concluded, "events have proved that the blood of their sovereigns was offered up to strange gods." He admitted: "These efforts, in both cases, were worth making, but they finally discovered that a legitimate republic required principles to which the people of both nations were altogether strangers." Clearly distinguishing his countrymen from their immoral European contemporaries, the lawyer simultaneously warned them not to lose their Republican virtues. "When the citizens of the United States become strangers to these principles," he assured them, "they are no longer free." New Englanders also considered the corruption of European women, whether they became immoral as the English or masculine as the French, as anti-Republican, and contrasted it with the Republicanism of their own wives and daughters.[43]

Publications characterizing Britons and Frenchmen as anti-Republican almost synchronically increased in scale and tempo after the turn of the century. In addition to individual reasons for each of the European nations to be traced at a certain time in a certain way lying mainly in the foreign relations of the United States, we can also find explanations in transformations within the new world that are true for both images of the British and the French. Although today Americans still compare themselves with Europeans and still have an ambiguous view of them, by the early nineteenth century New Englanders passed the stage of an infant nationalism that struggled with the classification and definition of the American nation. Descriptions of the British and the French published in the first two decades of the nineteenth century show that New Englanders had developed an idea of what distinguished their national character from Great Britain and France. After the young American nation had survived its first decade facing party divisions and doubts about the republic's economic, social, and moral stability, and in spite of remaining fears, it went into the new millennium with increased self-confidence. The victorious outcome of the War of 1812 further intensified the faith in the United States. As Joyce Appleby argues, after Jefferson's election Americans were more convinced that they lived in a privileged country enjoying political, economic, social, and religious liberties. The growing number of articles in New England newspapers and books emphasizing the failure of the British and the French to sustain such liberties seem to support Appleby's analysis of American self-perception in reaction to Jeffersonian policies.[44]

Early Republican nationalism in New England did not go so far as to exclude British and French people on principle from their own imagined community. Already defining the United States as a country open to everybody who shared Republican ideals and embodied Republican virtues, New England celebrated the French general Marquis de Lafayette as a Republican hero when he returned to tour America in 1824.

CHAPTER 4

Hero of Liberty: New England Celebrations of General Lafayette during His Visit in 1824–1825

Following a formal invitation from Congress and President Monroe, the French aristocrat and hero of the American Revolution, the Marquis de Lafayette, visited the United States in 1824 and 1825.[1] During this trip, the French visitor traveled twice through New England. As in the Southern and Western states, on his tour through New England people of all classes, gender, and ages celebrated him as a martyr for liberty, as a model Republican and as a founding father. These celebrations always followed the same pattern: local militia troops escorted the "nation's guest" into the town through arches covered with evergreen, flags, and patriotic slogans. Accompanied by bells and cannon salutes, Lafayette paraded through excited crowds waving their white handkerchiefs (often decorated with the hero's portrait). Later, local politicians gave glorifying speeches underlining Lafayette's friendship with Washington and his sacrifices for liberty in the American as well as in the French Revolution. Emphasizing his attachment to the American people, Lafayette met with veterans, children, and other ordinary citizens. He visited Revolutionary battlefields, schools, orphanages, and hospitals.

Fifty years after the War of Independence, these celebrations of the French aristocratic general provided powerful means to evoke the memory of the Revolution and to reinvent Republican virtues. By praising Lafayette's benevolence and disinterestedness, New England leaders hoped to counter the selfishness and individualism that emerged with the commercialized society. Many reports of Lafayette's parades through individual towns emphasized the large numbers of women and children enthusiastically welcoming the visitor. With such accounts authors wanted to prove the success of "Republican mothers" in raising patriotic children and serving as Republican role models. At a time when the election of 1824 underlined partisan factions, the festivities served as unifying rituals because different social, political, gender, and age groups participated in them and shared an admiration of a common idol. Accounts in local newspapers reporting about Lafayette fetes in places near and far—in other New England towns as well as in the South and the West—established a collective imagination of common national virtues and festivities. New Englanders, who often excluded the South in their definition of the American nation, now imagined themselves as part of a union that shared common values and memories. Interestingly, this nationalism sometimes also comprised exclusionary tendencies. By portraying Lafayette as an advocate for freedom for slaves, New England papers tried to exclude Southern slaveholders from the New England ideal of the American nation.

Furthermore, New Englanders defined their nation in contrast to Europeans when they stressed Lafayette's Americanism. In their orations both Lafayette and his hosts emphasized American prosperity, which in New England minds indicated American superiority. This superiority, the speakers and their audience were convinced, sprang from a virtuous American people and democratic American institutions. In his speeches, Lafayette himself praised American democracy and Republican virtues. In their celebration of Lafayette, New Englanders distinguished themselves at the same time from the French. Ironically, numerous biographies of the French visitor supported the New England image of the French as failing Republicans. They praised Lafayette's effort to establish Republican virtues and liberty in France, and contrasted his humanity and righteousness with the cruelty and greed of the French people. Many authors of Lafayette's life story participated in the creation of a horrifying and chaotic image of the French Revolution. They also pictured the Napoleonic era as one of limited liberties and pointed out that Lafayette defended freedom when he—in contrast to other Frenchmen, who willingly accepted Napoleon's system—publicly opposed the Napoleonic regime.

Lafayette's visit was not only a successful nationalistic enterprise, but also a lucrative commercial event. The Revolutionary Hero was another trophy that made New England nationalism a profitable business. Booksellers, local artists, tailors, instrument and box makers, ceramic and glass manufacturers, all wanted to make money on the cult of the French hero. Souvenir books on Lafayette's life and visit filled print shops throughout New England. In addition to works by New England authors, New Englanders sometimes even sold translations of French "memoirs."[2] During the festivities, women, men, and children proudly wore ribbons and badges featuring portraits of Lafayette. Lawyer and Congressman Stephen Longfellow, for example, purchased a silk ribbon with a Lafayette engraving for the ceremonies in his hometown of Portland, Maine, which Lafayette visited in June 1825. Many patriotic New Englanders dressed up with gloves and waistcoats decorated with Lafayette's profile when they attended the festivities. They also brought home souvenirs portraying the famous guest on ceramics, pottery, glass, and wooden boxes. In their Lafayette euphoria, New Englanders drank from Lafayette mugs, pitchers, and bottles, and dined from Lafayette plates. Owners of hotels, taverns, and inns expected better business of guests who could associate their house with the famous French guest. The Thompson Hotel in Connecticut tried to attract travelers with a signboard showing Lafayette journeying the country in his coach. A "Hotel Lafayette" opened in Boston right in time for the hero's visit to the city in 1824. Significantly, Chichester, New Hampshire, tavern owner Joseph Warren Leavitt was so enthusiastic about Lafayette staying at his inn that he himself produced a painting showing the famous visitor to one of his guestrooms.[3] A local musical instrument maker in Pittsfield, Massachusetts, felt that Lafayette's brief stop at the small town was a reason to build a commemorative Lafayette snare drum.[4]

These memories of Lafayette's visit to New England still persist today. Travelers in the region will find Lafayette streets and roads in many towns throughout New England. Visitors to New Hampshire can even climb Lafayette Mountain. Simple historical markers such as street names establish Lafayette as a part of daily life in present-day New England.[5]

The Christian name of the general and statesman was Marie Joseph Paul Ives Roch Gilbert du Motier, Marquis de La Fayette. He was born in 1757 in the French province Auvergne. In 1771, at the age of fourteen, the young aristocrat joined the French army. Four years later he married and entered court life at Versailles. After the outbreak of the American Revolution, driven by a desire for glory, he decided to support the American colonies in their fight against Great Britain. Although Louis XVI denied permission, the twenty-year-old Lafayette left for the colonies and served as a major general in the Revolutionary army. He became a close friend of General Washington, with whom he fought in the Battle of Brandywine that took New York City from the British. When Lafayette returned from France with some French troops ready to fight for the American cause in 1781, colonists entrusted him with the defense of Virginia. In the famous Battle of Yorktown, Lafayette trapped the English commander Lord Cornwallis and forced him to surrender. This contribution to the military conclusion of the War of Independence made the French general a hero throughout America.

Back in France, inspired by his experience in America and ideas of the Enlightenment, the general opposed the Old Regime, in which only the privileged classes enjoyed economic and political freedom. In 1789, he took a seat as a deputy of the nobility in the national assembly, the Estates General. After the fall of the Bastille on July 14, 1789, Lafayette commanded the National Guard, but his decision to fire on a mob forced him to retire. As a supporter of a constitutional monarchy, he presented a draft of the Declaration of the Rights of Man in 1791. In spite of his dislike of the radicalization of the French Revolution, he fought in the war against Austria and Prussia. By 1792, Jacobin plans far exceeded Lafayette's moderate ideas. The general wanted to protect the king and the queen from mob action. A mob attack on the royal family caused such a dispute between Lafayette and Robbespierre's followers that Lafayette had to flee across enemy lines. Austria kept him as a prisoner of war until Napoleon obtained his release from jail in 1797. When he was finally allowed to return to France in 1799, Lafayette publicly disagreed with Napoleon's government and played a major role in the emperor's abdication in 1815. With the Bourbon restoration Lafayette became a political leader in the liberal opposition. At the age of sixty-three Lafayette again commanded the national regard in the July Revolution of 1830. Although an influential figure in the American and French Revolution, he had lost his popularity among the French people by the time of his death in 1834.[6]

The Founding Father and Benevolent Philanthropist

During his tour through the United States in 1824 and 1825, Lafayette visited New England twice. After he landed in New York City in mid-August 1824, Boston was his first destination. From here he continued his trip to Marblehead, Newburyport, Portsmouth, and then back to Boston. The French guest then returned to New York by way of Worcester, and Hartford, from where he traveled through Pennsylvania, Maryland, and Virginia and reentered New England after a visit to Pittsburgh and Buffalo in the summer of 1825. He reached Boston right in time for the fiftieth anniversary of the Battle of Bunker Hill on June 17.

The returning Revolutionary general constituted a medium through which New Englanders could remember and reinterpret their struggle for Independence. Following an invitation from the city of Portland, on his second visit the popular hero went to the newly established state of Maine. Even before Lafayette arrived in their town, numerous reports about Lafayette fetes in other places gave New Englanders a clear idea of how they would celebrate the guest. Such readings inspired people to prepare identical festivities in their own hometown.[7]

In expectation of Lafayette's visit New Englanders erected Liberty Trees and arches with patriotic banners welcoming him, decorated the streets with flowers, and illuminated their windows with candles. Members of each community composed marches and songs, and wrote poems to honor the general. Men and women enthusiastically bought ribbons, badges, gloves, and handkerchiefs with Lafayette's portrait to wear on the occasion. Dressed in their finest clothes they filled the streets to watch Lafayette's entry into their town. Bells and canon salutes gave the parades, reviews of troops, meetings with veterans, or visits of hospitals and schools, a particular festive atmosphere. Waving their handkerchiefs and strewing flowers, New Englanders burst with sentimental and patriotic pride when they saw their hero. For the fifteen months of Lafayette's visit to the United States, local New England newspapers and journals constantly gave reports very much like one in the *New England Galaxy* about his reception in Worcester. The author reported from the celebration that the "scene was one which we have no ability to describe—it makes breath poor and speech unable." Then he described the "long train of military, consisting of... the finest troops in this division—the cheering of the enthusiastic crowd, mingled with roar of cannon, the martial music, and the ringing of bells—the waving of handkerchiefs and the bright eyes which sparkled every window," all to welcome the aristocratic visitor.[8]

In 1824 and 1825, New Englanders developed such an enthusiasm to celebrate their French guest because after three decades of searching for their American identity and attempting to classify their young nation in comparison to Europe, there was a moment where they were convinced that they surpassed their contemporaries on the other side of the Atlantic. As a European who had risked his life for the American colonies and praised the young nation for its libertarian virtues, Lafayette confirmed such feelings of American superiority. Lafayette's visit was a moment in New England history, when the ambivalence toward Europe, the uncertainty whether to reject

European culture or adopt it as a model, seemed to be resolved. New Englanders celebrated the security and national self-consciousness they were gaining. Part of this was, of course, their rediscovery of the Revolution, which they regarded as an event that had established all the virtues that distinguished them from Europeans. New Englanders' excitement about the new historical memory of the struggle for Independence and their clearly defined idea of superiority over the old world erupted in the celebrations for Lafayette.

Lafayette's public performances tended to be emotional, especially when he met with Revolutionary War veterans. According to contemporary newspapers, the general's recognition of old comrades moved everybody, including the spectators, to tears. Although the style of the celebrations was semi-royal with bells ringing, canons fired, lighted candles in the windows, and laurel wreathes decorating the streets, speakers and numerous articles about the Lafayette celebrations emphasized his ordinary appearance. This and his interest in patients in hospitals and asylums, and students at schools, helped to present him as a model Republican and philanthropist. Advertisements in local newspapers inviting everybody who did not yet have a chance to meet him created the image of a hero who was close to the people. Books and newspapers strengthened the image of Lafayette as an ordinary man who advocated equality, by reporting about his emotional intermingling with the people and by stressing his dislike of titles. Biographies, children's books, and newspaper articles emphatically announced that Lafayette had dropped his aristocratic title "Marquis" many years ago because it was "inconsistent with his well known principles and professions of liberty." Now, they said, the European aristocrat was proud to be called "General."[9]

Meetings with veterans of the Revolutionary War emphasized the mutual affection of the French general and the veterans, who in this case represented the American people. This was obvious not only in the tearful reunion scenes, but also in stories of old soldiers who insisted on being introduced to Lafayette. Such anecdotal stories not only indicated the veterans' affection for the French Revolutionary hero, but also that they demanded to be honored as well for their own service for their fatherland. An article in the *Portsmouth Weekly Magazine* about a veterans' event in New York combined both patterns. The article said that when General Lafayette received visitors in New York, an elderly man was kept aside. After insisting on his meeting with Lafayette, the old man walked up to the hero and asked him whether he remembered him? Lafayette recognized the veteran immediately, called him by his name, reached out for his hand, and responded: "Yes, you assisted me off the field of battle, when wounded."[10]

These meetings with veterans celebrated Lafayette as caring for his soldiers and regarding them as equals. In an oration to the Boston Society of the Cincinnati, for example, Lafayette himself expressed this by calling the other veterans "companions." The Society of the Cincinnati often participated in Lafayette ceremonials. Lafayette's visit was an important event for the local branches of the society, which was founded in 1783 by veteran officers of the Revolutionary War to promote patriotism. The members of the hereditary society often represented the local elite. The celebrations also honored ordinary soldiers and presented them as Republican heroes. With their performance at these festivities and Lafayette as their famous representative, veterans managed to gain a lot of public attention and applause. When the French guest spoke to the Boston Cincinnati on August 27, 1824, he described the American Revolution and its veterans as virtuous. "It is to me a delightful gratification," he said "to recognize my surviving companions of our revolutionary army—that army so brave, so virtuous, so united by mutual confidence and affection. That we have been the faithful soldiers of independence, freedom and equality." Moreover, he extended his praise to the contemporary Republican society resulting from the Revolution, when he stressed his happiness to "have lived to see those sacred principles secured to this vast Republic."[11] The large number of reports of Lafayette festivities in the New England print media increased the already strong effect of the propaganda at the local celebrations themselves. Furthermore, it enabled those communities that Lafayette did not visit to feel part of American collective culture simply by reading about it.

As with descriptions of New England towns and images of the French and the British, the celebrations of Lafayette's visit defined the new American nation as one of equality and liberty. There were, however, always signs that New Englanders at the same time feared anarchical consequences from those ideals. They celebrated equality, but nevertheless believed in the natural leadership of a talented elite and favored a system in which ordinary people zealously fulfilled their tasks and accepted their social position. A Revolutionary War anecdote about Lafayette and the loyal soldier Charley introduced such an attitude as truly Republican. The story in the *Portsmouth Weekly Magazine* pictured Charley as a Republican hero, who content with his rank rejected a promotion with which Lafayette wanted to reward him for his service. In this narrative, Lafayette sent Charley as a spy to mingle among the troops of Lord Cornwallis. When Charley returned after a successful mission, he brought several British deserters with him. Pleased with Charley's loyalty and bravery, Lafayette offered to promote him to corporal. With Republican modesty and honesty, Charley rejected the opportunity to achieve a higher rank. "I have ability to discharge the duties of a common soldier, and my character stands fair," he replied, "but should I be promoted, I may fail, and lose my reputation." Of course, even if Lafayette was presented as an ordinary man with human emotions who mingled with ordinary soldiers, the style of the receptions—the toasts, dinners, inscriptions, poems, songs, and marches in his honor—clearly distinguished him from other veterans. As this story shows, the figure of Lafayette could be used by progressive New Englanders to push ideas of liberty and social flexibility as well as by the old guard. This anecdote of Charley, who knew his place in society, was an opportunity for conservatives to promote obedience and the maintenance of the *status quo* in social hierarchy.[12]

As Lloyd Kramer and Anne Loveland have shown, Lafayette's visit opened the opportunity to revive the memory of the Revolution and to invent the tradition of a virtuous American people. At a time when most founding fathers were dead or retired from the public sphere, Americans could identify the French Revolutionary hero as the last surviving founder. Speeches and ceremonies throughout New England introduced Lafayette as a Revolutionary veteran and consequently linked him with the foundation of the nation. Americans often compared the French guest with Washington and pointed out that the two men had been close friends. Inscriptions, like the one on the Liberty Tree in the Boston Market, often read: "Washington and Lafayette. A Republic not ungrateful." Souvenir mugs, pitchers, and plates were decorated with portraits of the first president and the French hero facing each other.[13] At a dinner the Massachusetts Mechanic Association gave for Lafayette in Boston in June of 1825, the participants sung a song connecting Lafayette's first visit to fight for American independence with his visit in 1824–1825 to receive the nation's gratitude for this heroic act:

> When darkness spread Columbia o'er
> And lightning from the war clouds fell;
> Our Champion left his native shore,
> And fought the fight of Freedom well;
> And proud her patriot armies greet
> The gallant, youthful LAFAYETTE

Again he comes in happier hours,
His children's tears his steps attend,
He treats his more than native shores,
Their patriot, soldier, father, friend;
And see united nations met
To hail again their LAFAYETTE.[14]

The Massachusetts Charitable Mechanic Association was a fraternity of craftsmen founded by Paul Revere. With events such as this dinner for Lafayette, artisans made an attempt to gain public attention and recognition of their contribution to the American Revolution. They wanted their public representations with the Revolutionary hero to inspire their countrymen to connect them with their nation's history and to see them also as personifications of Republican virtue. Furthermore, their public appearance with a national hero confirmed the higher social status that they had hoped to achieve in the new republic. The representation of Freemasons at Lafayette celebrations is remarkable given the increasing anti-Masonry sentiment in the 1820s. In particular Evangelicals blamed the powerful upper-class members of the Freemason lodges for excluding women, drinking, and possessing an undemocratic attitude. By demonstrating their connection to the national hero and his Republican values, the Masons attempted to transform public opinion and regain legitimacy.

In addition to his meetings with veterans and visits to battlefields, Lafayette's trip to see eighty-eight-year-old John Adams in Quincy, Massachusetts, and his return to Boston for the fiftieth anniversary of the Battle of Bunker Hill, consolidated the connection of his tour with the memory of the Revolution. At the anniversary of the Revolutionary battle, the French hero laid the cornerstone for the new Bunker Hill Monument that was to replace the wooden obelisk on top of the Charlestown hill. The event attracted thousands of spectators and later schoolchildren had to learn parts of the speech Daniel Webster gave at the occasion by heart. In his address, the well-known politician and lawyer drew the usual picture of the Puritans civilizing the wilderness and of American Revolutionaries establishing a libertarian and egalitarian nation. He especially honored Revolutionary veterans and described the death of General Warren as a heroic patriotic sacrifice.[15]

Most of the numerous books published to satisfy New Englanders' desire to know all about Lafayette's life traced the Revolution and his role in it extensively. A biography that appeared in Hartford, Connecticut, for example, began with two general chapters on the

Revolutionary War, before it treated the Frenchman's arrival and heroic contribution. In their speeches, many orators such as Boston mayor Josiah Quincy and newly elected President John Quincy Adams sought to revive what they regarded as Revolutionary Republican traditions and appealed to their audience to introduce their children to these values. Harvard Professor George Ticknor supported such attempts when he talked about a Revolutionary tradition of a virtuous American people that lived on in young Republicans and was also to be passed to the next generation. In his *Outlines of the Principle Events in the Life of General Lafayette*, Ticknor described Lafayette as an agent of Revolutionary Republican virtues to the country's next two generations. The visit of the Revolutionary hero "offers us . . . one of the great actors, from this most solemn passage in our national destinies," the Cambridge author explained, "and thus enables us to transmit yet one generation further onward, a sensible impression of the times of our fathers; since we are not only permitted to witness ourselves one of their foremost leaders and champions, but can show him to our children." In the mind of New England elites, as a historical hero and a model Republican, Lafayette fulfilled the double purpose of reviving the memory of the Revolution and appealing to young Republicans to live up to the ideal of a Republican citizen. This tradition, the professor rejoiced "brings, in fact, our revolution nearer to us, with all the highminded patriotism and selfdenying virtues of our forefathers."[16]

George Ticknor was born in Boston in 1791 as the son of a schoolteacher, who later became a wealthy merchant. He attended Dartmouth College. After his graduation, he traveled through Eastern cities in the United States, where letters from John Adams introduced him to local and national leaders. The young Bostonian dined, for example, with James Madison and visited Thomas Jefferson in Monticello. In 1815, his desire to continue his studies and his curiosity about European culture brought him to Germany, where he entered the University of Goettingen. Ticknor was a truly transatlantic person; he went to France, Switzerland, Italy, Spain, Portugal, and the Netherlands. In all these places he met with the leading intellectuals and established long-lasting friendships with these Europeans, which he maintained by writing letters and revisiting when he returned to Europe years later. One of his close European friends was the English writer Robert Southey, whose description of early nineteenth-century British society was reprinted in Boston. In 1819, Ticknor returned to the United States and accepted a position of teaching languages at Harvard. Eager as many American intellectuals to prove to skeptical Europeans that the new nation was able to produce significant literature, he published many short stories. A large number of them appeared in the *North American Review*.

As with Frederick the Great and George Washington, Lafayette was celebrated as a disinterested and benevolent patriot. Books and newspaper articles established him as a model Republican working toward the common good and as a transatlantic advocate of liberty. The parades, dinners, and other festivities were rituals in which New Englanders confirmed the Republican values, which they believed the French general embodied. In an attempt to fight the materialism and selfishness that evolved with commercialization, politicians, teachers, and lawyers writing about Lafayette's life centered on the sacrifices the general had made in his struggle for liberty on both sides of the Atlantic. As a perfect Republican patriot, they stressed, he never accepted any reward, neither a title nor money. In contrast, the aristocrat lost his fortune, spending some of it in support of the American War of Independence and the rest through confiscation during the French Revolution. As the Prussian King Frederick II, early Republican publications portrayed General Lafayette as a philanthropist, who always cared for his soldiers and the poor.

Souvenir books for children and adults told the same stories about Lafayette over and over again. They brought to the attention of their readers how Lafayette left his native country, his family and friends, and all his properties and wealth to risk his life for the liberty of the American colonists. Moreover, he did not mind spending his fortune for the American cause, and pointed out that he himself paid for a vessel to sail to the colonies. The children's book *Lafayette: or Disinterested Benevolence* described how Lafayette "raised, clothed, and armed a whole regiment of soldiers, and distributed among them articles he had brought with him" once he arrived on American shores. Proving his disinterested devotion to the cause of liberty, the Frenchman demurred when Congress appointed him a major general. After the War of Independence, New Englanders learned, the general returned to France and continued his struggle for the rights of man in the French Revolution. Completing the image of Lafayette as a martyr for liberty, Lafayette biographies described the Frenchman's sufferings when held in horrible Prussian and Austrian prisons during the French Revolutionary Wars. One of the newspaper clippings on Lafayette and his visit, which Eliza Quincy carefully collected in her scrapbook, summarized what the biographies told in much greater details:

> Lafayette left his friends, his wealth, his country, his prospects of distinction, his wife, and all sources of domestic bliss, to assist a foreign

> nation in its struggle for freedom.... He fought for that country, he fed and clothed her armies, he imparted of his wealth to her poor. He saw her purpose accomplished, and her government established on principles of liberty. He refused all compensation for his service. He returned to his native land, and engaged in contests for liberty there... was imprisoned by a foreign government, suffered every indignity and every cruelty that could be inflicted.[17]

Constantly drawing lines between Lafayette's glorious contributions during the Revolutionary War and his Republican virtues displayed during his tour through the United States almost forty years later, newspapers published an anecdote indicating that Lafayette still, after losing his wealth, was too modest to expect any financial reimbursement for his service. The anecdote was published in reaction to an ongoing debate in Congress how much of a compensation to allow the popular veteran. New Englanders followed the debate with great interest and gave their opinions in letters to their local newspapers. John Newhall, another Massachusetts collector of newspaper clippings on Lafayette, pasted a letter "of an old veteran" arguing for the financial allowance next to the anecdote advertising the French guest's disinterestedness in it. When a member of Congress apologized for the opposition, so the story said, Lafayette replied: "I, sir, am one of the opposition. The gift is so munificent, so far exceeding the services of the individual, that had I been a member of congress, I must have voted against it."[18] On December 21, 1825, Congress finally voted to pay Lafayette 2,000 dollars and to give him 24,000 acres of public land in Florida.

Transforming Lafayette from a military genius into a role model of a Republican, politicians and journalists called him a "philanthropist" in their welcoming orations and newspaper reports. Authors of periodicals and biographical books contributed to that image with stories describing Lafayette's care for his soldiers and the poor, as well as his commitment to human rights. It was this devotion to work for the good of other people, these publications claimed, that had created the Revolutionary generation's love and admiration for Lafayette. Their readers witnessed this deep affection at the emotional reunions of the French general with Revolutionary War veterans. An anecdote about a veteran's hospitality toward the French general in a Portsmouth periodical supported this image. When the "very poor" Connecticut veteran heard that Lafayette had lost his fortune, he said: "As poor as I am, I should love to have him come and live with me all his life." In his *Sketch of the Tour of General Lafayette* the Portland author John Foster explained why the veterans felt such love for Lafayette.

> "During his military career in America, the Marquis displayed that patriotism, integrity, humanity, and every other virtue which characterizes real greatness of soul," he wrote, "His manners being easy, affable, and engaging, he was particularly endeared to the officers and soldiers under his command; they admired, loved, and revered him as their guide and support when in peril, and their warmest friend when in perplexity and trouble."

A children's book on Lafayette gave an example of his caring attitude in a story about an old soldier who could hardly walk and was blind, but insisted to be introduced to Lafayette. The reason for his being so desperate to meet the general was to show him that he did not forget how Lafayette shared his blanket with him, when he lay wounded and shivering in the neighboring tent.[19]

Highlighting Lafayette's particular virtuousness and considering that early Republicans might find it hard to resist un-Republican behavior in a seductive commercial society, New England biographers of Lafayette underlined that he grew up as a wealthy aristocrat, was "reared in the lap of unlimited luxury, surrounded by every thing conducive to physical happiness," and nevertheless became a "genius of republicanism."[20] This praise of the French aristocrat as a first-class Republican in spite of his noble origin established the idea that a true Republican always followed the ideals of liberty, equality, and disinterestedness with no regard to the social and economic context. Some New Englanders might have concluded that in a nation of true Republicans, commercialism was not a threat to people's virtues. Advocates of commercialism would have been able to argue that even a life in luxury could produce a good Republican.

Unifying the Nation: New England's Self-Integration

Lafayette's visit to the United States not only evoked memories of the Revolution and promoted Republican virtues, but also unified the nation. In a time when the election of 1824 between Andrew Jackson and John Quincy Adams split the country along partisan lines,[21] and New England and other Northern states often excluded the South from their imagined nation, the common interest in celebrating the French guest united Republicans and Federalists, as well as Northerners and Southerners. In New England the fetes around Lafayette did more than fire American nationalism. For the duration of Lafayette's tour through the states, they transformed a national identity that was imagined in New England's own terms into the notion that all states shared a common history, collective values, and collective achievements. New Englanders thought that Northerners, Southerners, Federalists, and Republicans all celebrated Lafayette in the same way, followed the same rituals, and praised the same virtues. The actual unifying effect, however, did not so much lie in the process of Americans in Maine, Virginia, and Kentucky celebrating in a common style. It was rather New Englanders reading about identical parades and dinners in Southern and Western towns that created the imagination of shared virtues. Reading reports about welcoming events for Lafayette in places near and far led New Englanders to define their national identity in national terms. Moreover, such reports indeed created a common culture. When inhabitants of Portland, Maine, followed newspaper reports about celebrations in New York City and Washington, they probably wanted to compete and imitated them in their own festivities. With their attempt to create a consciousness of that unification among their countrymen, New England elites wanted to increase the nationalistic effect of Lafayette's tour. For that purpose, Harvard Professor Ticknor praised the visitor for bridging partisan fractions and connecting Americans in different places through a newly inflamed Republican spirit. The visit of Lafayette, he was convinced, "is doing much to unite us [as a nation]. It has brought us together, who have been separated by long lives of political animosity.... It makes a holiday of kind and generous feelings in the hearts of the multitudes that throng his way, as he moves in triumphal procession from city to city." At his reception by the Massachusetts legislature, Lafayette himself accentuated the attachment to the union that he had experienced on his tour through the states. Appealing to the audience's federal loyalty, he underscored that it was this attachment to the union "on which resides the safety of these states, and the hopes of mankind."[22]

Like their common admiration of Lafayette, the celebration of Frederick the Great might indicate that Northerners and Southerner shared a taste in national heroes, at least to a much bigger extent than New England nationalists wanted to believe. Even if the media of Frederick celebrations differed from North to South, both regions were attracted to the German king.

In addition to people from various regional and partisan backgrounds, this inclusive process united New Englanders of different class, age, and gender. Women, men, children, parents, grandparents, mill workers, farmers, merchants, and manufacturers all celebrated together. Again, reading about all these groups joining in common festivities played a significant role in intensifying a revitalized sense of community. Newspapers often emphasized how everybody enthusiastically participated in fetes in the streets and on school campuses, around historical monuments and in city halls. The *Portsmouth Weekly Magazine*, for example, quoted a New York paper commenting on the inclusive character of Lafayette processions in Connecticut: "It is impossible" says the *New York Daily Advertiser*, speaking of the progress of Lafayette, "to travel through the towns of Connecticut and not feel a part of enthusiasm which pervaded all classes." To give an example, the article reported about coachmen proudly wearing ribbons and joining in the patriotic excitement of the crowd: "Even the poor lads who drove the carriages entered fully into the common feeling, and seemed proud of their honors. They wore silk ribbons fastened to the button holes of their waistcoats, by way of distinction." Although some New England leaders still feared anarchical chaos as a consequence of a truly egalitarian equal society that did not protect its natural elite of talented men, others worried that commercialization increasingly widened the gap between rich and poor. Fetes celebrated by all sorts of people and reports emphasizing this social intermingling eliminated fears of growing social distinctions at least for the time of Lafayette's visit.[23]

Strikingly, beside veterans, women and children seemed to dominate the welcoming ceremonies for Lafayette. Expressing their love and admiration of the Revolutionary hero with tears, flowers, songs, and poems, they stood at the center of the festivities. Observers of those scenes then praised the ladies' and students' Republicanism in their written accounts. Some reports of Lafayette events gave the impression that women were most prominent among patriotic spectators. Stressing the large number of the female viewers, John Foster, for example, noted in his report of Lafayette's entrance into Boston "the windows of the streets through which the General was to pass, were thronged with females." He perceived the Boston women as so excited that they could not even wave their handkerchiefs. In an attempt to promote patriotic Republicanism among women, New England intellectuals describing processions and other celebrations in their books and articles wanted to state that Republican women earned the attention and respect of men. Of course, this idea was reversible: in this imagery great Republican men such as Lafayette enjoyed all the love and admiration of their female counterparts. Foster drew such a picture of mutual admiration and respect between Republican men and women when he wrote about Lafayette's meeting with John Hancock's widow. When the French general passed by John Hancock's house, Foster recounted, "The Mayor said to him, there sits the widow of your deceased friend. He immediately caught her eye, and, in the most enthusiastic manner, pressed his hand upon his heart. She burst into tears, and exclaimed, I have now lived long enough."[24]

The experience of the Revolution, when women's production of daily necessities was essential for the boycott of British goods and their initiative of running farms and shops enabled their husbands to fight, opened the public realm for American women. Of course, Republican ideology, ideas of liberty and equality, also contributed to the expansion of women's sphere. The Revolution had helped women to attain a public importance. In the early republic, Americans of both genders recognized that women also fulfilled obligations to the state by raising good Republicans and honoring Republican symbols. As Mary Ryan has shown in her study of New York, New Orleans, and San Francisco, by 1825 women had entered the public sphere as spectators at parades and other civic ceremonies. Even if they could not yet get involved as main actors, women had begun to occupy public places and events.[25]

Although the stage was not open for women orators yet, at New England civic rituals celebrating General Lafayette they could nevertheless display their patriotism and Republican sentiments in songs. As in the speeches given by their husbands and brothers, the songs women sang expressed America's affection and gratefulness to Lafayette and glorified him as a hero of liberty. With a strong patriotic tone in their singing, women confirmed the image of their country as the land of freedom. To early Republican New Englanders, women's contribution to the nationalistic festivities was so important that papers also printed songs performed by women outside the region. John Newhall pasted the copy of a tune sung by a ladies' choir in Wilmington, Virginia, in his scrapbook. Like many of his fellow countrymen, Newhall's patriotic feelings rose when he read the words the Wilmington women sang. The female performance filled early Republicans with pride of their Republican women. Songs such as this also inspired their patriotic imagination:

> Hear us! Hear us! n'er [never] thou leave us,
> Take our lingering, long farewell!
> Thou who erst did'st aid to give us,
> All the joys we now can tell.
> Vetran hero! Friend to Freedom!
> In our hearts thou'dt ever dwell.
>
> May the richest loon of heaven,
> Pay thee for the good thou'st done;

And to us may it be given
To behold thy setting sun.
Vetran Hero! Friend of Freedom!
Take the Fruits thy valor won.

Leave no more these peerless mountains,
Every hearth a home for thee;
All these plains, these crystal fountains,
All, are fraught with liberty.
Vetran Hero! Friend of Freedom!
Rest thee with the brave and free.[26]

In the New England celebrations of General Lafayette as well as in the reporting of them, women played an active role as translators of the nation's enthusiasm for the French guest. More than behind-the-scene producers and buyers of patriotic household goods, in Lafayette festivities women acted as performers of patriotic Republicanism either on the stage or as a participating audience.

The involvement of children in the ceremonies also displayed women's exemplary Republicanism. Boys and girls reciting poems, singing patriotic songs, and wearing badges expressing their admiration for the general, indicated their mother's success in raising a new Republican generation. Children were omnipresent in the repetitive and pompous celebrations of Lafayette. In the yard of the Connecticut State House in Hartford, 800 children expected the French visitor. Their badges said, "Nous vous animons Lafayette (We love you Lafayette)." When he entered Boston in 1824, the *Boston Evening Gazette* estimated that more than 2,500 schoolchildren wearing ribbons with Lafayette portraits lined up along the Boston Common to welcome him. On Lafayette's way to the Massachusetts State House, about two hundred girls in white dresses strew flowers in his path. Boys and girls in vessels on Boston's Charles River especially delighted Lafayette's secretary August Levasseur, who accompanied the general on his trip. As in Hartford, Boston, and many other towns, New Englanders sent their children to welcome the French visitor when he came to Portland in 1825. The *Christian Intelligencer* reported: "More than a thousand little lads and misses belonging to the schools, were stationed on the side-walk in Free street, the former had on their hats a printed inscription 'Welcome Lafayette.'"[27]

The display by children of Republicanism and patriotism confirmed the reinvented tradition of American Republican virtues. Books and newspaper articles drew a constant picture of boys and girls participating in the celebrations and in creating a cult of the

French veteran. Several publications retold, for instance, the story about a six-year-old Boston girl crowning Lafayette with a garland of flowers, which she made of her own bouquet. The children's book *Lafayette or Disinterested Benevolence,* describing the day of Lafayette's visit in a Boston family, began with some paragraphs picturing the youngest son's excitement and curiosity about the French hero. After little David had witnessed Lafayette's entrance into the city, he was too impressed to eat his dinner. He even forgot his table manners and constantly interrupted his parents with questions about the exotic visitor. With such stories, New England authors wanted to prove the next generation's Republican spirit. At the same time, they supported the image of Lafayette as a role model that helped to revive and pass on virtuous Revolutionary traditions.[28]

The celebration of the Marquis de Lafayette in New England was an inclusive process. While New Englanders generally did not regard Southerners as true Americans, when Lafayette toured the United States they for a short moment in time changed their attitude and imagined their countrymen in the South to participate in the national welcoming of the Revolutionary hero. Lafayette's visit constituted a brief moment in the early republic when New Englanders predominantly imagined the American nation as a union sharing the same characteristics and goals.

Although New England fetes of Lafayette defined the nation in such national terms, sometimes this image conflicted with the otherwise widespread idea of New England's superiority within the United States. New Englanders saw Lafayette as a hero of liberty, who extended his struggle for freedom to black Americans. Transforming Lafayette into a New England hero, the author of *Lafayette or Disinterested Benevolence* pictured the French general as an advocate for the poor and for African Americans. "But Lafayette, though born in affluence, though his parents were among the nobles of the earth," he explained to his young readers, "has always, like a true gentleman been condescending and kind to the poor, and to the Africans." In his biography of Lafayette, Ticknor emphasized that the Frenchman had always opposed the slave trade and had spent large sums on buying slaves in a French colony in order to educate and free them. Written from the perspective of slaves, a poem in the *Columbian Centinel* defined Lafayette as the savior of black Americans. In the poem, blacks appealed to the general to continue his struggle for liberty and to try to convince Southerners to free their slaves. The first verse argued that slavery did not concur with the ideals of the Revolution, which naturally implied that Southern society ignored virtuous Revolutionary principles. “Approving in age what you did in your youth, / In fighting for Freedom, for glory, and Truth, / You can't be contend to see us enslav'd, / By freemen who laud you for valor that saved?” the African voices claimed. In his ongoing fight for freedom, they hoped, Lafayette could use his popularity to lead Southerners on the right path to free their slaves and become true Republicans:

> We therefore solicit assistance from you,
> As one to whom deference is own'd to be due;
> If millions to you have surrendered the heart,
> Direct them, O General; to act the good part,
> To take off our fetters with wisdom and grace,
> To treat us as brothers—tho' sable our race.[29]

By imagining Lafayette as liberator of the slaves, New Englanders again defined the nation in their own terms and indicated that they wanted the South to adopt the New England way. It is important to emphasize that when New Englanders reinvented their history and present by imagining their region as a free, white republic and excluded Southerners from their vision of America, they were only gradually emancipating their own slaves. In 1800 New Englanders were still holding 1,488 slaves. Rhode Island only passed a final abolition bill in 1843, New Hampshire in 1848, and constitutional interpretations of emancipation in Massachusetts and New Hampshire were ambiguous during the years of the early republic. Emancipation statutes throughout New England delayed freedom for children born to slaves until they reached their twenties and denied freedom to slaves over thirty years of age. Moreover, New Englanders treated free people of color like slaves and they only found them worthy of their freedom if they also behaved like slaves. In New England white people expected free African Americans to be disorderly and to cause chaos, a form of racism that helped them to justify the slave-like conditions black New Englanders often lived in. New England's much celebrated lack of slavery was a myth that served as a cover for racial oppression and a justification for New England chauvinism. Often privileged New Englanders and Southern planters shared racist attitudes. The myth of a free and white New England had not much to do with a reality that meant racial exploitation and discrimination of African Americans in the region.[30]

Interestingly, on his tour through the Southern states Lafayette himself was very careful not to confront his Southern hosts directly with his attitude toward slavery, but he constantly indicated his sympathy for African Americans when he visited their schools and met with a few black callers. Lafayette stopped, for example, at a few slave cabins in the Carolinas, and met a delegation of black men in New Orleans.

Even if the festivities followed the same pattern throughout the entire country, the existence of slaves in the South distinguished Lafayette's visit there from his experience in the North. In some Southern cities such as Savannah, Georgia, and Fredericksburg, Virginia, newspapers announced that slave owners should keep their slaves from the streets and especially from the areas where Lafayette's procession went through. Obviously, some Southerners, who tried to hide their slaves from Lafayette, were aware of their guest's abolitionist sentiments and perhaps also of the problematic situation of owning slaves in a republic that claimed liberty as a key value. Although Lafayette, with his desire to return praise to the American people, did not openly criticize slavery, he challenged Southern culture when he met with a slave in Savannah, who had accompanied his master in the Revolutionary War. This meeting demonstrated that Savannah could not really hide its slaves and emphasized the role of blacks in the Revolutionary War. If New Englanders read about Southerners attempting to make their slaves invisible, they certainly felt confirmed in their anti-Southern sentiments, but they must have also been able to identify with such a common tendency of denial in their own region.[31]

If slaves changed the environment of the repetitive celebration patterns in the South, Indians had a similar effect on festivities on the Western frontier. By meeting with several Indian chiefs in Alabama, for example, Lafayette showed respect to Native Americans and expressed interest in their culture and situation and wanted to get firsthand accounts on it. Therefore, he met among others an Indian who was educated by white Americans but returned to Indian Territory because he preferred the Native American lifestyle. Lafayette called the treaties white Americans made with the Indians unfair, but still acknowledged that they followed mutual agreements. Levasseur even went so far to say that he found the white man always the aggressor. White Americans recognized their guest's favorable attitude toward Indians and responded accordingly. The governor of Mississippi showed Lafayette his collection of Indian relics, which suggested a shared interest in Native American culture, and gave his guest an Indian garment as a gift.[32]

In spite of this segregational tendency Lafayette's visit to New England was strictly a unifying event. New Englanders especially imagined it as such. Ironically, celebrations of the French guest also enabled New Englanders to define their collective identity against the French. Lafayette biographies always included a description of his role in the French Revolution and his negative opinion of the Napoleonic system. Both subjects gave New England writers the opportunity to confirm the negative picture of Revolutionary and Napoleonic France as well as of the French people's Republican inability. The reaction to Lafayette's French origin is another aspect in which New England celebrations differed widely from those in the South. The South, in contrast to New England, had nevertheless a number of inhabitants of French descent. Emphasizing and celebrating their common roots with the French guest, some Southerners awaited Lafayette with bilingual welcoming songs and groups of French descendents made sure to address Lafayette as, for example, in Charleston, South Carolina. Southern newspaper accounts of Lafayette's tour through the region constantly reported not only meetings with French citizens and French decedents, but more generally emphasized the presence of French culture, such as French language, French or bilingual newspapers, and French theatre in places such as Columbia and Charleston, South Carolina, Savannah, Georgia, and New Orleans, Louisiana. Familiar French voices also addressed Lafayette and his travel companion Levasseur in some new Western states. Levasseur noticed French voices at a reception in Missouri. This shows that the unity that New Englanders perceived during Lafayette's trip through the United States was not always as strong as they imagined it. Southerners of French origin did most likely not share New Englanders' anti-French ideas or at least not whole-heartedly.[33]

Lafayette the American

In his book about Lafayette's public identity, Lloyd Kramer concludes that the French general's visit to the United States combined the following three themes: a virtuous American Revolution; successful Republican institutions; and American prosperity indicating the superiority of these American institutions. Lafayette's praise of American institutions and virtues opened a window for Americans to express their nationalism. My study complicates our understanding of this creation of the American nation by arguing that in their cult of Lafayette, early Republicans defined their nation against the French. Biographies of Lafayette joined other publications in the early 1820s in emphasizing the failure of the French Revolution and the lack of liberty in French post-Revolutionary society. The celebrations of Lafayette as a hero of the American Revolution and Lafayette's confirmation of its success in establishing a model republic provided a stronger contrast between the virtuous American Revolution and the failed French Revolution than other descriptions. Lafayette's opinion of Napoleon as summarized in New England biographies also agreed with the general New England picture of the Napoleonic system as one of limited civil liberties. Strikingly, even in their celebrations of their French hero General Lafayette, New Englanders used France as an antithesis for the image of their own nation.[34]

Wherever Lafayette visited, he praised New Englanders' success in cultivating and civilizing the country, particularly in establishing Republican institutions. In his answer to an address of the mayor of Boston, Lafayette emphasized how happy he was to "witness the prosperity, the improvements, that have been just reward of noble struggle, virtuous morals, and truly republican institutions." In his report of Lafayette's visit to the United States, John Foster said that when the general toured Worcester County in Massachusetts, he "was delighted with the fine country which he had seen, and the excellent improvement, and cultivation which he had witnessed." Furthermore, the Massachusetts author proudly pointed out how Lafayette connected the nation's prosperity with its Republican institutions. The French general described New England as industrial, democratic, and outstanding in its wide range and high quality of education. Lafayette, Foster wrote, "saw the best proof of a great, prosperous, and happy people, in the rapid advancement of the polite and useful arts, and in the stability of our free institutions." Lafayette's praise of democratic institutions confirmed New Englanders' pride in their colleges, courts, and churches. With such statements about the high level of civilization of the young nation, Lafayette supported New England's definition of itself and of the nation. Lafayette's confirmation certainly strengthened the region's idea that it embodied the nation, especially when articles about other parts of the country seemed to show that their fellow Americans had also adopted New England ways. Many Bostonians may well have had that in mind, when they read the reprint of a speech by the Tennessee orator William Gibbes Hunt, which stressed the civilization process in the new Western territories. "Even in these remote western regions where at the time of his first arrival on our continent, the voice of civilization had scarcely been heard," Hunt had said, "[Lafayette] now finds richly cultivated fields, thriving villages, and even populous cities, adorned with art, and science, and taste, and all that can render life comfortable and delightful." Descriptions of Lafayette processions and other public fetes also celebrated New Englanders as true Republicans. Confirming this image of educated, grateful, and civilized inhabitants of the region, Foster proudly wrote that when Lafayette retired to his lodgings after a military parade in Boston, "he had . . . a fine sample of the Boston Mob: a collection of Intelligent, Rational, and Independent Freemen, publicly testifying their gratitude to a national benefactor."[35]

This emphasis on civilization and cultivation served even more as a means to express American superiority over Europe rather than New England superiority within the United States. New Englanders found the celebrations themselves to exceed any great European ceremonies. Even if such classifications of New England festivities were exaggerated, ordinary New Englanders proudly absorbed them as praise for their patriotic culture. The author of a *Biographical Sketch of the Life of the Marquis De La Fayette* compared Lafayette's landing in New York City with European receptions and thought Lafayette's welcome in America surpassed any similar events organized by Europeans. "We have seen the reception of great events in Europe—we have read of the landing of King William, the entrée of George the fourth in Ireland, and Louis the 18th in Paris," he enumerated, "but never witnessed a more splendid display, or more cordial, generous and spontaneous feeling than that of yesterday on the landing of General Lafayette." The fact that all sorts of people participated in the festivities and unrestrictedly attended events also gave evidence to New Englanders of the high Republican standard of their country. In France, Foster claimed, this was not the case at all. When Lafayette embarked from the French port in Havre, he reported, police prevented people from giving Lafayette a farewell, soldiers closed the roads and "guarded the scene."[36] In the New England mind, the glamorous and actually royalistic celebrations of the French visitor showed the high level of cultivation America had achieved and the birth of Republican civilization. The costly festivities also indicated the new nation's prosperity, which of course proved the success of the Republican virtues they displayed. The story of Lafayette's life then contrasted this American "paradise of liberty" with a chaotic and oppressive France.

Biographies of Lafayette painted the history of the French Revolution as one of an anti-libertarian and anti-Republican revolution. The French Revolution was so inhumane and cruel, they argued, that it had been an act of liberty to protect the royal family from the violent French mob. During some celebrations of Lafayette, New Englanders even transformed Louis XVI into an advocate of liberty. At a dinner party in Boston, Chief Justice Isaac Parker toasted the

French king: "The memory of Louis 16th—Those who have aided the cause of liberty should not be forgotten, although they have worn crown." Biographies of the French visitor depicted Lafayette as a defender of freedom because he had spoken up for the liberty of the royal family as he had spoken up for the liberty of the common people. Furthermore, he had saved the royal family when one night an angry mob stormed the gates of Versailles and intended to assassinate the king and the queen. Like many other stories about French cruelties against their royal family, Lafayette biographies stressed that French violence did not stop at mothers and children. The angry mob at Versailles, one biographer noted, wanted to murder Marie Antoinette although she appeared at the balcony with her children. Lafayette protected her from the outraged crowd by kissing her hand in order to show the people that, although he supported the Revolution, he still respected the queen. With their royalist toasts and stories about Lafayette saving the royal family, New Englanders wanted to manifest such acts as part of a global struggle for liberty. When Lafayette visited Yale College, the president not only emphasized how impressed the guest was with the institution, but also that in France he has himself "been the active friend of science, and of universal instruction. So great has been his zeal for teaching every child that the ultra Royalists have charged him with a design to corrupt all the youth of the nation by infusing republican notions." New Englanders were aware that when Lafayette returned from Austrian imprisonment to post-Revolutionary France, he was deeply disappointed with the results of the Revolution. Under the reign of Napoleon, who Lafayette thought jeopardized civil liberties, he continued his fight for freedom by publicly announcing his opinion and voting against Bonaparte's appointment to consul for life.[37]

A remarkable Lafayette anecdote in the *Boston Monthly Magazine* in similar terms contrasted the United States as the "land of liberty" with France as the "land of despotism." Newspaper editors found the story so powerful in evoking nationalism that the editor of the *Boston Commercial Gazette*, where the article appeared first, "was requested to put it into [the *Monthly Magazine*] as a place where it could more readily be found." Lafayette fans read that their hero had a vision of the Goddess of Liberty appearing to him when he was praying for freedom in a prison in Prussian Magdeburg. When he "murmured an imprecation against despotic power, united with a mental prayer for the long lost liberties of man," the Goddess agreed to show him the future. She first took him to a country that was obviously Lafayette's native France, where the "silence of despotism reigned." Then

Lafayette and the goddess crossed the Atlantic, and the goddess brought him to a "paradise of liberty" where hardworking, intelligent people cultivated a wilderness, built towns and industries, and established democratic institutions. Lafayette immediately identified this place as his "beloved America."

> "The place was changed—oceans were passed, and other worlds were in view," the article said leading the readers to the ideal country of liberty. "Nature was here exhibited on her broadest scale...man seemed in the morning of his existence," the description began, "putting on all the energies of his character; immense forests were receding before the busy inhabitants of the country,...and cities were springing up, as it were, by a magic spell; industry, plenty, knowledge, and happiness, went hand in hand, in the journey of man."

Defining the United States as a refugee for the oppressed, the Goddess of Liberty introduced it as "the last great Asylum of oppressed humanity." In Lafayette's vision, liberty made America a strong empire. Only partisan divisions disturbed harmony and idyll in America. But the anecdote introduced a positive solution. Americans' Republican spirit soon helped to overcome the problem of party division: "The sun of empire shone with a bright and morning ray, and nothing disturbed the scene, excepting now and then a little transient cloud of party spirit shot across the horizon, and obscured, for a short season, the goodly aspect; but the angel of political wisdom was on the wing, and chased the mists away." The story also helped to invent a Revolutionary tradition, when it described how Lafayette envisioned himself among other Revolutionary heroes such as "Washington, Knox, Hamilton and Warren" guarding over the young nation.[38]

By celebrating Lafayette as a Revolutionary veteran and a model Republican, New Englanders Americanized the French visitor. This process is obvious in the anecdote about Lafayette's vision. The Frenchman called the United States "my beloved America" and took up a seat among American national heroes. The image of Lafayette that the celebrations and biographies drew described him as an American. It agreed with the ideal of a true American Republican introduced in so many other publications of the time. Moreover, in their feting and writing, New Englanders expressed that they perceived the French visitor as an American. The Boston *Columbian Centinel* listed a toast where a New York alderman called Lafayette "the Adopted Child of the Nation." At a dinner for the popular guest, the inhabitants of Salem, Massachusetts, decorated Lafayette's seat with a garland of flowers that said: "Lafayette in America—Where can one better be than in the bosom of his family." In *Lafayette or Disinterested Benevolence,* little New England children read that Lafayette called himself the "American veteran."[39] The implication was clear: To be American one had not necessarily to be born in the United States. Anyone who came to the United States and displayed American Republican virtues could adopt an American identity. In the American collective identity, common characteristics and symbols replaced the organic connection with the land and blood bonds that partly defined European identities.

As much as Lafayette served as a figure to shape early Republican American nationalism, America also molded its hero. Lafayette's experience with American society and culture in the Revolutionary War had a lasting impact on the young Frenchman. In France he promoted American ideas and sought the friendship of other Europeans who had an interest in the new world. Like many European travelers in New England, Lafayette became Americanized during his first visit to the new world. The enthusiasm of Lafayette and his fellow European visitors to the new world indicates that they adopted American values and replaced their traditional European ideas.

Lafayette's visits to New England during his tour of the United States constituted a rare moment in the early republic, when New Englanders integrated themselves into an American identity. They envisioned themselves as participants of a collective American culture without perceiving their own region as the only true Republican model, which the other regions had to follow. Although such a feeling of regional superiority appeared in some speeches and writings, in general the manifestation of American predominance over Europe, and especially France, overshadowed it. New England's celebration of Lafayette as a hero of liberty was an inclusive process that united different generations, professions, men, and women. New Englanders began to imagine the South and the West sharing their American identity. They saw themselves as part of the American people instead of the nation's defining element. The reason for this, of course, was that reading newspaper articles about Lafayette fetes in other parts of the country, New Englanders saw Southerners and Westerners praising and displaying the very same values they had defined as truly American. For a moment partisan and regional differences diminished; although it has to be mentioned that the presence of slaves and Americans of French origin in the South and Native Americans in the West did in fact make a difference in celebrations in these regions.

Overall, however, Lafayette's visit enabled Americans to stress common values and to define their nation nationally. But as all holidays, Lafayette festivities constituted a break from the routine and allowed people to escape into an ideal world for the time of the celebration. Certainly, they helped to bridge some gaps and left a general feeling of community behind, but in their everyday life New Englanders still dealt with regional, social, religious, and political differences.

CHAPTER 5

Separation for the Nation: The Movement for Maine's Statehood

"Take us by the hand, introduce us into the American family, & make us part of that Great republic, destined as we hope to become the pattern of freedom, the pride of nations, and the glory of the world."[1] With these lines the Portland newspaper *The Eastern Argus* fostered the separation of Maine from Massachusetts. Nationalistic language such as this article from 1816 claimed that as a state, Maine would strengthen the nation by contributing to its Republican virtue. This rhetoric finally convinced the people of Maine that their district should separate from Massachusetts to become a state. Mainers debated statehood for thirty-six years before a state of Maine was established in the spring of 1820. The movement for separation began shortly after the American Revolution in 1784, just a year after the peace treaty with Great Britain was signed. The regional, social, religious, and political differences that set New Englanders apart drove this campaign. Ironically, although these differences led some Mainers to seek separation from Massachusetts, a collective New England national identity helped this separation movement to succeed. Mainers came to believe that a state of Maine would fulfill the New England American ideal much better than the district.

The State of New Hampshire split Maine and Massachusetts not only geographically, but it also separated a prosperous established community with a powerful Congregational Church from a more isolated frontier community where radical sects attracted more and more members. The social, religious, and political gap between Massachusetts and the district of Maine widened during the early years of the republic. Local conditions—such as the lack of institutionalized authorities of courts and churches, isolation from the market, and sectarian religion—shaped the identity of many people in Maine. There was a similar division between Maine's coastal centers, which shared social and economic structures with Massachusetts, and the towns in the interior where poor settlers felt deprived of their liberties by Massachusetts' proprietors and the Congregationalists church establishment.

The lack of support from coastal communities, who feared a disruption of connections to commercial and financial Massachusetts, repeatedly halted the movement for separation. But after 1800, self-confident Maine merchants and the growing number of religious dissenters merged in the new Democratic-Republican Party and pushed for separation from Federalist and Congregational Massachusetts. Interestingly, in spite of the local differences it was an appeal to common New England values and a common New England cause that paved the way. Maine statehood succeeded in 1820 as part of the Missouri Compromise, which helped to preserve a balance between Northern and Southern states in the U.S. Senate. It was the combination of regional and national loyalty of New England nationalism that emerged between 1790 and 1820 that finally animated Mainers to push for statehood for their district.[2]

In 1791, shortly before the first campaign for separation failed, Daniel Davis, a young lawyer, employed New England nationalism to argue for Maine statehood. In an address to the people of Maine that was filled with pride of his country's new constitution, he explained to his audience how a state of Maine would increase patriotism among its inhabitants. He emphasized that Mainers would gain "dignity" and "respectability" when their district becomes a state. Furthermore, he said, patriotism would rise once Maine became aware of a well-managed Maine government, talented Maine men in public offices, and the resulting prosperity. Besides laying the groundwork for strong political and economic arguments that proponents of separation used in following decades, Davis emphasized that two more New England senators would strengthen the region's power in Congress.

According to Davis the new federal government and constitution opened up an opportunity for Maine's independence from Massachusetts. Mainers' lack of governmental experience, he claimed, was no longer an argument against a state. "Several objects of legislation which are the most difficult to manage," he pointed out, "are, by that U.S. constitution, taken out of the hands of the state government; and referred to the Legislature of the Union. This must be . . . a great relief to those, whose lot it may be to administer a government, without the necessary experience."[3] Maine statehood, he continued, would strengthen the republic by moving its institutions closer to the people. The republic would profit from more frequent Supreme Court sittings, a state government in the midst of the people, the opportunity for talented men to participate in that government, and reduced governmental costs.

Despite Davis's argument, in the 1792 referendum for separation, voters in Maine rejected it by a margin of 2,074 votes in favor to 2,524 votes against. Votes in 1797 and 1807 again rejected separation. Although the vote in 1797 approved statehood by 373 votes, the Massachusetts General Court ruled that this was an insufficient number. The legislature considered Mainers uninterested in separation because only a few more than five thousand citizens, out of a population of almost one hundred thousand, went to the polls.[4] New England nationalism failed to convince the majority of Maine's inhabitants that it was an advantage for the district to become a state.

Paradoxically, the final success of the movement did not express a strong Maine identity. Instead, an emerging New England nationalism drove that success. Mainers believed that a state of Maine would enhance New England virtues among them. Like New Englanders, the people of Maine imagined New England virtues to define the nation and were, therefore, convinced that Maine statehood would raise their nation's glory. As early as 1795, James Sullivan, a lawyer who later became governor of Massachusetts, writing in his history of Maine, praised Mainers' Republicanism as a prospective contribution to the nation's stability. Sullivan exemplified the combination of local attachment and a regional nationalism that constituted the ideology of many New Englanders. He defended the religious dissenters in Maine against Massachusetts Congregationalism. At the same time he was a conscious New England nationalist working to increase the region's national political power. Sullivan was a unifying figure in Massachusetts politics; at the same time he was supporting Maine dissenters he was also a leading lay spokesman for the Congregational Church. Like many contemporaries, Sullivan compared the United States to Europe, which led him to develop a dislike for the French Revolution and to express his pride in his nation during the 1790s.[5]

Advocates for a separation of Maine from Massachusetts forcefully employed the argument that bringing civilization to the wilderness was a crucial element of New England's regional American identity. They claimed a separation from Massachusetts would intensify civilization in Maine. Colleges, in which New Englanders took special pride, would develop to their full capacity. Settlement of the wilderness would be encouraged. Maine forest would be transformed into cultivated agricultural landscapes as New Englanders promoted them as models for the entire nation. Manufactories would be built and those industries would open the door for progress and prosperity. A state of Maine, as separatists described it, fit exactly the New England that early Republican New Englanders imagined and celebrated. Sullivan's history of Maine as well as paintings and engravings of Maine houses, towns, colleges, and landscapes indicate a sense of a Maine identity but they speak even more for a strong New England identity. These images were identical with many other depictions of New England. Mainers aimed to live up to the New England ideal; and by 1820 separatists persuaded them that statehood intensified Republicanism, prosperity, education, and other New England characteristics. For Mainers, the separation from Massachusetts was a regionalist and nationalistic goal.[6]

Interestingly, the leaders of the separation movement before and after the turn of the century belonged to opposing political groups, but they generally used similar arguments. Before 1800 a minority of Portland Federalists, like Daniel Davis, led the movement for separation. They found that Boston Federalists did not act in their interests. In the early nineteenth century, however, members of the rising Democratic-Republican Party took over the movement for Maine statehood. Like their predecessors, they wanted to be freed from the authority of Massachusetts Federalists. Some members of the new party had been Federalists before and had switched to the new Democratic-Republican Party.

The leader of the Maine Jeffersonians, William King, was a ship owner and wealthy merchant from Bath, who would later be Maine's first governor. Like Sullivan, King had been a Federalist. He probably saw a state of Maine as a better place than Massachusetts to pursue his political career and to reach his ambitious goals to win a prestigious public office. After he resigned as Maine's first governor in 1821, he became a U.S. commissioner to negotiate a treaty with Spain.

James Sullivan was the son of a schoolteacher from Berwick, Maine, and a self-made rising figure in Massachusetts politics. In the mid-1790s he became frustrated over the exclusion of social climbers such as himself by the Federalist elite. Sullivan was one of the most prominent members of the emerging Democratic Republican Party. His moderate views enabled him to keep his office as attorney general even under a federalist administration until he became governor in 1807. As many other New England nationalists, he was as an incorporator of the American Academy of Arts and Science and a founder of the Massachusetts Historical Society, and helped founding the young nation's literary and historical institutions.

Although Jeffersonian Democrats engineered the campaign for separation, Federalists did not automatically fall into opposition. Some still wanted Maine to become a state. A pamphlet, which was the product of a convention on separation that met at the Portland Episcopal Church in 1794, argued that independence from Massachusetts would strengthen New England virtues in Maine. "The present state of education is disproportioned to our ability," the authors claimed, because the Massachusetts government did not pay enough attention to Maine's literary institutions. Furthermore, they said, not only the arts and sciences, but also agriculture and manufactures "would probably flourish" in a state of Maine.[7]

William King himself, the movement's leader, lived up to the New England ideal of industry. In his hometown of Bath he established two banks, an insurance company, and Maine's first cotton mill. In the first two decades of the nineteenth century, the new separatists pushed these arguments of a state of Maine as the New England ideal with increasing vehemence and a stronger rhetoric than their predecessors. Beginning in 1815, the *Eastern Argus*, Portland's Democratic-Republican newspaper, published numerous articles promoting separation. With the growing number of Democratic-Republicans in Maine, the *Argus* helped to spread the argument for statehood among a larger audience than Federalist separatists of the late eighteenth century could ever reach.

The fast-growing number of new immigrants settling on Maine's frontier constituted an expanding audience for separatist arguments. These new settlers felt betrayed by the Massachusetts government. Immigrants' aim for property clashed with the patriarchal attitude of Massachusetts' great proprietors and their sectarian religious beliefs caused antagonisms with Massachusetts' Congregationalists. While their predecessors had not been sympathetic to the settlers' grievances, the new Democratic-Republican separatists embraced them. King played a major role in the passage in the 1811 "Toleration Act," which abolished Massachusetts' compulsory tax to support the Congregational Church. Even if some merchants in the coastal towns still feared that the coastal trade would suffer from separation, it seemed that at the end of the first decade of the nineteenth century it was almost common sense that Maine would be a state at some point.

Coastal Mainers feared economic damage through separation because their coastal trade would suffer. A Federal "Coasting Law" required every vessel passing a noncontiguous state to pay a tax. Nevertheless an 1809 schoolbook predicted Maine statehood. As an answer to the question, "When will Maine become a separate State?"

schoolchildren read in their *Maine Spelling Book* that it could not be long "considering the rapid settlement of the country, and the many inconveniences to which we are subject." Proudly the spelling book emphasized that Maine will soon be "ranked with other American States."[8]

The Embargo of 1807 and the War of 1812 also helped the prospect of separation. Jefferson's embargo imposed U.S. neutrality in the Napoleonic Wars, and harmed Maine's economy. In the War of 1812, British occupation lasting for almost the duration of the war caused even bigger economic losses in Maine. Disappointed by Massachusetts' failure to protect the district from the British, and frustrated with their economic situation, Mainers felt more and more enthusiastic about separating from the Bay State. In the fall of 1815, the *Eastern Argus* reported that during the war separation had not been a topic because Mainers, as good Americans, had done everything to support their homeland. "Our only enquiry," the paper claimed was, "for the fate of our countrymen." After the war, however, the article continued, separation became "soon . . . a topic of conversation almost as general as the war itself."[9]

But most important for the success of the separation movement was the appeal to a common New England identity. According to statehood advocates, the government of Massachusetts did not allow Mainers to fully develop their virtues. The Bay State prevented Mainers from fully living up to their Republican potential because it did not encourage settlement of the Maine wilderness, did not grant freedom of religion, nor did it support colleges and manufactories. These were all points that New Englanders saw as indications of their high level of civilization.

Civilizing a Wilderness

The image of New England as a civilized wilderness, which played such a crucial role in the creation of a New England identity, helped to direct the people of Maine toward a decision for the district to separate from Massachusetts. In an area where thousands of new settlers arrived every year looking for land in the backcountry, the clearing of the forest was a daily struggle.[10] Mainers proudly decorated their houses with images picturing the process. An 1802 overmantel from the Lazarus Hathaway House in Paris, called a "View from Paris Hill," depicted the clearing of the forest and advance of civilization in the town of Paris. The unknown amateur artist placed hardworking Mainers cutting trees at the center. A refined lady in an elegant dress riding her horse through the cleared forest and a village with a church and some public buildings in the distance represent the advent of civilization. Although the people of Maine were proud of their emerging civilization, they believed they could enhance the process if they were no longer limited by the Massachusetts legislature.[11]

Advocates of separation argued that the Massachusetts legislature acted in the interest of great proprietors and made it difficult for settlers to turn Maine into a cultivated New England American landscape. An anonymous author who called himself "Independence" maintained in an 1816 newspaper article that Massachusetts lawmakers were not concerned about Maine's prosperity. They did not support settlement, he complained. "I apprehend that the [Massachusetts] legislature have not discovered much anxiety for our growth or prosperity," he wrote. "Their encouragements to settlers have been miserable. Vast tracts of land have been sold to monopolizing speculators, whereby settlements have been prevented and those tracts remain a wilderness." Maine settlers thought that they had fought the Revolution not only for national independence, but also for free access to the wilderness and local autonomy. They felt betrayed by proprietors' claim for payments for the land that in their eyes was already their property. Settlers had adopted a Lockean view on property and labor: by turning the wilderness into a cultivated landscape, they insisted, they gained the ownership of the land. Settlers rebelled in the first two decades of the new republic, but in 1808 they had to accept a compromise. The Betterment Act granted them ownership of the improvements they had made. But they had to pay the wild land value to the proprietors. Dissatisfied with this solution, settlers regarding cultivated landscapes as a New England characteristic identified with the statehood movement. They agreed with separatists that Maine's independence would put an end to all burdens that prevented them from fulfilling their patriotic task of cultivating the land. In addition to Lockean ideas and encounters with the proprietors' agents, a strong regionalism, defining civilization as a major New England American value, pushed them toward separation from Massachusetts.[12]

Similar to other New Englanders, Mainers' civilization of the wilderness meant an expansion of agriculture and trade as well as the establishment of meeting houses, colleges, and manufactories. In their publications on separation, the local elite implied that cultivation and civilization were patriotic enterprises. Even if the first generation of separatists had addressed these issues in the late eighteenth century, the new generation rising in the early nineteenth century utilized such rhetoric much more aggressively. Their identification with the frontier settlers and recognition of the settlers' contribution to the civilization of the wilderness helped to evoke a regional national loyalty among frontier Mainers that served more and more as a convincing argument for statehood. An anonymous author in the *Argus* enthusiastically promised that people "whose ambition would be to encourage Agriculture, Manufactories & Trade—build up our literary and religious institutions and adopt a liberal system for the improvement of our wild lands" would govern a state of Maine.[13] As separatists sketched, a state of Maine would increase education, freedom of religion, industry, and prosperity significantly.

From the Puritans to Timothy Dwight, New Englanders emphasized education as a central New England value and described it as part of the civilization process. John Brown's 1822 painting depicts how Bowdoin College, chartered in 1794, helped civilize the Maine frontier.[14] The prestigious brick buildings, the manicured campus, and elegantly dressed students and professors illustrated the advent of civilization in the wilderness. With its emphasis on the college buildings, Brown's "Bowdoin Campus" resembles Alvan Fisher's two popular paintings of Harvard College.

Mainers wanted to participate in New England's celebration of its high level of education. They shared the belief that education produced model Republicans. Along those lines, "A Federalist" in an 1819 *Portland Gazette* maintained that Maine colleges did not get enough support from the Massachusetts government. In a state of Maine, he said, these literary institutions could grow to their full potential. By emphasizing a higher quality in education as an advantage of separation, Mainers linked statehood with a New England identity. They also saw it tightly connected to another New England virtue: prosperity. In 1819, the *Eastern Argus* stressed that an improved system of education would increase Maine's prosperity and so would strengthen Maine's New England character. The paper also made the point that education always had been an important virtue in the region, that it was a New England tradition.[15]

Although post-Revolutionary Republicanism and traditional Puritanism shared an emphasis on education, the idea of New England and America as a model for the rest of the world; pride in cultivating the wilderness; Republican ideology; and the market revolution also added concepts to the New England value system. These clashed with New England's Puritan heritage; the prospect of greater religious autonomy for dissenters and a materialistic interest in economic benefits conflicted with Puritan Congregationalism and simplicity.

In his *History of the State of Maine,* William Williamson, a Democrat who later served as acting governor of the new state, also declared education an important Maine value. Like other New Englanders, he found education the precondition for Republicanism. "Education," he announced, "has been esteemed by every age since the country was settled as the guardian spirit of civil and religious liberty, and the main supporter of a republican government." Williamson was a firm advocate of separation and felt a strong loyalty to Maine. Even before Maine became a state, he began to research and write a history of Maine. In a letter to Isaac Lane in December 1820 asking for information on Lane's hometown, Williamson announced that he wanted to collect information on every town in the new state. In Williamson's mind, Maine fulfilled the New England ideal. Education was one field where he thought he could find proof of that fact. In his history of Maine, which he published in 1832, Williamson gave a detailed description of more than five pages of how education had always been a major concern in Maine.[16]

Spokesmen for the separation movement extended the argument of Dwight and others that education tempered religious zeal and encouraged liberal and democratic attitudes. They affirmed that education also led to prosperity. With their idea of education as an initiator of liberal attitudes and affluence, early Republicans moved away from the traditional Puritan notion, which emphasized education as a means of self-reflection and a necessity for a godly community. In August 1819, an anonymous author in the *Eastern Argus* tempted Mainers' regionalism when he predicted prosperity for a state of Maine. This prosperity would spring from a high level of education: "It only requires the powerful influence of the institutions for education which have existed from the birth of New England settlements to confirm its hopes of full prosperity."

Mixing local, regional, and national loyalties, separatists pointed out that Maine had ideal natural conditions to prosper in the New England way. Rivers and harbors on the seacoast, combined with an "active spirit of commercial enterprize [*sic*]" among its inhabitants, connected Maine with world markets. As a result of such international trade, they imagined canals would be built and manufactories and mills be constructed. Furthermore, Maine agriculture would boom from the cultivation of what separatists regarded as "fertile [Maine] land." In November 1815, an *Argus* author wrote: "I contend... that we are not only capable of becoming a great Commercial and Manufacturing—but a very respectable Agricultural State."

Such a promise satisfied everybody—Jeffersonians who wanted an agricultural nation and Federalists who envisioned the United States as an industrial country. Beginning in 1815, the *Eastern Argus* ran a series of articles under the headline "the District of Maine," where arguments for separation could be published. Moses Judkins from Castine was so convinced of the paper's positive effect that he wrote a letter to King proposing a general distribution among the common people. Furthermore, he wondered whether the government might pay for the production of those newspapers.

Publications in the *Argus* show that the second generation of separatists was able to address their nationalistic arguments to many more people then their predecessors in the post-Revolutionary period. Separatists invited Mainers to imagine a glorious future for Maine as a leading New England state. In 1816 a separation pamphlet concluded: "In fine, she [Maine] wants nothing but fostering care of a legislature, devoted to her prosperity, and ready to aid the enterprise of men of public spirit and capital, to make her the most wealthy and powerful of the Northern States."[17]

Separatists also appealed to Mainers' pride in being good New England Republicans just as regional nationalists praised them. They emphasized that the people of Maine were as good Republicans as the people of Massachusetts and were, therefore, ready to govern themselves. The people of Maine, they claimed, "would adopt a constitution and form of government as excellent in its provisions and as judicious in its limitations as that of any State in the union." Proudly, some stated that Mainers could even be compared to classical Republicans of antiquity, who were in many respects models for American Republicans. Shortly before Maine became a state, D. Long (probably Daniel Long) wrote to William King: "The persevering…fidelity, & integrity of the people of Maine, should not suffer by a comparison with the best days of the Republics of Greece and Rome."

Mainers found themselves not only virtuous enough for self-government, but also thought that their countrymen would respect their Republicanism much more, if they practiced their virtues in their own state. Separatists praised Maine's Republican virtues to persuade the people to separate from Massachusetts. Moreover, they pronounced that good Republicans would not consider their own selfish interest, but only the common interest of the district. Citizens, the *Argus* reminded its readers, were not supposed to ask: "How will it [separation] affect my interest, the interest of my particular friends, or the interest of my party." Such thinking, the newspaper maintained, belonged to the commercial realm: "Such sordid motives may well fit the seller & the purchaser, but they ill become the citizen." The *Argus* utilized Mainers' New England identity by appealing to their Republican virtue of working for the common good, which early

Republicans saw as the only legitimate interest to consider in a political decision. Separatists increasingly used the stabilizing regional American identity to promote their cause.[18]

Starting in 1815 Federalists responded to Democratic-Republicans' campaign for statehood with a series of articles in the *Portland Gazette*. Here they disputed Republican claims about the advantages of separation and vehemently argued against Maine statehood. The suffering of the coastal trade and an increase in expenses for government were the major reasons the *Portland Gazette* authors listed for their case against separation, especially in the beginning of their newspaper battle between the statehood advocates and antiseparatists.

Soon, antiseparatists also started to refute their opponents' strong New England nationalistic arguments. Like the separatists, they appealed to their readers' pride in Maine, but also tried to utilize a local loyalty to Maine rather than a regional loyalty to New England. A state of Maine, they claimed, would not increase New England virtues such as education and an individual effort to work toward the common good; the district itself was already virtuous enough, they said. Authors of the *Portland Gazette* emphasized that Maine already had good colleges and honorable men in public offices, and that there was nothing to be improved by a separation from Massachusetts. Furthermore, antiseparatists destroyed romantic regionalist hopes of an expansion of New England through an increasing migration to its frontier. They assured their readers that the wave of emigration of farmers to Ohio would not diminish with Maine statehood, as separatists had promised. A state of Maine would not increase immigration because the reason why migrants moved westward instead of to the Maine frontier was not Maine's dependence on Massachusetts, but the warmer Western climate that promised profits with less labor.[19]

By 1816 it was clear that it was no longer a question *whether* Maine became a state or not but, as the *Maine Spelling Book* had already put it in 1809, a question of *when* Maine became a state. It was not only the articles in the *Eastern Argus* that helped to spread propaganda for separation among ordinary Mainers. Separatists also promoted their cause on a much more personal level. Like the religious revivals of the time, the movement for separation spread through personal contacts. After the War of 1812, separatists felt that the collective New England American identity among their neighbors was strong enough to respond to direct and personal appeals in their propaganda. Samuel Whiting, a leading separatist, lawyer, and *Argus* author, reported to King in 1816 that "friends of separation" worked hard to convince the people that a state of Maine would be good for them. These advocates of separation were riding into nearby towns, discussing the issue with their neighbors and distributing pamphlets. By 1816, the New England national identity, to which Maine separatists appealed, was strong enough to help the separation movement to gain support. This becomes particularly obvious in contemporary images of Maine houses, towns, ports, and landscapes. Mainers portrayed their district as a part of New England. Their visual works cannot be distinguished from those depicting Massachusetts or New Hampshire. These images could have been used to illustrate travel journals on any part of New England.[20]

In 1800, twelve-year-old Sophia Sewall Wood Monroe, for example, painted the Barrell Homestead in York, which was the most impressive house in her hometown.[21] Her painting shows an elegant house with a big barn surrounded by refined fenced in farmlands. Like other New England girls, Sophia depicted New England civilization. In addition to the buildings of the house and the barn, a row of young trees, which were planted in a line separating the Barrell property from the road, especially underlines the degree of cultivation of Maine lands.

Other images show seaports and their surrounding landscapes, emphasizing economic activity and prosperity. A number of works focused on Portland present it as a prosperous city vigorously engaged in the coastal trade. In his 1807 painting "Signals at Portland Lighthouse," (see figure 5.1) Lemuel Moody, a known Maine draftsman, emphasized Portland's mercantile and seafaring activity including all the signal flags of Portland merchants registered at the Portland Head Lighthouse. Views of Casco Bay, Cape Elizabeth, the city of Portland and Portland's waterfront strengthen Moody's message. Schooners, ships, churches, lighthouses, and warehouses all contribute to the image of a progressive commercial center. At the same time, James Akin, a Philadelphia engraver who briefly visited New England, produced a similar image of Portland on his Certificate of the Portland Marine Society.[22] In addition to pictures of a shipwreck and ships passing a lighthouse, he included a hospital as an example of Portland's fine public buildings as well as a view of the harbor showing the warehouses at the waterfront. Portland—with its harbor, public buildings, and vessels—was also the favorite subject of young Maine girls in their embroidery. Mary Rea instructed the students in her Portland boarding school to create such images of their city.[23]

Although it was apparent by 1816 that Maine would eventually separate from Massachusetts, it was not accomplished for another four years. In the referendum on separation on May 20, 1816, a majority of Mainers (10,391) voted in favor of separation and only 6,501 voted

Figure 5.1 Lemuel Moody, *Signals at Portland Lighthouse*, watercolor 1807, collections of the Maine Historical Society

against it. But again, a large number of Mainers did not make a public decision at all. About 10,000 out of 37,000 Mainers bothered to go to the polls. For that reason, a committee appointed by the Massachusetts Senate, dominated by Harrison Gray Otis, agreed to authorize a convention of Maine delegates to meet and discuss the issue in Brunswick. After a second vote on separation on September 2, delegates from 137 Maine towns met in the Brunswick Congregational Meeting House. Massachusetts residents showed even less public interest in the issue of separation. Massachusetts newspapers published the election results of each town, but did not usually provide any commentary on the vote. The September vote had brought more people in Maine to the polls, but it had attracted those who rejected separation in much higher numbers. This time 12,000 Mainers voted yes and 10,382 voted no. This result complicated the situation at the Brunswick convention. The conflict between separatists and antiseparatist hardened. Antiseparatists accused separatists of fraud and corruption. Finally the Massachusetts General court ruled to dissolve the convention and not to take any further steps toward a separation of Maine from Massachusetts.[24]

Strengthening a New England America

Most Mainers who voted against separation probably shared a strong New England identity with the separatists, but they lived in coastal towns and still feared losses in their profitable coastal trade would result from separation. This changed in the spring of 1819, when William King, supported by his half-brother, New York Senator Rufus King, induced Congress to repeal the "Coasting Law." Consequently, a broad majority of Mainers, stimulated by their strong New England identity, finally decided in favor of separation. The final vote on separation on July 26, 1819 resulted in an undeniable victory for separatists with a majority of 10,000 votes. A resounding 17,091 Mainers voted in favor of separation and only 7,132 against it. Separatists persuaded their fellow Mainers to vote for separation from Massachusetts, although their opponents published more articles in the *Portland Gazette* in the spring and fall of 1819 than separatists did. The fears antiseparatists expressed about Maine statehood during that time emerged from traditional Federalist concerns about growing threats to the republic. Antiseparatists believed a state of Maine would create anarchy and chaos. But interestingly, although they repeated these fears in their articles, in 1819 they no longer rejected separation as vehemently as they did in the years before.

In July the *Portland Gazette* even published an essay by "An Old Man" pleading his case for separation. Stressing his age and his bonds with the very early national period, he referred to anti-Federalist arguments from the constitutional debates in the late 1780s. As a member of the founding generation, he felt entitled to engage the classical thesis that only small republics could maintain virtue among their citizens. This was an idea anti-Federalists had used two decades earlier to argue against a large federal United States. Small republics, the old man said implying that he was talking about a prospective state of Maine, produced great men. This author of the Federalist *Portland Gazette* even shared logic with his Republican opponents who had repeatedly built their campaign for separation on the classical argument for small republics. Separatists praised the federal system and emphasized how its structure supported the establishment of new states, which would be small republics.

In 1816, a report in the *Eastern Argus* on a Lincoln County separation convention reminded readers of the nature and advantages of the federal system: "The leading principles of our federative system refer the details of local legislation to comparatively small and convenient sections of the country." Praising the national political system, the article concluded that these principles at the same time "confide our great national and commercial interests to the general government." A state of Maine would share a right of protection against foreign invasion with all other states. After Mainers felt that they had just been denied this right in the War of 1812, the prospect of being defended by the national government probably convinced some, especially merchants, to support Maine statehood. After the War of 1812, separatists elevated the separation question more and more to a national level. They not only tempted Mainers' nationalism, but also pretended that Mainers could not enjoy basic American rights and freedoms as long as they lived in a district.[25]

Even as separatists and antiseparatists split along party lines, Mainers of all parties shared a loyalty to their region and nation. In their campaign from 1815 to 1819, separatists again and again employed antiparty rhetoric in order to affirm that all Mainers, Federalists and Republicans, participated in a common cause. By emphasizing that statehood for Maine was not a partisan issue but rather of interest for all, separatists strategically utilized the strong New England American identity that had emerged over the previous three decades. When they appealed to Mainers' New England nationalism, separatists hoped to animate their opponents to overcome partisan allegiance and support the "common" regional and national good. Democratic-Republicans even tried to connect to their Federalist predecessors by integrating the struggle for Maine statehood into a collective Maine history. Maine's first settlers claimed that they "who occupied the highest place in the affections of their fellow citizens were years ago, advocates for separation." By describing the separatist movement as a historical struggle of the district, Democrats downplayed the role of parties.

From the beginning of their newspaper controversy with the Federalists in 1815, Democratic-Republicans emphasized that the debate about the separation was not influenced by party spirit. They invented a nonpartisan tradition of the separation movement by asserting that the petitions for separation to the Massachusetts Legislature in 1787 and 1792 had not been motivated by party bonds. Underlining their exemplary Republican effort, separatists suggested that they were not committed to the interest of any political party. They also bolstered their pretension to work for the improvement of Republican virtue when they lamented party divisions and rejected partisan motives of their movement. In February 1816 an author, who called himself "Old York" promoted separation alluding to the un-Republican divisive nature of partisan activities. "It must be a pleasing reflection to every well-wisher of Maine," he stated, "that in the revival of the subject [of separation], it is divested of all those hateful features of party animosity, which has so long divided our country."[26]

On the state level, cooperation between Republicans and Federalists on the issue of separation of Maine from Massachusetts was already a reality. By 1816, many Massachusetts Federalists were willing to allow Maine to separate because it removed the Maine Democratic-Republicans from Massachusetts politics. Furthermore, they thought that a state of Maine strengthened the federal government. The nonpartisan rhetoric increased the effectiveness of separatists' argument that a state of Maine worked in favor of Republicanism and promoted a New England America. Gaining strength in 1816, separatists put their appeal more and more on a national level. They invited Maine Federalists to join them in their nationalist cause and to subdue their party affiliation. In a clever campaign, they labeled partisan attachments as "local feelings," implying that party feelings were unpatriotic. In an explicit attempt to arouse Mainers' nationalism, separatists called upon all people in the district to join in the common cause of separation: "Republicans and Federalists! Let us join in one common cause—let us cordially unite in placing Maine in our great confederacy, an independent State.... It is a question in which we are all mutually interested—and it ought to call forth the exertions of all our citizens, regardless of local feelings."

Pushing Mainers to vote for separation in the May election of 1816, separatists linked the day of the election, which was the 20th of May, with the Fourth of July. By predicting a local jubilee as great a celebration as the national holiday of Independence Day, separatists again tried to apply Mainers' national loyalty for their own purposes.[27]

In actuality, the day when Maine became a state would never be celebrated, neither in the years following separation nor at any other moment in time.

Like all New Englanders by the beginning of the third decade of the nineteenth century, Mainers were proud of their nation and its Republican qualities that in their mind distinguished it so clearly from European countries. At the same time a local attachment bound them to Maine. It was exactly this combination of national and local loyalty that defined the collective identity in early nineteenth-century New England. The people of Maine could link both loyalties when they lurched to the idea of their district becoming one of America's "great" Republican states. Filled with nationalistic enthusiasm and high expectations of Maine's future role in the American republic, a separatist in the *Eastern Argus* wrote that Maine would "soon form a strong and important link in the great chain of the American Union."[28] Republican patriotism of the late eighteenth and early nineteenth century held that citizens obtained liberty in return for their patriotic loyalty. Especially at the Brunswick Convention, separatists argued that the people of Maine would only experience all the rights of freeborn Americans in a state of Maine. Self-government, advocates of separation claimed, was the right of every American and, therefore, it was unpatriotic to exclude Mainers from that freedom. In this rhetoric, separation from Massachusetts became a Republican right.

The selectmen of Meuer in Somerset County, one of Maine's remote inland communities, summarized how the freedom of self-government was a Republican liberty Mainers could not be restrained from. They intimated in convention on September 30 that no patriot or advocate of equal rights would reject Mainers such basic Republican rights.

> It would be ungenerous to . . . indulge the jealousy that any considerable number of our brethren in the district of Maine should even harbor a wish, to exclude from the right, so many freeborn Americans, . . . a right which every lover of equal rights, every real patriot, must rejoin to see freely exercised, by every member of that body politic, to which we belong.

Furthermore, separatists claimed this freedom as a New England tradition. Relying again on Mainers' regionalism, a writer in the *Eastern Argus* emphasized that the people in the New England colonies had always been convinced that they were born free and equal. A separation broadside for the vote in July 1819 reversed this argument and maintained that Mainers had to earn freedom and independence by voting for separation. Claiming national importance for the decision on Maine statehood, separatists announced: "The eyes of all America are upon you." They appealed to the voters to "convince the world by an overwhelming majority that you deserve FREEDOM AND INDEPENDENCE."[29]

Northerners also associated a state of Maine with nationalistic symbols and values. A New Yorker signing as "A Native of old Massachusetts" suggested in a letter to William King that the new state, be named not Maine, but Washington. Addressing his belief in Maine's important future national role, the New Yorker wanted to persuade King to merge his regionalist loyalty with his nationalistic pride and express Maine's new national rank by relating it to the greatest national hero. "Sir, The District of Maine being soon destined to attain an important rank in the Union permit me to hope that you will use your influence to consecrate this event by adopting the sainted name of Washington, thus combining whatever is good and great and glorious." Turning Maine into a monument for George Washington, the New Yorker thought, would put the new state in the favor of the entire country. Like many of his contemporaries he was excited about establishing another means to keep the memory of the nation's glorious history alive. Naming the new state Washington, the New Yorker concluded, would "elevate a monument of gratitude to the memory of our political Fathers, associate the future history of the State with the recollection of his virtues, and the duration of his fame, and propitiate the best wishes of the whole Country." In their publications, separatists always pointed at any support of their cause coming from people who did not live in Maine. The *Argus* published, for example, two articles in favor of separation. One was a copy from a local paper in Utica, New York, the *Colombian Gazette*, and the other came from the Massachusetts *Salem Gazette*.[30]

Interestingly, Massachusetts papers avoided the debate about Maine statehood. Some, as for example, the *Salem Gazette,* published articles presenting pro-separation as well as articles presenting anti-separation arguments. Massachusetts residents generally seemed to believe the people in Maine should decide whether or not they wanted to remain part of the Bay State. Nine days before the referendum, the *Boston Daily Advertiser* wrote that the question of separation was now entirely in the hands of the people of Maine and that the reason why many members of the Massachusetts legislature had voted for the referendum was not because they were in favor of separation, but because they believed only Mainers could make that decision. If people in Massachusetts opposed a state of Maine, it was mostly out of a strong feeling of local loyalty. They thought that the separation was not necessary because the Massachusetts government had treated Maine well and that the few advantages that statehood would bring for Maine were not worth the big and expensive step.

In March 1820, the *Salem Gazette* emphasized with a sentimental tone that Maine and Massachusetts did have a "favorable" and "happy connection." Many expected Boston to remain Maine's commercial center. A sense that it was rather hurt feelings of local pride that prevailed among many in Massachusetts than real opposition is especially strong in an article in the Boston *Columbian Sentinel.* The piece, full of Massachusetts pride, questioned the ability of Mainers to read and understand the referendum. It suggested that the text of the referendum misrepresented the conditions of separation and that its proponents were indeed "false coloring" the facts on Massachusetts property in Maine. Emotionally, it concluded that Massachusetts only agreed to Maine's separation because the terms were clearly in her favor. But this sentiment was not dominating. The *Boston Patriot*, for example, reprinted articles and poems from Maine newspapers, throughout the month of July 1819, demanding a "bigger slice" of land for the new state.[31]

As much nationalistic rhetoric as Mainers and their supporters employed in their debates on Maine statehood, in its final phase Maine statehood became part of a great sectional crisis. A state of Maine helped to solve the conflict between Northerners and Southerners about whether the new state of Missouri should be a slave or a free state. The prospective state of Maine pushed through by the force of a sectional New England nationalism got entangled in the first sectional conflict of the young American nation.

Preventing Southern Dominance

After the majority of the people had voted for statehood in July 1819, the admission of Maine as a state appeared to be only a formality. When the bill from the House of Representatives admitting Maine reached the Senate in December, it was clear that further obstacles had emerged. The question of Maine statehood became part of the dispute over the Missouri Territory. The debate whether Missouri would be admitted to the Union as a slave or free state set off an intense sectional debate between Northern and Southern legislators. The political controversy started in 1819 when Congressman James Tallmadge of New York proposed the gradual emancipation of Missouri slaves. The Northern majority in the House of Representatives blocked Missouri's admission as a state in reaction to white Missouri's rejection of Tallmadge's proposal. A heated debate over the issue continued into 1820. Southerners argued that Congress could not impose conditions for statehood that slavery was a state internal issue, and that Congress could not interfere with slaveholders' property rights. When Maine applied for statehood, Speaker of the House Henry Clay of Kentucky saw this as an opportunity to maintain the balance of free and slave states. Ironically, Clay was a slaveholder, but he strongly believed in compromise as the essence of the political process. He, therefore, worked out a compromise to end the debate that split North and South: Maine would be admitted as a free state and Missouri as a slave state; the remaining territory north of the 36–30 parallel would be closed off to slavery.

The admissions of Maine and Missouri had been joined. Maine was caught in the conflict over whether Missouri was to be "free" or "slave." Attached to the Maine bill was an amendment not to restrict slavery neither in Maine nor in Missouri. The linkage of Maine statehood to the Missouri controversy frustrated Mainers. With the admission of Alabama in the same month, the U.S. Senate was evenly divided between North and South. Now the Senate represented eleven states from each region. Mainers became aware that unless Missouri was admitted as a slave state, Maine would not be admitted or at least not be admitted as a "free" state.[32]

This constituted a real dilemma for separatists who had propagated statehood by appealing to a New England identity that emphasized the un-Republican character of the slave South. Even the driving force in the separation movement, William King, first opposed statehood if it was linked to an expansion of slavery. As the pioneer in the New Orleans cotton trade with Liverpool, the merchant William King personified the paradox of the New England antislavery standpoint.

As all New Englanders, Mainers had come to exclude the South from their imagined nation, although a good number of them made a fortune from the Southern labor system. Furthermore, slavery had existed in all New England colonies including Massachusetts and continued to exist during the early republic. It was indeed only gradually abolished in the years after the Revolution at the same time when New Englanders claimed that they were better than their Southern countrymen because they did not own slaves. Moreover, from the beginning of the separation movement separatists had argued over and over again that a state of Maine would increase Northern influence in the Senate and limit Southern power within the U.S. government. New England virtues would then dominate national politics. As early as 1791 Daniel Davis pleaded that two more senators from a Northern state would strengthen the interest of the North. Repeating that point in a much more vehement manner than Davis, the *Argus* reminded its readers, for example, in December 1815, that representatives of Maine in the Senate "would, among other good effects, tend greatly to quiet the minds of some of our Northern folks, who have of late been much alarmed at the great increase of Southern influence by the formation of new States in that section of our country. It would be balancing the scale by the addition of a little Northern influence."

In the same year the *Argus* blamed Southerners for resisting a separation of Maine from Massachusetts because they did not find Mainers capable of self-government. Linking everybody who agreed with the un-American Southerners, the Democratic paper called that statement against a state of Maine a "slave driver" argument. The fact that New Englanders excused each other of using a "slave driver argument" shows how successful they were in erasing their own slave-owning past and present and how they believed themselves in their invention of New England as a free society. The link between Maine statehood and the Missouri debate combined a prospective increase of New England power in the federal government with an expansion of slavery.[33]

Mainers, who had proudly emphasized their New England character, felt uncomfortable about an establishment of a state of Maine that helped the Southern plantation economy to expand westward. They felt that the coupling of a Missouri slave state and a state of Maine, the fact that an extension of slavery was the price for a separation from Massachusetts, was "unjust to the people of Maine," as an article in the *American Advocate* put it.[34] It was unjust because they had to compromise with the ideals defining their collective identity. This shows how ambitiously New Englander worked on an image of their region that claimed that New England was white and free and scrupulously denied the existence of New England slaves. But finally after the people of Maine and their representatives in the national government struggled with this over the winter of 1820, the Missouri Compromise was acceptable to them because it nevertheless forbid slavery north of the line 36°30" in the Louisiana Territory. This at least enabled New Englanders to maintain their self-image of a morally superior people. More importantly, the state of Maine kept the balance between Northern and Southern states in the Senate. On March 15, 1820, after more than three decades of debate and campaign, Maine became the twenty-third state of the Union.

The day of Maine "Independence" was not much different from any other ordinary day in the life of the people of Maine. Mainers did not rest from work or parade through their streets. There were no celebrations as separatists had predicted in 1816. Beside an "Independence Ball" in Portland on the 16th of March, there was not much going on in the new state. Massachusetts papers favorably reported a joyful atmosphere among the people in Portland, and flags displayed on ships in the harbor. Considering Mainers' New England American identity, the quiet style of the celebrations is not surprising. The people of Maine were proud to be New Englanders and Americans. They were proud that their new state was part of the Union and stood for New England values in that Union, but they did not find a reason to fete anything that symbolized Maine in particular. On March 14, the *Argus* applauded in separatists' regular New England nationalistic language that with a state of Maine "another glory is added to the star spangled banner."[35]

The degree to which the inhabitants of Maine subscribed to a New England identity becomes obvious in the visual depictions Mainers created of their towns and landscape in the years after Maine was admitted as a state. Paintings and engravings of Maine from the period after 1820 portrayed New England values as cultivated landscapes, neat towns, sophisticated houses, and public buildings, and a hardworking people. The best example is Jonathan Fisher's painting "A Morning View of Blue Hill Village" (cover of this book). Jonathan Fisher was a landscape painter, but also Blue Hill's Congregational pastor; a farmer, poet, and scientist. Resembling many other similar pictures of rural New England, Fisher's work shows meadows, separated by stonewalls, in the foreground with two women and a man working for further progress. The village of Blue Hill with its white houses and church steeples is in the background as another symbol of civilization. A schooner on the docks of Blue Hill presents New England's industry in the coastal trade. Works such as Jacques Gerard Milbert's "View of Hallowell" from 1820 and "View of Augusta," painted by an unknown artist in 1825, fulfill a similar pattern. All depict typical New England towns and villages.[36]

A painting from a Portland amateur woman artist indicates that ordinary people felt much more as New Englanders than Mainers. The new state of Maine itself did not have a special meaning to the people. It was only in the context of their region and their nation that Mainers paid particular attention to symbols of their state. In 1832, Anna Bucknam painted Congress Street in Portland as she remembered it in the early 1820s, when the first State House was still in her hometown, before it was moved to the new capital of Augusta. Interestingly, "The First State House" does not focus on the State House; it is rather a view of Congress Street with the church, the courthouse, another elegant brick building, well-dressed people, and orderly trees at the end.[37] Bucknam did not put the State House at the center of her work. She seemed to be more interested in the entire street and its attributes of civilization.

The history of the movement for Maine statehood shows that New Englanders at the frontier differed from their countrymen in the coastal centers, due to different religious, economic, and political structures. New Englanders at the frontier often belonged to religious sects rather than large denominations, and were isolated from the market and institutions as courts and the established churches. The history of the separation of Maine from Massachusetts further reveals that New Englanders shared a strong regional national identity in spite of these differences. It was this New England American loyalty that directed the majority of the people of Maine to support the separation from Massachusetts. Especially during the last period of the movement when separatists needed to convince the people in the coastal towns, the nationalistic regionalism helped to bridge gaps between the coast and the frontier. After the War of 1812 had consolidated the New England nationalism that had been growing since the beginning of the century, separatists systematically engaged elements of that identity; for example, the civilization of the wilderness and the Republican and patriotic character of the people, in order to attract Mainers to their movement.

Advocates of a state of Maine used the expanding print media as well as personal contact to urge people to join them. After the first isolated and rudimentary movement in the late eighteenth century, separatists transformed their campaign into a professional activism employing the modern ideology of nationalism and modern means of communication. The people of Maine were proud New Englanders and intended, like everybody in the region, to spread New England values throughout the nation. They were satisfied with their contribution to that process because a state of Maine set at least a free Northern state against the "Southern" slave state of Missouri, and helped to delimit the northward extension of slavery. The establishment of the state of Maine is an indicator of the strength of the new regional nationalism and the success of the New England intellectual elite in creating and promoting that ideology.

Although many Mainers differed from their Massachusetts contemporaries in their religious culture and beliefs, Maine separatists avoided the issue of religion in their campaign. With its large number of religious dissenters, Maine became a hot spot where Puritan heritage and the post-Revolutionary Republicanism clashed. While Puritan tradition demanded dominance of the Congregational establishment, the new Republicanism promoted religious freedom and provided ideological support to the dissenters. One of the few publications that mentioned the area's sectarian character was Williamson's history of Maine. In his work, William Williamson portrayed freedom of religion as a unique Maine virtue and emphasized the number of different sects enjoying such liberty. Contrasting his state with Europe, he also made a point that some of these sects had been brutally persecuted in Europe. The reason for the reluctance to involve religion in the argument for statehood was probably that New Englanders of all denominations still shared a strong Protestant identity, which overshadowed religious differences.[38]

CHAPTER 6

God's People: The Creation of a Protestant Nation

Three days before Christmas in 1820, the Presbyterian minister James Sabine gave a sermon celebrating the second centennial of the landing of the Pilgrims at Plymouth. Speaking from his pulpit in the Essex Street Church in Boston, Sabine combined a number of images and ideas that defined early Republicans' national identity in New England. The immigrant from old England praised such New England virtues as modesty, simplicity, and hard work and admired New Englanders' Republican sacrifice of their individual interests for the common good. Implying New England's superiority to other "nations," Sabine emphasized that these traditions furnished the region with a unique history and character. He linked his regionalist statements with a strong nationalist appeal. At the time of the sectional crisis of the Missouri Compromise, he did not want his sermon to spur the emotions and attitudes that divided the nation. "I do not forget that New England is a part, and but a part, of a great nation," he assured his parishioners. But after the clergyman repeated how he himself and New Englanders in general felt loyal to the United States, he nevertheless heartily highlighted the region's peculiar virtues again. Repeatedly praising New England, Sabine alluded to the region's leading role within the nation. Furthermore, he joined other regionalists who imagined New England culture spreading throughout the entire country. Enthusiastically, Sabine claimed that New England had already molded the nation's character.

New England nationalists such as Sabine vehemently ignored the history of Southern states and the role Southern history played in shaping the new nation. Nevertheless, Virginia not Massachusetts is the oldest colony. New Englanders reinvented American history by completely disregarding Southern history. With this attitude it became easy for them to overrate the importance of their own regional history.

The careful denial of any disloyalty to the union that Sabine included in his sermon distinguished clergymen from other elites who helped create New England's collective identity. In contrast to lawyers, professors, and writers who helped engineer this identity, clergymen often tried to legitimize the regionalist character of their nationalism by emphasizing their national loyalty and denying any sectional feelings of superiority, but then reaffirming New England's uniqueness as a mere fact. In many cases they still implied New England's role as a model for the entire nation. Sabine, for example, added to his proclamation of federal loyalty that "still, New England has her own character, and this character is more distinctly spiritual, than that of any other nation under heaven."[1]

James Sabine participated in a larger cultural movement portraying the New England identity as a religious identity. He predicted that in the future the United States would depend even more on their people's piety than on a strong military force or a prospering economy. The vehement articulation of the idea that religion was an essential element of the New England identity was also unique to the regionalist rhetoric of New England ministers. When James Sabine preached to his Boston parish he gave a sermon that many of his colleagues, including those who belonged to other denominations, could have given as well. Even if they believed in different doctrines, Presbyterians, Congregationalists, and Baptists all propounded the same general ideas of New England nationalism to their growing audiences. The collective identity that emerged during the early years of the republic provided a source of unity in the Second Great Awakening. Church membership doubled during the religious revivals and exposed many New Englanders to such nationalist religious ideology. The regional nationalism promoted in sermons reached New Englanders not only in coastal centers such as Boston and Portland, Maine, but also in the smaller towns and frontier settlements as, for example, Weatherfield, Connecticut and Middlebury, Vermont.

With his promotion of Christian New England nationalism, Sabine fit the pattern of a typical New England minister; but he also shared the views English tourists who came to travel the region and in their comments contributed to its glorification. Sabine was born in Farnham, England. It was only in 1818, two years before he gave his sermon on the Pilgrims, that he crossed the Atlantic and moved to Boston with his family. Sabine is a good example of how easy the transition from a European to an American identity was for some immigrants. The English-born minister probably compared himself and his Atlantic crossing with the experience of the Pilgrims—believing that he shared

the priority of religion with these New England settlers. Religion, he reminded his listeners, had been the reason that their forefathers had left England and settled in the American wilderness: "Let me direct your attention to the *single object* which called your Fathers to this land. WAS IT NOT RELIGION? RELIGION ALONE? RELIGION INDEPENDENT OF EVERY THING BESIDE ITSELF?" Because religion brought their ancestors to this country, he argued later, it should always continue to shape the New England identity. Sabine was able to take pride in his own contribution to New England religious life. He had founded the very church where he spoke that morning.[2]

At a time when the Second Great Awakening split the New England clergy, New England nationalism was a strong ideology that unified not only the clergymen, but also laymen across denominational lines. The emphasis on religion as part of the New England identity strengthened the revival movement and provided a bond for the different religious sects. Furthermore, it connected the evangelists with the established churches as well as revivalists and orthodox believers.

Religious newspapers addressing different groups also participated in the creation of the New England national identity. They published articles glorifying the first settlement, praising New England virtues and landscapes, celebrating heroes such as General Lafayette and picturing the British and the French as failed Republicans. Orthodox Presbyterians, and Congregationalists read articles on these issues in the *Christian Spectator* and the *Christian Observer*. The *Religious Intelligencer*, *Connecticut Evangelical Magazine*, *The Advisor of Vermont Evangelical Magazine*, and *Piscataqua Evangelical Magazine* engaged all evangelicals in such subjects. Journals writing for specific religious sects also took part in this process. The *Christian Herald*, which focused on Baptist and Methodist readers, and the *Religious Informer*, which paid special attention to a Freewill Baptist audience, published articles promoting a New England American identity. In their individual journals, religious leaders could reaffirm the New England nationalist ideas they introduced in their sermons and appeal to their followers to feel a part of the newly invented New England nation. Although newspapers addressing Methodist audiences participated in the publication of New England nationalist ideas, Methodist ministers hardly joined their Presbyterian, Congregational, and Baptist colleagues in giving sermons with such contents. Even if Methodists participated in the new nationalist culture, they certainly played as an active role as other denominations. Universalists, the group who was in vanguard of dissent with the Standing Order by the 1820s, but remained a minority throughout the nineteenth century and disappeared at the end of the century, did not engage very much in the culture of American nationalism in New England.

New England's clergy played an important role in the creation of a national identity in New England even in nonreligious publications. Ministers such as the Unitarian William Emerson and Congregationalist Jedidiah Morse wrote and promoted New England history. Joseph Conforti calls Morse the "geopolitical patriarch of New England's republicanized collective identity in the young nation." In his publications *The American Geography* (1789) and *The American Universal Geography* (1793), the Congregational minister expressed pride in New England's cultural homogeneity and contrasted it with the, in his eyes, diverse and raw South. For Morse, the best example of the New England landscape of white towns, which he believed brought about a Republicanized version of traditional Puritan virtues, was the Connecticut River Valley. In his description of what appeared to him as the heartland of New England, Morse promoted the region as the civic model for the rest of the nation. With its depiction of New England as a cultural region, Morse's geography appealed very much to Federalists and they applauded Morse as one of the leaders of their secessionist movement. Congregationalists Timothy Dwight, who was a close friend of Morse, and Jonathan Fisher created visual and literary depictions of New England landscapes and villages.[3]

Especially in their sermons, revivalist as well as orthodox preachers addressed these issues and shared a common New England nationalist language, although their diverse doctrines led to different worldviews. The biggest difference was probably various ideas of the role of the individual in conversion and salvation. By emphasizing the conversion experience, revivalists granted ordinary people more responsibility and decision-making powers. After the turn of the century, New England ministers widened their popular appeal dramatically by engaging with a much broader spectrum of the population.

In the early nineteenth century, dissenters took advantage of the rising political platform of Republicans and used it to operate more democratically. At the same time, Congregationalist became disillusioned with Federalists magistrates, with whom they have had very tight connections during the 1790s. Their disappointment with the Federalist officials, who lost political power after 1800 and no longer offered political support, led Congregationalists to open up to new organizational forms on the grassroots level. The Unitarian crisis played a role in that process as well by dividing Congregationalists and, therefore, weakening their alliance with the elites. Unitarians continued to focus on the upper segment of New England society, while Orthodox clergy adopted more democratic ideas of leadership. As a result, Republican Congregationalists and dissenters began to operate in similar ways and both succeeded in appealing to broad audiences. Through print culture, clergymen reached a larger audience than just the congregation gathering to listen to their preaching. During the early republic, a large number of sermons were published and contributed to the effect of the spoken words. The broader popular appeal, democratic organization, and growing exposure through print culture of New England ministers tremendously increased their influence on the emerging national identity.[4]

Like other members of the New England elite class, religious leaders talked about the civilization of the wilderness and praised New England virtues, but they extended the usual catalogue of celebration of the region by emphasizing religion as a part of New England's collective identity. With the Second Great Awaking leading to an increase in church membership, the early years of the republic constituted the perfect time to define America as a Protestant nation. In their constant attempt to win new souls, ministers restated the idea that New Englanders were God's chosen people over and over again. The numbers of conversions were very important for the status of a minister and regional nationalism certainly attracted people from different ages, professions, and social backgrounds. The religious advocates of a New England regionalism and nationalism compared New Englanders and Americans with the people of Israel, claiming that God had always been on the side of the American people, especially New Englanders, as he had been on the side of the Israelites. The idea of an alliance between God and the people of New England added a strong religious argument to the usual assertions of New England superiority. Such statements were general enough to appeal to different religious groups. Disagreements in beliefs, such as whether individuals could be instruments in their own salvation process or not, did not conflict with that general loyalty to the region and nation. It seemed that ministers of different denominations found it necessary to use that New England nationalist rhetoric in order to be able to compete with other churches and sects.[5]

The Quakers and Shakers did not fit into this picture. Although New Englanders proudly emphasized their Republican virtues, they did not always live up to them when it came to religion. Catholics, Jews, and Quakers could not vote in several New England states. In the early republic, New Englanders seemed to feel especially ambiguous about the Shakers. The sect appeared to embrace some New England values, but denied others. Moreover, Shakers not only differed from other New Englanders in their lifestyle, they also did not participate in the creation of a New England identity. Although many people observed Shaker villages with suspicion, some tried to find New England virtues in these utopian communities. New England nationalism was so strong that it even evoked an effort to include religious and social outsiders as the Shakers.

Protestant Virtue and the Exemplary New England Patriot

New England ministers and preachers of different denominations cooperated with lawyers, historians, professors, writers, and artists in forging people's imagination of their region and nation. In sermons and religious newspapers, early Republican New Englanders confronted the same images of New England landscapes and virtues as they were introduced in travel books, almanacs, and on paintings and household utensils. In concert with their worldly contemporaries, religious leaders pictured New Englanders and their ancestors as benevolent, disinterested, modest, hardworking, educated, and pious. Although many other architects of a New England identity also included piety in their canon of the region's virtues and also stressed the centrality of Protestantism in the collective identity, clergymen argued that piety was intertwined with all other New England values. They introduced a collective identity that was molded by Protestant religion.[6]

Listening to sermons and reading religious publications in the late eighteenth and early nineteenth century, New Englanders came to believe that piety constituted the basis for all their virtues because in the religious nationalistic discourse religion seemed to strengthen all other characteristics. Lecturing his parishioners in Albany, New York, on the New England Pilgrims, the Presbyterian pastor and native New Englander John Chester emphasized that it was not morality in general that distinguished the first New England settlers, but more specifically a biblical "Scriptural" morality. Chester was born in Weatherfield, Connecticut, in 1785, the son of a colonel in the Revolutionary Army. After he graduated from Yale, he preached in different towns in Massachusetts and moved to New York in 1810, first to Cooperstown and then to Albany. In Albany, he contributed to the town's level of civilization by founding the first women's academy and the Albany Academy.

Like Chester, Jacob Burnap argued in a sermon which he preached in Merrimack, New Hampshire that piety produced other New England virtues. "New England people were noted for their good morals and industrious habits," the Congregational minister said, and implied that these sprang form "their strict adherence to religious institutions." He also praised the first New England settlers: "Our ancestors were men of solid piety and true patriotism. They were venerable for those endowments that were conducive to the wellbeing [*sic*] of a community and ornamental to the human character."

At the New England Society of New York, which transplanted New Englanders had founded in 1805 to maintain and promote New England culture, the Presbyterian Gardiner Spring explained to his audience of New England admirers that it had been the Pilgrims' religiosity that had helped them create strong civil and religious institutions. Members of the New York New England Society drank toasts to "The Universal Yankee nation!" In an article on New England schools, the Evangelist Reverend Greenwood (as he styled himself) extended the usual argument that education was essential to bring up Republican citizens. He insisted that not just education, but religious education, was a precondition for a prosperous nation. His emphasis on rather traditional religious education in contrast to a more general education, which was a Republican ideal, clearly shows that time-honored Puritan ideals did not always merge smoothly with new Republican ones. Greenwood explicitly pointed out religious education to ensure that it would not lose its significance in the new republic. New England ministers found religious education at least as important as secular education for the success of the new republic. If he wanted to show a stranger the source of his nation's greatness, Greenwood proudly stated, he would not guide the visitor to the economic centers, army posts, newly constructed roads and canals, but lead him to the most remote schools in New England, where children were still studying the Bible. According to religious propagandists for New England nationalism, piety and patriotism were the most important New England virtues. The Reverend Burnap, for example, presented them as typical characteristics of his ancestors. He thought these New England traditions deserved special praise because they ensured the well-being of the entire community and they also distinguished the individual character.[7]

During the Second Great Awakening New Englanders experienced the social and political influence of Protestantism every day when they witnessed and often engaged themselves in the work of interdenominational abolition, temperance or missionary societies. During the revivals, religious leaders played an important role in directing the values as well as social and political activities of their large number of followers. Most importantly, the revival movement not only led to the establishment of missionary, abolition, and temperance groups, it also allowed ministers to successfully create and promote a Protestant New England nationalism. In a time when the market revolution dissolved traditional social ties, and westward migration isolated people from their families and friends, just as other institutions and ideas of the religious revival the New England American identity offered them a new sense of community and belonging.

For ministers regional nationalism was an ideal ideology to spread the values of self-discipline, soberness, and hard work among ordinary people. It also provided them with a tool for trying to avoid a situation like that of France, where the Revolution had replaced religion with secular nationalism. In contrast to France, the new American republic as New England ministers imagined it was shaped by the powerful ideology of religion. Moreover, ministers wanted some reinvented Puritan traditions to join with new Republican values in defining the new collective identity. Sometimes attempts of New England ministers to enforce Puritan culture met with resistance. New Englanders in New York City often boycotted emerging entertainments such as theatres, popular horse races, dances, and Sunday boat excursions. Gardiner Spring, for example, thought that theatre-going encouraged licentious habits and was outraged over Sabbath breaking. In 1821, Spring and other Sabbatarians even won the support of Mayor Allen when they boycotted newspapers that advertised Sunday pleasure trips. The entertaining events nevertheless remained very popular among New Yorkers and newspapers were able to defend the boat excursions as innocent.[8]

By linking Republican virtues and piety, New England's religious leaders merged the Republican idea of civic virtue, the interest in the common good, with the Protestant ideal of Christian benevolence. In his important study of public Christianity in Southern New England, Jonathan Sassi concludes: "When ministers discussed virtue, they put a Protestant slant on an often secular and republican term." Sassi's observation is true for all of New England. The New England clergy also underlined the interdependence of church and state. Employing popular concern about the survival of the republic, they claimed that only a vital Christianity among the people could ensue its security.[9]

Even if the Great Awakening established a focus on the individual and their interests, early Republican religious leaders still promoted the model of Protestant benevolence, especially when joined with Republican virtue. James Sabine, for example, warned his congregation: "Let no man seek his own: but every man another's wealth." With that approach ministers responded to the selfish individualism that they felt had emerged as an evil component of the market revolution. In this respect New England nationalism was ambiguous. On the one hand it included praise of industry and commerce as symbols of civilization; but on the other hand it sometimes involved rejection of commercialism, because New Englanders were afraid that a focus on economic success eradicated traditional Republican virtue. The New England identity reflected the ambivalence of individuals as well as of early Republican society in general. Many welcomed the prospect of economic well-being, but also thought that commercialism corrupted order in all areas of life. The solution the New England clergy offered their congregations was to desire commerce in order to increase New England values such as education, the arts and sciences, and industry, but at the same time to never allow it to become their major priority. They implied that only if commerce became the number one priority in people's life would it lead to luxury and corruption. They preached that instead of commerce, God should be the focus of New Englanders' life. Such a collective divine obligation, religious leaders proposed, would control the evil side effects of the region's commercialization. Ministers praised Americans' wealth as a sign of greatness, but criticized the money-driven culture—especially in the context of slavery. Ironically, ministers rarely addressed the issue of New England's own slaves, New England's profits from Southern slave labor, or racist attitudes in New England. With the expansion of the market revolution and the emergence of abolitionism in the first decades of the nineteenth century, ministers expressed such criticism more and more vehemently.[10]

In their campaign to promote piety, ministers tried to convince New Englanders that religion was the key to the persistence of prosperity and Republican virtue. They spread a strong message among early Republicans by maintaining that it was not only necessary for the people to be seriously religious in order to guarantee the survival of the republic, but also to work toward prosperity. By tying the market economy and Republicanism to religion, they argued, New Englanders would be able to avoid such destructive vices as selfishness, greed, and corruption. Jacob Burnap employed material values when he wanted to promote religion among his New Hampshire audience. He told them, "To prolong public prosperity, to avert national calamity, and prevent destruction, let every individual be persuaded to fear God, and keep his commandments. This is the direct way to promote public prosperity and personal welfare and safety."[11]

The clergy hoped to encourage New Englanders to maintain traditional ideals so that they would play a role in defining the Republican collective identity, especially because they were aware of the fact that traditional virtues did not always shape new Republican values but sometimes clashed with them. Jedidiah Morse Republicanized Puritanism in order to make it attractive to a new Republican generation. He hoped that through this reinvention of Puritan tradition, New England's "ancient" pious "habits" would always thrive among the people. Like many advocates of New England nationalism, Morse believed that only latter-day Puritanism would secure Republican virtue. Appealing to his listeners to reestablish traditional values, John Chester painted an image of better times in New England history. In the early nineteenth century New Englanders used such nostalgia increasingly as a strategy to criticize social, economic, and political changes. The cofounder of the Albany Female Academy underscored how order and obedience had prevailed in the lives of the Pilgrim fathers and had secured their happiness. "Then there was some meaning in the terms master and servant," he taught his New York listeners, "subordination and obedience were common in the family and school-room, the shop and the counting-house, and order and happiness were the consequences." The fact that Chester helped establish a women's academy indicates that he was rather a progressive than a conservative, backward-looking person. His rhetoric of the good old orderly society was basically a means to increase people's pride in their history and to provide a model for the prevention of chaos and anarchy. A call for traditional values did not necessarily interfere with the ministers' aim for social progress.[12]

The civilization of the wilderness was as much a major topic in religious speeches as it was in other articulations of New England nationalism. Religious spokesmen praised the early settlers in the usual way for building towns, bridges, and roads, planting fields and gardens, and cultivating the wild landscape. Often they added that the wilderness had offered a divine refuge from the worldly corruptions of Europe. Responding to the ambivalent attitude that some New Englanders had toward the uncivilized aspects of the American landscape, religious leaders reminded their contemporaries that the wilderness had been a place where their ancestors were able to exercise pure religion. Religious freedom and purity were the rewards New England's first settlers received for living in "savage" nature. The clergy stressed that the wilderness had not only provided shelter from worldly but also from religious corruption. An 1811 article in *The Advisor of Vermont Evangelical Magazine* pointed out that the New England fathers settled in the uncivilized country "to seek, in the wilds of America, a refuge from the corruptions of the world, and tranquility in their adherence to the pure religion of the gospel."

John Chester described the establishment of religion in a "savage" place as the most important part of the civilization process. "The wilderness, which they found filled with savages, destitute alike of civilization and culture; where the worship of god was unknown," he wrote, "has become joyful with improvement, and vocal with praise." Later, he added, the New England ancestors found in the wilderness what "civilization and refinement had denied them."[13] New England ministers concluded that it was this religious legacy that defined New England patriotism.

If New Englanders wanted their nation to flourish, so the region's religious leaders preached, they needed to maintain both traditional Protestant and new Republican virtues. These religious advocates of New England nationalism pushed that argument even further than New England's early historians. While historians of the Pilgrims and Puritans presented these virtues as New England traditions, ministers implied that as loyal Protestant Americans their virtuous heritage obliged New Englanders to preserve this heritage because only a virtuous and religious nation could prosper and outshine European competitors. In a sermon entitled "National Glory," the Unitarian minister Winthrop Bailey warned that "in order that glory may dwell in our country the people must be diligent and virtuous." Profligates, drunkards, duelists, and swearers, he said to his audience in Brunswick, Maine, were certainly not patriotic citizens. In contrast, they dishonored their country by rejecting God and by showing a lack of interest in the well-being of their neighbors. Speaking to his coastal community about irreligious, unruly, and drinking contemporaries, Bailey probably referred to Maine's frontier settlers, with whom he and his Brunswick neighbors did not always seem to share their own civilized, sober, and Protestant virtues. To Federalists, of course, such vices were the result of Jeffersonian democracy. The message sent by New England preachers was clear: It was both Protestantism and Republican virtues that defined a patriot. Daniel Chaplin, a Congregational minister from Groton, Massachusetts, expressed that idea most explicitly in an 1815 sermon. A good Republican and patriot, Chaplin said, had to be a good Christian as well:

> If you wish to contribute to the salvation of our beloved country in this day of our calamity, if you seek the prosperity of this town, and the public in general, be persuaded to impress on your minds the necessity of practicing all duties of Christianity. If you do this, you will be a good citizens, good townsmen, sound patriots, and happy Christians.[14]

Even if ministers started to value grassroots concerns after the turn of the nineteenth century, and increasingly linked piety and patriotism by inventing a profoundly religious national identity, they rejected certain forms of nationalist activity. Like the Unitarian minister Bailey, most New England clergymen were opposed to drinking and did not find it an appropriate way to celebrate the American nation. Ministers condemned the consumption of alcohol and the mingling of sexes during Fourth of July festivities. A strong influence of religion and traditional Puritan values of sobriety and orderliness, they thought, promised to free the new nationalism from such vicious side effects.[15]

The Unitarian Bailey, Presbyterians Sabine and Chester, and Congregationalist Chaplin all cooperated to invent a Protestant New England nation. Naturally, more than any other group ministers pictured New England as a traditionally religious region. They claimed that religion had been the major condition of the divine charter of New England. That the region's history demanded New England nationalism to be religious appeared to be only the logical conclusion of their argument. Along those lines, Sabine explained to his fellow Bostonians: "New England must be a religious nation. This was the chief article in the original charter, granted by the king of Zion." Such a national religious identity, they stressed, was more virtuous than nationalism based on strong military power, on a high level of civilization, and on economic prosperity. Sabine intensified the argument in an attempt to convince his listeners that God disliked a pure economic, militaristic, and political nationalism. The Congregational minister envisioned the rise of a new nationalism. This new "American" form of nationalism was determined by the number and by the influence of churches and ministers:

> The political character of nations is wearing off, and a moral character is now demanded by the great Monarch of the Universe. In a few years, a nation's glory and greatness will not be calculated upon the number of her armies, or the force of her navy; upon her mercantile strength and influence—her civil and scientific renown; but upon the sum of righteousness in the land—upon the number and purity of her churches—and faithfulness of her ministers—upon the influence of moral institutions, and upon the interest she takes in the conversion of the world.

By arguing that God favored a nation that defined itself in religious terms, Sabine implied that God would support such a nation and favor it over others. This idea certainly appealed to the first generation of independent Americans, who wanted to feel superior to

Europeans. Religious leaders threatened their congregations with the loss of the privileges that they were so proud to have, such as community, education, prosperity, and freedom, if they rejected the Protestant ideal. This was also an effective means to promote the image of a Christian patriot; it also helped them to continuously stress the centrality of Providence, which the Congregational establishment had used for a long time to explain history, to predict the future, and to warn from its downfall through sins.[16]

Members of different Protestant groups drew a largely consensual picture of New England's history, people, and virtues. Their sermons sometimes made an attempt to claim the New England heritage for their own branch of Protestantism. In his *Church History of New England*, the Baptist leader Isaac Backus argued that contemporary Boston Baptists were hardly distinguishable from their ancestors of the Plymouth colony. They still embodied all the traditional virtues of a godly life, and only differed in their practice of christening infants. An article in the *Advisor of Vermont Evangelical Magazine* maintained that the Puritans "were distinguished for their adherence to evangelical truth." Rewriting New England history, the Vermont journal suggested that the Puritans had been evangelicals. Revivalists often wanted to link themselves with the Puritans to profit from their historical legacy. In 1805, the *Piscataqua Evangelical Magazine* published a biography of the Puritan John Cotton, who had been a leading member of the first generation of New England settlers. This article implied that Cotton had been a prototype of an Evangelist. In contrast to this portrayal, Cotton clearly distanced himself from Antinomians such as Anne Hutchinson when it became obvious that they remained a minority, although he first sided with religious dissenters. Cotton was always concerned about his own popularity and wanted to maintain his status. The account of Cotton in the evangelical magazine indicates the intensity with which members of Evangelist sects admired New England virtues. The biographical article described Cotton as hardworking, pious, sober, and loyal. By linking themselves with New England's history and its major figures, evangelists participated in the promotion of the region's identity. Moreover, they hoped that their self-integration into that identity legitimized their group and placed them on the same level with the traditional established churches.[17]

Ministers believed that New Englanders were particularly responsible for the fate of the nation's glory. They thought the region's inhabitants were obligated to perform what they introduced as traditional New England virtues because they believed in New England's duty to spread its values throughout the country. Like worldly engineers of American identity in New England, religious leaders defined the values they wanted to promote as New England traditions. When John Chester complimented the region's excellence in education, for example, he maintained that the majority of American civil and religious leaders from other parts of the nation had been educated in New England: "The interest of learning have steadily advanced, and multitudes of men, of the first eminence, in every part of the United states, and every department of civil and professional life, have been educated in New England." The Second Great Awakening indeed helped to increase the number of colleges in New England by leading to the foundation of a number of Protestant schools throughout the region. Already during the eighteenth-century students from the Mid-Atlantic region and the South sometimes attended New England colleges, but Chester pushed that fact beyond a legitimate claim. Ministers further accentuated their point that the New England way improved the entire nation by portraying New Englanders as a people who were chosen by God to fulfill an exemplary role. Sabine, for instance, introduced the idea that God had arranged for New England settlers to distinguish themselves from other people through their political talent: "God so ordered it, that a great proportion of the New England men . . . soon gave a distinct character and indeed no small importance to their body politic."[18]

Religious leaders were the group of New England nationalists that addressed the issue of the region's leading role within the United States most frequently and most directly. Although they were fully aware of the dividing and sectionalist effect of their ideas, they embedded their regionalist concepts into their nationalism. Their loyalty to their nation consisted of regionalist imaginations and attachments.

God's Chosen People

Presbyterians, Congregationalists, Baptists, and other evangelicals agreed that New England's history and character marked the region as superior not only over other nations, but also over other regions within the United States. This superiority, they believed, sprang from New England's piety and Republicanism. Their regionalism often merged with a loyalty to the nation. As an outstanding region, ministers repeatedly explained to their listeners, New England had molded the national American character and raised it above all other nations. In their mind, New England's excellence was at the heart of American superiority. James Sabine concluded from New England's history that the character of the region was "distinct from the character of all other nations on the face of the whole earth." Gardiner Spring praised his New England ancestors as a superior "race." "America has not seen a more manly and gigantic race," he boasted, "than that which took possession of this western wilderness during the first century after the landing at Plymouth." The *Vermont Evangelical Magazine* wrote, "No people on earth may so justly pride themselves upon their ancestors as the New Englanders." Sabine and his colleagues imagined that this New England virtuosity shaped the national character.

New England ministers played a major role in creating and stabilizing the new regional American identity. With their nationalistic idea of New Englanders as a superior and chosen people they responded to the collective insecurity and anxiety caused by the westward migration to the new frontier areas, the dislocation from family and friends, and dissolution of personal ties in the workplace accompanying the market revolution.

From the 1790s on, all these changes had increasingly undermined a collective sense of community, stability, and security. The ministry not only responded to that collective deficit by offering new religious ideas and institutions to replace the fading identity, but also by supplying their fast-growing numbers of followers with an elaborate nationalistic culture. They gave the New England nationalistic ideology a religious legitimacy by emphasizing the history of God's special relationship with the New England people. And again, they also wanted to ensure an influential role for themselves in the new republic. By pleasing their audience with such praise of the region, ministers probably hoped to endorse their own popularity. This was particularly true for the Congregational establishment when they started to struggle with a decline of power and reorganization after the turn of the century. In the 1780s and 1790s the Congregational Church had still been dominant and enjoyed a number of privileges. They had by far the most numerous churches and ministers, and sufficient income to provide security. All this gave them an advantage in organization and influence.

When the number of dissenters rose dramatically in the nineteenth century and the Unitarian Crisis caused the loss of Congregationalist power, ministers began to adopt new forms of organization and developed an interest in an interdenominational effort to campaign for religiosity. They employed the energy of the revivals and began to promote a collective agenda of Protestant nationalism in order to guarantee themselves a continuous role of leadership and influence in the new republic. An interdenominational effort existed especially after 1812, when partisan competition declined and peace in the Atlantic world was finally restored. As Jonathan Sassi argues: "The ministers budding nationalism provided a noticeable point of interdenominational consensus in the years following the War of 1812."[19]

Gardiner Spring was born in 1785 in Newburyport, educated at Yale College, and worked as a Presbyterian pastor in New York after 1810. He imagined the influential role of New England to be the original reason for the divine charter of the New England settlement. As a native New Englander Spring applauded the expansion of New England virtues among New Yorkers who already identified with their Northern neighbors. Emphasizing the national benefit of New England's morality, he expressed his ideas to his fellow New Yorkers: "The settlement of New England was designed to have a very important influence on the character, prospects, and usefulness of the American nation." To drive home his point, Spring repeated that not only New Englanders gained from the region's virtues, but that these virtues helped the entire country to rise as an empire.

Spring's regionalist nationalism, his idea of a benevolent American empire molded by New England morality and piety, went hand in hand with his strong commitment to the reform movement. In 1816, he helped to found the American Bible Society. He also served on the interdenominational boards of the American Tract Society and the American Home Missionary Society. Spring's activity demonstrated his belief in the strength of common Protestant ideals and in cooperation across sectarian lines. Furthermore, Spring and his New England colleagues who worked for these reform societies also saw them as organizations to expand New England ideals.[20]

Many New Englanders commented on the superiority of their region over the South. Religious leaders, however, often coupled their statements on New England's outstanding qualities with a confirmation that they did not want to disparage other regions. Still New Englanders began to make anti-Southern remarks in the early 1790s. They condemned the three-fifths clause in the Federal Constitution with which Northerners accepted slavery in the South and a numerical disadvantage in federal elections for the sake of the union.

These cultural and ideological differences between North and South did not fade away once the nation was founded and the union established, but rather became more obvious. Over the following three decades, New Englanders continued to exclude Southerners from their vision of the American nation, but they never indicated that they reflected on their own sectional bias. Ordinary New Englanders did not seem to perceive their sectionalism and, even if they did, they did not regard it as an ideology that clashed with their nationalism. Some wealthy Northerners, however, rather identified with the Southern elite than with middling people in their own region. In places such as Philadelphia where Southerners owned second homes, attended school, and liked to travel, class united more than section divided: "Planters and Philadelphians saw each other far less as Southerners and Northerners than as fellow aristocrats."[21] A common lifestyle and discomfort with the opportunities that Republican society had opened up for ordinary people sometimes united the Northern and Southern elites.

New England clergymen, however, were conscious of emerging divisive tendencies. Their involvement in the slowly emerging antislavery movement might explain their heightened awareness. In contrast to the majority of their fellow New Englanders, they clearly addressed the issue. They already feared that ideas of New England dominance could work against a feeling of national unity and pride. Therefore, religious leaders often assured their audience that they did not have regionalist intentions, but, ironically, after emphasizing their national loyalty they never missed the opportunity to restate New England's predominance.

John Chester, a peer of Gardiner Spring and also a Presbyterian, shared the belief that it was New England wisdom, patriotism, and piety that had produced the independence of the United States. After demonstrating how New England had deserved a high rank on the scale of "nations," he assured that although the praise of New Englanders and their ancestors was just, he did not intend "to detract from, or deny the merits of other colonies." Having demonstrated his nationalism, the minister repeated to his New York audience that it was New England spirit and wisdom that had established the glory of America's "great empire." Inviting his New York parishioners to identify with their New England ancestors, Chester continued to praise New England's positive influence throughout the entire nation. The effects of the "noble exertions" of "our fathers," he said, "have been felt, and will continue to be felt, through every portion of our country." As an example, the pastor mentioned the impact of the New England political system. The "free" political institutions of the United States were, according to him, molded by New England's "perfect... pure democracy."[22]

At the time of the Missouri Compromise, when sectionalist tendencies were stronger than ever before, both Chester and Sabine linked regionalist rhetoric with a firm nationalist appeal in their sermons. Many other contemporaries did not deny that their belief in superior

New England virtues degraded the South. One reason for the ministers' exceptional proclamation might have been the ideal of Christian brotherly love, or that they saw it as their mission to unite the opposing sections. Gardiner Spring, for example, felt sympathetic to Southern slaveholders when abolitionism in New England grew in the decades preceding the Civil War. Perhaps ministers wanted to legitimize the idea of New England's dominance by rejecting its exclusive nature. Most likely, they were as ardent nationalists as they were regionalists. They hoped that in the future, Americans' regional and national loyalties would completely melt into a single affection for the nation.

Chester prophesied such a national identity. The American people, he envisioned "will soon melt down into a mass, possessing the good qualities of all, and form one character. Local prejudices will vanish, and we shall all surrender sectional and peculiar names, for the proud distinctive appellation of Americans."[23] As convincing as this nationalistic enthusiasm may have sounded, the native New Englander preaching for over an hour on the preeminence of New England virtues to a New York audience certainly envisioned a uniform American character that was shaped by the New England model. The combination of these statements shows how tightly New Englanders linked their regionalism and nationalism.

The nationalism of New England clergymen contained in general the same exclusive elements as the nationalism of professors, lawyers, merchants, and statesmen. In comparison to these other groups of New England nationalists, ministers addressed the idea of the superiority of New Englanders much more directly and even more frequently. Even Chester, who denied that he intended to deprecate the South, spoke with a sectionalist voice in the very same sermon. He praised Northerners for setting themselves apart from Southerners by despising slavery and embracing Republican values such as religion, liberty, and education. Depicting Protestantism as the ideology that created all these virtues, Chester asserted that the Northern states were populated by descendents of persecuted Protestants. Like many New Englanders, religious leaders not only excluded Southerners from their nation as they imagined, but made it clear that Europeans also did not fit the virtuous American character. Sabine, who had exchanged his old English identity with a New England self, warned Bostonians not to become like their European contemporaries and long for luxuries. Such an attitude, he emphasized, would cause a wide gap between rich and poor. The immigrant pastor assured his audience that New England would experience mass poverty just like England, France, and other European countries.

With such statements, the clergy supported the image of European inequality, which was presented in countless newspapers. Again, these anti-European statements served as a reminder to withstand materialistic values of the market economy by embracing more traditional virtues of piety. Ministers also contrasted the United States and New England with France and contrasted American Protestant virtue with French Catholic vice. They emphasized the difference between New England American piety and European superstition and tyrannical hierarchy. Interestingly, with this disparity New England clergymen placed European monarchy in the same category as religion.[24]

The Congregational minister Abiel Abbot illustrated American superiority in a comparison of the United States with Great Britain and France. While American superiority over England was most clearly reflected in her religious strength, the Massachusetts minister found that his country and France differed in every respect. Underlining America's exceptional character, he said: "Look at France; is she like America?" Answering his rhetorical question, he continued: "No, blessed be God, neither in her crimes nor her miseries." Interestingly, Abbot used New England's image of France to prove his argument that Americans resembled the people of Israel in their virtues, which had earned both people God's special affection. The only common event Catholic France and the Protestant United States shared, he declared, was their revolutions; however, the opposite nature of the American and the French Revolution demonstrated French Catholic vices and American Protestant virtues. "I will just remark; in one respect France and America are alike," Abbot lectured his Haverhill parishioners, "they have both been in a state of revolution. America spoiled hers not by one drop of blood, shed by civil hands; but France, shall I not say, has rendered hers accused by the blood of millions of her own citizens." In the late 1790s, Congregational ministers very much opposed the French Revolution's turn to terror and, therefore, moved into the Federalist camp. They accused Jeffersonians of creating dangerous fractions and even treated them as religious dissenters. In their sermons, Congregationalists often accused the French, Democratic Republicans, and sectarians at the same time of infidelity.[25]

In the first decade of the nineteenth century the majority of Congregational ministers, who still believed in Federalist ideals although they felt deeply disappointed with the Party, compared Democratic-Republicans with the French. Jefferson's election evoked among them a negative perspective of the nation's future. Many New England clergymen did not like to be governed by a Virginian; and especially not by Jefferson, with his French sympathies. These Federalist ministers feared that the new president would copy the anarchy and secularism of the French Republic. Even if they claimed nonpartisan attitudes, they still believed in a Jeffersonian conspiracy.

Certainly, New England Protestants from different denominations shared Francophobe anti-Catholicism and anti-French statements and they continued to express such attitudes in the 1810s and 1820s. At the beginning of the War of 1812, which would intensify the emerging New England nationalism, the Maine clergymen Winthrop Bailey preached against an alliance with France, picturing the French people as the antithesis of New Englanders. Although he viewed the French as greedy anti-Republicans, he saw the biggest contrast between Americans and the French in the two peoples' religion. Building on traditional Anglo-American anti-Catholicism, Bailey called France the "modern Antichrist." In his eyes, the French government was opposed to religion and, therefore, did not respect human rights. Bailey's logic against an American-French alliance was that New England virtues and French vices clashed to such an extent that the two people would never be able to find a common interest. "There is no common character, nor can there be a common interest," he assured, "between the protestants, the dissenters, the puritans of New England, and the papists, the infidels, the atheists of France; or between our free, republican institutions, and the most merciless tyranny, that ever heaven suffered to afflict mankind." Ministers confirmed their parishioners' belief that the United States (under the leadership of New England culture) after they had freed and protected themselves from European vices in the Revolutionary struggle did now outshine other nations. Inspired by this idea, Reverend Greenwood wrote in his article on New England schools that "free from the rusted fetters of the old world; and in the beauty and dignity of that peace they stand up now, self-government, orderly, and independent, a wonder of nations."[26]

Early Republican religious leaders synthesized the ideas of New England American superiority, the divine character of New England's original charter and piety as the key New England virtue in the powerful image of Americans as God's chosen people. By promoting the concept that God's providence had been manifested in the settlement and progress of United States, clergymen reaffirmed the close bond between American nationalism and Protestantism. Ministers construed an American history which proved that God had selected them as his people: God, they rejoiced, had been always on their side, sending diseases to kill New England Indians, helping Puritan settlers to survive in the wilderness, increasing New England's population, and letting New Englanders win the War of Independence against the British.

During the early years of the republic, New England ministers often compared Americans to the Israelites, God's chosen people from the Old Testament. This was, of course, not a new idea. New England clergy had compared New England with Israel for a long time. But after the young nation was founded, this comparison experienced an emotional revival. In 1799, Abiel Abbot enthusiastically celebrated the favor Americans and ancient Israelites shared: "Happy art thou, O Israel: who is like unto thee, O people saved by the Lord, the shield of thy help, and who is the sword of thy Excellence!" Older sermons tracing the "New English Israel," as for example, Samuel Dexter's sermon given in Dedham, Massachusetts, in 1738, were now reprinted. On Thanksgiving 1799, Abiel Abbot revealed to his Haverhill congregation how the "American Israel" had emerged as a common term. "It has been often remarked that the people of the United States come nearer to a parallel with Ancient Israel, than any other nation upon the globe," the Congregational minister stated proudly. "Hence, 'Our American Israel,' is a term frequently used; and common consent allows it apt and proper." The fact that a translation of a French history of the ancient Israelites was published in Vermont in 1813 shows the popularity of the idea.[27]

Portraying Americans, and especially New Englanders, as present-day Israelites enabled ministers to appear modest, because they could praise their region and nation in an indirect way. Many of such sermons simply focused on the divine favor that Israelites had enjoyed, and indicated their glorification of Americans only by underlining the similarity of the two people. By using such terminology, early Republican ministers built on John Winthrop's and other seventeenth-century Puritans' invocations. During the colonial settlement of New England, terms such as New Israelites did not indicate an American identity but a sense of a "transatlantic community of English saints." In an 1815 sermon that he gave in his Baptist Church in Bristol, Rhode Island, Barnabas Bates compared the afflictions of the ancient Israelites with the sufferings of the American colonists under George III. Bates belonged to the group of New England nationalists who emigrated from Europe. He was born in Edmonton, in England, in 1785, and came to New England as a young boy when his parents immigrated to the new world. Although he drifted to Unitarianism, he was able to keep his job because he was a highly respected member of his community. Like many local members of the elite in the early republic, Bates was a freemason and a master of the local Masonic lodge. Bates was against slavery and used his position as port collector in Bristol, Rhode Island, to prevent the efforts of some slave smugglers.

In 1820, twenty-one years after Abiel Abbot had preached to the people of Haverhill on the resemblance of the American people and ancient Israelites, his colleague Joshua Dodge similarly traced the issue of Americans and Israelites before the same church. Dodge wanted to augment the national pride of his Massachusetts community, when he stressed, just as Abiel Abbot had years before him, how divine government and virtue had distinguished Israel from all other nations. They were "a highly favoured people," he assured, emphasizing at the same time the "elected" status of Americans. Like many New England nationalists, he also urged his audience to teach their children about the unique character of the United States. Using the Israelites as an example, he wanted to encourage his congregation to tell the next generation of Americans about their people's special covenant with God. The people of Israel, he told them "were instructed to make known, and familiarize to their children [with] the wonderful interpositions of Heaven in behalf of their nation."[28]

The image of Americans as God's chosen children fulfilled a twofold purpose. It promoted American nationalism and at the same time defined the United States as a religious nation. At the time of the Second Great Awakening, when American Protestantism continued to split into different sects, the rhetoric about an American Israel offered stability and unity. Ministers were interested in defining Americans as a deeply religious people to promote their own profession and fill their churches. They wanted to avoid that secularism dominated American Republicanism. The English had perceived themselves as God's people, especially during the English Civil War under Oliver Cromwell. Cromwell had used such language to animate his army. The idea that God had chosen Americans instead of the English as his favored people endorsed feelings of American superiority toward the former mother country. Again although ministers preached that the entire nation had been chosen by God, all these sermons implied that New Englanders had very much contributed to this favorable condition. Most examples of God's providence for the American people that New England clergymen mentioned were examples from New England's history. Some clergymen, such as Samuel Dexter, talked specifically about "New Englanders" instead of "Americans."

Fitting in the Shakers

Congregationalists, Presbyterians, Baptists, Freewill Baptists, and Unitarians all helped shape a New England American identity in spite of their different doctrines and religious practices. These religious groups could cooperate because they still shared a common culture and loyalty to their region and nation. The Shakers, whose micro-societies had a different structure and were rather isolated from the dominant society's politics and events, did not participate in that creative process.

In their religious writings, Shakers did not comment on New England landscapes and characteristics, nor did they say anything about the British and the French or God's special relationship with the American people. The Shakers built villages throughout New England between the 1790s and the mid-1820s, and focused on their religious beliefs and practices of dancing and singing. Some New Englanders felt threatened by the growing sect because of its distinct lifestyle. Shakers lived in utopian communal villages. Their founder, Mother Ann Lee, established a celibate lifestyle and their communities were split into male and female living quarters, which clearly distinguished them from the typical New England village. In a society where private property was seen as an essential right, Shakers integrated their possessions in the communal property as soon as they entered the sect. Some New Englanders were afraid that the spreading Shaker culture threatened New England virtues. In reaction to those fears, Shakers were accused of robbing their members of their property and destroying families. Between 1818 and 1822 Mary Dyer, a woman who had lived with the Shakers after her husband's conversion, published pamphlets condemning the Shakers for drunkenness, fraud, lying, extreme abuse, and debauchery.[29]

But few New Englanders adopted such extreme views of the Shakers. Even if they found the Shakers' communal and gender-segregated life outlandish, they still tried somehow to integrate them into their image of New England and to discover some New England values in the Shaker communities. It is not surprising that New Englanders depicted the Shakers as a group destroying families and robbing their members of their property, but it is remarkable that they still made an effort to imagine the Shakers as fellow New Englanders. The New England American identity was so strong that New England intellectual leaders, as for example, Benjamin Silliman, attempted to fit them in the harmony of New England life that was so present in early Republican books, newspapers, and speeches. Consequently, a small controversy developed around Mary Dyer's book. A pamphlet denying Dyer's charges appeared in 1824, picturing the Shakers as honest, moral, kind, and charitable people. New Englanders were indeed able to find New England virtues such as modesty, simplicity, and industriousness in the Shaker villages because the Shakers pursued perfection and productivity, established prosperous villages, and created simple but practical furniture and buildings. Accounts that ascribed such characteristics to the Shakers enabled New Englanders to imagine the sect as a part of their region's culture, fitting the pattern at least in some respects. Most importantly, with their neat, industrious villages the Shakers seemed to help in cultivating the wild American landscape.

In his journal of his trip from Hartford to Quebec, Yale professor Benjamin Silliman expressed his perception of the Shakers as a group of hardworking, neat, and civilized people.

> "The utmost neatness is conspicuous in their fields, gardens, courtyards, out house, and in the very road; not a weed, not a spot of filth," he wrote. "Their wood is cut and piled, in the most exact order; their fences are perfect; even their walls are constructed with great regularity.... The production of their industry and skill... are distinguished by excellence of workmanship."

In 1817, the *Boston Weekly Magazine* stressed the Shakers' contribution to the civilization of the American wilderness. Not only did Shakers cultivate their kitchens, gardens, and fields, the Boston periodical claimed, but they even took excellent care of their lands. The article portrayed Shaker property as part of the American picturesque scenery:

> Even their mountains are capable of cultivation to their summits, and their hills and valleys rich in the production of every thing necessary for the sustenance of man. Here may the eye enjoy the magnificence of a mountain scenery, without the view of those huge and rugged precipices, those deep and gloomy glens, which usually compose and deform it. There is throughout the whole scene, a striking conformity of art to nature.

The Boston magazine even implied that the Shakers were good Republicans because their neighbors benefited from their example. With all their civilization, industry, modesty, and neatness, the article implied, the sect contributed to the common good. It also described the sect as an "enlightened" community.

Although some travelers described Shaker villages as part of the New England landscape, there were no paintings or engravings illustrating such accounts before the mid-1830s. The reason for this scarcity of Shaker village views might have been the Shakers' own disinterestedness in New England nationalism. To the degree the Shakers ignored the collective New England identity, their neighbors belonging to other religious groups defined their world in terms of their regional nationalism. Given this fact, it is even more surprising that New England travelers and newspaper editors depicted the sect as part of the New England landscape and people. New Englanders' search for their region's values in Shaker communities indicates an inclusive quality of early Republican collective identity in New England.[30]

The inhabitants of early Republican New England split into numerous different religious groups with diverse religious doctrines and practices. The argument, especially advocated by the Baptist Isaac Backus, against taxes supporting the region's traditional Congregational Church caused long disputes. Although the religious diversity certainly caused tensions, New Englanders belonging to different sects were unified by a strong Protestant New England American loyalty. The consciousness that they shared an idea and attachment to their region and nation helped early Republicans to unite across sectarian lines. Ministers of different denominations used the strong regional nationalism to promote religion in general and to win members for their church in particular. With an effective rhetoric defining New Englanders and Americans as God's chosen people, they forged the long-lasting tie between Protestantism and American nationalism. Their strategy was probably especially successful because they presented their ideas as the conclusion that emerged naturally from the region's history. Refurbished New England traditions defined New England America as a superior and Protestant nation.

With the New England virtue of religious freedom, early Republican ministers reinvented another tradition that strengthened the region's collective identity. By declaring freedom of religion a traditional New England right, religious leaders legitimized religious pluralism. Moreover, they transformed the religious diversity that resulted from religious freedom into a New England value. Inspired by their regionalist nationalism, New England ministers then imagined that the New England virtue had become a national virtue.

Gardiner Spring, for example, told the members of the New York New England Society how the entire nation had profited from the impact of New England's tradition of freedom of conscience and how religious freedom was now an American characteristic. Statements such as Spring's gave New Englanders who had left their region and moved to the new Western territories and Mid-Atlantic states a sense of pride that their migration had contributed to the spread of New England ways and Republicanism. Spring said: "That the American States have not been so slow to learn, is in no small degree owing to the high sense which our fathers cherished of the rights of conscience. It is now an unquestioned axiom, that religious freedom is the sacred and inviolable right of every man." Religious freedom, the Presbyterian pastor proudly continued, had been an American virtue admired by the entire Western world since the founding of the Plymouth colony and religious freedom was such an important element of the American identity that every patriot should celebrate and defend it. Speeches introducing first a collective image of America molded by New England values and secondly religious pluralism as a New England American virtue offered New Englanders an ideology that even celebrated their diverse religious beliefs and at the same time united them through a common pride in their region's superiority.[31]

While New Englanders excluded Europeans and Southerners from their imagined American identity, they attempted to include dissenting religious groups, including the Shakers. The effort of some New Englanders to reinvent the Shaker communities as a particular form of New England villages, in spite of the fact that the Shakers struck them as social and economic outsiders, indicates the strength and success of the regional American identity that emerged among the first independent generation. It was the pride in their region that shaped New Englanders' nationalism during the early years of the republic. With sectional differences becoming more and more obvious and even causing a federal crisis in 1819, New Englanders needed to keep the harmonious image of their region alive, even if it meant inclusion of utopian religious groups such as the Shakers.

Regional and national identities were tightly interwoven in New England in the late eighteenth century and early nineteenth century. This hybrid of loyalties was, of course, shaped by Protestantism. New England religious leaders played a crucial role in the creation of American nationalism in the early republic by uncompromisingly promoting a national identity, which was shaped by Protestantism. In a republic that granted religious freedom, the French example of secular Republicanism caused fears among the ministers that religious anarchy or blasphemy might soon define the new nation. The divisive experience of the partisan struggles between Federalists and Jeffersonian Republicans and the Second Great Awakening both provoked a desire for unity among New England religious leaders. While they advocated different doctrines, the various denominations shared a common interest in promoting Protestantism and piety in order to prevent a secularization of American Republicanism.

As a result New England religious leaders claimed that the survival, progress, and prosperity of the new nation depended on the piety of the people. They wanted their mass audiences to believe in Protestantism as the single most important value system in the American republic. Republicanism and Protestantism emerged as a strong ideological combination that defined early American nationalism.

Although ministers emerged as ardent advocates and engineers of the new nationalism, some identified flaws in the Republican ideology. They saw materialism, an emphasis on secular education, and frivolous forms of patriotic celebrations as dangerous side effects of the new Republican ideology that could eliminate Republican virtue. Sometimes new Republican values seemed to be built on Puritan traditions, which added a sense of collective history, but at other times ministers warned their audiences of the need to preserve those traditions against threatening elements of the market revolution and a Republican society. The religious character of American nationalism demonstrates the widespread success of the ministers' campaign.

Conclusion

In the years between 1789 and 1825, New Englanders struggled to define and redefine their identity in the newly created environment of the independent American nation. They inhabited a nation that had been an object of imperial greed for more than one and a half centuries; a nation most of whose culture was rooted in Europe and had no natural relation to the land. It had been the focus of struggle between the European great powers. It was a nation built on a Republican political system feared by its European counterparts because of its possible revolutionary influence in the old world. Europeans observers predicted the young American republic would not survive longer than a few years.

In this setting of European heritage and competition, New Englanders, as all Americans of the first independent generation, struggled with the classification of their new nation in the Atlantic world. As a result, an ambiguity between imitating European culture and rejecting old-world characteristics and ideals emerged as a central element of the new American nationalism. New Englanders selected some European values, such as those personified by the Prussian Frederick the Great and the French General Lafayette, as models. Others, however—above all collective characteristics that New Englanders ascribed to the British and the French—served as contrasts to their own American identity. Although early Republican New Englanders excluded Europeans from their imagined community, with these European elements their nationalism was nevertheless a transatlantic phenomenon.

The foundation of their nation led New Englanders not only to compare themselves with Europeans, but also with their Southern countrymen. The new American nation-state united former colonies with different social, economic, and cultural systems and forced its members to compromise. Regional differences and the size of the young nation encouraged New Englanders to imagine the nation in terms of their own region. They could only imagine their national community through the lens of their own New England culture. A regional nationalism thus emerged.

Although the common revolutionary cause against the British had initially united Northern and Southern colonies, the prevailing differences between the regions exerted a critical influence upon New Englanders' nationalism. Americans in Northern states close to New England, who were often migrants from the region, integrated themselves in this emerging sectional identity. Only some New Englanders wanted to break away from the South; but many thought Southerners should adopt New England values in order to become true Americans in the New England sense. In the New England mind, the American nation had to be New Englandized to fulfill the ideal of the New England model. To a certain degree New Englanders constructed their national identity in contrast to Southerners.

Both trends, the ambiguity toward Europe and the ideal of New England dominance within the nation, characterized American nationalism in New England from the late eighteenth century onward. While the images that defined the regional American nationalism did not change over time, the tone of its rhetoric became more assertive and the regional nationalistic ideas began to root deeper and deeper in the minds of ordinary people. The first pivotal step in that process was the election of 1800. Even if a Federalist culture persisted in New England after the Jeffersonian election, Jeffersonian politics and the rhetoric of the new social, economic, and political freedom convinced New Englanders to live in a privileged country enjoying all kinds of civil and religious liberties. This belief helped to increase the self-consciousness of young Republicans, especially when they compared themselves with Europeans. The idea that the new world was now superior to Europe became more and more persuasive. By 1825 New Englanders felt much more confident about the level of civilization of their nation in contrast to European countries. Especially after the War of 1812, the tone in statements excluding the British and the French from the imagined New England America became more aggressive, although a transatlantic culture continued. Although many New Englanders had not wanted the war initially, its outcome nonetheless confirmed some of the attributes their regional nationalism had praised. In the eyes of early Republicans, the War of 1812 proved the lasting quality of the young republic, its superiority over England, and God's favor of their country. Maybe even those New Englanders who had wanted to break away from the South were able to feel some pride or gain some belief in their nation as a whole after the Hartford Convention failed in initiating New England's secession from the union. A more accepting attitude toward the union could have led to confidence in American values and less dependence on

European culture among New Englanders, even if they still strongly believed that Southerners had to adopt New England values in order to become true Americans. After 1815, New Englanders still integrated European values and ideas into their own culture, and they still had an ambiguous attitude toward their contemporaries on the other side of the Atlantic, but they no longer felt so anxious about their own position. Moreover, they now had a pattern of established ideas and the experience of another military victory that in their minds raised their nation above European countries. After Federalists' aim at secession failed in the Hartford Convention, New Englanders began to sometimes emphasize their loyalty to the union and seemed to accept the union more easily. At the same time, they started to focus even more on promoting their rights and standing within the union by pushing the idea that Southerners had to go through a New Englandization before they could be accepted as true Americans.

Simultaneously, as their national confidence developed, New Englanders' regional self-respect grew. In the first three decades of the nineteenth century, they became more and more convinced of the legitimacy of New England's dominance within the United States. This is particularly obvious in the successful regionalist rhetoric that proponents of the separation of Maine from Massachusetts used in their campaign. The events of the Hartford Convention show how substantiated the regional consciousness was in 1815. At this moment, some political leaders of the region were willing to announce secessionist aims. After the war, sectional tensions seemed to have grown more powerful than ever before.

New Englanders' feeling of superiority toward the South was a double-edged sword. At the same time when they took increased pride in their New England America, New Englanders also became anxious about the divisive force of that regional American identity. Their solution to the problem was to New Englandize the rest of the nation, as actually happened in some frontier areas settled by New England migrants. This attitude that all Americans should adopt the exemplary Republican virtues of New England only slowly widened the gap between North and South. The sectionalism that shaped the United States from the late 1850s on emerged in the first half of the century largely in New England.

The Missouri Compromise of 1820 is a crucial marker in the hesitant process of the emergence of sectionalism in New England. Ironically, Mainers could only achieve their goal of fulfilling the New England American ideal and becoming perfect New England Americans by allowing the institution of slavery to expand. This is also a moment when New Englanders began slowly to recognize the sectionalist character of their regional nationalism. Especially from 1820 on the ministry addressed the issue in their sermons, when they emphasized that they were loyal to the nation in spite of their deep pride in their region. This awareness did not weaken the regional nationalism; to the contrary, it rather increased its intensity. After 1819, New Englanders imagined their American identity more distinct and superior to a Southern identity than ever before. In the early 1820s the new sense of separate tensions created insecurity among the region's inhabitants, but the concept of New England as the embodiment of America, and the region's mission to New Englandize the rest of the country, had grown so strong that it dominated the public mind. A widespread idea of New England as a model for American nationalism, Republicanism, and Protestantism created strong feelings of pride, belonging, stability, and superiority among New Englanders, which diminished worries about sectional sentiments.

The aim to spread New England nationalism throughout the country was interwoven with early antebellum reform movements. Propagating moral values such as sobriety, self-control, and religiosity, reformers could find their own values even in the Spartan self-discipline of the Prussian King Frederick II or the selfless generosity to the American people of General Lafayette. Not only did the virtues of the missionary societies and the New England nationalist ideology overlap, but it was also often the same people who created and promoted missionary and nationalist ideas. Many advocates of the new regional nationalism were members of one or more reformist societies. In addition to the important role the New England ministry played as propagandists for the regional nationalism, and the inherent praise of Protestantism as part of the general nationalist rhetoric, this link between the missionary societies and New England nationalism is a strong indicator for a symbiosis of Protestantism and nationalism in early Republican New England. In late eighteenth- and early nineteenth-century America, nationalism did not fill the need for explanations for human suffering and death caused by an enlightened secularization as argued by Benedict Anderson. In New England, the older religious and newer nationalist ideologies rather merged. Together, religion and nationalism provided New England leaders with a strong pattern of ideas. These enabled them to evoke loyalty to the young American nation, unite New Englanders of different sexes, social class, from urban coastal centers, and rural frontier areas, adjusting them to the social, political, and economic system that resulted from the founding of the republic and the market revolution.

The new nationalism combined two ideological strains that had played an important role in bringing about the American Revolution: the heritage of Puritan religious importance and religious impulse from the First Great Awakening on one hand, and the Enlightenment values of Revolutionary leaders such as Benjamin Franklin on the other. In their writings, speeches, paintings, and craftwork, advocates of New England nationalism emphasized the combination of piety and Republicanism over and over again. In the imagery of early Republican nationalism, New Englanders and their model Frederick the Great embodied Republican as well as Protestant virtues.

When New Englanders compared themselves with the British and the French, they also emphasized their own Republican virtue and the failure of contemporary Europeans to live up to those standards. They, of course, contrasted their own Protestant virtues with French Catholic vices and even distinguished their own religious virtuosity from the corrupt English Protestantism. Denominational differences did not interfere with this collective Protestant identity. Moreover, New England nationalism created a feeling of Protestant unity among people belonging to different religious groups. Congregational, Presbyterian, Baptist, Methodist, and Unitarian ministers cooperated in creating and promoting the Protestant New England American identity.

The regional nationalism emerging in early Republican New England constituted the major force that united the region's people across denominational, party, gender, class, and geographical lines. New Englanders' lifestyles and attitudes differed depending on whether they sympathized with Federalists or Democratic Republicans, whether they lived in Boston or Fryeburg, Maine, whether they worked as a farmer or a manufacturer, whether they were Congregationalists or the Baptists. They were all confronted with the same nationalist rhetoric and images in their daily lives. Of course, we have to take their different backgrounds into account when we think about their collective identity. The texts and images that were part of the nationalist propaganda have to be seen as events that changed slightly with every reader or observer. Different audiences reacted and interpreted nationalistic pieces differently. A story about General Lafayette's aristocratic origin and wealth, for example, could have been used to argue that luxury could not disguise a model Republican, but also that a virtuous Republican did not desire such wealth, and values such as freedom were much more important to him.[1]

The nationalist rhetoric appealed to various groups of New Englanders because it included a cluster of different, at times ambiguous, values. Although it praised economic progress as part of the civilization process, it always placed it in a rural setting, underlining the agricultural character of the New England nation. Such images probably pleased both Federalists and Jeffersonian Republicans. Furthermore, the emphasis on the civilization of the wilderness appealed to Boston's great proprietors, who invested in frontier lands; but as long as it somehow enabled frontier settlers to find themselves and their contribution to that cultivation in such pictures as well, they joined their wealthy counterparts in identifying with it. This becomes especially clear in the final phase of Maine's statehood movement. As soon as separatists included frontier settlers in their campaign, the movement was able to unite the people from the coast and the hinterland successfully. Depictions of industrial enterprises in Western and Northern New England evoked hopes among rural people to soon live in a world that combined the best of the agricultural and industrial sector. Especially when they read about the corrupt commercialism in England and the poverty it created in the dirty industrial cities, they thought more positively of New England mills built in small towns and surrounded by farmland. New England nationalists created images and descriptions of the region's landscapes and towns that were stylized and thus New Englanders living in many different places could identify with them. Notions that the New England way was spreading created collective hopes that even if local conditions were not yet ideal, they could still be transformed by establishing regional virtues.

Encouraged by books, newspaper articles, and pictures decorating their homes, New Englanders envisioned their region to be a place superior to Europe and also to the Southern states, a place that embodied true American values and defined the young American nation. This belief helped to even out political, economic, and religious differences between them, and enabled them to cope with social and economic changes caused by the market revolution.

The symbiotic combination of regionalism, nationalism, and Protestantism distinguishes early American nationalism in New England from modern European nationalism that emerged simultaneously on the other side of the Atlantic. In some European nations, as for example, in France, nationalism gave birth to a more centralized collective identity, which was supposed to eradicate regional loyalties. In contrast to many European leaders, the New England elite utilized regional loyalty to establish a strong national identity.

Notes

Introduction

1. See David Potter, "The Historian's Use of Nationalism and Vice Versa," in Don Fehrenbach, ed., *History and American Society: Essays of David M. Potter* (New York: Oxford University Press, 1973), 75.
2. Perry Miller introduced the term the "New England mind" in his sequence *The New England Mind: The Seventeenth Century* (New York: Macmillan, 1939) and *The New England Mind: From Colony to Province* (Cambridge, Massachusetts: Harvard University Press, 1953), x. For the new understanding of nations as inventions, see Benedict Anderson, *Imagined Communities: Reflections on the Origins and Spread of Nationalism* (London: Verso, first published, 1983, revised edition, 1991); Eric Hobsbawm, *Nations and Nationalism since 1780: Programme, Myth, Reality* (Cambridge, England: Cambridge University Press, 1990); and Eric Hobsbawm and Terence Ranger, eds., *The Invention of Tradition* (Cambridge and New York: Cambridge University Press, 1983). For this approach, see also Ernest Gellner, *Nations and Nationalism* (Oxford: Oxford University Press, 1983).
3. David Waldstreicher, *In the Midst of Perpetual Fetes: The Making of American Nationalism, 1776–1820* (Chapel Hill, London: University of North Carolina Press, 1997). Linda Kerber, *Federalists in Dissent, Imagery and Ideology in Jeffersonian America* (Ithaca: Cornell University Press, 1970).
4. P. Simon Newman, *Parades and the Politics of the Street: Festive Culture in the Early American Republic* (Philadelphia: University of Pennsylvania Press, 1997); Len Travers, *Celebrating the Fourth: Independence Day and the Rites of Nationalism in the Early Republic* (Amherst: University of Massachusetts Press, 1997). In their important works Waldstreicher, Newman, and Travers stress the role of ordinary Americans in the formation of a national political culture in the early republic. They argue that ordinary Americans challenged the hegemony of the elites, when they participated in public rituals and festivities. This culture, they emphasize, was molded by political partisanship. Waldstreicher shows how Federalists and Democratic Republicans used print culture to claim legitimacy and delegitimize their opponents. Federalists promoted order and state authority, while Republicans propagated popular sovereignty. See Joyce Appleby,

Inheriting the Revolution: The First Generation of Americans (London: Harvard University Press, 2000).

5. Timothy H. Breen, "Ideology and Nationalism on the Eve of the American Revolution: Revisions Once More in Need of Revising," *Journal of American History* 84 (June 1997): 34.
6. Engaging with the work of historians such as Linda Colley and John Brewer, who show how Britons in the eighteenth century constructed their national identity against the French, can help Americanists to uncover further exclusionary tendencies of early American nationalism. John Brewer, *The Pleasures of the Imagination: English Culture in the Eighteenth Century* (London: Fontana Press, 1997); Linda Colley, *Britons: Forging the Nation 1707–1837* (London: Pimlico, 1992). A good summary of the character of the New England identity from the region's first settlement to the mid-twentieth century is Joseph Conforti's *Imagining New England: Explorations of Regional Identity from the Pilgrims to the Mid-Twentieth Century* (Chapel Hill: University of North Carolina Press, 2001). Conforti gives an overview of the development and change of New England regionalism over a long time period, but he does not place it into a transatlantic context. For a strong argument on how wealthy Northerners and Southerners in Philadelphia united along class lines and were bound together through education, lifestyle, and a distrust of the capacity of ordinary people see Daniel Kilbride, *An American Aristocracy: Southern Planters in Antebellum Philadelphia* (Columbia: University of South Carolina Press, 2006).
7. A study that describes exactly this process of isolation from the familiar community and new social relationships at the workplace is Paul Johnson, *A Shopkeeper's Millennium: Society and Revivals in Rochester, New York, 1815–1837* (New York: Hill and Wang, 1978). Johnson takes Rochester, New York, as an example, but economic change caused the same transformation in many small New England towns. For the social and economic changes brought about by the market revolution, see Charles Sellers, *The Market Revolution: Jacksonian America, 1815–1846* (New York: Oxford University Press, 1991). Although Sellers focuses on the three decades following the War of 1812, some of the developments and effects of the market revolution that he describes can be found in the two decades before. Steve Watts scrutinizes the impact of the market revolution in the period between 1790 and 1820; see Steve Watts, *The Republic Reborn: War and the Making of Liberal America, 1790–1820* (Baltimore: John Hopkins University Press, 1987). He shows how the production for the market transformed the social perception, political judgments, economic endeavor, and private sensibility.
8. In his pathbreaking study of reading in rural New England, William Gilmore shows that even New Englanders in remote areas had access to European publications; see William Gilmore, *Reading Becomes a*

Necessity of Life: Material and Cultural Life in Rural New England, 1780–1835 (Knoxville: University of Tennessee Press, 1989). Biographical essays of the architects of the New England nationalist ideology in the *American National Biography* show their various backgrounds and their common education, transatlantic interest and activity in missionary, literary, and scientific institutions; see *American National Biography*, ed. John Arthur Garraty and Mark Christopher Carnes (New York, Oxford University Press, 1999).

9. For the sewing box Jane Otis Prior made, see Nina Fletcher Little, *Neat and Tidy: Boxes and Their Contents Used in Early American Households* (New York: E. P. Dutton, 1980), 136–137. With their engagement with the full range of material culture the works of Linda Colley and John Brewer served as a model for this study. Brewer and Colley illustrate how paintings, household decorations, and utensils can not only contribute to our understanding of the character of the collective identity that was invented, but also of the interaction between elites and masses; see Colley, *Britons* and Brewer, *The Pleasures of the Imagination*. Another outstanding study of collective identity that uses visual sources is Simon Schama's *Embarrassment of Riches: An Interpretation of Dutch Culture in the Golden Age* (New York: Knopf, 1987).
10. Appleby, *Inheriting the Revolution*. In her study of the first generation of Americans after American Independence, Appleby studies the new collective identity on the national level and convincingly argues that the North shaped the image of the new nation. Appleby gives a vivid description of that Northern image, on which I want to build in this book and take her argument a little further to claim that New England played a dominant role in shaping that image.
11. Eckhart Hellmuth's analyses of the cult of the Frederick II after his death in 1786 in Germany inspired my study of the strikingly similar celebration of the Prussian monarch in New England; see Eckhart Hellmuth, "A Monument to Frederick the Great: Architecture, Politics and the State in Late Eighteenth-Century Prussia," in *Rethinking Leviathan: The Eighteenth-Century State in Britain and Germany*, ed. John Brewer and Eckhart Hellmuth (London: German Historical Institute; Oxford: Oxford University Press, 1999) and Eckhart Hellmuth, "Die 'Wiedergeburt' Friedrichs' des Großen und der 'Tod fürs Vaterland': Zum Patriotischen Selbstverständnis in Preußen in der zweiten Hälfte des 18. Jahrhunderts," in *Nationalismus vor dem Nationalismus*, ed. Reinhard Stauber and Eckhart Hellmuth (Hamburg: F. Meier, 1998). Hellmuth engages a wide range of visual sources; my research suggests that with a few exceptions such sources do not exist in the New England version of the story. For the popular image of George Washington I relied on Paul Longmore, *The Invention of George Washington* (Berkeley: University of California Press, 1989) and Patricia Anderson, *Promoted to Glory: The Apotheosis*

of George Washington (Northampton, Massachusetts: Smith College Museum of Art, 1980), which gives a great overview over the visual depictions of the first president. An excellent study of the transformation of a popular leader into a symbol for his times is John William Ward's book on the celebration of Andrew Jackson as a popular hero, *Andrew Jackson: Symbol of an Age* (New York: Oxford University Press, 1953).

12. The idea to study how New Englanders used the British and the French as juxtapositions for their own identity sprang from Linda Colley's argument that the British constructed their collective identity in opposition to what they imagined to be the national character of the French, see Colley, *Britons*, 5. Here she summarizes:

    Time and time again, war with France brought Britons, whether they hailed from Wales or Scotland or England, into confrontation with an obviously hostile Other and encouraged them to define themselves collectively against it. They defined themselves as Protestants struggling for survival against the world's foremost Catholic power. They defined themselves against the French as they imagined them to be, superstitious, militarist, decadent and unfree.

13. Most works on Lafayette's tour through the United States in 1824 were published a few decades ago, as, e.g., Anne C. Loveland, *Emblem of Liberty: The Image of Lafayette in the American Mind* (Baton Rouge: Louisiana State University Press, 1971) and Marian Klamkin, *The Return of Lafayette, 1824–1825* (New York: Charles Scribner's Sons, 1975) and there was a need for a new study of the event. But also more recent works such as Lloyd Kramer's *Lafayette in Two Worlds: Public Cultures and Personal Identities in an Age of Revolution* (Chapel Hill: University of North Carolina Press, 1996) explain the unifying effect of Lafayette celebrations and point to the creation of Revolutionary memory during the ceremonies, but they do not place the Frenchman's visit in the context of regional nationalism. Furthermore, these works do not trace the issue of anti-French propaganda in biographies of Lafayette.
14. The most recent publication on the movement for Maine statehood is Ronald Banks's *Maine Becomes a State: The Movement to Separate Maine from Massachusetts, 1785–1820* (Middletown, Connecticut: Wesleyan University Press, 1970), which is a traditional history that provides the basic events, numbers, and chronology of the movement as well as a descriptive summary of the ongoing debate between separatists and their opponents in the Portland newspapers. An interesting selection of essays on religion, economy, architecture, and statehood in early Republican Maine is *Maine in the Early Republic: From Revolution to Statehood*, ed. Charles Clark, James Leamon, and Karen Bowden (Hanover: University Press of New England, 1988). Alan Taylor's analysis of the struggle for Maine lands between frontier

settlers and Massachusetts' great proprietors lays out the cultural, social, political, and economic differences between Maine and Massachusetts; see Alan Taylor, *Liberty Men and Great Proprietors: The Revolutionary Settlement on the Maine Frontier, 1760–1820* (Chapel Hill: University of North Carolina Press, 1990).

15. In their studies of the Great Awakening in New York City and Rochester, New York, Paul Johnson and Carroll Smith Rosenberg emphasize the strong political and cultural influence of evangelist ministers; see Paul Johnson, *A Shopkeeper's Millennium: Society and Revivals in Rochester, New York, 1815–1837* (New York: Hill and Wang, 1978) and Carroll Smith Rosenberg, *Religion and the Rise of the American City: The New York City Mission Movement, 1812–1870* (Ithaca: Cornell University Press, 1971). The best study of New England ministers in the early republic is Jonathan Sassi, *A Republic of Righteousness: The Public Christianity of the Post-Revolutionary New England Clergy* (New York: Oxford University Press, 2001).

Chapter 1 New Englandizing America

1. Joyce Appleby makes a strong argument that the new American nation emerged in the image of the North, see Joyce Appleby, *Inheriting the Revolution: The First Generation of Americans* (London: Harvard University Press, 2000). See also David Waldstreicher, *In the Midst of Perpetual Fetes: The Making of American Nationalism, 1776–1820* (Chapel Hill, London: University of North Carolina Press, 1997) and Lewis P. Simpson, *Mind and the American Civil War: A Meditation on Lost Causes* (Baton Rouge: Louisiana State University Press, 1989). For a similar argument on early Republican regionalism in New England, see Joseph Conforti, *Imagining New England: Explorations of Regional Identity from the Pilgrims to the Mid-Twentieth Century* (Chapel Hill: University of North Carolina Press, 2001). For the clash of New England ideals with the emerging entertainment culture in New York City, see Edwin Burrows and Mike Wallace, *Gotham: A History of New York City to 1898* (New York: Oxford University Press, 1999), 452–455.
2. The first institution that resulted from the movement was the Massachusetts Historical Society, founded in 1791, followed by the Boston Athenaeum, founded in 1807, the American Antiquarian Society, founded in 1812, the Rhode Island Historical Society, founded in 1822, and numerous state and local societies established in the following one and a half centuries. See Julian P. Boyd, "State and Local Historical Societies in the United States," *The American Historical Review* 40 (1934): 10–34. Boyd argues that the movement was clearly dominated by New England: "A fact which remains substantially true to the present time is that historical societies were most numerous and drew the widest support in the areas covered by

New England expansion; the Southern states have never, until very recent years, revealed a commensurate interest in such institutions" (15–16). See Wilbur Zelinsky, *Nation into State: The Shifting Symbolic Foundations of American Nationalism* (Chapel Hill: University of North Carolina Press, 1988), 221, 230. On Southerners' ideas about their history and landscape, see Joan Cashin, "Landscape and Memory in Antebellum Virginia," *Virginia Magazine of History and Biography* 4 (1994): 477–500. Hannah Adams, *A Summary History of New England* (Dedham, Massachusetts: H. Mann and J.H. Adams, 1799); Hannah Adams, *An Abridgement of the History of New England* (Boston: Etheridge and Bliss 1805, 1807). It was also printed in Boston, by Belcher and Armstrong, 1807 and reprinted in London, by Morris, Dunstable, 1806; Jeremy Belknap, *History of New Hampshire* (Dover, New Hampshire: J. Mann and J.K. Remick, 1812). A first edition of Belknap's history was published in Boston in 1791 and reprinted in 1792 and 1793; an unauthorized version appeared in Boston in 1813; William Bradford, *A Descriptive and Historical Account of New England in Verse* (Boston: Munroe and Francis, 1794); William Hubbard, *A General History of New England from the Discovery to MDCLXXX* (Cambridge: Hilliard and Metcalf, 1815); Thomas Hutchinson, *The History of Massachusetts from the First Settlement* (Boston: Manning and Loring, 1795, 1803). It was also published in London in 1795; Jedidiah Morse, *A Compendious History of New England Designed for Schools and Private Families* (Newburyport, Massachusetts: Thomas and Whipple, 1809); Thomas Robbins, *An Historical View of the First Planters of New England* (Hartford, Connecticut: Gleason and Co., 1815). "New England's Memorial by Nathaniel Morton," *The Monthly Anthology and Boston Review* 7 (1809): 62–67; "History of New England by Daniel Neal," *The Monthly Anthology and Boston Review* 7 (1809): 346–352, 414–421; "Neal's History of New England," *The Monthly Anthology and Boston Review* 8 (1810): 105–106; "Review of an Abridgement of the History of New England for the Use by Hannah Adams," *The Monthly Anthology and Boston Review* 2 (1805): 538–541; "A Compendious History of New England by Jedidiah Morse," *The Monthly Anthology and Boston Review* 2 (1805): 541–548; "Review of an Abridged History of New England by Hannah Adams," *The Literary Miscellany* 2 (1806): 291–295; "The Literary Review: A Summary History of New England by Hannah Adams," *The Columbian Phenix and Boston Review* 1 (1800): 129–132; "Adams' History of New England," *Portfolio* 4 (1807): 309–310; "Adams' History of New England," *The Monthly Magazine and American Review* 1 (1799): 445–449; "Belknap's Observation on History," *The American Museum or Universal Magazine* 7 (1789): 294. Even medical doctors studied these histories; see "Nathaniel Morton's New England Memorial," *Philadelphia Medical and Physical Journal* 1 (1804): 59.

3. "Review of an Abridgement of the History by Hannah Adams," 538–540. See also "Adams' History of New England," 445. Here the reviewer wrote: "A succinct, clear, comprehensive, and judicious view of the subject she has chosen, seems to have been the only scope of her ambition. Minute details and intricate inquiries, were foreign to her plan." Other examples are "Review of an Abridged History of New England by Hannah Adams," 291–295; "The Literary Review," 129–130; "A compendious History of Newengland by Jedidiah Morse," *The Monthly Anthology and Boston Review* 2 (1805): 541–548.
4. George B. Kirsch, "Jeremy Belknap: Man of Letters in the Young Republic," *New England Quarterly* 54 (1981): 33–53 and Leonard Tucker, *Clio's Consort: Jeremy Belknap and the Founding of the Massachusetts Historical Society* (Boston: Northeastern University Press, 1990).
5. John McAleer, *Ralph Waldo Emerson: Days of Encounter* (Boston: Little, Brown, 1984) and Evelyn Barish, *Emerson: The Roots of Prophecy* (Princeton: Princeton University Press, 1989).
6. Conforti, *Imagining New England*, 82. James N. Green, *Mathew Carey, Publisher and Patriot* (Philadelphia: The Library Company of Philadelphia, 1985) and Richard C. Cole, *Irish Booksellers and English Writers* (London: Mansell, 1987).
7. "Review of an Abridgement of the History of Newengland for the Use by Hannah Adams," 538. See also Robbins, *An Historical View of the First Planters*, 247. Here Robbins wrote: "The settlement of New-England is a very important event in the history of mankind." Brissot de Warville, *New Travels in the United States* (Boston: J. Bumstead, 1797), 59. John Melish, *Travels through the United States in the Years 1806, 1807, and 1809, 1810 & 1811* (Philadelphia: T. and G. Palmer, 1815, reprinted, 1970), 70; Benjamin Silliman, *Remarks, Made on a Short Tour between Hartford and Quebec, in the Autumn of 1819* (New Haven: S. Converse, 1820), 40; "Tour in New England by an Englishman," *The Connecticut Magazine or Gentlemen's and Ladies' Monthly Museum* 1 (1801): 14. Timothy Dwight tried to awake his readers' interest in history even in his travel descriptions by stressing its importance again and again; see Timothy Dwight, *Travels in New England and New York* (New Haven: S. Converse, 1821–1822). One example is as follows: "No sober New Englander can read the history of his country without rejoicing that god had caused him to spring from the loins of such ancestors, and given him his birth in a country whose public concern were entrusted by their management" (Vol. I, 121). Another example is in his account of Plymouth: "The remainder of the day we spent with our Plymouth friends in examining the antiquities of this place, so interesting to every New Englander" (Vol. II, p. 4). "Adams' History of New England," *The Monthly Magazine and American Review* 1 (1799): 445. See also "Cursory Thoughts on the first Settlement of New England," *The American Museum or Universal*

Magazine 5 (1789): 46. The author saw history as essential because of its educational effect: "The history of one's nation, and the principal events that take place in it, in a country like ours, the generality of the people may be well acquainted...And such an acquaintance, I am persuaded, would have the happiest effect upon civil and religious life. History hath been defined 'as philosophy reaching by example.'"

8. "The Literary Review: A Summary History of New-England by Hannah Adams," 129; "A Historical View of the First Planters of New England," *The Connecticut Evangelical Magazine and Religious Intelligencer* 4 (1812): 361. See also Robbins, *An Historical View of the First Planters*, 14:

   > To the fortitude, to the labour, of our ancestors, we are indebted for the inheritance of these fruitful fields which were cleared by their toil and defended by their valour. From their wisdom and virtue, we have received a still more precious heritage, in those social institutions, civil, moral, and literary, which are the source of our undisturbing prosperity. From their piety, their faith, their prayers, have been transmitted to their descendants, the order, improvement, and purity of our churches, with all those...institutions, which now constitute the distinguished ornament of this portion of our country.

   In "The Character of New England Colonists," *The American Review and Literary Journal* 2 (1802): 480, the publishers wrote as follows: "We shall be happy hereafter to witness, on subjects of greater magnitude and more durable interest....Nothing can tend more to invigorate the generous feelings of our nature than the habitual recollections of the virtues, the sufferings, and constancy of those from whom we derive our birth." Perry Miller, *Errand into the Wilderness* (Cambridge: Belknap Press, 1956), 1–15; Sacvan Bercovitch, *The Puritan Origins of the American Self* (New Haven: Yale University Press, 1975); Waldstreicher, *Perpetual Fetes*, 251–269.

9. See, e.g., "The Character of New England Colonists," *The American Review and Literary Journal* 2 (1802): 480–483; "Circumstances, which Formed the Character of New England Inhabitants," *The Monthly Register, Magazine and Review of the United States* (New York) 1 (1805); and William Tappan, *New England and Other Poems* (Philadelphia: J.H. Cunningham, 1819).

10. Compare Waldstreicher, *Perpetual Fetes*, 255–256. As examples for the numerous accounts on celebrations, see "The Character of New England Colonists," 480–483 and Abiel Abbott, *A Discourse Delivered at Plymouth December 22, 1809, at the Celebration of the 188th Anniversary of Our Forefathers in that Place* (Boston: n.p., 1810). For the New England Society of New York, see *The New England Society Orations: Addresses, Sermons, and Poems Delivered before the New England Society in the City of New York, 1820–1885*,

ed. Cephas Brainers and Eveline Warner Brainers (New York: The Century, 1901). For the New England Society of Philadelphia, see Tappan, *New England and Other Poems.*

11. "Circumstances, which Formed the Character of New England Inhabitants," 64; Dwight, *Travels*, II, 204–205, and also 218–219. Other examples are "A Historical View of the First Planters of New England," 448. Here the author concluded his description of the American wilderness with picturing the Pilgrims "in a most howling wilderness, inhabited by pagan savages and wild beasts, a dreary winter approaching, no shelter from the tempest, and, as yet, no place of abode." In "A Historical View of the First Planters of New England," *The Connecticut Evangelical Magazine and Religious Intelligencer* 6 (1813), the following description appears: "They were surrounded with numerous savage enemies. They were few in number. Their country and climate was unfavorable to any rapid advancement. A great portion of people were destitute of property and whole unacquainted with the labor of wilderness" (49). The author also praised the Puritans for undertaking the adventure: "It is not easy to conceive of a greater undertaking than that of a man who leads a colony to a distant wilderness" (42). "Conduct of the People of New England," *The Monthly Register, Magazine and Review of the United Sates* 1 (1805): 242. Here Plymouth Rock is depicted as "a barren wilderness, inhabited only by savage men and beasts." See also Tappan, *New England and Other Poems*, 6.
12. "It communicated to the emigrants, those wonderful energies of mind and body which enabled them to triumph over all obstructions, and to draw from an inhospitable, savage country, at once, a tolerable support, soon a comfortable livelihood, and ultimately, immense affluence, with refinement and luxuries." See "Circumstances, which Formed the Character of New England Inhabitants," 64; Charles Shaw, *Topographical and Historical Description of Boston* (Boston: Oliver Spear, 1817), 148. See also "The Character of New England Colonists," 481. In his speech at the annual festival of the first colonists John Quincy Adams described how they moved to an "untried soil, a rigorous climate and a savage wilderness for the sake of reconciling their sense of religious duty." "Cursory Thoughts on the first Settlement of New England," 45–46.
13. "A Historical View of the First Planters of New England," 89. See also "Circumstances, which Formed the Character of New England Inhabitants." The author stressed that "love of freedom was the predominating feature of their character" (57). Later he concluded his description of the civilization of the wilderness with the following words: "By those sons of hardihood and enthusiasm was New England first peopled" (65). In "The Character of New England Colonists," 480–481, the author listed the virtues of New England settlers as follows: "Christian grace, patience and heroic martyrdom"

(480), and emphasized the religious reasons for their emigration from England. They moved to an "untried soil, a rigorous climate and a savage wilderness for the sake of reconciling their sense of religious duty ..." (481). Dwight, *Travels*, I, 122. Dwight appealed to his readers to connect the contemporary New England landscape with the character of the inhabitants:

> Had you traced the hardships and discouragements with which these settlements were made, had you seen the wilderness converted by them into fruitful fields, had you surveyed the numerous, cheerful, and beautiful towns and villages which under their forming hand have sprung up into desert, you would regard this mighty work as an unanswerable and delightful proof of both the enterprise and the industry of this extraordinary people.

14. "Circumstances, which Formed the Character of New England Inhabitants," 57.
15. "A Historical View of the First Planters of New England," 41. "Cursory Thoughts on the first Settlement of New England," 46. For divine providence in general, see also Elias Boudinot, *Elias Boudinot's Journey to Boston in 1809*, ed. Milton Halsey Thomas (Princeton: Princeton University Press, 1955), 78 and Robbins, *An Historical View of the First Planters*, 60–61, 69, 75, 241–243. As another example for God's influence on the Indians, see "A Historical View of the First Planters of New England," 449: "They had now to contend with the inclement seasons, with innumerable privations, in a constant fear of a savage foe. But God has prepared their way before them. A desolating plague, which prevailed among the natives about three years before, had nearly depopulated those parts of the country." See also, Simpson, *Mind and the American Civil War*, 44.
16. Such souvenirs were, e.g., copies of Benjamin Burt's tankard with an engraved view of the Charles River; see Benjamin Burt, Silver Tankard, Boston, ca. 1786, in *Eighteenth-Century American Arts: The M. and M. Karolik Collection*, ed. Edwin J. Hipkiss (Cambridge, Massachusetts: Harvard University Press, 1941), 221.
17. Melish, *Travels through the United States*, 70; Warville, *New Travels in the United States*, 59; Silliman, *Remarks, Made on a Short Tour*, 40; William Strickland, *Journal of a Tour in the United States of America, 1794–1795*, ed. J.E. Strickland (New York Historical Society, 1971), 209; "Tour in New England by an Englishman," 14. He continued, "I was agreeably surprised to find this convenience [of a coach], instead of the open caravan in the Pennsylvania and New York states. I observed also with pleasure... the attention and excellent accommodation on the road." See also Belknap, *History of New Hampshire*, 61. Here he wrote: "Within these last twenty years, the country has been much improved in respect to roads; and the communication between the distant parts of it is become, in a great measure, easy and commodious." In Dwight, *Travels*, II, 146, He

wrote about roads in Maine: "The road from Brunswick to Bath…is in the main a good one.…A new one is nearly finished in the turnpike manner." Sarah Weld Clark Crehore, *Journal of a Trip to Maine*, 1807, Crehore Family Papers, Massachusetts Historical Society, Boston. Philip Stansbury wrote the following about Montpelier, Vermont: "The hotels shone bright from their windows," Philip Stansbury, *A Pedestrian Tour of Two Thousand Three Hundred Miles, in North America: To the Lakes,—the Canadas,—and the New England States, Performed in the Autumn of 1821* (New York: Myers and Smith, 1822), 238. For a remark on the elegance of the bridge he crossed from Cambridge to Boston, see also Boudinot, *Journey to Boston in 1809*, 33.

18. Dwight, *Travels*, II, 99. See also Belknap, *History of New Hampshire*, 56: "Amidst these wild and rugged scenes, it is amusing to observe the luxuriant sportings of nature. Trees are seen growing on a naked rock; their roots either penetrate some of its crevices, or run over its surface." See also, "New England, a Poem by William Morrell," *The American Apollo* 1 (1792). In the introduction the author said about the land: "It hath not at any time been manured and husbanded, yet it is very beautiful in open lands, mixed with godly woods, and again open plaines" (124). "Account of the White Mountains," *The Journal of Science and the Arts* 2 (1817): 392–399.
19. Boudinot, *Journey to Boston*, 24. Dwight, *Travels*, II, 99. For a comparable characterization of the landscape around Burlington, Vermont, see Henry Gilpin, *A Northern Tour: Being a Guide to Saratoga, Lake George, Niagra, Canada, Boston Etc.* (Philadelphia: H.C. Carey and I. Lea, 1825), 238. Here he wrote: "The hills presenting many handsome acclivities, show us flourishing farms, advancing rapidly towards a thorough cultivation. Often behind them, and often rising immediately from the road, objects invested with awful grandeur, are finely contrasted with this smiling scenery. On the north side…rocks…form wild, rugged and magnificent counterparts to the rude mountains on the eastern continent." Philip Stansbury gave a very similar description of the Burlington area: "The river flows through a gap between the mountains, where some violent convulsion has rent them asunder, and after dashing down ledges of rocks, rolls past our feet, black and deep, and spreads away upon the left amongst islands and flowery meadows" (Stansbury, *A Pedestrian Tour*, 236).
20. George Adams Boyd, *Elias Boudinot* (Princeton: Princeton University Press, 1952).
21. Dwight, *Travels*, II, 82. Deering, Journey from Falmouth to Boston, 1814, Maine Historical Society. Elias Boudinot described the coastal countryside North of Boston, between Ipswich and Newbury, simply as "broken and rough." Good roads were not enough to get him excited; see Boudinot, *Journey to Boston*, 57. In

the closing chapter of his book "The Wilderness Should Turn a Mart," William Cronon explains how the European Americans' civilization of the wilderness had changed New England's ecological system by 1800; see William Cronon, *Changes in the Land: Indians Colonists, and the Ecology of New England* (New York: Hill and Wang, 1983), 159–170. For the perception of the American wilderness, see John William Ward, *Andrew Jackson. Symbol of an Age* (New York: Oxford Univ. Press, 1953), 40. Compare Roderick Nash, *Wilderness and the American Mind* (New Haven: Yale University Press, 1967), 55–60.

22. See Peter M. Briggs, "Timothy Dwight 'Composes' a Landscape for New England," *American Quarterly* 40 (1988): 359–377 and John F. Sears, "T. Dwight and the American Landscape," *Early American Literature* 11 (1976–1977): 311–321. For an excellent study of the cult of the picturesque in eighteenth-century England, see John Brewer, *The Pleasures of the Imagination: English Culture in the Eighteenth Century* (London: Fontana Press, 1997). Even a tourist pocket book taught its readers about picturesque views of nature and towns; see George Temple, *The American Tourist's Pocket Companion, or, A Guide to the Springs and Trip to the Lakes* (New York: D. Lonwoth, 1812), 57, 62.

23. Silliman, *Remarks, Made on a Short Tour*, 11, 13. For other examples of these picturesque ideas, see W.L. Smith, Journal of 1790–91, *Proceedings of the Massachusetts Historical Society* 1917, 40, 43–44, 53:

> From a high hill which I ascended there is a very magnificent prospect of an extensive range of country, some miles around Plainfield—a highly cultivated plain interspersed with woods and surrounded by beautiful hills, illuminated by a bright sun, opened a charming view just as I reached the brow of the hill, and struck me with an agreeable surprise. (40)
>
> The whole way from Norwich the country is thickly settled, farm houses in sight constantly, the country well-cultivated, meadows, hills, and distant woods rising one above the other...the whole a most romantic country, thickly settled, highly cultivated, and adorned both nature and art. (43)
>
> The town of Farmington is seen at a distance and the whole is extremely picturesque. At the top of the mountain is a curious pond surrounded with rocks and woods, in a very romantic situation. (44)

In Temple, *Pocket Companion*, 60, 64, the author described one of his suggested tours as follows: "Our sight regaled with the extensive meadows and well cultivated farms, on Connecticut river, and panning through the neat village of Charleston" (60). See also Stoddard Family Papers, Massachusetts Historical Society, Boston. See also remarks by the Scotswoman Frances Wright D'Arusmont, *Views of Society and Manner in America: A Series of Letters from that Country to a Friend in England during the Years 1818, 1819 and 1820* (New York: n.p., 1821), 220.

24. Chandos Michael Brown, *Benjamin Silliman: A Life in the Young Republic* (Princeton: Princeton University Press, 1989).
25. Dwight, *Travels*, II, 82.
26. Dwight, *Travels*, I, 103, see also 122. For the struggle between frontier settlers and proprietors, see, e.g., Alan Taylor, *Liberty Men and Great Proprietors: The Revolutionary Settlement on the Maine Frontier, 1760–1820* (Chapel Hill: University of North Carolina Press, 1990).
27. Ralph Earl, *Looking East from Denny Hill*, painting, 1800, in Alan Emmet, *So Fine a Prospect: Historic New England Gardens* (Hanover, New Hampshire: New England University Press, 1996), 2.
28. Large trees, which are painted on the left and right side of a rural scene. For the view of Haverhill see Mrs. Green, *A View of the Town of Haverhill*, drawing 1812–1814, Trustees of the Haverhill Public Library, in *The Landscape of Change: Views of Rural New England, 1790–1865*: [exhibition], February 9–May 16, 1976, Old Sturbridge Village, Sturbridge, Massachusetts, Figure 1.
29. Dwight, *Travels*, I., 92. See also William Tudor, *Letters of the Eastern States* (New York: Kirk and Mercein, 1820), 302. An article on the White Mountains in the London Journal of Science compared especially plants with their European counterparts, "Account of the White Mountains," *The Journal of Science and the Arts* 2 (1817): 392–399.
30. Dwight, *Travels*, III, 92. The Boston author William Tudor even saw ruins as unattractive relicts of the feudal system:

    Our picturesque objects of an artificial kind, are vastly fewer than those in older countries. The total absence of ruins deprives us of what is an abundant source of associations in Europe . . . in truth we have no other way to turn the edge of reproach on this account than by boldly assuming, that the landscape is better without them:—that the sight of these grisly, hideous remains, conjure up the ideas of baronial oppression, feudal slavery, and monkish delusion;—that in those mouldering [*sic*] dungeons were formerly immured the victims of priestly or lordly tyranny;—and those ruined walls once protected a few lawless despots. (Tudor, *Letters of the Eastern States*, 271)

31. For the important role of the local community in dominating and shaping ideas about national politics and virtues in the early republic, see also Thomas Bender, *Community and Social Change in America* (New Brunswick, New Jersey: Rutgers University Press, 1978), 78–86. Joseph S. Wood, *The New England Village* (Baltimore: John Hopkins University Press, 1997), 71–87, 114–134. For the fact that New England towns were actually built in the early republic, see also Stephen Nissenbaum, "New England as Region and Nation," Chapter 2 in Edward L. Ayers et al., *All over the Map: Rethinking American Regions* (Baltimore: Johns Hopkins University Press, 1996), 43–46.

Boudinot, *Journey to Boston*, 33–34, 55. For the chance of the use and design of churches, see Edmund W. Sinnott, *Meetinghouse and Church in Early New England* (New York: Bonanza Books, 1963), 71–74 and Elise Lathrop, *Old New England Churches* (Rutland, Vermont: The Tuttle Publishing Co., 1938).

32. Silliman, *Remarks, Made on a Short Tour*, 39, 40, 380–381. Northern newspapers gave the same picture in their numerous accounts of towns; see "Description of Boston," *The New York Magazine or Literary Repository* 5 (1795): 387–388; and "Salem Described," *The Massachusetts Magazine* 4 (1792): 85–86.
33. For the images see, Daniel Bell, *Framingham Common*, oil painting, Framingham, 1808, in Nina Fletcher, *Country Arts in Early American Homes* (New York: Dutton, 1975), 32; Joseph Stewart, *Maria Malleville Wheelock* (Hanover, New Hampshire, 1793), in Nina Fletcher, *Little by Little: Six Decades of Collecting American Decorative Arts* (New York: E.P. Dutton, 1984), 264; Jane Otis Prior, sewing box, 1822, in Nina Fletcher Little, *Neat and Tidy. Boxes and Their Contents Used in Early American Households* (New York: E. P. Dutton, 1980), 136–137.
34. See Sophia Stevens Smith, *View of North Branford, Connecticut*, embroidery, 1818, owned by Mrs. Henry Coe, in *American Samplers*, ed. Ethel Stanwood Bolton and Eva Johnston Coe (New York: Dover Publications), Plate 68.
35. See Rebecca Davis, mourning picture, painting, ca. 1815, in Fletcher, *Little by Little*, 142; and *Boston State House*, dinner service, Rogers and Son, in A.W. Coysh, *The Dictionary of Blue and White Transfer Ware* (Woodbridge, Great Britain: Antique Collectors' Club, 1990), 48.
36. For praise of Boston as an elegant and sophisticated place that compares to European cities; see Melish, *Travels through the United States*, 78–79; Boudinot, *Journey to Boston*, 34; "Tour in New England by an Englishman," 14; and "Description of Boston," *New York Magazine or Literary Repository* 5 (1795). Philip Stansbury found Boston similar to London because of its narrow streets and plain buildings (Stansbury, *A Pedestrian Tour*, 256). For Dwight's complaints about Boston, see Dwight, *Travels*, I, 353–355, 362.
37. Joseph Wood also argues that the nineteenth-century settlement ideal—which shaped the process of rebuilding of New England towns—included rural and urban elements; see Wood, *The New England Village*, 131–160. See Appleby, *Inheriting the Revolution*, 241.
38. Writers mentioned New England colleges especially to emphasize the region's high level of education, see the following. For authors praising colleges beside Dwight, see Tudor, *Letters of the Eastern States*, 120–122; Tappan, *New England and Other Poems*, 16. For Fisher's paintings of Harvard College, see Agnes Morgan, *Harvard Honors Lafayette* (New York: Garland Press, 1975), 118–121.

39. Edward Augustus Kendall, *Travels through the Northern Parts of the United States in the Years 1807 and 1808* (New York: L. Riley, 1809), Vol. 3, 131.
40. Boudinot, *Journey to Boston*, 36, 46. For similar enthusiasm for the houses and buildings, see also Warville, *New Travels in the United States*, 73; Temple, *Pocket Companion*, 60; Silliman, *Remarks, Made on a Short Tour*, 387, and Tudor, *Letters of the Eastern States*, 302.
41. See Ralph Earl, Oliver and Abigail Ellsworth, painting, 1792, in Emmet, *So Fine a Prospect*, 1; and Artist Unknown, fireboard, Banister House, Brookfield, Massachusetts, ca. 1790, in Nina Fletcher Little, *American Decorative Wall Painting*, 1700–1850 (Sturbridge, Massachusetts: Studio Publications, 1952), 30.
42. Alvan Fisher, *The Vale*, watercolor, 1820, in Emmet, *So Fine a Prospect*, 8. Boudinot, *Journey to Boston*, 42–43. On early Republican New England gardens, see Emmet, *So Fine a Prospect*.
43. Dwight, *Travels*, II, 14; Boudinot, *Journey to Boston*, 24. Compare the description of Boston merchant Charles Stoddard in his journal of a tour in July 1820, Stoddard Family Papers, Massachusetts Historical Society: "The scenery is around is quite romantic, and the stream well improved by factories of several kinds; the principals of which are for the fabrication of bottom goods, as the manufactory of threads. These factories are 8 or 10 in number, and all apparently in a flourishing condition." See also Temple, *Pocket Companion*, 56, 58, and 65. Other examples are "Description of Boston," 387–388 and "Salem Described," *The Massachusetts Magazine* 4 (1792): 85–86. Already the French tourist Warville thought that it was industrial and commercial sites rather than colleges that defined New England, Warville, *New Travels in the United States*, 58, 61–62. He wrote: "It is remarked, that, in countries chiefly devoted to commerce, the sciences are not carried to any high degree. This remark applies to Boston. The university certainly contains men of worth and learning, but science is not diffused among the inhabitants of the town."
44. Published in 1794 *Greenfield Hill* launched the myth of the New England town as a new Eden, which had been shaped over almost two centuries beginning with William Bradford's *Of Plimmoth Plantation*, into the new republic. Bradford's poem saw a revival in the early republic; it was published in the *Collections of the Massachusetts Society*: "A Descriptive and Historical Account of New England in Verse From a Ms. of William Bradford, Governour of Plymouth Colony," *Collections of the Massachusetts Historical Society* 3 (1794): 77–84. *The Major Poems of Timothy Dwight, with a Dissertation on the History, Eloquence, and Poetry of the Bible* (Gainesville, Florida: Scholarly Facsimiles and Reprints, 1969), 381, 378. He assures that the inhabitants of New England towns tasted "every good / Of Competence, of

independence, peace / And liberty unmingled; every house / On its own ground, and every happy swain / Beholding no superior, but laws, / And such as virtue, knowledge, useful life / And zeal exerted for the public good, / Have raised above the throng." Morse had argued that republican New England virtues had been formed by the institutions of New England towns even before Dwight published his travel books. Dwight was very much influenced by the ideas of his close friend Morse, see Conforti, *Imagining New England*, 95.

45. "On New England Republicanism," *The American Museum or Universal Magazine* 12 (1792): 303, 304; Belknap, *History of New Hampshire*, 171. Here he wrote:

    It has been confidently asserted by Europeans writers . . . that the climates of America . . . are unfriendly to health . . . these . . . effects are ascribed to putrid exhalations from stagnat water, to a surface uncleared, uncultivated. . . . If such remarks were intended to be confined to the low plains in the southern States, the propriety of them might not perhaps be disputed.

    Jedidiah Morse and his role are discussed in chapter 6.
46. Wright, *Views of Society and Manners in America*, 221. Patricia Brady describes Wright's attitude toward the slave South in "Carnival of Liberty: Lafayette in Louisiana," *Louisiana History* 2000 (41): 37. See also the account of Warville, *New Travels in the United States*, 71. For an example of Dwight's description of the town governments, see Dwight, *Travels*, I, 179–182.
47. Silliman, *Remarks, Made on a Short Tour*, 19.
48. Boudinot, *Journey to Boston*, 52. For the same distinction between New Englanders and the British, see "Essay on New England," *Monthly Anthology and Boston Review* 4 (1807): 658. For this characterization of New Englanders, see also Gilpin, *A Northern Tour*, 255.
49. Wright, *Views of Society and Manner in America*, 221; Silliman, *Remarks, Made on a Short Tour*, 19.
50. Boudinot, *Journey to Boston*, 27. He wrote as follows:

    Through Connecticut, a Traveller cannot but be pleased with the high state of Cultivation prevailing in every quarter. But no sooner does he pass into Rhode Island, than he is astonished at the Contrast, without being able to account for the fact. On enquiring into this Phoenomenon, we were answered, that in the Country, they have neither Churches nor Schools.

    For Jeremy Belknap, see Lawrence Buell, *New England Literary Culture: From Revolution through Renaissance* (London: Cambridge University Press, 1986), 313. Edward Kendall described the farmers of Maine as indolent and said that among them "low dissipation" and drinking habits "were by much far too common" (Kendall, *Travels through the Northern Parts of the United States*, Vol. 3, 81). He mentioned that there were not many educated and wealthier people in Maine (110). On Morse's and Dwight's perception of Rhode Island, see Conforti, *Imagining New England*, 100. For Belknap's experience in Dover and his opinion on the people of the town, see Tucker, *Clio's Consort*, 10, 12–13, 17–19, 20–22, 70, 124.

51. Isaac Weld, *Travels through North America and Canada, 1795–1797* (London: J. Stockdale, 1799, also published Paris, 1800, The Hague, 1801).
52. "Parallel between New England and Great Britain," *Monitor* 1 (1801): 284; John Goldie, *Diary of a Journey through Upper Canada and some New England States, 1819* (Philadelphia: privately published, 1910), 51.
53. "Tour in New England by an Englishman," 81–82; Dwight, *Travels*, I, 123.
54. Dwight, *Travels*, IV, 244; "Parallel between New England and Great Britain," 283. Morse was another New England nationalist, who claimed that New England education was most generally diffused among all ranks of New Englanders; see Conforti, *Imagining New England*, 97.
55. Melish, *Travels through the United States*, 78–79; "Tour in New England by an Englishman," 83. For piety, see "New England, A Poem by William Morrell," 124. In his introductory letter the editor of the poem wrote this about New England: "I never came in a more godly country in all my life."
56. Dwight, *Travels*, I, 368. See also "Tour in New England by an Englishman," 84. Here the author wrote: "Justly accounted [New England is] the best settled country, with the most steady and best informed inhabitants in the Union." John Melish wrote: "The fruits of attention to the improvement of the mind…are very apparent in the deportment of citizens of Boston, who are intelligent" (Melish, *Travels through the United States*, 78–79). "Parallel between New England and Great Britain," 283. "Our common people," Dwight asserted, "are far better educated than [those of England and Europe], both in the school and in the church" (Dwight, *Travels*, IV, 244).
57. Wright, *Views of Society and Manner in America*, 306; Silliman, *Remarks, Made on a Short Tour*, 30.
58. Boudinot, *Journey to Boston*, 40; Silliman, *Remarks, Made on a Short Tour*, 32–33; Melish, *Travels through the United States*, 79; Tappan, *New England and Other Poems*, 7. Compare also Dwight, *Travels*, I, 366. He said the following about Bostonian women: "The best bred women here are charming examples of grace and amenity." See Mary Spence to Graeme Keith Spence, Portsmouth, NH, June 16, 1802, Spence-Lowell Collection, Huntington Library, San Marino, California.
59. "A Yankee Trick," *The New England Farmer* 1823 (1): 208. Boston. Another example for such an anecdote is *"Morristown Ghost" or "Yankee Trick" Being a True, Interesting, and Strange Narrative*

(USA, n.p., 1815). It is about a Yankee who exploits the superstition of the people in Morristown, New York, in order to make money. When the Yankee schoolmaster from Connecticut moved to the town, he claimed that he could communicate with spirits and that the spirits promised wealth for the community. However, in order to become wealthy, the Yankee said, the townspeople needed to give money to the spirits. Shortly after, two other Yankees moved to the area and helped the schoolmaster to set up ghost appearances and strange noise to scare the townspeople. It was a lucrative enterprise for the Yankees, although in the end the townspeople found out that it was a trick. See also Micah Hawkins, *The Sawmill, or, a Yankee Trick* (New York: J. Harper, 1824), "Yankee Jump," *The Christian Telescope and Universalist Miscellany* 1825 (1): 172 (for the same story, see "A Yankee Exploit," *The Portsmouth Weekly Magazine* 1825 (1): 2), "Diversity. Original Anecdote: Yankee Manners, in Days of Old," *Balance and Columbian Repository* 1801 (1): 4 and "Yankee Tricks," *The Portfolio* 1809 (2): 533. For examples of the increasing number of publications after 1930, see Rufus Charles Maclellan, *The Foundling, or, Yankee Fidelity. A Drama in Two Acts* (Philadelphia: King & Baird, 1839); Thomas Chandler, *Judge Haliburton's Yankee Stories* (Philadelphia: Lindsay & Blackston, 1849, published in Halifax in 1836); Morris Barnett, *Yankee Peddler, or, Old Times in Virginia* (New York: Samuel French, 1858); and Philip Paxton, *A Stray Yankee in Texas* (New York : Redfield, 1853).

60. In America everything was bigger than in Europe. See, e.g., the introductory letter of "New England, A Poem by William Morrell," 124–125: "The increase of corne is fare beyond expectation....And cattle do prosper very well, and those that are bredd here farr greater than those with you in England." Another example is "Essay on New England," *Monthly Anthology and Boston Review* 4 (1807): 658. Silliman even found that English tourists displayed social superiority in their attitude toward innkeepers and especially toward their servants, see Silliman, *Remarks, Made on a Short Tour*, 33–34. Boston was described as identical to any European city. "Tour in New England by an Englishman," 14; "The Virtue of New England People," *Gentlemen and Ladies' Town and Country Magazine* 1 (1789): 310; and Melish, *Travels through the United States*, 78. Frenchman Warville found New England manners very British; see Warville, *New Travels in the United States*, 58: "In their whole manner of living the Americans in general resemble the English."

61. Dwight, *Travels*, I, 214. In another place he stressed the Englishness of Bostonians:

> They are all descendants of Englishmen, and of course are united by all the great bonds of society: language, religion, government, manners, and interest...they speak the English language in the English manner, are Protestants, hold the great

> principle of English liberty, are governed voluntarily by the English common law...under a constitution essentially copied from the British....Although they are republican, and generally Congregationalists, they are natively friends of good order and firm government, and feel the reputation of Old Massachusetts in much the same manner as an Englishman feels the honor of Old England. (365)

Philip Stansbury clearly distinguished between American and Canadian rural people: The former were in his view austere and "unambitious" peasants, and the latter "plain, open-hearted, merry-making farmers," Stansbury, *A Pedestrian Tour*, 233. For a tendency of American almanacs to publish pro-British and anti-French essays even during the 1770s, when the French supported the American cause, see Waldstreicher, *Perpetual Fetes*, 45.

62. Appleby, *Inheriting the Revolution*, 239–268.
63. "Salem Described," 85.
64. "Tour in New England by an Englishman," 81; "Character of the inhabitants of New England," 335. The New England poet William Tappan also emphasized that his region was not corrupted by the Southern labor system; he wrote, "Unscorched [*sic*] by burning heat and Southern blast, / The bracing North, confirms thy ruddy cast" (Tappan, *New England and Other Poems*, 7). Some authors emphasized the uniqueness of the Northern States, as, e.g., Edward Kendall, who wrote,

> That part of the United States which comprehends what are variously called the Northern States...and which retains its ancient name New England, is, in many particulars, distinguishable from the remainder. It differs, not only in its climate, nut in the history of its colonization, in the objects of many of its institutions, in its modes of thinking and manners of life, in its civil occupations, and perhaps in its political interests. (Kendall, *Travels through the Northern Parts of the United States*, III; Dwight, *Travels*, I, 366)

65. "Character of the inhabitants of New England," 335. Already Warville argued that the abolition of slavery in New England had led to prosperous industries, see Warville, *New Travels in the United States*, 59. For the perception of African Americans and slavery in New England compare Joanne Pope Melish, *Disowning Slavery: Gradual Emancipation and "Race" in New England, 1780–1860* (Ithaca: Cornell University Press, 1998). Melish argues that despite of 150 years of slavery, New Englanders constructed their region as a place where the institution did not exist. By inventing New England in those terms they juxtaposed themselves with the South.
66. See Warville, *New Travels in the United States*, 155 and Smith, Journal of 1790–91, 50. For Morse's, Webster's, and Dwight's perception of the South, see Conforti, *Imagining New England*, 87–88, 106–107.

From 1786 to 1787 Morse served as the Congregational pastor of Midway, Georgia.

67. Melish, *Disowning Slavery*, 15.
68. For New Englanders attitude toward race and New England's history of slavery, see Melish, *Disowning Slavery* and John Wood Sweet, *Bodies Politic: Negotiating Race in the American North, 1730–1830* (Baltimore: John Hopkins University Press, 2003).
69. Dwight, *Travels*, III, 186 and *Travels*, I, 8. "The Virtue of New England People," 310. For an argument that the mobility of New Englanders roused hopes for the New Englandization of the nation, see also Conforti, *Imagining New England*, 93. The article in *The Reformer* is cited in Richard Lyle Power, "A Crusade to Extend Yankee Culture, 1820–1865," *The New England Quarterly* 13 (1940): 638–653, 638.

Chapter 2 A Prussian Monarch—an American Hero: Early Republican Royalism and Parallels between the Cult of Frederick the Great and Celebrations of the First American President

1. Eckhart Hellmuth, "A Monument to Frederick the Great: Architecture, Politics and the State in Late Eighteenth-Century Prussia," in *Rethinking Leviathan: The Eighteenth-Century State in Britain and Germany*, ed. John Brewer and Eckhart Hellmuth (London: German Historical Institute; Oxford: Oxford University Press, 1999); Eckhart Hellmuth, "Die 'Wiedergeburt' Friedrichs' des Grossen und der 'Tod fuers Vaterland': Zum Patriotischen Selbstverstaendnis in Preussen in der zweiten Haelfte des 18. Jahrhunderts," in: *Nationalismus vor dem Nationalismus*, ed. Reinhard Stauber and Eckhart Hellmuth (Hamburg: F. Meier, 1998). Hellmuth talks about a sort of "reincarnation" of the Prussian king. For the time period between 1786 and 1825, the index to the American Periodical Series lists forty-eight anecdotes on Frederick II published in New England, twenty-five published in Philadelphia, and twenty-six published in New York periodicals. See *An Index to the Microfilm Collection of the American Periodical Series* [CD-ROM] (Ann Arbor, Michigan: University Microfilms International, 1979).
2. Among the numerous biographies of Frederick II, the following selection are suggested for a good overview and different perspectives: Gerhard Ritter, *Frederick the Great: A Historic Profile* (Berkeley: University of California Press, 1968); Thomas Carlyle, *History of Frederick II of Prussia, Called Frederick the Great* (Chicago: University

of Chicago Press, 1969); Peter Gooch, *Frederick the Great, the Ruler, the Writer, the Man* (Hamden, Connecticut: Archon Books, 1962); and Theodor Schieder, *Frederick the Great* (New York: Longman, 2000).

3. "Odes on the King of Prussia's Victories," *The American Magazine and Monthly Chronicle for the British Colonies* 1 (1758): 240–241, 280:

   Great Frederick's deeds do still require
   More ample praise
   Let his great acts the verse inspire
   And tuneful be thy lays
   Illustrious HANNIBAL of old,
   CAESAR the brave and SCIPIO bold,
   For battles won stand high enroll'd
   In hist'rys page!
   Let FREDERICK'S name with theirs be told
   The hero of his age!

   Another example for divine qualities in one of these odes is as follows: "Tis he! I hear him from afar, / Thund'ring like the God of War; / To Rosbach's plain, in dread array, / The god-like hero bends his way!" (240). On the enthusiasm for Frederick II during the Seven Years' War in Great Britain, see Manfred Schlenke, *England und das Friderizianische Preussen, 1740–1763: Ein Beitrag zum Verhaeltnis von Politik und Oeffentlicher Meinung im England des 18. Jahrhunderts* (Muenchen: Karl Alber, 1963). As examples of the countless articles on the Prussian king in Colonial publications, see "View of the King of Prussia passing through Leipzig," *The American Magazine and Monthly Chronicle for the British Colonies* 1 (1757): 243; "Thanksgiving Sermon for the Victories of the King of Prussia," *The American Magazine and Monthly Chronicle for the British Colonies* 1 (1757): 441; "Poem on the King of Prussia," *The American Magazine and Monthly Chronicle for the British Colonies* 1 (1757): 550; "The King of Prussia's Parallel with Julius Caesar," *The New American Magazine* 1 (1758): 618; "Character of the King of Prussia," *The New American Magazine* 1 (1758): 321; William H. Dilworth, *Das Leben und heroische Thaten des Koenigs von Preussen, Friedrichs des III [Life and Heroic Actions of Frederick III King of Prussia]* (Germantown: Christoph Saur, 1761); and *Hoechstmerkwuerdige Prophezeyung von wichtigen Kriegs und Welthaendlen: in welcher von dem glorwuerdigen Koenig von Preussen geweissagt wird* (Philadelphia: Henrich Miller, 1760).

4. See Copper tobacco box, in Nine Fletcher Little, *Boxes and Their Contents Used in Early American Households*, 80; and Worcester jug, in *Antiques* 61 (1962): 316.

5. For the German anecdotes copied by American editors, see following German eighteenth-century periodicals: *Berlinische Monatsschrift*, *Braunschweigisches Journal*, *Deutsches Museum*, *Journal aller Journale*,

Journal des Luxus und der Moden, *Journal von und für Deutschland*, *Neue Bunzlauische Monatsschrift*, *Neue Litteratur und Völkerkunde*, *Patriotisches Archiv für Deutschland*, *Schlesische Provinzialblätter*, *Stats-Anzeigen*, *Teutscher Merkur*. The best source to find access to the German anecdotes is the so-called Goettinger Periodical Index. The index lists 250 articles on Frederick the Great, see *Index deutschsprachiger Zeitschriften 1750–1815* (Hildesheim: Deutsche Forschungsgemeinschaft, 1989). See Joyce Appleby, *Inheriting the Revolution: The First Generation of Americans* (London: Harvard University Press: 2000), 239–268. In her study of the first generation of Americans after American Independence, Appleby works on the national level and convincingly argues that the image of the new nation was shaped by the Northern states. Appleby gives a vivid description of that Northern image, but she does not mention the dominant role that New England played in shaping it.

6. Thomas Cooke, *I'll Love You Ever Dearly: Sung by Mr. Taylor: From the Operatic Anecdote of Frederick the Great* (Philadelphia: G. Willig's Musical Magazine, 1815, 1817, 1818, 1819 and New York: W Dubois, 1817). See also Thomas Cooke, *Roll Drums Merril: Frederick the Great. When I Was an Infant* (Philadelphia: G. Willig, 1820, 1824) and W. Dimond, *Third Night of the Broken Sword: On Friday Evening, May 2, 1817, Will Be Presented, the New Operatic Drama, in 3 Acts, of Frederick the Great…* (New York: n.p., 1817). See also *King Friedrich Wilhelm the First: The Story of the Youth of Frederick the Great: A Historical Drama in Four Acts* (n.p., 1800). Plays on Frederick II were also performed in Washington and Fredericksburg, Virginia; see, e.g., *The Two Pages of Frederick The Great, a Comic Piece, in Two Acts: From the French, as Performed at the Theatre Royal, Covent Garden, by John Poole* (Washington: Davis and Force, 1823) and *Theatre… Mr. Cadwell's Benefit: Monday Evening, Sept. 12, 1825; Will be Presented, Shakespeare's Celebrated Tragedy of Romeo and Juliet…After which, a Petit comedy, called The Two Pages, or Frederick the Great* (Broadside, Fredericksburg, Virginia, 1825). Dieudonne Thiebault, *Original Anecdotes of Frederick the Great, King of Prussia, and of His Family, His Court, His Ministers, His Academies, and His Literary Friends* (Philadelphia: E. Bronson, 1806). It was also published in Philadelphia: E. Bronson, 1816; Philadelphia: Etheridge and Bliss, 1806; and New York: I. Riley and Co., 1806. For the large number of books on Frederick the Great in New England libraries, see William Gilmore, *Reading Becomes a Necessity of Life: Material and Cultural Life in Rural New England, 1780–1835* (Knoxville: University of Tennessee Press, 1989), 339, n. 86.
7. Washington to Lafayette, May 10, 1786, in *The Papers of George Washington, 4, April 1786–January 1787*, ed. Albot and Dorothy Twohig (Charlottesville, London: University Press of Virginia, 1992),

420. For Washington's wish to get a bust of Frederick the Great, see Paul Longmore, *The Invention of George Washington* (Berkeley: University of California Press, 1989), 60, 303, n. 47.

8. *Boston Gazette*, November 6, 1786; *Connecticut Journal*, November 22, 1786, the first part of this article was also published in *United States Chronicle*, November 30, 1786. An exception to the unemotional reaction was "Ode to Death," *The New Haven Gazette and Connecticut Magazine* 1 (1786): 339–340.
9. For the celebration of Frederick in Germany, see Hellmuth, "Die 'Wiedergeburt' Friedrichs des Grossen," 31–33.
10. "King of Prussia," *The Boston Magazine* 14 (1817): 54. "Anecdote of the King of Prussia," *The New Haven Gazette and the Connecticut Magazine* 2 (1787): 69–70, 170, here 70; the same anecdote appeared in *The Boston Weekly Magazine* 12 (1816): 48. In the later version of the anecdote, the soldiers and grenadiers were "full of enthusiasm and admiration, they exclaimed 'Thou art still our old Frederick; thou partakest every danger with us.'"
11. They showed. e.g., his strict but just treatment of his officers and troops; see "Anecdote of Frederick the Great," *Lady's Miscellany or Weekly Visitor* 11 (1810): 76, 92. In 1795 a Pennsylvania German published a poem very much like the ones being read during the French and Indian War:

    Von Gottes Gnaden Friedrich,
    Der Himmel segne, Dich
    Weil du bist gluecklich in der Schlacht,
    Und hast gedaempft des Feindes Macht,
    Von Gottes Gnaden Friedrich,
    Der Himmel segne Dich
    Den Ruhm hat dieser grosse Held,
    Wohl in der ganzen Welt,
    Wer so tapfere Voelker fuehrt,
    Und sie auch sonst kommandiert,
    Mit seinem Degen in dem Feld,
    Friedrich der grosse Held.

    [From God's mercy Frederic, / Heaven bless you, / Glory has this big hero, / in the whole world, / who leads people so bravely, / und commands them also otherwise, / with the rapier in the field, / Frederic the big hero.]; Edwin Wolf, *Lied vom Koenig von Preussen* (Pennsylvania: n.p., about 1795). In John O'Keefe's musical *Patrick in Prussia*, Patrick says: "Why at present my country does not want my services, and I thought it should want them, that they would not prove less deserving of George by being for the present under the tuition of so regular a disciplined a master as Frederick" (John O'Keefe, *Patrick in Prussia or, Love in a Camp: A Comic Opera* [Philadelphia: Henry Taylor, 1791], 7). One example for the publication of Frederick's military writings is "The King of Prussia's

Letter to Gen de Tauenzin," *The New Haven Gazette and the Connecticut Magazine* 1 (1786): 45–46.

12. "New Anecdotes of the late illustrious Frederick II," *The American Magazine* 1 (1787): 605–609. For another example, see Prince de Charles Joseph Ligne, *Letters and Reflections of the Austrian Field-Marshal Prince Ligne: Containing anecdotes hitherto unpublished of Joseph II, Catherine II, Frederick the Great* (Philadelphia: B. Graves, 1809), 22. Here Ligne described how simple but kind his reception was when he visited the king at a military camp. Compare also "Anecdote," *The Philadelphia Minerva* 4 (1798): 54. It shows how Frederick's modest behavior worked in his favor:

    When the king of Prussia and the Emperor met at Beisse, they once happened to come to the bottom of a flight of stairs, and neither would go up first, and take precedence on the other. They stood and bowed, and... complimented and each politely wished to give the way to the other at last the king of Prussia got behind the Emperor and pushed him forward, "Ho: Lord!" said the Emperor "if you begin to manevre [maneuver] with me I must unavoidably go anywhere you please!" and walked up first.

    For another example that underlines Frederick's sense of humor, see "Anecdote," *The New Haven Gazette and the Connecticut Magazine* 38 (1788): 8.

13. Thiebault, *Original Anecdotes of Frederick the Great*, Vol. 1, p. 108. In another place he explained how the king also wanted everybody else to adopt this simple style: "Fifthly, in fine, never to present myself before the king but in a plain and simple dress. This last precaution suited admirably with the principles of Frederick. He exacted, that the heads of the principal mercantile houses, his ministers of state, and especially financiers, should display a certain luxury" (13). Even the royal castle was to be furnished in that Spartan style: "The furniture of the castle was old-fashioned, and rather simple than otherwise" (124). *Memoirs of John Quincy Adams, Comprising Portions of His Diary from 1795 to 1848*, ed. Charles Francis Adams (Philadelphia: J. B. Lippincott & Co., 1874–1877), Vol. 6, 209. Compare a story about Frederick's successor in the *Rural Magazine*, "Anecdote," *The Rural Magazine* 1 (1798): 4. It said:

    On the king of Prussia's accession to the throne, his cook thought it a matter of course to increase the number of dishes on the royal table; but Frederick William III. no sooner perceived the change, than he ordered the dishes to be reduced to their former number; observing that he did not see why he should eat more, being king, than he had done when Prince Royal.

The story in "The King of Prussia's Skill in Revenue," *The New Haven Gazette and the Connecticut Magazine* 1 (1786): 370, said the following:

> The King of Prussia, whose parsimony and rigid economy never allowed him to indulge his fancy in the gaudy [*sic*] of splendor of other monarchs, used to send every year a snuff-box set in diamonds of about 5000 crowns value together with fifteen hundred pounds sterling to Prince Henry as a new years gift. He had likewise a service of solid gold, which he never used but to celebrate his brother's birthday.

14. See, e.g.: "Anecdotes of Frederick II," *Ladies Weekly Museum* 17 (1805): 848; "Character of the late King of Prussia," *The Massachusetts Magazine* 3 (1791): 571–572; "Notice of Frederick the Great," *Cabinet* 1 (1811): 74; "On the Intelligence of Frederick II," *Ladies' Weekly Museum* 2 (1813): 48. These stories described him as being too strict and harsh on his people and especially soldiers.
15. "Original Anecdote," *The Time Piece and Literary Companion* 2 (1797): 5.
16. Washington to the Comte De Rochambeau, On July 31, 1786, in *The Papers of George Washington, 4, April 1786–January 1787*, 492. For Frederick's II attitude toward the American Revolution, see Hans Karl Gunther, "Frederick the Great, the Bavarian War of Succession and the American War of Independence," *Duquesne Review* 16 (1971): 59–74 and Paul Leland Haworth, "Frederick the Great and the American Revolution," *American Historical Review* 9 (1904): 460–478.
17. Elise Lathrop, *Early American Inns and Taverns* (New York: Tudor Publishing Company, 1926), 168, 179. For George Elliot naming the town in 1786, see Clifton S. Hunsicker, *Montgomery County, Pennsylvania: A History*, 2 Vols. (New York: Lewis Historical Publishing Company, 1923), 340; and *History of Montgomery County, Pennsylvania*, ed. Theodore W. Bean (Philadelphia: Everts and Peck, 1884), 1118.
18. On the concept of Republicanism, see Gordon Wood, *The Creation of the American Republic, 1776–1787* (Chapel Hill: University of North Carolina Press, 1969) and James T. Kloppenberg, "The Virtues if Liberalism: Christianity, Republicanism, and Ethics in Early American Political Discourse," *Journal of American History* 74 (1987): 9–33. On the market revolution and its impact on collective values, see Steve Watts, *The Republic Reborn: War and the Making of Liberal America, 1790–1820* (Baltimore: Johns Hopkins University Press, 1987).
19. "The Gatherer," *Parlour Companion* 2 (1818): 88. For the same story, see "Frederick the Great," *Ladies Weekly Museum* 16 (1804): 819.
20. Pathbreaking in the research of patriotism, see Rudolf Vierhaus, "Patriotismus—Begriff und Realitaet einer moral-politischen

Haltung," in Rudolf Vierhaus, *Deutschland im 18. Jahrhundert. Politische Verfassung, soziales Gefuege, geistige Bewegung* (Goettingen: Vandenhoeck and Ruprecht, 1987). One example for a story that described Frederick as religiously tolerant appeared in a 1787 edition of the *New Haven Gazette and Connecticut Magazine.* Again, the modern-minded Prussian monarch was contrasted with his intolerant English counterparts. "The subject and advantage of toleration are very little understood by the orators of England. The late king of Prussia was the only Prince of modern times that could avail himself of all its advantages," argued the American editor in his introduction to the German anecdote. He continued:

> In Neufchatel, Mr. Pitit Pierre, a Calvanistic [*sic*] clergyman, had doubts of the eternity of hell torments, and therefore never alluded them to them in his sermons. The orthodox preachers alarmed the people, and Mr. Pitit Pierre was suspended. The ministers...obtained a memorial to the king, to oblige Mr. Pitit Pierre to preach on hell torments, and to punish him. The king wrote at the bottom of the memorial, "If the people of Neufchatel choose to be eternally damaged, so be it;—but the King requires that the conscience of the minister be not molested." ("Anecdote of Frederick II" *The Boston Weekly Magazine* 1 [1824]: 2; "Anecdote of the King of Prussia," *The New Haven Gazette and the Connecticut Magazine* 2 [1787]: 170).

A similar version of that story was published in *The Herald of Life and Mortality* 2 (1819): 58–59. For another similar story, see "Anecdote of Frederick the Great," *The New Haven Gazette and the Connecticut Magazine* 3 (1788): 47. It said:

> Professor Eberhard, of Halle, was some years ago appointed, by the upper consistory, preacher of Charlottenburg. The townsmen who had fixed on another person, protested against Eberhard to the consistory, because he had written the apology for Socrates. This objection was considered as insufficient; and they were ordered to submit. On this they represented to the King that they could not think of trusting the care of their souls to a man, who had affirmed that the cursed heathen Socrates was saved. His Majesty, who was sorry to hear the worthy philosopher cursed, wrote to them in reply: "I insist on Socrates being saved, as also on Eberhard becoming your preacher."

See also "Frederick anecdote," *American Museum or Universal Magazine* 10 (1792): 108. It said: "The bible (said the late king of Prussia) is a staff, which God put into the hands of blind men to guide their steps. But they, instead of applying it to that use, immediately began to wrangle and dispute about its length, breadth, and thickness; and concluded by knocking each other over the pate with it." The same image was drawn of other Prussian kings reigning during the early Republic. The New Haven *Religious Intelligencer* reported that the Prussian King Frederick William III founded a university, which "Provision is made for Evangelical and Catholic Faculties"; see *The Religious Intelligencer* 42 (1819): 674. At the same time Frederick William was pictured as the protector of Protestantism; see "Religious Sentiments of the King of Prussia," *The Religious Intelligencer* 23 (1826): 366–367.

21. "A Faithful Lad," *The Boston Magazine* 1 (1802): 115. Thiebault extensively described the king's tied [tight] schedule and his long working hours; see Thiebault, *Original Anecdotes of Frederick the Great*, Vol. 1, 57–64.
22. See "Anecdote of the late King of Prussia," *The Philadelphia Minerva* 2 (1796): 94 and "Anecdote of Frederick the Great," *The New Haven Gazette* 3 (1788): 47. In 1800, the *Columbian Phenix and Boston Review* published a poem by the Frederick II, "Philosophy of an Hero," *The Columbian Phenix and Boston Review* 1 (1800): 315. For the image of Frederick as a philosopher and advocate of the arts and sciences, see, e.g., Thiebault, *Original Anecdotes of Frederick the Great*, Vol. 1, 69, 124. Here he wrote about the king's five libraries and his habit to divide his books into two classes, one he wanted to read only once, and another he "wished to study and have recourse to from time to time during his life. In another place he asked, "Ought I to mention in this place his patronage of the arts, and the taste he had acquired them?" Thiebault also had an extensive chapter on Frederick's educational impact: "His Academy, his schools, and his Friends literary and Philosophical" (Vol. 2, 281–333).
23. John Quincy Adams, *Letters on Silesia: Written on a Tour through that Country in the Years 1800, 1801* (London: L. Budd, 1804), 372. See also William H. Seward, *Life and Public Services of John Quincy Adams* (Auburn: Derby, Miller and Company, 1849), 72. New England periodicals also wrote about the educational effort and impact of Frederick's successors. The Boston *Christian Observer* and New Haven *Religious Intelligencer* reported that Fredrick William III founded several universities and that he personally directed their curriculum, faculty, and so on; see "Prussia," *Christian Observer* 3 (1805): 180 and *The Religious Intelligencer* 42 (1819): 674. Here the king is quoted to have said:

    > Now that by the aid of the most high, peace and order are restored in Europe, I have resumed that subject, [the education of the rising generation] which is the ground work of all true strength of a state, and highly important to the general welfare of the people. And I have earnestly resolved to bring the whole public concern and means of instruction and improvement in my countries, to as great a degree of perfection as is possible and commensurate to the grandeur of the object.

    New Englanders with their admiration of cultivated landscapes also could identify with the image of Frederick as a farmer. For this, see

The American Farmer 3 (1821): 104. Here it said, "Frederick of Prussia, who deserves to be no less celebrated as a political economist, than as a successful commander, expended upwards of a million of dollars annually in the agricultural improvement of his kingdom . . . and by this judicious expenditure, he enriched his subjects and filled his treasury to overflowing." See also Adams, *Letters on Silesia*.

24. Adams, *Letters on Silesia*, 135, 362. For another example of a comparison of Silesia and his native country, see page 76. Adams stressed again and again that Frederick "treated this province [Silesia] always as a favourite" (135) and how he improved it:

    > At the time of his conquest, education had seldom made an object of the concern of governments, and Silesia, like the rest of Europe, was but wretchedly provided, either with schools or teachers [. . .] Frederic issued an ordinance, that a school should be kept in every village, and that a competent subsistence should be provided for the schoolmaster, by joint contribution of the lord of the village, and of the tenants themselves. (362)

25. William Vans Murray to J.Q. Adams, April 3, 1802, American Historical Association, *Annual Report*, 1912, 705. For a sense of a clear division between North and South in Van Murray, see Linda Kerber, *Federalists in Dissent: Imagery and Ideology in Jeffersonian America* (Ithaca: Cornell University Press, 1970), 35.
26. Thiebault, *Original Anecdotes of Frederick the Great*, Vol. 1, 41. For stories on his nephew, see, e.g., "Anecdotes of the Late King of Prussia," *The American Moral and Sentimental Magazine* 1 (1797): 25–262. The story told how Frederick's nephew threw his shuttlecock three times at the desk where the king was writing. The king took it away from the boy and the prince threatened Frederick to return it, which the king did and said, "You are a brave boy, you will never suffer Silesia to be taken from you." Stories about Frederick's youth also show him as a human being suffering under his strict, militant father who had heart for his philosophical son; see, e.g., *King Friedrich Wilhelm the First: The Story of the Youth of Frederick the Great. A Historical Drama in four Acts* (n.p., 1800).
27. For the role the family metaphor played in the creation of an collective American identity in the early nineteenth century, see Amy Murrell Taylor, *The Divided Family in Civil War America* (Chapel Hill: University of North Carolina Press, 2005), 8–9.
28. "Opinion of Frederick II on Field of Sports," *Christian Observer and Advocate* 5 (1806): 482; "Anecdotes of Frederick II," *Ladies Weekly Museum* 17 (1805): 848; for the same story, see "New Anecdotes of the late illustrious Frederick II," *The American Magazine* 1 (1787): 605–609; "Biography of Frederick the Great," *The Nightingale* 1 (1796): 223–225. For another example of an anecdote on the king's justice, see "Anecdote of the King of Prussia," *The Atheneum* 4 (1824): 165.

29. "Justice of King Frederick," *Boston Magazine* 1 (1784): 286–287; for the same story, see *The Emerald or Miscellany of Literature* 30 (1808): 463–464. A similar story told how Frederick changed his plans for the gardens of his castle Sans-Souci in order not to have to remove a mill that was owned by the same family for generations. See "New Anecdotes of the late illustrious Frederick II," 606–607.
30. "King of Prussia," *The Boston Weekly Magazine* 14 (1817): 54–55.
31. "Notice of Frederick the Great," *Cabinet* 1 (1811): 74. For a similar version of the story, see "Frederick the Great," *A Repository of Polite Literature* 2 (1811): 74.
32. For a British cult of service to the state and West and Copley, see Linda Colley, *Britons: Forging the Nation 1707–1837* (New Haven: Yale University Press, 1992), 177–183. Quilted spread, *The Death of General Wolfe at the Battle of the Plains of Abraham*, 1785, in *America's Quilts and Coverlets*, ed. Carleton L. Safford and Robert Bishop (New York: Dutton, 1972), 120–121.
33. John Trumbull, *The Death of General Joseph Warren at the Battle of Bunker Hill*, painting, 1786.
34. Abigail Adams, *Letters of Mrs. Adams, the Wife of John Adams*, 2 vols. (Boston: Charles C. Little and James Brown, 1840), Vol. 1, 126–127; Irma B. Jaffe, *John Trumbull, Patriot-Artist of the American Revolution* (Boston: New York Graphic Society, 1975) and *John Trumbull: The Hand and Spirit of a Painter*, ed. Helena Cooper (New Haven: Yale University Art Gallery, 1982), 30–33. As now English artists and because of their close connection to the king, West and Copley could not undertake the series of Revolutionary War paintings themselves, and, therefore, encouraged Trumbull to do it.
35. For the Federalists' idea of social order, see Wood, *Creation of the American Republic*, 508. Wood argues that they wanted to maintain a hierarchy and an elite of "natural," talented leaders to prevent riots, chaos, and anarchy. See also Kerber, *Federalists in Dissent*, Chapter 6 "Images of social Order," 173–215. For Federalist culture and the ideal of the gentlemen, see Alan Taylor, *William Cooper's Town: Power and Persuasion on the Frontier of the Early American Republic* (New York: A. Knopf, 1995) and *Liberty Men and Great Proprietors: The Revolutionary Settlement on the Maine Frontier, 1760–1820* (Chapel Hill: University of North Carolina Press, 1990).
36. Barry Schwartz, "The Character of Washington: A Study in Republican Culture," *American Quarterly* 38 (1986): 202–222. She argues that this depiction of Washington did neither express classical nor religious ideals, but needs to be interpreted as an indicator of the Anglo-American Whig tradition as described by Bernard Bailyn.
37. Elwin L. Page, *George Washington in New Hampshire* (Cambridge, Massachusetts: Riverside Press, 1932), 14.
38. "Account of the President's Reception at Trenton," *Massachusetts Magazine* 1 (1789): 318; Anonymous, "Arrivée Du President. De

New-York, 24 Avril 1789," *Courier De Boston* 1 (1789): 13. Translation: "toute la ville fut illumineé dans la soirêe." Compare Page, *George Washington*, 25–26. Here he quotes newspaper accounts of the celebration of Washington in Portsmouth: "'The Bell rang a joyful peal, and repeated shouts from grateful thousands, hail'd their Deliverer welcome.'...The salute of thirteen guns fired by three companies....The ships in the harbor...had broken out their colors." On royalistic elements of Washington's birthday celebrations, see Richard Norton Smith, *Patriarch: George Washington and the New American Nation* (Boston: Houghton Mifflin, 1993), 128–129 For the role of newspaper in inventing the American nation, see also David Waldstreicher, *In the Midst of Perpetual Fete: The Making of the American Nationalism, 1776–1820* (Chapel Hill, London: University of North Carolina Press, 1997), 108–112.

39. Anonymous, "Triumphal entry into Philadelphia," *The Philadelphia Monthly Magazine* 1 (1798): 300; Page, *George Washington*, 31–32. See Washington-biographer Richard Norton Smith's comments about Stuart's portraits in Smith, *Patriarch*, 264. Abigail Adams to Mary Cranch, August 9, 1789, quoted in *The Diaries of George Washington*, Vol. V, ed. Albot and Dorothy Twohig (Charlottesville: University of Virginia, 1976), 451. See also Romeo, "For the Philadelphia Minerva," *The Philadelphia Minerva* 1 (1795). Here the author emphasizes that "WASHINGTON is equally majestic" as any monarch. Also see "Triumphal entry into Philadelphia," *The Philadelphia Monthly Magazine* 1 (1798): "Not all the pomp of majesty ... could equal this interesting scene" (300). In her book *Parlor Politics in which the Ladies of Washington Help Build a City and a Government* (Charlottsville: University Press of Virginia, 2000) Catherine Allgor shows what influential role Washington women were able to play by using elements of European court etiquette and how they disliked Jefferson and Jackson's attempts to abolish such royal culture.

40. Anonymous, "From the Virginia Gazette, To General Washington, on the Late Conspiracy," *American Journal*, January 20, 1781.

41. For the cult of Frederick, see Hellmuth, "Die 'Wiedergeburt' Friedrichs." For the reaction to the death of Washington, monuments, paintings, and prints, see *Resolution of Congress for Perpetuating the Memory of General Washington, December 4, 1799*; *in Senate of the United States, May 8th, 1800: Resolutions of the Joint Committee Appointed on the Death of George Washington, Proposing a Statue and Monument in His Memory*, broadside (Philadelphia: n.p., 1800); Patricia Anderson, *Promoted to Glory: The Apotheosis of George Washington* (Northampton, Massachusetts: Smith College Museum of Art, 1980); Barbara Mitnick, *The Changing Image of George Washington* (New York: Fraunces Tavern Museum, 1989), 10, 40. For Washington images on needlework, drinking vessels,

porcelain, and so on, see "The Collector's Washington," *Antiques* 63 (1953): 124–127.

42. The birthday ode was published in Jedidiah Morse, *A True and Authentic History of his Excellency George Washington, Commander in chief of the American Army during the late War* (Philadelphia: Peter Stewart, 1790), 20–21. As another example for Washington's comparison with ancient heroes, see "Character of Washington Written in 1798," in *Memory of Washington: Comprising a Sketch of His Life and Character and the National Testimonials if [of] Respect: Also a Collection of Eulogy and Orations* (Newport, Rhode: Island Oliver Farnsworth, 1800), 7–12. Some eulogies found him even superior to ancient heroes; see "An Eulogium of General Washington," *The Massachusetts Magazine* 7 (1795): 428–429. Here he was also compared with Cincinnatus: "Like Cincinnatus, the Roman husbandman and General, he [Washington] left the implements of agriculture for the weapons of war; having successfully used them, he lays them down, and withdraw from the camp to his plantation, to resume the employments of a country life." For many more examples, see Garry Wills, *Cincinnatus: George Washington and the Enlightenment* (Garden City, New York: Doubleday, 1984). See also the chapter "Roman Virtue," in Howard Mumford Jones, *O Strange New World: American Culture: The Formative Years* (New York: Viking Press, 1964). Jones argues that Washington embodied classical ideals of the early Republic. For the comparison of Frederick the Great with ancient Roman heroes in German publications, see, e.g., Dieter Jenisch, Der Borussias elfter Gesang, *Neuer Teutscher Merkur* 2 (1792): 426 and Orwing, Auf Friedrichs, *Teutscher Merkur* 3 (1787): 57. For visual depictions of Frederick as an ancient hero, see G.W. Hoffmann, Friedrich des Zweiten Ankunft im Elysium, etching 1788, courtesy of the German Historical Museum, Berlin.
43. Cornelius Tiebout, *Sacred to Patriotism*, engraving, 1798, in Mitnick, *The Changing Image of George Washington*, 15.
44. "Eulogy on George Washington," *New England Galaxy* 3 (1820), 151; "The Collector's Washington," 124–127. See also Susanne Netzer, *Daniel N. Chodowiecki 1726–1801: Zeichnungen aus dem Besitz der Kunstsammlung der Veste Coburg, Katalog zur Ausstellung* (London: Goethe Institute, 1989), 127; and Andrea M. Kluxen, *Bild eines Königs: Friedrich der Große in der Graphik* (Limburg, California: Starke Verlag,1986), 136, 144.
45. George Washington, William Rush, Independence National Historical Park Collection, Philadelphia. For a picture of the sculpture, see Wills, *Cincinnatus*, 163. The Boston periodical *Gentlemen and Ladies' Town and Country Magazine* described him as a philosopher as early as 1789: "Brief Account of the Illustrious George Washington," *The Gentlemen and Ladies' Town and Country Magazine* (1789): 153.

46. "The Life of George Washington," *The Panoplist and Missionary Magazine* 2 (1810): 531, 526, 529, and 525. When he went to school at Westmoreland, the story said: "His character for truth was such, that, when the boys were in violent dispute respecting a question of, nothing was more common than for some little shaver to call out 'Well boys! George Washington was there; he knows all about it; and if don't [*sic*] say it was so, then we will give it up.'" For Washington's benevolence, see also "An Eulogium of General Washington," *The Massachusetts Magazine* 7 (1795): 428; and John Fitch, *A Sermon Delivered... as a Tribune of Respect for the Memory of General George Washington* (Peachah, Vermont: Farley and Goss, 1800). Often such publications stressed his magnanimity; see, e.g., "The Character of George Washington," *The Massachusetts Magazine* 4 (1792): 429.
47. "Lewis's Oration on George Washington," *The Monthly Magazine and American Review* 2 (1800): 126. This is one of many examples. Johann Erich Biester, Friedrich Gedicke, "König Friedrich der Große," *Berlinische Monatsschrift* 8 (1786): 280–281 [Original: "Er ist nicht mehr, der liebevolle Vater seines Volkes, der Schutzheld seiner Lande."]. For one of countless other German examples, see Anonymous, "Neuere Weltbegebenheiten," *Neue Bunzlauische Monatsschrift* 3 (1786): 281. Here it said: "*Er ist dahin, Friedrich II. der 75jährige Greis, und 46jährige Vater Schlesiens und aller seiner Provinzen.*" [He is gone, Frederick II, the 75 year old man, and 46 year old father of Silesia and all his other provinces.]
48. Edward Savage, *The Washington Family*, painting, 1796, in Mitnick, *The Changing Image of George Washington*, 32.
49. See, e.g., "The Life of George Washington," *The Panoplist and Missionary Magazine* 2 (1810): 525 and "Portrait of General George Washington," *The New York Magazine or Literary Repository*, 2nd series (1797): 99.
50. See Daniel Chodowiecki, *Der Todt Friedrichs des Zweyten*, etching, 1792, in Eckhart Hellmuth, *Nationalismus vor dem Nationalismus*, 31; John James Barralet, *Apotheosis of Washington*, engraving, 1800, in Wills, *Cincinnatus*, 26; and John Trumbull, *Study for the Apotheosis of Washington*, in Wills, *Cincinnatus*, 69.
51. For the apotheosis of Frederick the Great, see Hellmuth, "A Monument to Frederick the Great," 321. For a discussion on the apotheosis of Washington compare Wills, *Cincinnatus*, 74–79. As an example for the deification of Washington in written sources, see "An Eulogium of General Washington," *Massachusetts Magazine* 7 (1795): 428. The article contains the following quotation: "The hero of America [fought] from the godlike motif of freeing his country from thraldom [*sic*]." For the depiction of Washington as godlike, see also Jones, *O Strange New World*, 263–264; Schwartz, "The Character of Washington," 202, and Marcus Cunliffe, *George*

Washington: Man and Monument (Boston: Little, Brown and Company, 1958), 6–7. For the religious iconography of Washington, see also Robert Peter Hay, "George Washington: American Moses," *American Quarterly* 21 (1969): 781–791; and James H. Smylie, "The President as Republican Prophet and King: Clerical Reflections on the Death of Washington," *Journal of Church and State* 18 (1976): 233–252. For the Puritan dogma in American culture, see Sacvan Bercovitch, *The Puritan Origins of the American Self* (New Haven: Yale University Press, 1975). For the intermingling of religious, liberal, and Republican ideas during the early republic, see Kloppenberg, "The Virtues of Liberalism," 9–33.

52. For the Chinese glass painting after Barralet, see C.L. Crossman, "China Trade Paintings on Glass," *Antiques* 95 (1969): 375. For Peale's painting, see Anderson, *Promoted to Glory*, 36. For *The Apotheosis of Benjamin Franklin and George Washington,* see ibid., 55–57. For the "tomb mourning" pictures, see Will, *Cincinnatus*, 79 and Anderson, *Promoted to Glory.* For the wallpaper picturing the Washington monument in Enfield, Massachusetts, see the slide collection of the Society for the Preservation of New England Antiquities; the item is not numbered and, therefore, there is no further information available.
53. For such German pictures of the death of Frederick, see Hellmuth, "Die 'Wiedergeburt' Friedrichs' des Grossen." For the engraving in the McCann house, see *Beauport: The Sleeper-McCann House* (Boston: David R. Godine, 1991), 88–89. See Daniel Chodowiecki, *Friedrichs des Einzigen Todt*, etching, 1790, in Hellmuth, *Nationalismus vor dem Nationalismus*, 31; and Patchwork quilt, *The Death of General Washington*, 1800–1810, in *America's Quilts and Coverlets*, 120–121.

Chapter 3 Failed Republicans: Images of the British and the French

1. James Kirke Paulding, *A Sketch of Old England, By a New-England Man*, Vol. I (New York: Charles Wiley, 1822), 3.
2. In the eighteenth century the British, e.g., constructed their national identity against the French; see Linda Colley, *Britons: Forging the Nation 1707–1837* (London: Pimlico, 1992) and John Brewer, *The Pleasures of the Imagination: English Culture in the Eighteenth Century* (London: Fontana Press, 1997).
3. *Ladies Port Folio*; *Merrimack Magazine and Ladies' Literary Cabinet*, and *The Boston Weekly Magazine or Ladies Miscellany*; *The Christian Herald*, *Religious Informer*, and *Christian Spectator*; *The New England Farmer*; *The Atheneum*, *The Massachusetts Magazine*, and *The North American Review*.

4. Edward Everett from Dorchester, Massachusetts, was also a Harvard graduate and studied abroad at the University of Goettingen.
5. The best account of Tudor's life is in Clifford K. Shipton, *Sibley's Harvard Graduates*, Vol. 17 (Boston: Harvard University Press, 1975).
6. "A Foreigner's Opinions of England, Comprised in a Series of Free Remarks by Christian August Gottlieb Gohde. Translated from the Original German by Thomas Horne, Boston: Wells and Lilly, 1822," *Christian Spectator* 5 (1823): 313–324, 320. For a portrait of "dandies," see also "The Hermit in London or Sketches of English Manners," *The Atheneum or, Spirit of the English Magazines* 4 (1818): 173–176.
7. Anonymous, "English Pride," *The Monthly Magazine and American Review* 2 (1821): 135–141, 139. The author wrote:

   We must voluntarily narrow... [the bounds of joviality and companionship] still further [he wrote], by acknowledging the supremacy of a new friend—the daemon [*sic*] of Luxury. Enjoyment of our friend's society was formerly considered the rational object of dinnerparty; but you now invite them that you may exhibit your superior magnificence, and, by exciting their envy or anger, do your best towards converting them into enemies.
8. Robert Southey, *Letters from England by Don Manuel Alvarez Espriella* (Boston: Munroe, Francis and Parker, 1808), 52. For other statements on greed in British society, see Diary of Dr. Walter Channing 1810–1812, Walter Channing Papers, Massachusetts Historical Society, Boston. Here Walter said that a Prussian travel companion was "disgusted with the manners of the greed in private life."
9. William Austin, *Letters from London* (Boston: Pelham, 1804), 17–18. For social effects of commercialism, see also Southey, *Letters from England*, 287. He found the theatres supporting the immorality of the new merchant class:

   The commercial system has long been undermining the distinction of ranks in society, and introducing a worse distinction in its stead. Mushrooms are every day starting up from the dunghill of trade, nobody knows how, and family pride is therefore become a common subject of ridicule in England; the theatres [*sic*] make it the object of a safe jest, sure to fiad [*sic*] applause from the multitude.
10. "Anecdote of An English Nobleman," *The Massachusetts Magazine* 6 (1794): 478; see Paulding, *A Sketch of Old England*, 11. Here Paulding talked about a class of Englishmen that "once gave a character to England.... It was this honesty, this inflexible regard to principle, which made amends for the absence of those easy and sprightly manners, which attach a stranger.... This class is, however, I regret to say, daily mouldering [*sic*] away amidst the speculating extravagance, and splendid pauperism of the times."

11. Benjamin Silliman, *A Journal of Travels in England, Holland and Scotland... in the years 1805 and 1806*, 3 Volumes (New Haven: S. Converse, 1820), 278. I was "completely disgusted with a place, which [he wrote], although superlatively elegant, is, I am convinced, a most successful school of corruption" ("The English Justice," *New England Galaxy and Masonic Magazine* 50 [1818]: 4).
12. Austin, *Letters*, 62. He explained: "A servant is bound to lift the knocker once: should he usurp a nobleman's knock he would hazard his situation. A postman knocks twice, very loudly. A milkman knocks once, at the same time, sending forth an artificial noise, not unlike the yell of an American Indian." Silliman observed the exact same ritual of class distinction when he studied in Great Britain; see Chandos Michael Brown, *Benjamin Silliman: A Life in the Young Republic* (Princeton: Princeton University Press, 1989), 160.
13. Diary of Dr. Walter Channing, 1810–1812, Walter Channing Papers, Massachusetts Historical Society, Boston. Austin, *Letters*, 12. For a description of social differences, see also "Sketches of English High Life," *The Atheneum or, Spirit of the English Magazines* 9 (1821): 463–468; H. "English Pride," 135–141, 136; and "The Hermit in London," *The Atheneum or, Spirit of the English Magazines* 5 (1819): 179–180, 238–239. James Kirke Paulding also said that in Great Britain wealth was not reward for hard work; see Paulding, *A Sketch of Old England*, I, 23.
14. William Tudor, *Letters of the Eastern States* (New York: Kirk and Mercein, 1820), 166; "A Foreigner's Opinions of England, Comprised in a Series of Free Remarks by Christian August Gottlieb Gohde. Translated from the Original German by Thomas Horne, Boston: Wells and Lilly, 1822," *Christian Spectator* 5 (1823): 313–324, 319; Paulding, *A Sketch of Old England*, I, 22, on beggars in Birmingham, see 81–82. New England newspapers often commented on poverty in Great Britain; see, e.g., "Britons Strike Home: England and America," *American Advocate*, October 2, 1819. The author wrote: "Britain? Look at her capital; view the scenes opening at, and around Manchester, see mothers disputing the scanty meals of starving infants; fathers, fired with the fury of despair, finding no relief in endless and unremitted toil, threatening to break down the last barriers of civil society."
15. Austin, *Letters*, 129. Silliman defined the British character in similar terms:

    The English servants are extremely assiduous and adroit; they are generally handsome well dressed men, and they ply the guest with such watchful attention, that, if for any reason he lays down his knife and fork, his plate is instantly caught away, and a clean one substituted. The manners of the gentlemen I think are marked by less suavity, than with us, and there is less gentleness in the tone of voice and in the turn of

> deportment. As to dress perhaps they are more punctilious. (Silliman, *A Journal of Travels in England*, 31)

16. "Journal of a Tour and Residence in Great Britain during the Years 1810 and 1811 by a French Traveler," *North American Review* 2 (1816): 242–271, here 246. For another example of gambling as a British vice, see "The Hermit in London, or Sketches of English Manners," 25–26. The author described the bad influence London society had on his cousin:

> The plain English of all this is, that my poor cousin is now enlisted under this Fashion banner, is a recruit of pleasure—an aspirante [*sic*] of sensuality—that he about to become the dupe of gamblers, and the imitator of the great,—that his moderate fortune is marked down for a finish,—and that he is on the high road to ruin. (26)

17. "English Manners at Different Periods," *The Atheneum or, Spirit of the English Magazines* 13 (1823): 261–263, here 263 and Silliman, *A Journal of Travels in England*, 149. For this see also Austin, *Letters*, 23–24; "The Hermit in London," *The Atheneum or, Spirit of the English Magazines* 5 (1819): 17–20; and "Sketches of English High Life," 463–468, 466. Here the author wrote about his visit to a fair: "The English . . . do not appear, to advantage in a holiday-scene. Those who were not drunk were dull; and in the merriment of the former there was too much coarseness and brutality." For another example, see "The French and the English," *The Recreative Magazine* 1 (1822): 426–446, 431, where the author asked rhetorically: "What are the joys of society in England? They drink immoderately, and eat in proportion: they swear, they kick, they cuff, and, when tired of these enchanting pleasures, they hang and drown themselves." For English vices and "savage" manners, see also "The French and the English," 426–446.
18. "Female Dress," *The Emerald* 1 (1808): 272; "Packing Up after an English Country Ball," *The Atheneum or, Spirit of the English Magazines* 2 (1822): 148–150. A certain Mr. Blackwood underlined that English women did not show virtues such as simplicity: "The women for example . . . possess none of that innocent untempted [*sic*] simplicity, which is more than half the grace of virtue"; see Blackwood, "English Woman," *The Euterpeiad or Musical Intelligencer* 2 (1821): 25. For the immorality of the English, see also "English Nobility," *Something* 1 (1809): 102–103. Here the author wrote, "Every moral principle was at least as readily imbibed and encouraged in the palaces of the real nobility, as in the houses of the most prudent citizen" (102). For a similar picture of English and French women, see Tudor, *Letters of the Eastern States*, 189:

> It is difficult to compare our women with those of France and England, because their manners, as well as their dress, resemble neither entirely, but partake considerably of both. Their dress is

> less foppish and extravagant than the French; less crude and fanciful than the English. Their manners are less artificial and sparkling than the former; less bold and decided than the latter.

19. "From Goldsmith's Citizen of the World," *The Weekly Visitant* 1 (1806): 163; Paulding, *A Sketch of Old England*, Vol. I, 99, and "Character of the English Nation," *Merrimack Miscellany* 1 (1805): 26. For British rudeness and vulgarity, see also "Journal of a Tour and Residence in Great Britain during the Years 1810 and 1811 by a French Traveler," 242–271. The author wrote: "The tone of manners in England is often embarrassing to a stranger, there is so much coldness, so little officiousness, so much reserve, and so little sympathy...and the coarse imitations of this style of society, that are too frequently met with, are downright rudeness and vulgarity" (251–252). The Boston newspaper *Polyanthos* used language to exhibit British egoism. In an 1812 issue an anonymous author thought, "It is something remarkable, that in other languages, the pronoun of the first person singular is usually written with a small letter....The English are the only people, who have dignified the *little hero* with a capital," "English Egotism," *Polyanthos* 2 (1812): 44–45.
20. Paulding, *A Sketch of Old England*, Vol. I, 6.
21. Austin, *Letters*, 100–101; F. Hopkins, "Character of the English People," *New England Galaxy and Masonic Magazine* 3 (1820): 170. Here he wrote:

    > It is a vain to tell...[the Englishman] that there are many rivers in America in comparison of which the Thames is but a ditch, that there are single province there larger than all England, and that the colonies formerly belonging to Great Britain, but now *Independent States*, are vastly more extensive than England, Wales, Scotland and Ireland are all taken together.

    See also "Sketches of English Manners," *The Atheneum or, Spirit of the English Magazines*, 10 (1821): 65–69, 66. For statements on British arrogance, see "English Manners at Different Periods," 261–263, 261: "No nation has a higher opinion of itself than the English." and Austin, *Letters*, 16: "The English are said to hold all other people in contempt—the usual fault of islanders. But the English indulge a sentiment of disdain arising from comparison, rather than from any other cause."
22. Southey, *Letters from England*, 72; Hopkins "Character of the English People," 170. Here Hopkins uncovered following contradictions: "An Englishman will treat his enemy with great generosity, and his friend with ingratitude and inhumanity, he will be lavish of his wealth when he has but little of it, and become a misery wretch when fortune pours her favor in his purse....Today his heart expands with social benevolence; tomorrow he is cold, sullen and morose." See also "Sketches of English Manners," 65–69:

    > What a different animal an Englishman is at home and abroad! Abroad, he cannot move a step without abusing every thing and

> everybody...at home, he rails, with equal violence, at all the customs and institutions of his own country. At home, he is a lover of liberty, and an advocate for equal rights of mankind; abroad, he acts, like the Roman proconsuls in their provinces, as if the greatest part of the human species were brought into the world for no other purpose but to wait upon his pleasure.... Abroad he is an indefatigable sight-seer [*sic*], and will not pass through the obscurest town without an accurate scrutiny of every thing that a...place can point out to his notice;—at home he toses [*sic*] entirely this thirst for information, and I verily believe there are many Englishman who have lived in London, and yet know less of its curiosities than they do of Rome, Athens, or Thebes. (66)

In "English Manners at Different Periods," 261–263, the author wrote:

> One may observe...that they [the English] are neither valiant in war, nor faithful in peace, which is apparently by experience; for although they are placed in a good soil and a good country, they are wicked, and so extremely sickle, that at one moment they will adore a prince, and the next moment they would kill or crucify him. (261)

23. Austin, *Letters*, 73–74. He emphasized the worldliness and corruptness: "Whenever religion degenerates into ceremony, or becomes the crooked way of worldly ambition, it becomes a matter of mockery with the profane, and of indifference with the more serious" ("Sketches of English Manners," 65–69, 65). It continued about the English system: "But in England, where all must pay tithes to the parson, whether they attend his preaching or not, it affords an indubitable mark of the earnestness and sincerity of the religious feeling that distinguishes this country, to see so many sects, for conscience-sake, supporting ministers of their own by additional voluntary contributions." The middle part of the poem, "The Happy Life of an English Parson," *The New England Farmer* 4 (1825): 104, described privileges, possessions, and loyalty to Charles I:

> A wife that makes conserves; a steed
> That carries double when there's need;
> October store, and best Virginia,
> Tithe pig, and mortuary guinea;
> Gazettes sent gratis down, and frank'd,
> For which thy patron's weekly thank'd;
> A large concordance, bound long since;
> Sermons to Charles the First, when prince;
> A chronicle of ancient standing;
> A Chrysostom [*sic*] to smooth—thy hand in; The polyglot—three parts—my text,
> Howbeit [*sic*],—likewise—now to my next;
> Low here the Septuagint [*sic*],—and Paul,
> To sum the whole,—the close of all.

Paulding also wrote about the privileges of English bishops and corruptness of English clergy. Moreover, he criticized that the Anglican Church depended too much on the king; see Paulding, *A Sketch of Old England*, Vol. 2, 28–29, 32, 39–40.

24. William Sullivan to George Keith Taylor, Boston, August 28, 1812, Sullivan Collection, Huntington Library, San Marino. For New England's opposition to the war of 1812, see Paul A. Varg, *New England and Foreign Relations, 1789–1850* (Hanover: University Press of New England, 1983), 63–72; Steven Watts, *The Republic Reborn: War and the Making of Liberal America, 1790–1820* (Baltimore: John Hopkins University Press, 1987), 280–281, and David Waldstreicher, *In the Midst of Perpetual Fetes: The Making of American Nationalism, 1776–1820* (Chapel Hill, London: University of North Carolina Press, 1997), 257–261. As examples for sermons against the war, see David Osgood, *Solemn Protest against the Late Declaration of War, in a Discourse, Delivered on the Next Lord's Day after the Tidings of It Were Received* (Cambridge, Hilliard and Metcalf, 1812); John Lathrop, *Two Discourses Delivered in Boston* (Boston: Burditt and Co., 1812); A. Layman, *Address to the Clergy of New-England on Their Opposition to the Rulers of the United States* (Concord, New Hampshire: n.p., 1814). Osgood implied the war would destroy New England's identity that was partly built on trade and prosperity by emphasizing that this was on risk:

> Wealth has flown in our sea-ports [he said], every foot of ground belonging to them has risen in value more than a thousand per cent, many of them have risen spacious and splendid palaces, and our merchants have become princes in opulence, while every class of tradesmen, mechanics, and labourers, have had full and constant employment, and more than double wages. This prosperity from trade has extended and diffused its salutary and enlivening effects over the face of the whole country, into very town and village, and to the remotest settlements in the wilderness. (18–19).

New Englanders memorized the American Revolution often as a New England achievement; see William Tappan, *New England and Other Poems* (Philadelphia: J.H. Cunningham, 1819), 7: "Fair heaven, approving smiles on every toil, / And Freedom hovers o'er her native soil; / Here, at her altar beamed the sacred fire' / Whose lightning-spark a nation did inspire."

25. For the role of the Battle of New Orleans in strengthening American nationalism, see John William Ward, *Andrew Jackson: Symbol of an Age* (New York: Oxford University Press, 1953). For the celebration of the Battle of Lake Erie, see *Brilliant Naval Victory. Yankee Perry, Better than old English Cider*, Broadside (Boston: N. Coverly, 1813), Massachusetts Historical Society:

> Huzza! For the brave Yankee boys,
> Who touch'd up John Bull on lake Erie,

Who gave'em a taste of our toys,
From the fleet of brave Commodore *Perry.*
They were not made of 'lasses but lead,
And good solid lumps of cold iron,
When they hit JOHNNY BULL in the head,
They gave him a pain that he'll die on.
Now the *Niagara* bore down,
To giv'em a bit of a whacking,
The *Lawrence* came up and wore round,
And set her nice pounders [*sic*] a cracking.
They soon felt the *Scorpion's* sting,
And likewise the *Eriel's* thunder,
The *Porcupine* give'em a quill,
And made the Queen Charlotte knock under.
The *Somers* now gav'em a touch,
And the *Tygress* she give him a shock sir,
Which did not divert Johnny much;
For it put him in mind of the Boxer.
The *Trip* she was hammering away,
The *Oris* soon made'em smell powder
The brave Caledonia that day
Made her thunder grow louder and louder.
We gave'em such tough yankee [*sic*] blows,
That soon they thought fit to surrender;
That day made'em feel that their foes,
Were made in the masculine gender.
Poor Johnny was sick of the gripes,
From the pills that we gave them at ERIE,
And for fear of the stars and the strips,
He struck to brave Commodore PERRY.
Now as for poor old Johnny Bull,
If we meet him on land or on Sea sir,
We'll give him a good belly full,
Of excellent gun powder tea sir.
Old England is fam'd for her perry [*sic*] and beer,
Which quickly bewilders the brain,
But such PERRY as she's taken here,
She never will wish for again.
Huzza! For our brave Yankee Tars,
Who pepper;d the British merry,
Who fought for the stripes and the stars,
Under brave Commodore Perry.

For the War of 1812 as a catalyst in the symbolism of the British, see Watts, *Republic Reborn.*

26. Theodore Lyman, *A Few Weeks in Paris* (Boston: Cumming and Hilliard, 1814), 109–110. For other depictions of French love of

extravagance and luxury, see "The French and the English," 426–446, 437. Here the author wrote about the French: "Their ardent love of glory, joined to the most profound homage to the idol of court favour [*sic*]...the extravagance of their taste, than which nothing can be more contemptible, except the eagerness of all Europe to adopt it." In the "Review of John Scott's a Visit to Paris in 1814," *The North American Review* 2 (1816): 398–431, 404, the reviewer quoted John Scott's description of a French hotel room: "The room into which we were shewn [*sic*], gave strong evidence that we were not in England. It would have been fine and elegant, if it had not been out of repair, and dirty. Glasses of a size which we never see in our own country, but in the houses of persons of fortune, hung on the cheerless walls." "Nothing but French," *The Atheneum or, Spirit of the English Magazines* 1 (1817): 111–112; "The Reasons Why the French Have More Wit and Better Spirits than the English," *Literary Tablet* 2 (1804): 17–18, and "French Bombast," *The Atheneum or, Spirit of the English Magazines* 1 (1824): 324. As an example for statements about theatres, see "French Peculiarities," *The Atheneum or, Spirit of the English Magazines* 1 (1817): 606–610. The author assured: "Such a flexibility of character must inevitably pave the way to a variety of irregularities, and eventually to vices; time is wasted in theaters, at shows, or at the more dangerous occupation of the gaming table" (610). When Abigail Adams went to Paris in 1784 to join her husband she astonished over the number of servants one was expected to have, shocked how extravagance indicated one's social status, and wondered whether the French ever worked in between going to plays and spectacles; see David McCullough, "Abigail in Paris," *The Massachusetts Historical Review* 3 (2001): 1–19. For the French's love for parties, see "The French and the English," 426–446. Here the author wrote: "It is extremely well known, though almost incredible, that at Spa, to which the French nobility emigrated, during the earlier part of the revolution, the Lavals, the Luxembourgs...were dancing with all gaiety possible, while their castles were pillaged and destroyed in France" (441). About immoral arrangements within marriages, see "French Theater," *Merrimack Magazine and Ladies' Literary Cabinet* 1 (1806): 107. The article ridiculed the *Theatre Francais* as a place of scandals and marriage arrangements. About one play it said, "Its purpose is to ridicule the facility with which divorces are obtained, and the indelicate traffic of getting a husband or wife by advertisement or agency." The play was about an old man who married a young girl. Both are unhappy and find another couple with the reverse age difference and decided not to get divorced, but to switch partner. For a description of French gambling houses, see John Scott, *Paris Revisited in 1815* (Boston: Wells and Lilly, 1816), 167. For immorality, see also "Review of John Scott's a Visit to Paris in 1814." Here the author wrote: "That there is much immorality in France, that the foundations of society are at some point sapped, cannot, unfortunately, be denied" (400).

27. "Nothing but French," 111–112. Hardly any publication on such a French lifestyle as any other descriptions of the French appeared before 1800.

28. *Connecticut Courant*, Hartford, April 8, 1793; *Columbian Centinel*, Boston April 17, 1793. As his behavior at his execution shows, the paper argued that Louis

> appears not to be the man which his enemies reported. His heart was found—his head was clear—and he would have reigned with glory, had he but possessed those faults which his assassins laid to his charge. His mind possessed the suggestion of wisdom; and even in the last moment, when the spirit of life was winged for another world, his lips gave utterance to them, and he spoke with firmness and with resignation

and in a mourning tone it continued,

> Thus has ended the life of Louis XVI, after a period of four years detention; during which he experienced from his subjects every species of ignominy and cruelty which a people could insist on the most sanguinary tyrant. Louis XVI. Who was proclaimed at the commencement of his reign, the Friend of the People, and by the constituent Assembly, the restorer of Liberties—Louis who but a few years since he was the most powerful Monarch in Europe, has at last perished on the scaffold. Neither his own natural goodness of heart, had the fire to procure the happiness of his subjects, nor that…love which the French entertained for their Monarch, has been sufficient to save him from the fatal judgment.
>
> "At this time, when the King of France is represented in our Gazettes as a tyrant, oppressor, it is but just to insert the following imperfect justification of his character," the anonymous author wrote, "he has ever been a pattern of pure morals, of decent deportment and conversation. He never had either a mistress or favourite [*sic*], and has ever been the greatest enemy to pomp and luxury. The King's honesty and probity were so extremely great, that considering the debt of his ancestors so sacred, he saved the nation from bankruptcy." (*Concord Herald*, Concord, March 28, 1793)

See also *Columbian Centinel*, Boston, April 13, 1793 and *Concord Herald*, Concord, April 25, 1793. Both papers printed the speech that the king tried to give before his execution as proof for his good intentions.

29. *Salem Gazette*, April 16, 1793:

> On Friday morning the Dauphin stole down stairs—the sentry at the door asked him where he was going—"Into the street (replied the infant) throughout all Paris, to beg of the people

> not to kill my dear Papa." One of the guards carried him to the King; when he heard what the child had said, he burst into tears, and pressed him to his bosom. The King took leave of the Queen and his infant Son and Daughter, at five o'clock yesterday afternoon. The Queen was in a raving delirium.

Columbian Centinel, Boston April 17, 1793: "Madame Royale, the daughter of Louis XVI is dangerously ill. She received the sacraments on the day of her father's execution. That fatal event and the barbarity with which she is treated in prison [the rest of the sentence is unreadable]. . . . Madame Elizabeth, the late King's sister, is also in a languishing condition." *Salem Gazette*, April 23, 1793:

> The Queen of France, by all that can be learnt, is not in found mind: she is become, by the weight of her affliction, quite decrepid [*sic*]—her hair is turned grey [*sic*]—she constantly weeps, and takes little refreshment. The Princess Elizabeth is much in the same state, though her constitution is stronger—she eats and drinks, but seldom speaks. The daughter remains ill. The Prince royal, too young to feel like others, is in better health, but even he is strongly affected with the late events.

For the story on how the royal family refused to pass by Louis's room, see *Concord Herald*, Concord, May 2, 1793 and *Salem Gazette*, April 16, 1793. For a report on the fate of the crown prince, see *Columbian Centinel*, Boston April 17, 1793: "With respect to the Dauphin, some Members of the Convention have not scrupled to declare, that the apothecary could easily get rid of him. The Dauphin is lodged in the Mayor's house until the convention determine his fate; he is prevented seeing the Queen, the most favorable opinion of his punishment is perpetual imprisonment." Reports on the queen's execution also supported this image. They implied how badly Marie Antoinette was treated when they reported that she was "thrown into a common prison amidst the most wretched and abandoned criminals" and emphasized the French people's cruelty by emphasizing that the "enthusiasm of the great body of the people of France, is said to be as great or greater than ever," *Columbian Centinel*, Boston April 17, 1793, and *Connecticut Courant*, Hartford, April 15, 1793.

30. For Americans' enthusiastic reaction to the French Revolution, see David Brion Davis, "American Equality and Foreign Revolutions," *Journal of American History* 76 (1989): 729–752. Gary B. Nash traced the reaction of New England clergymen in "The American Clergy and the French Revolution," *William and Mary Quarterly* 22 (1965): 392–412. For the particular reaction of New Englanders, see Ann Butler Lever, "Vox Populi, Vox Dei: New England and the French Revolution, 1787–1801" (Ph.D. diss., University of North Carolina at Chapel Hill, 1972). David Waldstreicher and Len Travers describe the partisan character of celebration of the French Revolution; see Waldstreicher, *In the Midst of Perpetual Fetes*, 112–140 and Len

Travers, *Celebrating the Fourth: Independence Day and the Rites of Nationalism in the Early Republic* (Amherst: University of Massachusetts Press, 1997), 89–106.

31. "French Cruelty," *The Literary Tablet* 3 (1805): 26; "A Picture of the French Revolution," *Ladies' Port Folio* 1 (1820): 153–154. See also John Carr, *The Stranger in France* (Hartford: Oliver D. Cooker, 1804), 70–74. He told a story about an English woman who was married to a French aristocrat and very cruelly treated and imprisoned, raped, and guillotined during the Terror. Some stories pictured French women as heroes rescuing their husbands; see, e.g., "From an Interesting Anecdote of a Heroic Female during the French Revolution," *Ladies' Port Folio* 1 (1820): 11. Others praised the British for their hospitality toward French refugees; see "French Refugees," *The Atheneum or, Spirit of the English Magazines* 11 (1822): 284–285:

    > No event, either in ancient or modern times, ever created so many exiles as the French revolution, notwithstanding the difficulty which often occurred of escaping from the merciless fangs of the guillotine, by which so many thousands were immolated in the sacred name of liberty.... England, notwithstanding the longcherished [*sic*] national enemy, was the first, last, and best asylum of the French emigrants.

    John Scott refreshed the memory of the royal massacres when he imagined the connection Louis XVII made to the cruel past, when he returned to Paris after the restoration of the monarchy. He looked "upon an unchanged nation, who danced as enthusiastically around the heads that were stuck upon pikes, and held up in the faces of Louis the XVI and his Queen," Scott, *Paris Revisited*, 173. Memories of the horrors of the royal executions were also revived in biographies of General Lafayette, which were published in large numbers during his tour through New England in 1824–1825; see, e.g., *Memoirs of General La Fayette Embracing Details of His Public and Private Life, Sketches of the American Revolution, the French Revolution, the Down-Fall of Bonaparte, and the Restoration of the Bourbons* (Hartford, Connecticut: Barber and Robinson, 1825), 334–414.

32. "French Peculiarities," 606–610. For French women in male occupations, see also Blackwood, "English Woman," *The Euterpeiad or Musical Intelligencer* 2 (1821): 25. He said that French women do business like men: "They mix themselves with all the cares of their husbands and assist them in their trade and business...and they know as much, and often more, of the details of trade than their husbands." In his travel book on France John Carr also reported on the male lifestyle of French women, when he described how they went to the theatre even unattended by men; John Carr, *The Stranger in France* (Hartford: Oliver D. Cooker, 1804), 144. New Englanders

also imagined French women in male positions as spies under Napoleon; see "Account of the Female Spies in the Service of Napoleon," *The Atheneum or, Spirit of the English Magazines* 11 (1822): 459–465. Linda Kerber coined the term "Republican mother," in her book *Women of the Republic: Intellect and Ideology in Revolutionary America* (Chapel Hill: University of North Carolina Press, 1980). For a separation in a male and female sphere in early Republican New England, see Nancy Cott, *The Bonds of Womanhood: "Woman's Sphere" in New England, 1780–1835* (New Haven: Yale University Press, 1977).

33. "Review of John Scott's a Visit to Paris in 1814," 398–431, and Lyman, *A Few Weeks in Paris*, 83. "The French Peasant," *The New England Farmer* 1 (1823): 384:

    Hark, don't you hear the general cry
    Whose troubles ever equall'd mine
    How readily each stander [*sic*] by
    Replies, with captious echo "mine"
    Sure from our clime this discord springs
    Heaven's choicest blessings we abuse,
    And every Englishman alive,
    Whether duke, lord, esquire or gent,
    Claims, as his just prerogative,
    Ease, liberty, and discontent.
    A Frenchman often starves and sings,
    With cheerfulness and wooden shoes.

34. "Anecdote of a French Officer," *The Religious Informer* 1819 (1): 41. Discrimination and Persecution of French Protestants after the revocation of the Edict of Nantes were, e.g., described in "An Excellent Spirit Discovered in Saurin, a French Preacher, Who Was Banished by Lewis XIV, because He Was a Protestant," *The Christian Herald* 8 (1825): 45–46.
35. "The French Protestant Children," *The Guardian* 6 (1824): 391–393.
36. "Anecdote of a Noble Huguenot," *Ladies' Port Folio* 1 (1820): 109–110.
37. A. de Auborn, *The French Convert: Being a True Relation of the Happy Conversion of a noble French Lady from the Errors and superstition of Popery, to the Reformed Religion by Means of a Protestant Gardener, her Servant* (Berwick, Massachusetts: W. Phorson, 1795). To give just a few examples of the large number of reprints of the *French Convert*, there were two Boston editions of the book in 1793 and 1794, a 1794 edition printed in Haverhill, and a 1798 in Brookfield, Massachusetts. In New Hampshire it was published in Walpole in 1794, in Hartford and in New Haven in 1798.
38. For the perception of religion in France among the New England clergy, see Gary B. Nash, "The American Clergy and the French

Revolution," 392–412. He traced the reaction of New England clergymen in this article.

39. On Huguenots in New England, see Hammet Tilley, *The Huguenots in Rhode Island* (New York: n.p., 1896); Abiel Holmes, *Memoir of the French Protestants Who Settled in Oxford* (Worcester, n.p., 1826); Edwin Allen, *Some Huguenots and Other Early Settlers at the Kennebec River* (Portland: Maine Historical Society, 1892); Charles Washington Baird, *The History of the Huguenot Emigration to America* (New York: Dodd, Mead and Company, 1885); and Jon Butler, *The Huguenots in America: A Refugee People in New World Society* (Cambridge: Harvard University Press, 1983).
40. "Remarkable Instance of a French Soldier," *The Boston Weekly Magazine* 3 (1819): 76. For this, see also "A French Grenadier," *The Atheneum or, Spirit of the English Magazines* 8 (1820): 95. This story described how in a battle between the French and the British

    > a child by some accident escaped from a house in the midst of the scene of action, and run, unawed [*sic*] by the danger, into the narrow interval between the hostile fronts. One of the French grenadiers seeing the imminent danger of the child, grounded his piece; left the ranks in the hottest fire; took the child in his arms; and placed it in safety.

    A story of a French sailor, who risked his live swimming back to a sinking ship to rescue a mother and her child, falls in the same category, "Intrepidity of a French Sailor," *The Atheneum or, Spirit of the English Magazines* 1821 (8): 391. William Gilmore uncovered Frederick the Great and Napoleon among the favorite topics presented in early Republican New England libraries; William Gilmore, *Reading Becomes a Necessity of Life: Material and Cultural Life in Rural New England, 1780–1835* (Knoxville: University of Tennessee Press, 1989), 339, n. 86.
41. "Bonaparte," The *Boston Spectator* 1 (1814): 83. Scott, *Paris Revisited*, 182; "Madame Bonaparte: The Present Empress of the Gauls," *Merrimack Magazine and Ladies' Literary Cabinet* 1 (1806): 193; "Bonaparte," The *Boston Spectator* 1 (1814): 82–83, 119 ; "From the Literary Gazette: Memoirs of the Court of Napoleon Bonaparte," *The Atheneum or, Spirit of the English Magazines* 5 (1819): 292–293. See also "Description of Bonaparte," *The Monthly Anthology and Boston Review* 2 (1805): 571–574; "Anecdote of Bonaparte," *The Boston Weekly Magazine* 1 (1817): 131.
42. "Outlines of the Principal Events in the Life of General Lafayette," *The United States Literary Gazette* 2 (1825): 9–15, here 10; Tudor, *Letters of the Eastern States*, 32. John Scott also assured his readers that there were only a very few "honest and honest friends of liberty in France," Scott, *Paris Revisited*, 180.
43. Austin, *Letters*, 27.

44. Joyce Appleby, *Inheriting the Revolution: The First Generation of Americans* (London: Harvard University Press, 2000).

Chapter 4 Hero of Liberty: New England Celebrations of General Lafayette during His Visit in 1824–1825

1. Anne C. Loveland, *Emblem of Liberty: The Image of Lafayette in the American Mind* (Baton Rouge: Louisiana State University Press, 1971), 3.
2. See, e.g., *Biographical Sketch of the Life of the Marquis De La Fayette* (Exeter, New Hampshire: Gerrish and Tyler, 1824); *Lafayette or Disinterested Benevolence* (Boston: Francis Y. Carlile, 1825); *Memoirs of General La Fayette Embracing Details of His Public and Private Life, Sketches of the American Revolution, the French Revolution, the Down-Fall of Bonaparte, and the Restoration of the Bourbons* (Hartford, Connecticut: Barber and Robinson, 1825); *Memoirs of General Lafayette with an Account of His Visit to America and of His Reception by the People of the United States* (Boston: E.G. House, 1824); John Foster, *A Sketch of the Tour of General Lafayette, on His Late Visit to the United States, 1824* (Portland, Maine: A.W. Thayer, 1824); George Ticknor, *Outlines of the Principle Events in the Life of General Lafayette from the North American Review* (Portland: David and Seth Paine, 1825); and Frederick Butler, *Memoirs of the Marquis de La Fayette, Major-General in the Revolutionary Army of the United States of America, Together with His Tour through the United States* (Wetherfield, Connecticut: Deming and Francis, 1825). Frederick Butler was an educationalist from Wethersfield, Connecticut. He was a Yale graduate and in 1821 he had published a *History of the United States to 1820.* Souvenir books of Lafayette's tour are also mentioned in Marian Klamkin, *The Return of Lafayette, 1824–1825* (New York: Charles Scribner's Sons, 1975), 42–43. New England journals reviewed translations of French copies as, e.g., *The North American Review* 20 (1825): 147–180.
3. Joseph Warren Leavitt, *Lafayette at Leavitt's Tavern, Chichester, New Hampshire*, watercolor, 1825, in *Lafayette, Hero of Two Worlds: The Art and Pageantry of His Farewell Tour of America, 1824–1825* (Hanover: University Press of New England, 1989), 71.
4. For Longfellow's ribbon and advertisements for such ribbons and badges in Portland newspapers, see *Agreeable Situations: Society, Commerce, and Art in Southern Maine, 1780–1830*, ed. Laura Fecych Sprage (Boston: Northeastern University Press, 1987), 209–210. An example of similar advertisements in Boston newspapers is in Eliza Quincy's scrapbook, where she collected all kinds of articles on Lafayette and his visit; Eliza Susan Quincy, *Notices of the Visit of Lafayette to the*

United States, Quincy Papers, Massachusetts Historical Society, 56. See also Octavia Roberts, *With Lafayette in America* (Boston: Houghton Mifflin, 1919), 261. She quotes an advertisement in a Boston paper in August: "Likeness of General Lafayette, engraved by J.V.N. Troop Esq., printed on Satin, intended to be worn as a compliment to the General. They are printed to answer for Belts and Watch ribbons. Military Companies can be supplied with any number at the shortest notice. J.W. Goodrich, 3 State Street." For the Lafayette gloves and waistcoat, see *Antiques* 34 (1938): 96. For Lafayette mugs and pitchers, see *Sotheby's: The Bertram K. Little and Nina Fletcher Little Collection* (New York, January 29, 1994); and *Antiques* 40 (1941): 220. For bottles see *Antiques* 38 (1940): 226–227. For plates see *Antiques* 18 (1930): 394–395. The "Lafayette Hotel" in Boston is mentioned in Alfred F. Young, *The Shoemaker and the Tea Party* (Boston: Beacon Press, 1999), 139. For the drum see Robert Goler, *The Legacy of Lafayette: A Publication in Conjunction with an Exhibition on View at the Fraunces Tavern Museum* (New York: Sons of the Revolution, 1984). A catalog of the Winterthur Museum includes all kinds of Lafayette souvenirs mentioned earlier, which were produced or imported by New Englanders, *Lafayette, the Nation's Guest; a Picture Book of Mementos which Express the Respect and Affection of the American People for Lafayette* (Winterthur, Delaware: Henry Francis du Pont Winterthur Museum, 1957). See David Johnson, *Lafayette*, engraving on silk, 1825, courtesy, Maine Historical Society, Portland, Maine, in *Agreeable Situations*, 210; and Signboard of Thompson Hotel in Thompson, Connecticut, courtesy, Connecticut Historical Society, in Alan Forbes, *France and New England* (Boston: Walton Advertising, 1925), 18.

5. To list only a few examples of towns with Lafayette streets throughout New England: Salem, Saugus, Salisbury, Wakefield, and Worcester in Massachusetts; Seabrook, North Hampton, Portsmouth, and Lebanon in New Hampshire; Bridgeport, Norwich, Waterbury, and Hartford in Connecticut; Saco, Yarmouth, and Lewiston in Connecticut; and Rutland in Vermont.
6. Lloyd Kramer, *Lafayette in Two Worlds: Public Cultures and Personal Identities in an Age of Revolution* (Chapel Hill: University of North Carolina Press, 1996) and *Lafayette, Hero of Two Worlds*.
7. For Lafayette's itinerary, see Kramer, *Lafayette in Two Worlds*, 190.
8. *New England Galaxy* 7 (1824): 2. Children's books gave the same accounts of Lafayette events as reports from spectators; see, e.g., *Disinterested Benevolence*, 7. It described what a Bostonian family had seen during the festivities:

   > They had seen the arches, and columns entwined with evergreens and flowers; they had seen the flags and streamers flying from public buildings, and strung across the streets; they have seen thousands of people, of all ages, from hoary age to lisping infancy, from the neighboring towns, pouring into

> the city, dressed in their best clothes, to unite in a cordial welcome to the Nation's Guest.

As examples of countless similar reports on festivities throughout New England, see "Lafayette in Maine," *Christian Intelligencer* 5 (1825): 12, and a report about the reception in Marblehead, *Salem Gazette*, September 1, 1824.

9. *Biographical Sketch of the Life of the Marquis De La Fayette*, 3. A newspaper clipping in Eliza Susan Quincy's scrapbook read: "Many of our public prints still style him the Marquis Lafayette—The concise and elegant resolution, adopted by the citizens of Richmond, retain the same appellation. But it is a misnomer. Lafayette has formally and publicly abjured the designation, contenting himself with the honourable title of General, which he first gained in the American service," Eliza Susan Quincy, *Notices of the Visit of Lafayette to the United States*, Quincy Papers, Massachusetts Historical Society, 13. See also the children's book *Disinterested Benevolence*, 9. For an example of a newspaper advertising the opportunity to meet with Lafayette, see *Boston Daily Advertiser*, August 28, 1824: "By request of Gen. Lafayette the Committee of arrangements inform their fellow citizens, who have not been introduced to him, that the General will be happy to receive them at the State House this day between the hours of 10 and 12."
10. "General Lafayette," *The Portsmouth Weekly Magazine* 1 (1824): 3. Another story on the same page emphasized the attachment to Lafayette:

> General John Davis, of Chester county, Pennsylvania, who was a distinguished officer in the Revolutionary War, and an intimate of General LAFAYETTE, has for a length of time past been labouring [*sic*] under the paralytic stroke, so severe in its effects, as to deprive him of speech. A few day[s] since, one of his family apprised him of the arrival of /general LAFAYETTE in his country; he immediately, as nature's last effort, exclaimed, is he here? And the tears trickled down his aged Patriot's cheek—he was unable to utter more.

For an example of the emotional character of such meetings, see *Columbian Centinel*, August 28, 1824:

> Several of the humble but interesting Heroes of the Revolution took this occasion to welcome their good old General. Numerous incidents in this scene brought tears from many manly eyes.—One decrepit veteran, on crutches, was recognized by the General as a companion in arms at the memorable onset at Yorktown; other were recalled to recollection by events at Monmouth.

See also John Foster, *A Sketch of the Tour of General Lafayette*, 79, 136.

11. *Columbian Centinel*, September 1, 1824. On celebration of ordinary soldiers compare Alfred F. Young, *The Shoemaker and the Tea Party* (Boston: Beacon Press, 1999), 137.

12. "Lafayette and Charley," *The Portsmouth Weekly Magazine* 1 (1824): 2–3. For the "Lafayette's March" composed for the General's review of troops in Boston on August 30, 1824, see Klamkin, *The Return of Lafayette*, 38. For an example of a song sung by girls in Philadelphia, see "Lafayette," *The Portsmouth Weekly Magazine* 1 (1824): 3.
13. See Peter Maverick, *Washington and Lafayette*, cup plate, engraving, 1825, in *Lafayette: The Nation's Guest* (Winterthur, Delaware: The Henry Dupot Winterthur Museum, 1957), 19.
14. Loveland, *Emblem of Liberty*, 5, 35–36, 44; and Kramer, *Lafayette in Two Worlds*, 199. For Lafayette's praise as a Revolutionary hero and friend of Washington, see "General Lafayette," *Christian Herald* 8 (1825): 111; "Address of Dr. A. R. Thompson at Bunker Hill," *New England Galaxy* 7 (1824): 2; and Foster, *A Sketch of the Tour of General Lafayette*, 78, 98. For the song sung at the dinner in Boston, see John Newhall, Commonplace Book and Diary, 1825, Massachusetts Historical Society.
15. For Lafayette's visit to John Adams, see Klamkin, *The Return of Lafayette*, 36; the report of Lafayette's secretary August Levasseur, *Lafayette in America, in 1824 and 1825, or Journal of a Voyage to the United States*, 2 vols., trans. John D. Godman (Philadelphia: Carey and Lea, 1829), vol. 1, 62; and *Memoirs of General Lafayette with an Account of His Visit to America*, 172–173. For Lafayette laying the cornerstone for the new Bunker Hill monument, see *Lafayette, Hero of Two World*, 135 and William. E. Woodward, *Lafayette* (New York: Farrar and Rinehart, 1938). In his address to Lafayette at the Bunker Hill celebration, Dr. A.R. Thompson at Bunker Hill praised Lafayette as a Revolutionary hero: "This joyful occasion revives high national feelings and recollections, and . . . springs of gratitude to be reminding us of that interesting period of our history which gave to our country a gallant Hero, and to the right of mankind a steadfast Champion," *New England Galaxy* 7 (1824): 4. For Daniel Webster's address, see *An Address Delivered at the Laying of the Cornerstone of the Bunker Hill Monument* (Boston: Cummings, Hilliard and Co., 1825).
16. *Memoirs of General La Fayette Embracing Details of His Public and Private Life*; Ticknor, *Outlines of the Principle Events*, 33–34. For an extensive treatise of the Revolution in general, see also Butler, *Memoirs of the Marquis de La Fayette.* Ticknor assured that Lafayette's visit cannot fail to produce a moral effect on individuals and the people as a whole (32). Ticknor's biographical essay was as many of his writings also published in *The North American Review* 20 (1825): 147–180. In his welcoming speech, the mayor of Boston Josiah Quincy also created such a historical memory: "Your name, Sir—the name of Lafayette, is associated with the most perilous, and most glorious periods of our Revolution: with the imperishable names of Washington, and of that numerous host of heroes which adorn the

proudest archives of American history, and are engraven [*sic*] in indelible traces on the hearts of the whole American people," Foster, *A Sketch of the Tour of General Lafayette*, 95. So did John Quincy Adams in his farewell speech on Lafayette's departure from the United States in September 1825:

> You have been received with rapture by the survivors of your earliest companions in arms, you have been hailed as a long absent parent by their children, the men and women of the present age: And a rising generation, the hope of future time,... have [uttered] acclamations of joy at beholding the face of him whom they feel to be the common benefactor of all. You have heard the mingled voices of the past, the present and the future age. (Quoted in *Lafayette, Hero of Two Worlds*, 89)

17. Compare Loveland, *Emblem of Liberty*, 46–49. *Disinterested Benevolence*, 22–23. Quincy, *Notices of the visit of Lafayette to the United States*, 80. For examples of these stories, see *Memoirs of General La Fayette Embracing Details of His Public and Private Life.* Details about Lafayette's imprisonment can be found in Butler, *Memoirs of the Marquis de La Fayette*, 97–101, 113–151.
18. Newhall, Commonplace Book and Diary, 1825, Massachusetts Historical Society. See also *Memoirs of General La Fayette Embracing Details of His Public and Private Life*, 435–442. For the decision in Congress, see Peggy Robbins, "Return of Hero: General Lafayette Visits America in 1824 and a Grateful Country Celebrates," *American History Illustrated* 14 (1979): 37.
19. "General Lafayette," *The Portsmouth Weekly Magazine* 1 (1824): 3; Foster, *A Sketch of the Tour of General Lafayette*, 12. For the anecdote, see *Disinterested Benevolence*, 22. In an address by the Massachusetts Cincinnati, the speaker said: "We hail you, Sir, in union with the millions of our citizens, most respectfully hail you as a Statesman, as a Philanthropist, and as the early, inflexible and devoted friend, not only of our beloved country, but of the sacred principles of civil liberty and human rights" (*New England Galaxy* 7 [1824]: 4). See also *Columbian Centinel*, September 1, 1824, and the welcoming speech of the mayor of New Haven, quoted in Foster, *A Sketch of the Tour of General Lafayette*, 78.
20. Foster, *A Sketch of the Tour of General Lafayette*, 49. He continued with the following rhetorical question: "How can we appreciate the sincerity and ardour of that attachment to the rights of man, which stimulated him under such circumstances, to sacrifice at the shrine of Independence." For another example, see *Disinterested Benevolence*, 9.
21. On Lafayette's visit and the election of 1824, see Robert P. Hay, "The American Revolution Twice Recalled: Lafayette's Visit and the Election of 1824," *Indiana Magazine of History* 69 (1973): 43–62. Hay argues that Americans sought in their presidential candidates the Revolutionary virtues which they had found in Lafayette and that

Andrew Jackson won because he fulfilled these expectations to a greater extent than John Quincy Adams.

22. Ticknor, *Outlines of the Principle Events*, 36; Butler, *Memoirs of the Marquis de La Fayette*, 403. Descriptions of celebrations outside New England are, e.g., in Newhall, Commonplace Book and Diary; "Lafayette," 2, 3; Foster, *A Sketch of the Tour of General Lafayette*, 58–77, 88; *Biographical Sketch of the Life of the Marquis De La Fayette.*
23. "General Lafayette," *The Portsmouth Weekly Magazine* 1 (1824): 3. Anne Loveland pointed out that the appendix of the 1824 *New England Galaxy* emphasized the unifying character of Lafayette's visit—Loveland, *Emblem of Liberty*, 70. The author of *Biographical Sketch of the Life of the Marquis De La Fayette* was sure to address a readership consisting of all classes: "A Sketch of his life, at the present moment, when enthusiastic millions are paying the homage of their gratitude and respect to so old and so able an avenger of liberty, cannot fail of being acceptable to all classes of people" (3). See also Foster, *A Sketch of the Tour of General Lafayette*, 107. He reported that in the Massachusetts State House "nearly two thousand citizens, of all professions, ages, and conditions, were presented to him, with each of whom he affectionately shook hands."
24. Foster, *A Sketch of the Tour of General Lafayette*, 84, 101; see also 79–80. He wrote:

    > Many females, we observed, in the excess of feelings, suspended this token of welcome [waving of handkerchiefs], to gaze more intently at the object, whom they appeared alone to see in the whole procession, and many a fine eye was wet with the gush of a tear, which the rush of so many sublime and sympathetic emotions sent warm from the heart. (86)

    In another place he underlined Lafayette's respect to Republican women. At Franklin Hall in Portsmouth Lafayette met "about three hundred ladies . . . each of whom he took by the hand, and addressed with a passing compliment" (137).
25. For the transformation of the women's sphere through the Revolution and its Republican ideology, see Mary Beth Norton, *Liberty's Daughters: The Revolutionary Experience of American Women, 1750–1800* (Boston: Little, Brown, 1980) and Linda Kerber, *Women of the Republic: Intellect and Ideology in Revolutionary America* (Chapel Hill: University of North Carolina Press, 1980). For women in the public sphere in the years between 1825 and 1840, see Mary Ryan, *Women in Public: Between Banners and Ballot, 1825–1880* (Baltimore: John Hopkins University Press, 1990).
26. Newhall, Commonplace Book and Diary. For the song in Philadelphia, see "General Lafayette," *The Portsmouth Weekly Magazine* 1824 (1): 3. Like most songs this one was much longer than the Wilmington song.

27. *New England Galaxy* 7 (1824): 2; *Boston Evening Gazette*, August 28, 1824; Levasseur, *Lafayette in America*, vol. 1, 38–39; for children in Newburyport see page 73 and "Lafayette in Maine," *The Christian Intelligencer* 5 (1825): 12. For a typical emphasis on women and children in the audience, see Foster, *A Sketch of the Tour of General Lafayette*, 112: "On the Main street was a beautiful display of the misses and youths of several schools—The bells rung merry peals; frequent salutes were fired; and the ladies filled the windows of the houses, and joined in the welcome of their country's friend."
28. *Boston Evening Gazette*, August 28, 1824: "A beautiful little girl, about 6 years old, stepped forth, and begged leave to address the General; she was handed to the Mayor, and by him to the General, who saluted her—she took a garland of flowers from her own, and put it on his head." The same incident was described in Foster, *A Sketch of the Tour of General Lafayette*, 98.
29. *Lafayette or Disinterested Benevolence*, 29; Ticknor, *Outlines of the Principle Events*, 9; "Address to General Lafayette, from 'The Slaves' in the Land of Freedom," *Columbian Centinel*, October 20, 1824, quoted in Loveland, *Emblem of Liberty*, 70. For Lafayette as an advocate for the emancipation of American slaves, compare John T. Gillard, "Lafayette, Friend of the Negro," *Journal of Negro History* 19 (1934): 355–371.
30. For gradual emancipation and New Englanders' attitude toward free African Americans, see Joanne Pope Melish, *Disowning Slavery: Gradual Emancipation and "Race" in New England, 1780–1860* (Ithaca: Cornell University Press, 1998), especially Chapters 3, 5, and 6. For the virulent racism among wealthy Philadelphians in the first half of the nineteenth century see Daniel Kilbride, *An American Aristocracy: Southern Planters in Antebellum Philadelphia* (Columbia: University of South Carolina Press, 2006), 147–149.
31. See Klamkin, *The Return of Lafayette*, 102–103; and Kramer, *Lafayette in Two Worlds*, 218. For Lafayette's visits of black schools and meetings with African Americans, see Patricia Brady, "Carnival of Liberty: Lafayette in Louisiana," *Louisiana History* 2000 (41): 35. A 1997 publication by the Sons of the American Revolution builds on the stories of Lafayette's encounter with "French" Southerners and claims that people in New Orleans "honored" Lafayette because of their common Gallic origin. Furthermore, it assumes that it was just for its French Colonial history that Lafayette stopped in Mobile, Louisiana. It also drew the conclusion that the French visitor had a tendency to stay longer in "French" cities in order to observe Frenchmen under a Republican regime. See *General Lafayette: Citizen of Louisiana* (Baton Rouge: Sons of the American Revolution, 1997), 35, 41.
32. Klamkin, *The Return of Lafayette*, 138–142, 150; Kramer, *Lafayette in Two Worlds*, 218–219. See also Roberts, *With Lafayette in America*, 240–261.

33. *A Pilgrimage of Liberty: A Contemporary Account of the Triumphal Tour of General Lafayette through the Southern and Western States in 1825 as Reported by Local Newspapers* (Athens, Ohio: The Lawhead Press, 1944), 80, 103–104, 160, 164, 215.
34. Kramer, *Lafayette in Two Worlds*, 199, 214. Anne Loveland argued that Lafayette served as a judge over success or failure of the Revolution; his praise of American institutions enabled Americans to express their nationalism; Loveland, *Emblem of Liberty*, 37.
35. Quincy, *Notices of the visit of Lafayette to the United States*, 51; Foster, *A Sketch of the Tour of General Lafayette*, 142; "William Gibbes Hunt, an Oration in Honour of General Lafayette, Delivered in His Presence at Nashville, May 4, 1825. 'At the Request of the Grand Lodge of Tennessee,'" *The United States Literary Gazette* 2 (1825): 353 and Foster, *A Sketch of the Tour of General Lafayette*, 117. See also Butler, *Memoirs of the Marquis de La Fayette*, 403. For Lafayette praising Americans as good Republican citizens, see also Kramer, *Lafayette in Two Worlds*, 194.
36. *Biographical Sketch of the Life of the Marquis De La Fayette*, 24; Foster, *A Sketch of the Tour of General Lafayette*, 56–57.
37. *Columbian Centinel*, August 28, 1824; Foster, *A Sketch of the Tour of General Lafayette*, 81. For the story about Lafayette saving the royal family, see Ticknor, *Outlines of the Principle Events*, 13–16; *Memoirs of General Lafayette with an Account of His Visit to America*, 68–70 and *Memoirs of General La Fayette Embracing Details of His Public and Private Life*, 235, 268. The cruelties of the royal executions and massacres during the French Revolution are also described in Butler, *Memoirs of the Marquis de La Fayette*, 101–108. For Lafayette's opinion of Napoleon, see Ticknor, *Outlines of the Principle Events*, 26–29; *Memoirs of General La Fayette Embracing Details of His Public and Private Life*, 415; *Memoirs of General Lafayette with an Account of His Visit to America*, 103; and Butler, *Memoirs of the Marquis de La Fayette*, 183–185.
38. "The Vision of Lafayette in the Dungeon of Magdeburg," *Boston Monthly Magazine* 1 (1825): 22–24. The idea that the American spirit of liberty would help the young nation to emerge as a powerful empire appeared in a number of welcoming speeches for Lafayette. In his address at Lafayette's visit to Worcester judge Lincoln said, e.g.:

    > Wherever you go, General, the acclamations of freemen await you—their blessings and prayers will follow you. May you live many years to enjoy the fruits of the services and sacrifices, the gallantry and valor of your earlier days, devoted to the cause of freedom and the rights of man; and may the bright examples of individual glory, and of national happiness, which the history America exhibits, illustrate to the world, the moral force of personal virtue, and the rich blessings of civil liberty in

Republican Governments. (Foster, *A Sketch of the Tour of General Lafayette*, 141)

39. Hone's toast is quoted in *Lafayette Guest of the Nation: A Contemporary Account of the Triumphal Tour of General Lafayette through the United States in 1824–1825 as Reported by Local Newspapers*, ed. Edgar Ewing Brandon (Oxford, Ohio: Oxford Historical Press, 1950), 109. For the inscription on the Salem flower garland, see Levasseur, *Lafayette in America, Vol. I*, 72; *Lafayette or Disinterested Benevolence*, 27.

Chapter 5 Separation for the Nation: The Movement for Maine's Statehood

1. "Memorial on the Separation of Maine," *The Eastern Argus*, June 26, 1816.
2. See Stephen Marini, "Religious Revolution in District of Maine," in *Maine in the Early Republic: From Revolution to Statehood*, ed. Charles Clark, James Leamon, and Karen Bowden (Hanover: University Press of New England, 1988), 118–145; James Leamon, "Revolution and Separation: Maine's First Efforts at Statehood," ibid., 83–99; Stephen Marini, *Radical Sects of Revolutionary New England* (Cambridge, Massachusetts: Harvard University Press, 1982); and Alan Taylor, *Liberty Men and Great Proprietors: The Revolutionary Settlement on the Maine Frontier, 1760–1820* (Chapel Hill: University of North Carolina Press, 1990).
3. Daniel Davis, *An Address to the Inhabitants of the District of Maine, upon the Subject of their Separation from the present Government of Massachusetts* (Portland: Thomas B. Watts, 1791), 9, 25. For similar arguments, see *Address of a convention of delegates from twenty towns and five plantations within the counties of York, Cumberland and Lincoln, met by adjournment at Portland, on the twenty eighth day of January, one thousand seven hundred and ninety five to the people of said counties, on the subject of their separation from Massachusetts* (Portland: Thomas B. Wait, 1795).
4. Ronald Banks, *Maine Becomes a State: The Movement to Separate Maine from Massachusetts, 1785–1820* (Middletown, Connecticut: Wesleyan University Press, 1970), 32. Edward Stanwood gives slightly different numbers: 2,084 votes in favor and 2,438 in opposition; Edward Stanwood, *The Separation of Maine from Massachusetts: A Study of the Growth of Public Opinion*, 1784–1820 (Cambridge: John Wilson and Son, 1907), 15–17. In the 1797 election 2,785 voted in favor and 2,412 against; in 1807 there was a clear majority against the separation, 9,404 votes against and only 3,370 in favor, Banks, *Maine Becomes a State*, 39, 53.
5. James Sullivan, *The History of the District of Maine* (Boston: Thomas and Andrews, 1795), vii.

6. On Sullivan's history, see Charles E. Clark, "James Sullivan's History of Maine and the Romance of Statehood," in *Maine in the Early Republic*, 184–195. Clark argues that the history of Maine established Sullivan as a "spokesman for democratic romantic nationalism," 186. For depictions of Maine landscapes, towns, and houses, see *Agreeable Situations: Society, Commerce, and Art in Southern Maine, 1780–1830*, ed. Laura Fecych Sprague (Boston: Northeastern University Press); Neil Rolde, *An Illustrated History of Maine* (Augusta: Friends of the Maine State Museum, 1995); and *Maine in the Early Republic.*
7. *Address of a convention of delegates from twenty towns and five plantations within the counties of York, Cumberland and Lincoln.* For the convention, see Banks, *Maine Becomes a State*, 36–37.
8. Thomas Mellen Prentiss, *The Maine Spelling Book* (Portland: Adams and Patten, 1809), 132.
9. "The District of Maine," *The Eastern Argus*, November 8, 1815.
10. Alan Taylor estimates that the population of Maine tripled to almost one hundred thousand between 1775 and 1790; see Taylor, *Liberty Men and Great Proprietors*, 15.
11. Unknown artist, *View from Paris Hill*, overmantel 1802, courtesy, Maine Humanities Council, Portland, Maine, in Rolde, *An Illustrated History of Maine*, 57.
12. Independence, "To the People of Maine," *The Eastern Argus*, January 10, 1816. For the struggle between settlers and great proprietors, see Taylor, *Liberty Men and Great Proprietors.*
13. "To the Citizens of Maine," *The Eastern Argus*, May 15, 1816. The issue remained when Maine and Massachusetts discussed the conditions of statehood. A pamphlet found among the papers of the Longfellow family, probably printed in 1819, repeated the argument that Mainers invested a lot to improve the "wild lands" and it was Massachusetts that profited from them. The pamphlet claimed that the State of Maine should exercise sovereignty over all these lands so that they could be civilized and commerce and prosperity could be increased. See *The Conditions of Separation Considered*, pamphlet in manuscript ca. 1816–1819, Longfellow Family Papers, Maine Historical Society, Portland.
14. John Brown, *Bowdoin Campus*, painting 1822, courtesy, Bowdoin College Museum of Art, in Rolde, *An Illustrated History of Maine*, 59.
15. "The District of Maine," *The Eastern Argus*, August 17, 1819.
16. "A Federalist for Separation," *Portland Gazette*, July 13, 1819; William D. Williamson, *The History of the State of Maine* (Hallowell: Glazier, Masters and Co., 1832), here 686; he traced the history of education in Maine from page 686 to page 691; and William Williamson to Isaac Lane, December 16, 1820, Maine Historical Society. Already in 1795 the Convention on separation resulted in the assumption that the "present state of education is disproportioned to our ability," *An Address of a Convention of*

Delegates from twenty towns within the counties of York, Cumberland and Lincoln.

17. "The District of Maine." *The Eastern Argus*, December 13, 1815, August 17, 1819; *An Appeal to the People of Maine: Is It for the Interest of the District of Maine to Become a Separate State?* (n.p.: 1816), 3, 4. Moses Judkins asked William King: "Will not every Representative be willing to pay for 10 or 20 papers for distribution for a few Months?" Moses S. Judkins to William King, Castine, June 5, 1819, William King Correspondence, Box 17, Folder 3, William King Papers, Maine Historical Society. "The District of Maine," *The Eastern Argus*, November 29, 1815.
18. *An Appeal to the People of Maine*, 19. It also said: "We believe that the people of Maine collectively have as much regard to order and good government, and as much morality, as even the people of Massachusetts proper." D. Long to William King, August, January 14, 1820, William King Correspondence, Box 17, Folder 10, William King Papers, Maine Historical Society. In a letter to the *Argus*, an anonymous author from the Penobscot Bay area emphasized that the virtues of the people of Maine would be much better respected when Maine was a state instead of a district; see *The Eastern Argus*, April 6, 1819. For this, see also an anonymous letter from the Penobscot Bay in the *Eastern Argus*, April 6, 1819. In *The Eastern Argus*, November 8, 1815, the article concluded that citizens "should have a more worthy object; he should be the enquiry, will it be for the interest of the district, for its inhabitants generally, and for posterity; if so I am in favor, if not, I am opposed."
19. For the arguments about the costs of government and the damage to the coastal trade, see the *Portland Gazette*, e.g., March 12, March 19, March 26, May 7, 1816. As a representative for Lincoln county, Maine, Isaac Reed reported to the Massachusetts House of Representatives that the people of his county opposed separation because the coastal trade would suffer; see Isaac Reed to the Senate House of Representatives of the Commonwealth of Massachusetts, Longfellow Family Papers, Box 3, Folder 3, Maine Historical Society. For the praise of Maine colleges and political engagement of its population, see "Separation of Maine," *Portland Gazette*, February 27 and March 5, 1816. For separatists' argument that a state of Maine would end the "Ohio Fever" see e.g., "The District of Maine," *The Eastern Argus*, November 29, 1815.
20. See S.K. Whiting to William King, Portland, July 9, 1816, William King Correspondence, Box 14, Folder 7, William King Papers, Maine Historical Society. For the argument that "a point of no return had been reached" in 1816, see Banks, *Maine Becomes a State*, 67–68.
21. Sophia Sewall Wood Monroe, *Barrell Homestead, York, Maine*, watercolor, 1800, private collection, in *Agreeable Situations*, 74.
22. James Akin, *Certificate of the Portland Marine Society*, engraving 1807, courtesy, Maine Historical Society, in *Agreeable Situations*, 48.

23. For another example of a depiction of an elegant and representative Maine home see Montpelier. Summer Residence of Henry and Lucy Knox, in Taylor, *Liberty Men and Great Proprietors*, 122. For the works produced in Mary Rea's school, see Betty Ring, *Girlhood Embroidery: American Samplers and Pictorial Needlework, 1650–1850* (New York: A. Knopf, 1993), 258–261.
24. Compare Banks, *Maine Becomes a State*, 67–115. For a number of examples of pictures of Portland embroidered by little girls, see Ring, *Girlhood Embroidery*, 156, 163, 256, and 258. For reports on the vote in Massachusetts newspapers, see *Columbian Centinel*, May 25, 29, 1816; *Boston Daily Advertiser*, May 24, 1816; and *New England Palladium*, May 28, 1816.
25. "Lincoln County Convention on the Subject of Separation," *The Eastern Argus*, May 15, 1816. The article concluded: "The new state [of Maine]...would enjoy, equally with the other states, the protection of the federal government, in defending it from foreign invasion, and in suppressing domestic insurrection." From his analysis of the votes in 1816 Ronald Banks concluded that the votes against separation come from coastal towns; see Banks, *Maine Becomes a State*, 86. On the vote of September 26, 181, see Banks, *Maine Becomes a State*, 146. On August, 17, 1819 the *Portland Gazette* wrote: "There is something terrific to the imaginations of many in the idea of forming a new state....To some it seems very little short of a second chaos; and presents a perfect image of the most absolute and uncontrollable anarchy." For the argument on the advantage of small republics; see "An Old Man for Separation," *Portland Gazette,* July 20, 1819.
26. "The District of Maine" *The Eastern Argus*, November 8, 1815; Old York, "Separation," *The Eastern Argus*, February 6, 1816. See also "The District of Maine," *The Eastern Argus*, November 15, 1815. About a week later the *Argus* wrote: "But in bringing this subject before the public, I whish it to be distinctly understood that, it is without reference to the two great political parties, who have heretofore so unhappily agitated our Republic," *The Eastern Argus*, November 29, 1815.
27. *The Eastern Argus*, January 17, 1816; "Remember the 20th of May!" *The Eastern Argus*, March 19, 1816. The article proposed that May 20 "will become as celebrated in the annals of the state of Maine as the 4th of July in the history of the United States." It again asked Mainers to overcome party bonds: "On this day, let honest Federalists take by the hand the honest Democrats, and both say on this day we will unite." On the standpoint of Massachusetts Federalists, see Banks, *Maine Becomes a State*, 76.
28. "The District of Maine," *The Eastern Argus*, November 15, 1815. See also "The District of Maine," *Eastern Argus*, December 13, 1815 and "Memorial on the Separation of Maine," *The Eastern Argus*, June 26, 1816. On February 8, 1820 an article in the same series

said: "The district of Maine has knocked at the door to be admitted into the family of the republic."

29. Brunswick Convention, Comments of the Brunswick Convention on the Separation of Maine from Massachusetts, October 1816, Maine Historical Society, Portland. On October 4, 1816, the selectmen of Dearborn, who said in the same context: "Patriotism shall dictate to give us what we claim." The Selectmen of Avon and Strong referred to liberties gained in the American Revolution when they said: Mainers "suffered so much to obtain and support independence, and among inherent freeborn rights we have none dearer (next to liberty of conscience) than that of governing ourselves." Separation Broadside, in Banks, *Maine Becomes a State*, 138. See also "The District of Maine," *The Eastern Argus*, August 17, 1819.
30. "A Native of old Massachusetts" to William King, New York, September 3, 1819, William King Correspondence, Box 17, Folder 6, William King Papers, Maine Historical Society. For the articles from newspapers outside of Maine, see "Separation: From the Columbian Gazette (Utica New York)" and "The District of Maine," *The Eastern Argus*, March 12, 1816 and May 4, 1819.
31. *Boston Daily Advertiser*, July 17, 1819. See also *Salem Gazette*, July 23, 1819; *Salem Gazette*, March 21, 1820; *Columbian Sentinel*, July 24, 1819; *Boston Patriot*, July 17, 20, 21, 22, 23, 1819. For a typical brief informative note on the vote in favor of separation, see Anonymous, "After a Long and Arduous Struggle in the District of Maine," *Religious Intelligencer* 1 (1819), 43.
32. For Maine statehood and the Missouri compromise, see Banks, *Religious Intelligencer*, 184–204. Maine's demographics, which changed dramatically in the early 1800s, played a role as well. Maine did not have enough people to become a state right after the Revolution when the province only had a population of about ten thousand. Maine's population grew from ninety-one thousand in 1791 to nearly three hundred thousand in 1820.
33. "The District of Maine," *The Eastern Argus*, November 22 and December 5, 1815. For the argument of a stronger New England influence in the Senate, see also *An Appeal to the People of Maine*. The pamphlet said, "There can be no doubt, that the relative importance of Maine in a national point of view would, by her becoming a separate State, be vastly increased. Admitted a constituted member of the union, entitled to her equal representation in the Senate of the United States, her voice would have its equal influence" (4). For Daniel Davis statement, see Davis, *An Address to the Inhabitants of the District of Maine*, 9.
34. "Maine and Missouri," *American Advocate*, February 5, 1820.
35. The *Argus* advertised a ball to be held on March 16: "Independence Ball! Those Gentlemen who are desireous of joining a Ball on the Evening of the sixteenth the first day of the Independence of Maine,

are requested to meet this Evening, at col. Burnham's hotel to make necessary arrangements"; see "The District of Maine," *The Eastern Argus,* March 14, 1820. For articles in Massachusetts newspapers, see *New England Palladium and Commercial Advertiser*, March 24, 1820 and *Boston Patriot,* March 23, 1820.

36. See Jacques Gerard Milbert, *View of Hallowell*, painting 1820, courtesy, Museum of Fine Arts Boston, in *Maine in the Early Republic*, ed. Clark, Leamon, and Bowden, 56; and Unknown artist, *View of Augusta*, painting 1825, courtesy, Colby College Museum of Art, in *Maine in the Early Republic*, ed. Clark, Leamon, and Bowden, 169.
37. The paper of the painting has an 1832 watermark, but the church on the left burned down in 1825, so the image must depict an earlier scene when the church was still standing. See Anna Bucknam, *First State House, Portland, 1820*, painting 1832, courtesy of the Maine Historical Society and Maine State Museum.
38. See Williamson, *The History of the State of Maine*, 691.

Chapter 6 God's People: The Creation of a Protestant Nation

1. James Sabine, *The Fathers of New England: A Sermon Delivered in the Church in Essex Street, Boston, December 22, 1820, Being the Second Centennial Celebration of the Landing of the Fathers at Plymouth* (Boston: G. Clark & co., 1821), here 26. He said:

   > I do not forget that New England is a part, and but a part, of a great nation; that she has federal obligations; and that much of her character is involved in the whole Commonwealth. I trust that I have said nothing that will be so understood, as to be supposed to bear an aspect unfriendly to that grand and important confederation. But still, New England has her own character, and this character is more distinctly spiritual, than that of any other nation under heaven. New England is the early first fruits of the Millennial harvest, the wave sheaf to be presented before the Lord; the fruits of her increase therefore must be holiness to the Lord.

   Sabine introduced modesty as a New England tradition:

   > The Sons of New England repair every year to the shores where their Fathers first landed, and in frugal feast upon the humblest produce of the sea, perpetuate the character of a humble race of men, humble, not in opposition to greatness and the truest dignity, but a humility of the same character as distinguished the King of Zion when he was on earth, who made himself of no reputation. (4)

   He emphasized simplicity, when he said:

   > No! New England Fathers were not originally princes, or nobles... they were for the most part plain men of country life,

> men that had been habituated to cultivate the soil of their native land; they had estates of their own of greater or of less value, to which they attained either by inheritance from their fathers, or by persevering habits of industry and labour. (5)

2. Ibid., 14.
3. As examples for articles in the *Christian Spectator* and *Christian Observer*, see "Prussia," *Christian Observer* 3 (1805): 180; and "Opinion of Frederick II on Field of Sports," *Christian Observer and Advocate* 5 (1806): 482. Other examples are Rev. Greenwood, "Schools of New England," *The Religious Intelligencer* 1825 (10): 347; "A Historical View of the First Planters of New England," *The Connecticut Evangelical Magazine and Religious Intelligencer* 4 (1812); "General Lafayette," *Christian Herald* 8 (1825): 111; "Extract from a Journey in New England" *The Religious Intelligencer* 1822 (7): 349–350; "Extracts from a Journey in New England," *The Religious Intelligencer* 1823 (7): 724–727; "Anecdote of a French Officer," *The Religious Informer* 1819 (1): 41; "An Excellent Spirit Discovered in Saurin, a French Preacher, Who Was Banished by Lewis XIV, because He Was a Protestant," *The Christian Herald* 8 (1825): 45–46; "Review of the First Settlement of New England, a Sermon, Delivered in the South Parish in Andover," *The Advisor of Vermont Evangelical Magazine* 1811 (3): 112–118; and "A Foreigner's Opinions of England, Comprised in a Series of Free Remarks by Christian August Gottlieb Gohde. Translated from the Original German by Thomas Horne, Boston: Wells and Lilly, 1822," *Christian Spectator* 5 (1823): 318–324. For the New England nationalism of Jedidiah Morse, see the excellent chapter "Regionalism and Nationalism in the Early Republic. The American Geographies of Jedidiah Morse," in Joseph Conforti, *Imagining New England: Explorations of Regional Identity from the Pilgrims to the Mid-Twentieth Century* (Chapel Hill: University of North Carolina Press, 2001), 79–122.
4. For the democratization of many Congregationalists in the early nineteenth century and how they adjusted to similar forms of organization as the dissenters inspired by the platform of the Republican Party, see Jonathan Sassi, *A Republic of Righteousness: The Public Christianity of the Post-Revolutionary New England Clergy* (New York: Oxford University Press, 2001), 117–118, 131–136, 169.
5. For the importance of conversions for the popularity and status of a minister, see, e.g., Carroll Smith Rosenberg, *Religion and the Rise of the American City: The New York City Mission Movement, 1812–1870* (Ithaca: Cornell University Press, 1971), 53.
6. For the praise of New Englanders' disinterestedness, piety, and benevolence, see "Review of the First Settlement of New England," 112–113. For modesty and simplicity, see Sabine, *The Fathers of New England*, 4–5. For virtues such as morality, order, piety, and education, see John

Chester, *Sermon, in Commemoration of the Landing, of the New-England Pilgrims, Delivered in the Second Presbyterian Church, Albany* (Albany: E. and E. Hosford, 1820), 19–21; and Gardiner Spring, *A Tribute to New England: A Sermon Delivered before the New England Society of the City and State of New York, on the 22nd of December, 1820. Being the Second Centennial Celebration of the Landing of the Pilgrims at Plymouth* (New York: S.F. Lockwood, 1821), 19. For benevolence, see "Extract from a Journey in New England," *The Religious Intelligencer* 1822 (7): 349–350. For morality, piety, and hard working, see Jacob Burnap, *A Sermon Preached at Merrimac, December 22, 1829, Being Two Centuries from the First Settlement of New England* (Amherst, New Hampshire: Elijah Mansur, 1821), 7 and Joshua Dodge, *Sermon, Delivered in Haverhill, December 22, 1820, Being the Second Centesimal [sic] Anniversary, of the Landing of New England Fathers at Plymouth* (Haverhill: Burrill and Hersey, 1821), 9. Dodge wrote, e.g.: "The first settlers of New England were good men. Their morality and piety, their love of truth, and the purity of their motives are unquestionable."

7. Chester, *Sermon, in Commemoration of the Landing, of the New-England Pilgrims*, 19. Here he said that the New England settlers "were distinguished for the good old ways of Scriptural morality." Burnap, *A Sermon Preached at Merrimac*, 6. Daniel Chaplin, e.g., described the Pilgrims as very religious:

> The morals of the people at large were wonderfully pure. Profaneness [*sic*], debauchery, intemperance, lying, and disobedience to parents and other superiors were scarcely to be seen in New England. The Sabbath was observed with great strictness, as it ought always to be in a Christian country.... They feared God and faithfully adhered to his word as the rule of their faith and practice.

(Daniel Chaplin, *The Dispensation of Divine Providence Considered as Generally Corresponding with the Morale Character of a Nation, and the Morals of New England, a Sermon Delivered in Groton [Ma], January 12, 1815* [Cambridge: Hilliard and Metcalf, 1815], 8–9). Spring, *A Tribute to New England*, 19. Rev. Greenwood, "Schools of New England," *The Religious Intelligencer* 1825 (10): 347; here he wrote:

> If a stranger should inquire of me the principal cause and source of this greatness of my country, would I bid him look on the ocean widely loaded with our merchandise, and proudly ranged by our navy; or on the lands where it is girdled by roads and scored by canals, and burdened with the produce of our industry and ingenuity?: would not, would also not show him the schools, but lead him out by some winding highway among the hills and woods, and when cultivated spots grew small and infrequent, and the houses became few and scattered, and a state of primitive nature

> seemed immediately before us, I would stop...and...point out to him a lowly building...full of blooming happy children,...reading...a portion of the word of God.

For an emphasis on education, see Frederick W. Hotchkiss, *On National Greatness: A Thanksgiving Sermon Delivered to the First Congregation in Say-Brook, November 29th, 1792* (New Haven: Thomas and Samuel Green, 1792), 12. For the importance of the combination of religion and education, see also Pitt Clark, *On the Rise and Signalized Lot of the United Americans: A Sermon Delivered, February 19, 1795, on the Occasion of Thanksgiving* (Boston: Samuel Hall, 1795), 29. For the New England Society of New York, see Edwin Burrows, Mike Wallace, *Gotham: A History of New York City to 1898* (New York: Oxford University Press, 1999), 337.

8. For the Second Great Awakening and its political and social impact through the missionary and temperance movement, see Paul Johnson, *A Shopkeeper's Millennium: Society and Revivals in Rochester, New York, 1815–1837* (New York: Hill and Wang, 1978); and Carroll Smith Rosenberg, *Religion and the Rise of the American City: The New York City Mission Movement, 1812–1870* (Ithaca: Cornell University Press, 1971). For New Englanders' campaign against New York entertainments and the reaction of the city's inhabitants see Burrows and Wallace, *Gotham*, 452–455.
9. Compare James Kloppenberg, "The Virtues of Liberalism: Christianity, Republicanism and Ethics in Early American Political Discourse," *The Journal of American History* 1987 (74): 9–3. See Sassi, *Republic of Righteousness*, 51–53, 57, 129–130.
10. Sabine, *The Fathers of New England*, 11. For the ministers' condemnation of a money-driven society, compare Sassi, *Republic of Righteousness*, 192–193.
11. Chester, *Sermon, in Commemoration of the Landing, of the New-England Pilgrims*, 21; Burnap, *A Sermon Preached at Merrimac*, 24. In his 1795 sermon that he gave to his congregation in West Springfield, Massachusetts, Joseph Lathrop already emphasized that commerce was important for the American nation's civilization, but it should never become the first priority because it would then lead to luxury and corruption; see Joseph Lathrop, *National Happiness, Illustrated in a Sermon, Delivered at West-Springfield, on the 19th of February 1795* (Springfield, Massachusetts: Hooker and Stebbins, 1795), 12–13. Here he said:

> Commerce is, indeed, useful, and in some degree necessary to civilized and refined nations....It contributes to the increase of knowledge and the improvement of arts. It humanizes the manners, gives spirit to industry, and a spring to enterprize [*sic*]. But when it becomes the principal objects, it is dangerous to a people....It tends to luxury and corruption of manners.

12. Chester, *Sermon, in Commemoration of the Landing, of the New-England Pilgrims*, 6–7, 23. For Morse, see Conforti, *Imagining New England*, 97.
13. "Review of the First Settlement of New England," 112; Chester, *Sermon, in Commemoration of the Landing, of the New-England Pilgrims*, 6–7, 23. On the civilization of the wilderness, see also Sabine, *The Fathers of New England*, 10. Here he prided in the achievements:

    What a series of events, my brethren, in so short a time! a history perfectly unique! the annals of all world besides, afford no such record! In 30 years, a savage wilderness, unknown to civilized nations, for time immemorial, becomes a land of cities, of fields, of gardens, of churches—a land wherein every man dwells safely under his vine and under his fig-tree.

    See also Spring, *A Tribute to New England*, 11–12. He wrote:

    Like the pilgrims of other times, "the wandered in the wilderness in a solitary way; they found no city to dwell in." Notwithstanding the rigour of the climate, and the severities [*sic*] of a disease which had cut off nearly one half of the colony, very conspicuous were the divine guardianship and munificence toward these pious men.... In this short period, a world that had been little else than the resort of beasts of prey, was turned into fruitful fields and pleasant habitations; and a forest that had swarmed with savage men became peopled with the sons of the Most High.

    John Hubbard Church, *The First Settlement of New England: A Sermon, Delivered in the South Parish, in Andover, April 5, 1810* (Sutton, Massachusetts: Sewall Goodrich, 1810); and Burnap, *A Sermon Preached at Merrimac*, 10.
14. Winthrop Bailey, *National Glory* (Portland: Arthur Shirley, 1812), 7; Chaplin, *The Dispensation of Divine Providence*, 8–9. Bailey described a good patriot along the same lines:

    The object of his wished was that combination of circumstances; that union of private and general success with the prevalence and influence of moral habits, and the means, dispositions, and effects of religion, in which the true glory of a nation consists. This kind of patriotism is not, like the other, the production of a selfish and worldly disposition. It is the genuine offspring of that supreme love to God.... To this class of patriots every good man belongs. It is not his object to promote a party, or to secure an office. It is not his design to render this rich, and that dependent. His heart is fixed to the true welfare of his country. (3)

    In a different place he rephrased this definition: "Nations are of course as dependent on God, as individuals, and no one can be a patriot in the highest and best sense without that pious disposition, which the psalmist discovers. Without this disposition a person must be indifferent to the interests of his countrymen" (4). For Federalists' views on immorality, crime, and anarchy as results of Jeffersonian democracy, see Sharp and James Roger, *American Politics in the Early Republic* (New Haven: Yale University, Press, 1993), 127 and William C. Dowling, *Literary Federalism in the Age of Jefferson: Joseph Dennie and the Port Folio, 1801–1812* (Columbia, South Carolina: University of South Carolina Press, 1999).

15. See Sassi, *Republic of Righteousness*, 185–187.
16. Sabine, *The Fathers of New England*, 29; see also 27. Here he said: "The future and standing character of New England will entirely depend upon the regard she continues to pay to her original constitution. The great objects of the Fathers in planting this wilderness were, That there might be a pure gospel church—liberty of conscience—an asylum for the persecuted—and a people advancing in the science of church polity." In Chester, *Sermon, in Commemoration of the Landing, of the New-England Pilgrims*, 25–27, he again defines the Christian nation: "We learn the true sources of national prosperity and glory. 'The fear of the Lord is the beginning of wisdom, and to depart from evil is understanding. Righteousness exalteth [*sic*] a nation, but sin is the reproach of any people" (25). He illustrated the fatal consequences of a neglect of religion:

    > Family will be forgotten, quality of education will decrease, no more liberty and asylum for the poor, poverty and servitude. . . . Be assured, my brethren, when the inhabitants of this country shall become advocates of immorality, of loose and infidel opinions; when the bible shall be the subject of lawless criticism . . . then anarchy will follow as the herald of despotism, and national felicity and freedom, will be exiled and destroyed." (26–27)

    John Chester also emphasized the religiosity of the New England fathers; he said they "were distinguished for their love of the divine cause of religion, and for the honour of God their Father, Saviour, and Sanctifier," Chester, *Sermon, in Commemoration of the Landing, of the New-England Pilgrims*, 18. For Providence as the central theme that the Congregational establishment always emphasized and which did not lose its importance in the nineteenth century, see Sassi, *Republic of Righteousness*, 31–51.
17. Isaac Backus, *An Abridgment of the Church History of New England from 1602 to 1804* (Boston: E. Lincoln, 1804), 262. Here he wrote: "Our churches in general hold the doctrines of grace, Christian experience, and the importance of a holy life, much as the chief fathers of New England did. They differ very little from the fathers of Plymouth colony, only about infant baptism" ("Review of the First Settlement of New England," 113); Burnap, *A Sermon Preached at Merrimac*, 7; "A Concise View of the Character of the Rev. Mr. John Cotton," *The Piscataqua Evangelical Magazine* 1 (1805): 56–60. See Spring, *A Tribute to New England*, 19. He said

the Pilgrims' "character both for learning and for piety, and the circumstances attending their establishment, were a sufficient pledge of their disposition to promote their interest of knowledge, which they well knew to be one of the most pillars of the Church as well as the State."

18. Chester, *Sermon, in Commemoration of the Landing, of the New-England Pilgrims*, 23; Sabine, *The Fathers of New England*, 13.
19. Jonathan Sassi convincingly shows what impact their loss of dominance, the Unitarian Crisis, and the increase in the number of dissenters had on Congregational public Christianity; see Sassi, *Republic of Righteousness*, 117–123, 131–136, 145–149, 154.
20. Sabine, *The Fathers of New England*, 21; "Review of the First Settlement of New England," 112; Spring, *A Tribute to New England*, 14, 19–20. For the virtuous influence of New England on the national character and American superiority as a result of this, see also Chaplin, *The Dispensation of Divine Providence*, 6. The Congregational minister said:

    > God has done great things for us. He did wonderful things for those excellent men from whom we descended. Through his blessing, population and wealth have increased with a rapidity much beyond what other nations have commonly experienced…and the country which we inhabit, within a short period, has become one of the brightest spots on the face of the globe.

    A traveler visiting the Bunker Hill Monument reported in 1823 how the sight convinced him that the New England virtues leading to the victory over the British had raised the American character: "Now, as I had always, in early life, heard of Bunker's Hill, and had associated with that name, those displays of determined courage and prowess, which the beginning of a doubtful and perilous contest, raised the American character, and perhaps were closely connected with the result of the struggle" ("Extracts from a Journey in New England," 724–727). John Chester said New England "ranks high on the catalogue of Nation. It is filled with noble institutions—it is blessed with liberty—it is governed by law" (Chester, *Sermon, in Commemoration of the Landing, of the New-England Pilgrims*, 7).
21. Daniel Kilbride, *An American Aristocracy: Southern Planters in Antebellum Philadelphia* (Columbia: University of South Carolina Press, 2006), 2.
22. Chester, *Sermon, in Commemoration of the Landing, of the New-England Pilgrims*, 13, 23. Compare Sabine, *The Fathers of New England*, 26. See also John Lathrop, *Patriotism and Religion: A Sermon preached on the 25th of April, 1799* (Boston: John Russell, 1799) and Hezekiah Packard, *The Plea to Patriotism: A Sermon preached at Chelmsford* (Boston: William Greenough, 1795).
23. Chester, *Sermon, in Commemoration of the Landing, of the New-England Pilgrims*, 29.

24. Ibid. He said:

> The inhabitants , of all the northern parts of the Union, are at this moment distinguished for their hatred of slavery,—for their comparative good morals,—for their love of liberty,—for their attention to education,—and for their efforts to spread the gospel. And how is this population composed? For the most part of the descendants of PERSECUTED PROTESTANTS.

See Sabine, *The Fathers of New England*, 25. Here the Bostonian minister described the process that led to European poverty:

> To get rich and to gain large estates, and to shine in palaces and mansions—these are the objects pursued by men in Europe, in France, in Germany, in Holland, in England; but it must not be so in New England, not you forfeit your right to the soil. In all countries where there are the greatest masses of riches, there are also the greatest masses of poverty; the extremes of poverty and riches are nearly connected.

For the contrast between American piety and European superstition, see Lathrop, *Patriotism and Religion*, 16.

25. Abiel Abbot, *Traits of Resemblance in the People of the United States of America to Ancient Israel in a Sermon delivered at Haverhill, on the 28th of November, 1799, the Day of Anniversary Thanksgiving* (Haverhill: Moore and Stebbins, 1799), 18. About England, Abbot said:

> The central, and the parent state of New England, she is crowned with every blessing of salubrity [*sic*] of climate, fertility of soil, and maritime accommodations. In regard to means of religion, we are equally favored. Upon our shores landed the pilgrims, who were the acorn, from which has grown a noble oak. The sons of such fires, we have degenerated; but we have so far preserved their spirit, as to retain a respect for religion in its ministers, its sabbath, and its public worship. (24)

As another example for Anti-French sermons during the late 1790s, see also Jedidiah Morse, *A Sermon Preached at Charlestown, November 29, 1798, on the Anniversary of Thanksgiving in Massachusetts: With an Appendix, designed to illustrate some Parts of the Discourse, exhibiting proofs…of French intrigue and influence in the United States* (Boston: Samuel Hall, 1798). For ministers' anti-French attitude and criticism of Republican and sectarian infidelity in the late 1790s, see Sassi, *Republic of Righteousness*, 75–78.

26. Bailey, *National Glory*, 9–11. He preached: "That the government of France is opposed to religion, and the rights, and interests of mankind, there can be no doubt; and in America we can yet express this opinion. Notwithstanding the pompous and extravagant pretensions of the French emperor, and his servile flatterers in styling him the avenger [of] rights and the protector of the liberties of the people." Greenwood, "Schools of New England," *The Religious Intelligencer*

10 (1825): 347. For fears of a Jeffersonian conspiracy and anti-French sentiments among Congregationalist after the election of 1800, see Sassi, *Republic of Righteousness*, 84–91.

27. Abbot, *Traits of Resemblance in the People of the United States of America to Ancient Israel*, 4, 6. Samuel Dexter, *Our Father's God, the Hope of Posterity: Some serious Thoughts on the foundation, Rise and Growth of the Settlement in New England* (delivered at Dedham, November 23, 1738, reprinted: Boston: Thomas Fleet 1796), see, e.g., 35. For a comparison of the American people and ancient Israelites, see also Joseph Lathrop, *National Happiness*, 13. The Congregational minister Pitt Clark combined that comparison with a strong statement on God's historical protection of New Englanders; see Clark, *On the Rise and Signalized Lot of the United Americans*, 7, 12–15. For the manifestation of God's providence, see among others Chester, *Sermon, in Commemoration of the Landing, of the New-England Pilgrims*, 27. For the idea that God had always been on the side of New Englanders and Americans, see William Rowland, *A Sermon, Delivered at Exeter, December 22, 1820, Being the Second Anniversary of the Landing of the Pilgrims of New England* (Exeter, New Hampshire: J.J. Williams, 1821), 4, 9–11. For the translation of the French history, see Claude Fleury, *A Short History of the Ancient Israelites with an Account of Their Manners, Customs, Laws, Polity*...(Burlington, Vermont: Stephen C. Ustick, 1813).
28. Barnabas Bates, *A Discourse Delivered to the Inhabitants of Bristol* (Warren, Rhode Island: Samuel Randass, 1815); Dodge, *Sermon, delivered in Haverhill*, 4. Compare Abbot, *Traits of Resemblance in the People of the United States of America to Ancient Israel*, 6–8. As another example for this comparison, see Rowland, *A Sermon, Delivered at Exeter*, 4. For the seventeenth-century use of such terms, see Conforti, *Imagining New England*, 29–30.
29. See Mary M. Dyer, *Portraiture of Shakerism, Exhibiting a General View of Their Character and Conduct* (printed for the author, 1822) and *A Brief Statement of the Sufferings of Mary Dyer Occasioned by the Society Called the Shakers* (Concord, New Hampshire: Joseph Spear, 1818), also printed in Boston by William S. Spear in the same year. For an account partly supporting Mary Dyer's description of the Shakers, see "Sect of Shakers in America," *The Atheneum* 2 (1825): 317–319.
30. Benjamin Silliman, *Remarks, Made on a Short Tour between Hartford and Quebec, in the Autumn of 1819* (New Haven: S. Converse, 1820), 42, 43. A similar description appeared in an article in the New York *Theological Magazine*, see "A Traveller [*sic*], Cambridge, 1796," *Theological Magazine* 1796, in Flo Morse, *The Shakers and the World's People* (New York: Dodd, Mead and Company, 1980), 68–69. The author portrayed the Shakers sharing New England values: "Their houses have a neatness beyond anything I have yet seen in our country.

Their farms, their gardens, their manufactories in iron, in brass and in tin bar traits of order and neatness....They themselves are plain, decent, and grave in their dress, language, and deportment." The article "Character of the Shakers," *Boston Weekly Magazine* 2 (1817): 7, 10, e.g., explains that "it is obvious, that their neatness, industry and improvements, must be daily producing beneficial public effects, by the power of their constant example on their neighbors." It also emphasized that the shakers lived without any luxury: "The temptation to extravagance in dress is removed, by their preserving the same unvaried quality and fashion in their garments, from one generation to another. They indulge not in the luxuries of the table, but content themselves mostly with the produce of their own lands." For visual depictions of Shaker villages, see Robert Emlen, *Shaker Village Views: Illustrated Maps and Landscapes by Shaker Artists of the Nineteenth Century* (Hanover, New Hampshire: University Press of New England, 1987); for an example of an early engraving from 1835, see page 140. For the pamphlet rejecting Mary Dyer's charges against the Shakers, see *A Review of Mary Dyer's Publication, Entitled a Portraiture of Shakerism* (Concord, New Hampshire: Jacob Moore, 1824).

31. Spring, *A Tribute to New England*, 18. Here he said:

> And what Christian, what patriot, but will rejoice that this most important principle has been so highly esteemed and so jealously guarded by the American people, that it holds a prominent place, not only in the several State Constitutions, but in the great bond of our National Confederation? Ever since the establishment of the Plymouth colony, the Western world has in this respect been unfolding a splendid and consoling prospect.

See also Dexter, *Our Father's God, the Hope of Posterity*, 21. Dexter maintained that the Pilgrims had pursued religious freedom: "The inhabitants of this Province have always had a just value for the civil Liberties, but free and secure enjoyment of their religious privileges."

Conclusion

1. For an appeal to historians to treat historical texts as events see John G.A. Pocock, "Texts as Events: Reflections on the History of Political Thought," in *Politics of Discourse: The Literature and History of Seventeenth-Century England*, ed. Kevin Sharpe and Steven N. Zwicker (London: 1987), 21–35. In his theoretical essay Pocock argues that historical texts should be interpreted in the same way as historical events, which do not have a stagnant but a shifting meaning depending on the personal context of the participant. Texts change their interpretation with every reader depending on his or her background and experience.

Bibliography

Primary Sources

Manuscripts

Brunswick Convention, Comments of the Brunswick Convention on the Separation of Maine from Massachusetts, October 1816, Maine Historical Society, Portland, Maine.

Crehore Family Papers, Massachusetts Historical Society, Boston, Massachusetts.

Deering, Journey from Falmouth to Boston, 1814, Maine Historical Society, Portland, Maine.

Longfellow Family Papers, Maine Historical Society, Portland, Maine.

Newhall Papers, Massachusetts Historical Society, Boston, Massachusetts.

Quincy Papers, Massachusetts Historical Society.

Sarah Weld Clark Crehore, *Journal of a Trip to Maine*, 1807, Crehore Family Papers, Massachusetts Historical Society.

Spence-Lowell Collection, Huntington Library, San Marino, California.

Stoddard Family Papers, Massachusetts Historical Society.

The Conditions of Separation Considered, Pamphlet in Manuscript ca. 1816–1819, Longfellow Family Papers, Maine Historical Society.

Walter Channing Papers, Massachusetts Historical Society, Boston.

William King Papers, Maine Historical Society.

Newspapers

Dailies

Boston Daily Advertiser, Boston, Massachusetts.

Boston Evening Gazette, Boston, Massachusetts.

Boston Gazette, Boston, Massachusetts.

Boston Herald, Boston, Massachusetts.

Columbian Centinel, Boston, Massachusetts.

Concord Herald, Concord, New Hampshire.

Connecticut Courant, Hartford, Connecticut.

Connecticut Journal, New Haven, Connecticut.

The Eastern Argus, Portland, Maine.

Portland Gazette, Portland, Maine.

Salem Gazette, Salem, Massachusetts.

Periodicals

Christian Observer, Boston, Massachusetts.

Christian Spectator, New Haven, Connecticut.

Courier De Boston, Boston, Massachusetts.

Merrimack Magazine and Ladies' Literary Cabinet, Newburyport, Massachusetts.

Merrimack Miscellany, Newburyport, Massachusetts.

New England Galaxy, Boston, Massachusetts.

The Advisor of Vermont Evangelical Magazine, Middlebury, Vermont.

The American Apollo, Boston, Massachusetts.

The American Magazine, Albany, New York.

The American Moral and Sentimental Magazine, New York, New York.

The American Museum or Universal Magazine, Philadelphia, Pennsylvania.

The American Review and Literary Journal, New York, New York.

The Atheneum, Boston, Massachusetts.

The Boston Spectator, Boston, Massachusetts.

The Boston Weekly Magazine, Boston, Massachusetts.

The Christian Herald, Portsmouth, New Hampshire.

The Christian Monitor, Boston, Massachusetts.

The Columbian Phenix and Boston Review, Boston, Massachusetts.

The Connecticut Evangelical Magazine and Religious Intelligencer, Hartford, Connecticut.

The Connecticut Magazine or Gentlemen's and Ladies' Monthly Museum, Bridgeport, Connecticut.

The Emerald or Miscellany of Literature, Boston, Massachusetts.

The Gentlemen and Ladies' Town and Country Magazine, Boston, Massachusetts.

The Guardian, New Haven, Connecticut.

The Journal of Science and the Arts, New York, New York.

The Ladies Weekly Museum, New York, New York.

The Lady's Miscellany or Weekly Visitor, New York, New York.

The Lady's Monitor, New York, New York.

The Literary Miscellany, Cambridge, Massachusetts.

The Massachusetts Magazine, Boston, Massachusetts.

The Monthly Anthology and Boston Review, Boston, Massachusetts.

The Monthly Magazine and American Review, New York, New York.

The Monthly Register, Magazine and Review of the United Sates, New York, New York.

The New England Farmer, Boston, Massachusetts.

The New Haven Gazette and the Connecticut Magazine, New Haven, Connecticut.

The New York Magazine or Literary Repository, New York, New York.

The North American Review, Boston, Massachusetts.

The Panoplist and Missionary Magazine, Boston, Massachusetts.

The Piscataqua Evangelical Magazine, Amherst, New Hampshire.

The Philadelphia Minerva, Philadelphia, Pennsylvania.

The Philadelphia Monthly Magazine, Philadelphia, Pennsylvania.
The Portfolio, Philadelphia, Pennsylvania.
The Portsmouth Weekly Magazine, Portsmouth, New Hampshire.
The Religious Informer, Enfield, Connecticut.
The Religious Intelligencer, New Haven, Connecticut.
The Rural Magazine, Rutland, New York.
The Time Piece and Literary Companion, New York, New York.
The United States Literary Gazette, Boston, Massachusetts.
Worcester Magazine, Worcester, Massachusetts.

Printed Works

A Review of Mary Dyer's Publication, Entitled A Portraiture of Shakerism (Concord, New Hampshire: Jacob Moore, 1824).

Abbot, Abiel, *Traits of Resemblance in the People of the United States of America to Ancient Israel. In a Sermon delivered at Haverhill, on the 28th of November, 1799, the Day of Anniversary Thanksgiving* (Haverhill, Massachusetts: Moore and Stebbins, 1799).

———, *A Discourse Delivered at Plymouth December 22, 1809, at the Celebration of the 188th Anniversary of Our Forefathers in that Place* (Boston, Massachusetts: n.p., 1810).

Abigail Adams, *Letters of Mrs. Adams, the Wife of John Adams, 2 vols.* (Boston, Massachusetts: Charles C. Little and James Brown, 1840).

Adams, Hannah, *A Summary History of New England* (Dedham, Massachusetts: H. Mann and J.H. Adams, 1799).

———, *An Abridgement of the History of New England* (Boston, Massachusetts: Etheridge and Bliss, 1805, 1807).

Adams, John Quincy, *Letters on Silesia: Written on a Tour through that Country in the Years 1800, 1801* (London, England: L. Budd, 1804).

Address of a convention of delegates from twenty towns and five plantations within the counties of York, Cumberland and Lincoln, met by adjournment at Portland, on the twenty eighth day of January, one thousand seven hundred and ninety five to the people of said counties, on the subject of their separation from Massachusetts (Portland, Maine: Thomas B. Wait, 1795).

An Appeal to the people of Maine: Is it for the Interest of the District of Maine to Become a Separate State? (n.p.: 1816).

Auborn, A. de, *The French Convert: Being a True Relation of the Happy Conversion of a noble French Lady from the Errors and superstition of Popery, to the Reformed Religion by Means of a Protestant Gardener, her Servant* (Berwick, Massachusetts: W. Phorson, 1795).

Austin, William, *Letters from London* (Boston, Massachusetts: Pelham, 1804).

Backus, Isaac, *An Abridgment of the Church History of New England from 1602 to 1804* (Boston, Massachusetts: E. Lincoln, 1804).

Bailey, Winthrop, *National Glory* (Portland, Maine: Arthur Shirley, 1812).

Bates, Barnabas, *A Discourse Delivered to the Inhabitants of Bristol* (Warren, Rhode Island: Samuel Randass, 1815).

Belknap, Jeremy, *History of New Hampshire* (Dover, New Hampshire: J. Mann and J.K. Remick, 1812).

Biographical Sketch of the Life of the Marquis De La Fayette (Exeter, New Hampshire: Gerrish and Tyler, 1824).

Boudinot, Elias, *Elias Boudinot's Journey to Boston in 1809*, ed. Milton Halsey Thomas (Princeton, New Jersey: Princeton University Press, 1955).

Bradford, William, *A Descriptive and Historical Account of New England in Verse* (Boston, Massachusetts: Munroe and Francis, 1794).

Brainers, Cephas and Eveline Warner Brainers, eds., *The New England Society Orations: Addresses, Sermons, and Poems Delivered before the New England Society in the City of New York, 1820–1885* (New York: The Century, 1901).

Brilliant Naval Victory: Yankee Perry, Better than Old English Cider, Broadside (Boston, Massachusetts: N. Coverly 1813).

Burnap, Jacob, *A Sermon Preached at Merrimac, December 22, 1829, Being Two Centuries from the First Settlement of New England* (Amherst, New Hampshire: Elijah Mansur, 1821).

Butler, Frederick, *Memoirs of the Marquis de La Fayette, Major-General in the Revolutionary Army of the United States of America, Together with His Tour through the United States* (Wetherfield, Connecticut: Deming and Francis, 1825).

Carr, John, *The Stranger in France* (Hartford, Connecticut: Oliver D. Cooker, 1804).

Chaplin, Daniel, *The Dispensation of Divine Providence Considered as Generally Corresponding with the Morale Character of a Nation, and the Morals of New England, a Sermon Delivered in Groton [Ma], January 12, 1815* (Cambridge, Massachusetts: Hilliard and Metcalf, 1815).

Chester, John, *Sermon, In Commemoration of the Landing, of the New-England Pilgrims, Delivered in the Second Presbyterian Church, Albany* (Albany, New York: E. and E. Hosford, 1820).

Church, John Hubbard, *The First Settlement of New England: A Sermon, Delivered in the South Parish, in Andover, April 5, 1810* (Sutton, Massachusetts: Sewall Goodrich, 1810).

Cooke, Thomas, *I'll Love You Ever Dearly: Sung by Mr. Taylor: From the Operatic Anecdote of Frederick the Great* (Philadelphia, Pennsylvania: G. Willig's Musical Magazine, 1815, 1817, 1818, 1819 and New York: W. Dubois, 1817).

———, *Roll Drums Merrily. Frederick the Great. When I Was an Infant* (Philadelphia, Pennsylvania: G. Willig, 1820, 1824).

Davis, Daniel, *An Address to the Inhabitants of the District of Maine, upon the Subject of their Separation from the present Government of Massachusetts* (Portland, Maine: Thomas B. Watts, 1791).

———, *Our Father's God, the Hope of Posterity: Some serious Thoughts on the foundation, Rise and Growth of the Settlement in New England* (delivered at Dedham, November 23, 1738, reprinted: Boston: Thomas Fleet, 1796).

Dimond, W., *Third Night of the Broken Sword: On Friday Evening, May 2, 1817, Will Be Presented, the New Operatic Drama, in 3 Acts, of Frederick the Great*...(New York, New York: n.p., 1817).

Dodge, Joshua, *Sermon, Delivered in Haverhill, December 22, 1820, Being the Second Centesimal [sic] Anniversary, of the Landing of New England Fathers at Plymouth* (Haverhill, Massachusetts: Burrill and Hersey, 1821).

Dwight, Timothy, *Travels in New England and New York* (New Haven, Connecticut: S. Converse, 1821–1822).

Dyer, Mary M., *A Brief Statement of the Sufferings of Mary Dyer Occasioned by the Society Called the Shakers* (Concord, New Hampshire: Joseph Spear, 1818).

———, *Portraiture of Shakerism, Exhibiting a General View of Their Character and Conduct* (printed for the author, 1822).

Foster, John, *A Sketch of the Tour of General Lafayette, on His Late Visit to the United States, 1824* (Portland, Maine: A.W. Thayer, 1824).

Fleury, Claude, *A Short History of the Ancient Israelites with an Account of Their Manners, Customs, Laws, Polity*...(Burlington, Vermont: Stephen C. Ustick, 1813).

Goldie, John, *Diary of a Journey through Upper Canada and Some New England States, 1819* (privately published Philadelphia, 1910).

History of Montgomery County, Pennsylvania, ed. by Theodore W. Bean (Philadelphia, Pennsylvania: Everts and Peck, 1884).

Hubbard, William, *A General History of New England from the Discovery to MDCLXXX* (Cambridge, Massachusetts: Hilliard and Metcalf, 1815).

Hunsicker, Clifton S., *Montgomery County, Pennsylvania: A History, 2 Vols.* (New York, New York: Lewis Historical Publishing Company, 1923).

Hutchinson, Thomas, *The History of Massachusetts from the First Settlement* (Boston, Massachusetts: Manning and Loring, 1795, 1803).

King Friedrich Wilhelm the First: *The Story of the Youth of Frederick the Great. A Historical Drama in four Acts* (n.p, 1800).

Lafayette or Disinterested Benevolence (Boston, Massachusetts: Francis Y. Carlile, 1825).

Lathrop, John, National Happiness, *Illustrated in a Sermon, Delivered at West-Springfield, on the 19th of February 1795* (Springfield, Massachusetts: Hooker and Stebbins, 1795).

———, *Patriotism and Religion: A Sermon preached on the 25th of April, 1799* (Boston, Massachusetts: John Russell, 1799).

———, *Two Discourses Delivered in Boston* (Boston, Massachusetts: Burditt and Co., 1812).

Layman, A., *Address to the Clergy of New-England on Their Opposition to the Rulers of the United States* (Concord, New Hampshire, 1814).

Levasseur, August, *Lafayette in America, in 1824 and 1825, or Journal of a Voyage to the United States, 2 vols.*, trans. John D. Godman (Philadelphia, Pennsylvania: Carey and Lea, 1829).

Ligne, Charles Joseph, *Letters and Reflections of the Austrian Field-Marshal Prince Ligne Containing Anecdotes Hitherto Unpublished of Joseph II, Catherine II, Frederick the Great* (Philadelphia, Pennsylvania: B. Graves, 1809).

Lyman, Theodore, *A Few Weeks in Paris* (Boston: Cumming and Hilliard, 1814).

Melish, John, *Travels through the United States in the Years 1806, 1807, and 1809, 1810 & 1811* (Philadelphia, Pennsylvania: T. and G. Palmer, 1815, reprinted, 1970).

Mellen Prentiss, Thomas, *The Maine Spelling Book* (Portland, Maine: Adams and Patten, 1809).

Memoirs of General La Fayette Embracing Details of His Public and Private Life, Sketches of the American Revolution, the French Revolution, the Down-Fall of Bonaparte, and the Restoration of the Bourbons (Hartford, Connecticut.: Barber and Robinson, 1825).

Memoirs of General Lafayette with an Account of His Visit to America and of His Reception by the People of the United States (Boston, Massachusetts: E.G. House, 1824).

Morse, Jedidiah, *A True and Authentic History of his Excellency George Washington, Commander in chief of the American Army during the late War* (Philadelphia, Pennsylvania: Peter Stewart, 1790).

———, *A Sermon Preached at Charlestown, November 29, 1798, on the Anniversary of Thanksgiving in Massachusetts: With an Appendix, designed to illustrate some Parts of the Discourse, exhibiting proofs...of French intrigue and influence in the United States* (Boston, Massachusetts: Samuel Hall, 1798).

———, *A Compendious History of New England Designed for Schools and Private Families* (Newburyport, Massachusetts: Thomas and Whipple, 1809).

Osgood, David, *Solemn Protest against the Late Declaration of War, in a Discourse, Delivered on the Next Lord's Day after the Tidings of It Were Received* (Cambridge, Massachusetts: Hilliard and Metcalf, 1812).

Packard, Hezekiah, *The Plea to Patriotism: A Sermon preached at Chelmsford* (Boston, Massachusetts: William Greenough, 1795).

Paulding, James Kirke, *A Sketch of Old England, by a New-England Man*, Vol. I (New York: Charles Wiley, 1822).

A Pilgrimage of Liberty: A Contemporary Account of the Triumphal Tour of General Lafayette through the Southern and Western States in 1825 as Reported by Local Newspapers (Athens, Ohio: The Lawhead Press, 1944).

Robbins, Thomas, *An Historical View of the First Planters of New England* (Hartford, Connecticut: Gleason and Co., 1815).

Rowland, William, *A Sermon, Delivered at Exeter, December 22, 1820, Being the Second Anniversary of the Landing of the Pilgrims of New England* (Exeter, New Hampshire: J.J. Williams, 1821).

Sabine, James, *The Fathers of New England. A Sermon Delivered in the Church in Essex Street, Boston, December 22, 1820. Being the Second Centennial Celebration of the Landing of the Fathers at Plymouth* (Boston, Massachusetts: G. Clark & co., 1821).

Shaw, Charles, *Topographical and Historical Description of Boston* (Boston, Massachusetts: Oliver Spear, 1817).

Silliman, Benjamin, *Remarks, Made on a Short Tour between Hartford and Quebec, in the Autumn of 1819* (New Haven, Connecticut: S. Converse, 1820).

Southey, Robert, *Letters from England by Don Manuel Alvarez Espriella* (Boston, Massachusetts: Munroe, Francis and Parker, 1808).

Spring, Gardiner, *A Tribute to New England: A Sermon Delivered before the New England Society of the City and State of New York, on the 22nd of December, 1820. Being the Second Centennial Celebration of the Landing of the Pilgrims at Plymouth* (New York: S.F. Lockwood, 1821).

Stansbury, Philip, *A Pedestrian Tour of Two Thousand Three Hundred Miles, in North America: To the Lakes,—the Canadas,—and the New England States, Performed in the Autumn of 1821* (New York: Myers and Smith, 1822).

Strickland, William, *Journal of a Tour in the United States of America, 1794–1795*, ed. J.E. Strickland (New York Historical Society, 1971).

Sullivan, James, *The History of the District of Maine* (Boston, Massachusetts: Thomas and Andrews, 1795).

Tappan, William, *New England and Other Poems* (Philadelphia, Pennsylvania: J.H. Cunningham, 1819).

Temple, George, *The American Tourist's Pocket Companion, or, a Guide to the Springs and Trip to the Lakes* (New York: D. Lonwoth, 1812).

Thiebault, Dieudonne, *Original Anecdotes of Frederick the Great, King of Prussia, and of His Family, His Court, His Ministers, His Academies, and His literary Friends* (Philadelphia, Pennsylvania: E. Bronson, 1806).

Ticknor, George, *Outlines of the Principle Events in the Life of General Lafayette from the North American Review* (Portland, Maine: David and Seth Paine, 1825).

Twohig, Albot and Dorothy, eds., *The Diaries of George Washington*, Vol. V (Charlottesville, Virginia: University of Virginia, 1976).

———, *The Papers of George Washington, 4, April 1786–January 1787* (Charlottesville, Virginia: University Press of Virginia, 1992).

Tudor, William, *Letters of the Eastern States* (New York: Kirk and Mercein, 1820).

Webster, Daniel, *An Address Delivered at the Laying of the Cornerstone of the Bunker Hill Monument* (Boston, Massachusetts: Cummings, Hilliard and Co., 1825).

Warville, Brissot de, *New Travels in the United States* (Boston, Massachusetts: J. Bumstead, 1797).

William Vans Murray to J.Q. Adams, April 3, 1802, American Historical Association, Annual Report, 1912, p. 705.

Williamson, William D., *The History of the State of Maine* (Hallowell, Maine: Glazier, Masters and Co., 1832).

Wright D'Arusmont, Frances, *Views of Society and Manner in America: A Series of Letters from that Country to a Friend in England during the Years 1818, 1819 and 1820* (New York: n.p., 1821).

Secondary Sources

Allgor, Catherine, *Parlor Politics in which the Ladies of Washington Help Build a City and a Government* (Charlottsville: University Press of Virginia, 2000).

Anderson, Patricia, *Promoted to Glory: The Apotheosis of George Washington* (Northampton, Massachusetts: Smith College Museum of Art, 1980).

Appleby, Joyce, *Inheriting the Revolution: The First Generation of Americans* (London: Harvard University Press, 2000).

Ayers, Edward L. et al., *All over the Map: Rethinking American Regions* (Baltimore: Johns Hopkins University Press, 1996).

Banks, Ronald, *Maine Becomes a State: The Movement to Separate Maine from Massachusetts, 1785–1820* (Middletown, Connecticut: Wesleyan University Press, 1970).

Barish, Evelyn, *Emerson: The Roots of Prophecy* (Princeton: Princeton University Press, 1989).

Bender, Thomas, *Community and Social Change in America* (New Brunswick, New Jersey: Rutgers University Press, 1978).

Bercovitch, Sacvan, *The Puritan Origins of the American Self* (New Haven: Yale University Press, 1975).

Boyd, Julian P., "State and Local Historical Societies in the United States," *The American Historical Review* 40 (1934): 10–34.

Breen, Timothy H., "Ideology and Nationalism on the Eve of the American Revolution: Revisions Once More in Need of Revising," *Journal of American History 84* (June 1997).

Brewer, John, *The Pleasures of the Imagination: English Culture in the Eighteenth Century* (London: Fontana Press, 1997).

Briggs, Peter M., "Timothy Dwight 'Composes' a Landscape for New England," *American Quarterly* 40 (1988): 359–377.

Brown, Chandos Michael, *Benjamin Silliman: A Life in the Young Republic* (Princeton: Princeton University Press, 1989).

Brown, Richard, *Knowledge Is Power: The Diffusion of Information in Early America, 1700–1865* (New York: Oxford University Press, 1989).

Burrows, Edwin and Mike Wallace, *Gotham. A History of New York City to 1898* (New York: Oxford University Press, 1999).

Butler, Jon, *The Huguenots in America: A Refugee People in New World Society* (Cambridge: Harvard University Press, 1983).

Cashin, Joan, "Landscape and Memory in Antebellum Virginia," *Virginia Magazine of History and Biography* 4 (1994): 477–500.

Clark, Charles, James Leamon, and Karen Bowden, eds., *Maine in the Early Republic. From Revolution to Statehood* (Hanover: University Press of New England, 1988).

Cole, Richard C., *Irish Booksellers and English Writers* (London: Mansell, 1987).

Colley, Linda, *Britons: Forging the Nation 1707–1837* (London: Pimlico, 1992).

Conforti, Joseph, *Imagining New England: Explorations of Regional Identity from the Pilgrims to the Mid-Twentieth Century* (Chapel Hill: University of North Carolina Press, 2001).

Cott, Nancy, *The Bonds of Womanhood: "Woman's Sphere" in New England, 1780–1835* (New Haven: Yale University Press, 1977).

Cronon, William, *Changes in the Land: Indians, Colonists, and the Ecology of New England* (New York: Hill and Wang, 1983).

Davis, David Brion, "American Equality and Foreign Revolutions," *Journal of American History* 76 (1989): 729–752.

Dowling, William C., *Literary Federalism in the Age of Jefferson: Joseph Dennie and the Port Folio, 1801–1812* (Columbia, South Carolina: University of South Carolina Press, 1999).

Emmet, Alan, *So Fine a Prospect: Historic New England Gardens* (Hanover, New Hampshire: New England University Press, 1996).

Fletcher Little, Nina, *American Decorative Wall Painting*, 1700–1850 (Sturbridge, Massachusetts: Studio Publications, 1952).

———, *Country Arts in Early American Homes* (New York, Dutton, 1975).

———, *Neat and Tidy: Boxes and Their Contents Used in Early American Households* (New York: E. P. Dutton, 1980).

———, *Little by Little: Six Decades of Collecting American Decorative Arts* (New York: E.P. Dutton, 1984).

Gillard, John T., "Lafayette, Friend of the Negro," *Journal of Negro History* 19 (1934): 355–371.

Gilmore, William, *Reading Becomes a Necessity of Life: Material and Cultural Life in Rural New England, 1780–1835* (Knoxville: University of Tennessee Press, 1989).

Green, James N., *Mathew Carey, Publisher and Patriot* (Philadelphia: The Library Company of Philadelphia, 1985).

Gunther, Hans Karl, "Frederick the Great, the Bavarian War of Succession and the American War of Independence," *Duquesne Review* 16 (1971): 59–74.

Habermas, Jürgen, *The Structural Transformation of the Public Sphere; Inquiry into a Category of Bourgeois Society* (Cambridge: MIT Press, 1989).

Haworth, Paul Leland, "Frederick the Great and the American Revolution," *American Historical Review* 9 (1904): 460–478.

Hay, Robert P., "The American Revolution Twice Recalled: Lafayette's Visit and the Election of 1824," *Indiana Magazine of History* 69 (1973): 43–62.

Hellmuth, Eckhart, "Die 'Wiedergeburt' Friedrichs' des Großen und der 'Tod fürs Vaterland': Zum Patriotischen Selbstverständnis in Preußen in der zweiten Hälfte des 18. Jahrhunderts," in: *Nationalismus vor dem Nationalismus*, ed. Reinhard Stauber and Eckhart Hellmuth (Hamburg: F. Meier, 1998).

———, "A Monument to Frederick the Great: Architecture, Politics and the State in Late Eighteenth-Century Prussia," in: *Rethinking Leviathan: The Eighteenth-Century State in Britain and Germany*, ed. John Brewer and Eckhart Hellmuth (London: German Historical Institute; Oxford: Oxford University Press, 1999).

Hunt, Lynn, *The New Cultural History* (Los Angeles: University of California Press, 1989).

Johnson, Paul, *A Shopkeeper's Millennium Society and Revivals in Rochester, New York, 1815–1837* (New York: Hill and Wang, 1978).

Kerber, Linda, *Federalists in Dissent: Imagery and Ideology in Jeffersonian America* (Ithaca: Cornell University Press, 1970).

———, *Women of the Republic: Intellect and Ideology in Revolutionary America* (Chapel Hill: University of North Carolina Press, 1980).

Kilbride, Daniel, *An American Aristocracy: Southern Planters in Antebellum Philadelphia* (Columbia: University of South Carolina Press, 2006).

Klamkin, Marian, *The Return of Lafayette, 1824–1825* (New York: Charles Scribner's Sons, 1975).

Kloppenberg, James T., "The Virtues of Liberalism: Christianity, Republicanism, and Ethics in Early American Political Discourse," *Journal of American History* 74 (1987): 9–33.

Kramer, Lloyd, *Lafayette in Two Worlds: Public Cultures and Personal Identities in an Age of Revolution* (Chapel Hill: University of North Carolina Press, 1996).

Lathrop, Elise, *Early American Inns and Taverns* (New York: Tudor Publishing Company, 1926).

———, *Old New England Churches* (Rutland, Vermont: The Tuttle Publishing Co., 1938).

Lever, Ann Butler, "Vox Populi, Vox Dei: New England and the French Revolution, 1787–1801" (Ph.D. diss., University of North Carolina at Chapel Hill, 1972).

Longmore, Paul, *The Invention of George Washington* (Berkeley: University of California Press, 1989).

Loveland, Anne C., *Emblem of Liberty: The Image of Lafayette in the American Mind* (Baton Rouge: Louisiana State University Press, 1971).

Marini, Stephen, *Radical Sects of Revolutionary New England* (Cambridge: Harvard University Press, 1982).

McAleer, John, *Ralph Waldo Emerson: Days of Encounter* (Boston: Little, Brown, 1984).

Melish, Joanne Pope, *Disowning Slavery: Gradual Emancipation and "Race" in New England, 1780–1860* (Ithaca: Cornell University Press, 1998).

Miller, Perry, *The New England Mind: From Colony to Province* (Cambridge, Massachusetts: Harvard University Press, 1953).

———, *Errand into the Wilderness* (Cambridge: Belknap Press, 1956).

Mitnick, Barbara, *The Changing Image of George Washington* (New York: Fraunces Tavern Museum, 1989).

Morgan, Agnes, *Harvard Honors Lafayette* (New York: Garland Press, 1975).

Murrell Taylor, Amy, *The Divided Family in Civil War America* (Chapel Hill: University of North Carolina Press, 2005).

Nash, Gary B., "The American Clergy and the French Revolution," *William and Mary Quarterly* 22 (1965): 392–412.

Nash, Roderick, *Wilderness and the American Mind* (New Haven: Yale University Press, 1967).

Newman, Simon, *Parades and the Politics of the Street: Festive Culture in the Early American Republic* (Philadelphia: University of Pennsylvania Press, 1997).

Norton, Mary Beth, *Liberty's Daughters: The Revolutionary Experience of American Women, 1750–1800* (Boston: Little, Brown, 1980).

Nissenbaum, Stephen, "New England as Region and Nation," Chapter 2 in E.L. Ayers et al., *All over the Map: Rethinking American Regions* (1996).

Potter, David, "The Historian's Use of Nationalism and Vice Versa," in: *History and American Society: Essays of David M. Potter*, ed. Don Fehrenbach (New York: Oxford University Press, 1973).

Ring, Betty, *Girlhood Embroidery: American Samplers and Pictorial Needlework, 1650–1850* (New York: A. Knopf, 1993).

Rosenberg, Carroll Smith, *Religion and the Rise of the American City: The New York City Mission Movement, 1812–1870* (Ithaca: Cornell University Press, 1971).

Ryan, Mary, *Women in Public: Between Banners and Ballots, 1825–1880* (Baltimore: John Hopkins University Press, 1990).

Safford, Carleton L. and Robert Bishop, eds., *America's Quilts and Coverlets* (New York: Dutton, 1972).

Sharp, James Roger, *American Politics in the Early Republic* (New Haven: Yale University, Press, 1993).

Schlenke, Manfred, *England und das Friderizianische Preussen, 1740–1763: Ein Beitrag zum Verhaeltnis von Politik und Oeffentlicher Meinung im England des 18. Jahrhunderts* (Muenchen: Karl Alber, 1963).

Schwartz, Barry, "The Character of Washington: A Study in Republican Culture," *American Quarterly* 38 (1986): 202–222.

Sears, John F., "T. Dwight and the American Landscape," *Early American Literature* 11 (1976–1977): 311–321.

Sellers, Charles, *The Market Revolution: Jacksonian America, 1815–1846* (New York: Oxford University Press, 1991).

Seward, William H., *Life and Public Services of John Quincy Adams* (Auburn: Derby, Miller and Company, 1849).

Simpson, Lewis P., *Mind and the American Civil War: A Meditation on Lost Causes* (Baton Rouge: Louisiana State University Press, 1989).

Sinnott, Edmund W., *Meetinghouse and Church in Early New England* (New York: Bonanza Books, 1963), 71–74.

Sprage, Laura Fecych, ed., *Agreeable Situations: Society, Commerce, and Art in Southern Maine, 1780–1830* (Boston: Northeastern University Press, 1987).

Stanwood, Edward, *The Separation of Maine from Massachusetts: A Study of the Growth of Public Opinion, 1784–1820* (Cambridge: John Wilson and Son, 1907).

Sweet, John Wood, *Bodies Politic: Negotiating Race in the American North, 1730–1830* (Baltimore: John Hopkins University Press, 2003).

Taylor, Alan, *Liberty Men and Great Proprietors: The Revolutionary Settlement on the Maine Frontier, 1760–1820* (Chapel Hill: University of North Carolina Press, 1990).

———, *William Cooper's Town: Power and Persuasion on the Frontier of the Early American Republic* (New York: A. Knopf, 1995).

Travers, Len, *Celebrating the Fourth: Independence Day and the Rites of Nationalism in the Early Republic* (Amherst: University of Massachusetts Press, 1997).

Tucker, Leonard, *Clio's Consort: Jeremy Belknap and the Founding of the Massachusetts Historical Society* (Boston: Northeastern University Press, 1990).

Varg, Paul A., *New England and Foreign Relations, 1789–1850* (Hanover, University Press of New England, 1983).

Vierhaus, Rudolf, "Patriotismus–Begriff und Realitaet einer moral-politischen Haltung," in: Rudolf Vierhaus, *Deutschland im 18: Jahrhundert. Politische Verfassung, soziales Gefuege, geistige Bewegung* (Goettingen: Vandenhoeck and Ruprecht, 1987).

Waldstreicher, David, *In the Midst of Perpetual Fetes: The Making of American Nationalism, 1776–1820* (Chapel Hill, London: University of North Carolina Press, 1997).

Ward, John William, *Andrew Jackson: Symbol of an Age* (New York: Oxford University Press, 1953).

Watts, Steven, *The Republic Reborn: War and the Making of Liberal America, 1790–1820* (Baltimore: John Hopkins University Press, 1987).

Wood, Gordon, *The Creation of the American Republic, 1776–1787* (Chapel Hill: University of North Carolina Press, 1969).

———, *The Radicalism of the American Revolution* (New York: A. Knopf, 1992).

Wood, Joseph, *The New England Village* (Baltimore: John Hopkins University Press, 1997).

Yokota, Kariann Akemi, "Post-Colonial America; Transatlantic Networks of Exchange in the Early National Period" (Ph.D. dissertation, University of California Los Angeles, 2002).

Young, Alfred F., *The Shoemaker and the Tea Party* (Boston: Beacon Press, 1999).

Zelinsky, Wilbur, *Nation into State: The Shifting Symbolic Foundations of American Nationalism* (Chapel Hill: University of North Carolina Press, 1988).

Zboray, Ronald J., *A Fictive People: Antebellum Economic Development and the American Reading Public* (New York: Oxford University Press, 1993).

Index

Abbot, Abiel, 187–190
Adams, Abigail, 8, 76, 78
Adams, Hannah, 17–21
Adams, John Quincy, 64, 69, 70–71, 104, 126–129
Akin, James, 156
Alexander, Francis, 39–40
American Revolution, and New England nationalism, 28, 65, 106, 114, 123–125, 137–138, 201
Anglophobia, 10, 87–105, 114–116, 197–198
Anti-Catholicism, 11–12, 51–52, 60, 90, 110–112, 187–188, 201
Appleby, Joyce, 4, 8, 52, 116
Armstrong, Samuel T., 68
Austin, William, 90, 92, 94, 99, 101, 115

Bates, Barnabas, 189–190
Barralet, John James, 82
Bell, Daniel, 33
Bell, William, 38
Belknap, Jeremy, 17–18, 43, 45
Biester, Erich, 81
Blue Hill, Maine, 166
Boston, Massachusetts, 6, 22, 26, 32, 35, 47, 53, 131, 133–134, 163, 202
Boudinot, Elias, 25–26, 32, 37–38, 44, 49
Bowdoin College Campus, depiction of, 152
British society
  and corruption, 89–93, 102–103
  and social inequality, 90–96, 102
British materialism, depiction of, 92–93
British people, and luxurious lifestyle, 89, 91–92
British Protestantism, 101, 103, 201
British vices, myth of, 91–92, 96–98, 100–103
British women, depiction of, 97–98
Brown, John and Nicholas, 55
Brunswick Convention, 158, 161
Buckingham, Joseph Tinker, 99–100
Bucknam, Anna, 166–167
Burlington, Vermont, 25, 33
Burnap, Jacob, 174, 175, 177

Carey, Matthew, 19–20
Channing, Walter, 90, 94–95
Chester, John, 174, 182
Chodowiecki, Daniel, 82
Civilization of the wilderness, idea of, 12, 16, 21–27, 29, 33–35, 43, 125, 141, 147, 150–152, 173, 178–179, 192, 202
Clay, Henry, 164
Collective identity, American, 2–13, 15–16, 24–28, 36, 41, 51–52, 63, 77, 95, 98, 137, 142, 161, 165, 170–177, 201–202
Commercialization, 66, 92, 127, 131, 177
Conforti, Joseph, 19, 172

Dartmouth College, 6, 126
Davis, Rebecca, 34

Democratic Republicans, *see also* Jeffersonians, 41–42, 107, 115, 187, 201
Democratization, 67
Dexter, Samuel, 190
Dwight, Timothy, 22–29, 35, 39, 42, 45–47, 51, 53, 56, 152–153, 172

Earl, Ralph, 29, 37
Edict of Nantes, 110, 113
Editors, 6–7, 9, 18–20, 63, 66–67, 88–89, 98–99, 110, 112, 140, 193
Education, 13, 31, 36–37, 42–49, 58–59, 68–69, 84, 99, 138, 152–153, 175, 177, 181–182, 195
Election of 1800, 198
Election of 1824, 118, 129
Emerson, William, 18, 172
English Civil War, effects of, 115, 190
Errand in the Wilderness, myth of, 21
European culture
  American imitation of, 8–9, 87, 197–199
  American rejection of, 1–3, 6–8, 11, 16–17, 87, 197–199
European patriotism, 67, 71, 75, 79–81, 83–84, 104
European travelers, 9, 24, 37, 46, 51–52, 91, 142, 197

Faneuil Hall, 34, 35
Federalists, 9, 20, 36, 38, 39, 41, 45, 54–55, 58, 88, 95, 129–130, 149, 153, 155, 159, 160, 172, 179, 194, 199
Fisher, Alvan, 38, 152
Fisher, Jonathan, 166, 172
Framingham, Massachusetts, 33
France, and aristocratic lifestyle, 104, 109–110
Francophobia, 10–11, 51, 64, 87–90, 103–110, 171, 187–189, 197, 201
Frederick II (the Great), king of Prussia
  comparison with George Washington, 77–85
  depictions of death of, 61–62
  as a father figure, 73, 77
  as a friend of the American Revolution, 65
  in General Ziethen anecdotes, 73, 75
  German cult of, 57, 60, 63–64, 66, 72
  life of, 58–59
  in Miller Arnold story, 73
  in operas and plays, 61
  as a philanthropist, 71–77
  pre-Revolutionary admiration of, 59–60
  as a Protestant hero, 9–10, 59–60, 68
  as a republican hero, 9, 65–70
French Huguenots, celebration of, 90, 110–113
French and Indian War, 59–60, 66
French Revolution, 1, 83, 88, 100, 105–108, 111, 114–115, 137–139, 187
French Terror, 108, 112
French Women
  depiction of, 106–108
  myth of defeminization of, 10, 89, 108

Gedicke, Friedrich, 81
Gilpin, William, 27–29
Gilmore, William, 61
God's Chosen People, myth of, 12, 23, 173, 182–183, 188–189, 193
Greenfield, Massachusetts, 42

Hartford Convention, 4, 55, 198–199

Harvard College, 36, 152
Huguenots, *see* French Huguenots, 110–114

Jeffersonians, *see also* Democratic Republicans, 41–42, 107, 115, 187, 201
Judkins, Moses, 154

King, William, 148, 149, 158, 164
King of Prussia, Pennsylvania, 65

Lafayette, Marquis de
 as an American, 118, 137–143
 in children's books, 122, 127, 129, 134, 142
 as liberator of slaves, 11, 118, 134–136, 142
 as a martyr of liberty, 11, 117, 127
 as a philanthropist, 120, 122–123, 127–129
 and Revolutionary War veterans, 122–128
 unifying effect of, 129–137
 women's admiration of, 117, 130–133
Lafayette celebrations
 in New England, 133–136
 in the South and in the Mid-West, 136–139
Lafayette souvenirs, 11, 118–119, 124, 127
Lenox, Massachusetts, 23, 33
Levasseur, August, 133, 136, 137
Louis XVI, depiction of, death of, 105, 109, 115, 119, 139
Lyman, Theodore, 38, 104

Market Revolution, 5, 66, 152, 176–177, 183, 195, 200, 202
Maine
 as an ideal New England state, 148, 154–156
 propaganda for statehood, 145–147, 155
 referendum of 1792, 147
 referendum of 1816, 156
 vote on separation 1819, 158, 161
Maine frontier, 12, 145, 149, 151–152, 155, 167, 179, 202
Maine separatists, 11–12, 148–149, 151–156, 158–162, 164, 166–167
Marie Louisa, French empress, 114
Massachusetts great proprietors, 29, 149, 151, 202
Melish, John, 24, 45, 47, 48, 55
Meetinghouses, 8, 31–33
Mid-Atlantic states, 9, 48, 53, 194
Mills, 31, 36, 39, 41, 153, 202
Missionary Societies, 175, 200
Missouri Compromise, 54, 146, 169, 185, 199
Moody, Lemuel, 156–157
Morse, Jedidiah, 17–18, 21, 42, 45, 54, 172, 178

Napoleon Bonaparte, 37, 85, 88, 109, 113–114, 140
New England
 comparison with Europe, 3, 5–11, 16–17, 24–39, 41–52, 58–67, 87–91, 94, 98–99, 115–116, 121–126, 139, 142, 186–189, 197–202
 comparison with the South, 2–3, 5, 15–16, 34–35, 42–43, 48, 52–58, 70, 118, 129–130, 169, 172, 184–186, 197–202
 cult of the picturesque, 15, 27–31, 38–39, 41, 192
 and education, 36–37, 42–43, 47–49, 58–59, 68–69, 84, 138, 152–153, 155, 175, 182, 186
 and feeling of superiority, 5–6, 36, 41, 46–48, 52, 55–56, 100, 103, 118, 121–122, 134, 137–139, 142, 169–170, 182–184, 187–188, 194

New England—*continued*
as a "middle landscape," 24, 26, 29, 41
and myth of social and racial equality, 8, 46, 53, 91–92, 94–96, 123, 132, 134–136, 163–167, 177
reinvention of, 3, 8, 22–23, 31–32, 35–36, 52–53, 55, 103, 135, 165, 176–178
New England accommodations, 24–25
New England characteristics, images of, 7, 15, 25, 35, 97
New England historiography, 16–24
New England landscapes, depiction of, 15–17, 22–32, 35–36, 38–41, 43–44, 97, 147–151, 171–172
New England ministers
and nationalism, 170–195
and critique of popular celebrations, 195
New England republicanism, 31–33, 42–44, 47, 49, 54–56, 65–67, 131, 133, 147–148, 153–154, 160, 168, 177, 182, 194–195, 200–201
New England slavery
gradual abolition of, 55, 134
effect on society, 55–56, 134–135, 164
New England souvenirs, 7, 11, 36, 60, 119
New England towns, as symbols of republicanism, 31–44, 166
New England virtues, as American virtues, 23, 31, 42, 45
New England women
and republican virtue, 49–50, 97–98
and regionalism, 7, 35–36
New Englanders
and ambivalence towards commercialization, 66, 92, 127, 131, 177
characteristics of, 44–52
in New York state, 9, 56, 78, 175–176, 193

Paulding, James Kirke, 87, 93, 96, 98, 99, 100
Peale, Charles Rembrandt, 82
Periodicals, 30, 44, 51, 57, 61–62, 84, 88, 97, 110, 128
Picturesque style
in New England, 15, 26–28, 30–31, 34, 38–41, 192
in England, 27, 31, 34, 38
Prior, Jane Otis, 7, 34
Protestantism, republicanization of, 193–195
Puritans, 21–23, 29, 97, 125, 152, 179, 181, 188–189
Puritan heritage, 13, 16–18, 22–24, 29, 31, 42, 68, 82, 91, 97–98, 103, 152–153, 168, 175–181, 188–189, 195

Reform movements, 6, 26, 95, 184, 200
Republican motherhood, 108
Republican virtues, 8, 11, 13, 16, 22–24, 44, 63, 66, 68, 72, 77, 88–89, 92, 97–98, 114–118, 128–129, 133
Republicanism, towns as symbols of, 31–44, 202
Ropes, Geroge, 37
Royal culture
Frederick's II dislike of, 64
in Washington D.C., 78
Royalism, 9, 57, 59–60, 64, 77–78, 102

Sabine, James, 169–171, 176, 180–183
Salem, Massachusetts, 30, 37, 60, 70, 98, 106, 142, 162–163
Samplers, and New England symbols, 7–8, 15–16, 25, 34–35, 83

Sassi, Jonathan, 176, 184
Second Great Awakening, 12, 170, 171, 175, 176, 194, 201
Sectionalism, 54, 184, 199
Shaker villages, 174, 192–193
Shakers, 173–174, 191–194
Silliman, Benjamin, 24, 27–28, 33, 44, 48–49, 93, 97, 191–192
Simpson, Louis P., 23
Smith, Sophia Stevens, 34
South
  and luxurious lifestyle, 8, 15, 70
  New Englandization of, 3, 5, 19–20, 50–58, 70, 198–199
Southern slavery
  New England perception of, 8, 53–55, 134, 164, 177
  and New England hypocrisy, 8, 53–56, 164, 177, 185–186
Southerners, New England description of, 3, 5, 48, 55, 103, 134–137, 185–186
Southey, Robert, 91, 97, 126
Spring, Gardiner, 175, 176, 183–186, 193
State service, cult of, 75–77
Stewart, Joseph, 34
Strickland, William, 24, 52
Sullivan, James, 147, 148

Tappan, William, 49
Thomaston, Maine, 7, 16, 34
Ticknor, George, 114, 126, 130, 134
Trans-Atlantic friendships, 117, 126
Trans-Atlantic royalism, 9, 57, 59–60, 64, 77–78
Trans-Atlantic patriotism, 10, 17, 67, 71, 75, 77, 79–81, 83–84
Trans-Atlantic Protestantism, 60, 112, 202
Tudor, William, 90–91, 95, 115

Van Murray, William, 70

Waldstreicher, David, 3–4, 5, 106
Warville, Brissot de, 24, 45
Washington, George
  as an ancient hero, 80, 83
  celebration of, 10, 77–84
  comparison with Frederick II, 10, 77–85
  death of, 77, 79, 81–93
  as a divine figure, 82–84
Webster, Noah, 54
Westward migration, as New Englandization, 2, 176
White Mountains, 22, 25, 27
Women, and collective identity, 7, 35, 49–50, 97–98, 131–133
Wood, Joseph, 31
Wood Monroe, Sophia Sewall, 156
Wright, Frances, 43, 45, 49

Yale College, 18, 27–28, 140, 184
Yankee, 8, 16, 50–52, 56, 115, 175